FIFTH EDITION

ISLAM
AND
HUMAN RIGHTS
Tradition and Politics

Ann Elizabeth Mayer
University of Pennsylvania

**WESTVIEW
PRESS**

A Member of the Perseus Books Group

Westview Press was founded in 1975 in Boulder, Colorado, by notable publisher and intellectual Fred Praeger. Westview Press continues to publish scholarly titles and high-quality undergraduate- and graduate-level textbooks in core social science disciplines. With books developed, written, and edited with the needs of serious nonfiction readers, professors, and students in mind, Westview Press honors its long history of publishing books that matter.

Find us on the World Wide Web at www.westviewpress.com.

Every effort has been made to secure required permissions for all text, images, maps, and other art reprinted in this volume.

Westview Press books are available at special discounts for bulk purchases in the United States by corporations, institutions, and other organizations. For more information, please contact the Special Markets Department at the Perseus Books Group, 2300 Chestnut Street, Suite 200, Philadelphia, PA 19103, or call (800) 810-4145, ext. 5000, or e-mail special.markets@perseusbooks.com.

Designed by Trish Wilkinson
Set in 10.5 point Adobe Garamond Pro

Library of Congress Cataloging-in-Publication Data

Mayer, Ann Elizabeth.
    Islam and human rights : tradition and politics / Ann Elizabeth Mayer. —
5th ed.
        p. cm.
    Includes bibliographical references and index.
    ISBN 978-0-8133-4467-6 (pbk. : alk. paper) — ISBN 978-0-8133-4465-2
(e-book) 1. Human rights—Islamic countries. 2. Human rights—Religious
aspects—Islam. I. Title.
KBP2460.M39 2012
341.4'80917671—dc23   2012011622

10 9 8 7 6 5 4 3 2 1

ISLAM
AND
HUMAN RIGHTS

Contents

Preface

Perspicacious readers will note that the title of this book is a misnomer. A more accurate title might be along the lines of "A Comparison of Selected Civil and Political Rights Formulations in International Law and in Actual and Proposed Human Rights Schemes Purporting to Embody Islamic Principles, with a Critical Appraisal of the Latter with Reference to International Law, Evolving Islamic Thought, and Relevant State Practice in the Middle East." The actual title stands as it is simply because it is the kind of rubric that people tend to consult when looking for material on human rights in Muslim milieus. That is, it has been selected for purely practical reasons despite its not being very informative. The reason why this book focuses on the Middle East is simply that my own research interests center on this region.

The reference to "Islam" in the book title is potentially misleading because I repudiate the commonly held view that Islam by itself determines the views on human rights that one finds in the Middle East. A central thesis of this book is that there is no Islamic consensus on a single Islamic human rights philosophy. The precepts of Islam, like those of Christianity, Hinduism, Judaism, and other major religions possessed of long and complex traditions, are susceptible to interpretations that can and do create conflicts between religious doctrine and human rights or that reconcile the two. Even where the discussion is limited, as it is here, to Muslims living in the area stretching from North Africa to Pakistan, one observes Muslims' attitudes toward human rights running the gamut from total rejection to wholehearted embrace.

Although human rights are debated in purely secular terms in many Muslim milieus, in the wake of the Islamic resurgence, questions of human rights, like other great political issues facing Muslim societies, cannot easily be severed from disputes that are raging about the implications of Islamic law for contemporary problems.

Whether in governments or in the opposition, many Muslims have recourse to interpretations of Islamic sources to develop positions supporting or condemning human rights. This has been dramatically illustrated in Iran, where the ruling clerics and dissident clerics who are at odds with the oppressive theocracy both invoke Islamic authority for their stances. In these circumstances, "Islam" has become both a vehicle for political protest against undemocratic regimes and a justification for the repression meted out by such regimes, often simultaneously expressing aspirations for democracy and equality and providing rationales for campaigns to crush democratic freedoms and perpetuate old patterns of discrimination.

The focus of this book is on the era since the emergence of the UN human rights system, when what are called here Islamic human rights schemes were produced—schemes in the sense of combinations of elements connected by design. As will be demonstrated, these schemes are designed both to mimic international law and to degrade the protections afforded by international human rights law. They embody highly selective and often less-than-coherent combinations of Islamic principles with extensive but unacknowledged borrowings from international human rights documents and rights principles in Western constitutions. These hybrid schemes offer truncated and diluted human rights that are emphatically rejected by the large segment of Muslims who endorse international human rights law.

As will be shown, these schemes can be criticized on a number of grounds, including oversimplifying and stereotyping Islamic doctrines, failures to acknowledge and address actual patterns of human rights abuses in the Middle East, a weak grasp of international human rights principles, misrepresentations of comparative legal history, imprecise legal methodologies, and the deliberate use of evasive and ambiguous formulations. These flaws should be ascribed to the failings of the authors, not to Islam per se.

Much of the secondary literature on the relationship between Islam and human rights is likewise flawed and must be cautiously used. Many works embody an uncritical approach that contributes little to an understanding of the subject. In many ways, the first edition of this book was inspired by a wish to correct common defects in the secondary literature, defects that should be summarized.

Many authors do not analyze and explain the criteria that are being employed to decide what does or does not qualify as "Islamic law," a term with a wide variety of potential connotations. One encounters failures to make needed differentiations respecting the categories involved, such as principles that are expressly set forth in the Islamic sources versus the historical patterns of diverging interpretations of these sources, which can alter over time. Authors may devote disproportionate attention to the classical theory of Islamic sources in use by premodern jurists, failing to explain how it happens that Islamic human rights schemes are studded with terms and concepts that have been borrowed from international law.

Treating Islamic law as static and mired in premodern jurisprudence, some authors may dismiss the relevance of new understandings of the sources, as if the progressive and reformist perspectives of contemporary Muslims did not count or were necessarily to be viewed as less legitimate than rules ratified by hoary Islamic tradition. Giving too much credence to the shibboleth that in Islam religion and state are one, people may overlook the existence of trends in Islamic thought that are supportive of a secular public domain, imagining that secular perspectives are antithetical to any Islamic worldview.

Comparisons of Islamic rights standards with their international counterparts, if undertaken at all, are frequently underdeveloped, with a common disposition to minimize the extent to which Islamic human rights schemes both borrow from international law and deviate from it. Writing in this area often reveals an unfamiliarity with how international human rights law developed, as well as a lack of awareness of how Muslims contributed to its formulation. In an ironic twist, human rights tenets originally promoted by representatives of Muslim countries may be mistakenly identified with Western values.

Specific analyses of how actual Islamization measures correlate with human rights violations perpetrated by governments in the Middle East are commonly wanting. Failing to consider how badly people suffer under corrupt despotisms, authors may choose to indulge in visions of harmonious societies whose members are united by a common Islamic ethos, imagining that Muslims willingly defer to official policies that claim Islamic authority. The ingrained tendency to downplay the degree to which Middle Easterners yearn for rights and freedoms may now be diminishing after the magnitude of popular uprisings of the 2011 Arab Spring conveyed how bitterly people in the region resent being left to the mercies of tyrannical ruling cliques.

In the following study, I am critical of governmental and ideological claims that unimpeachable Islamic authority warrants denying human rights, even though I understand that individual Muslims may freely decide to accept interpretations of the Islamic sources that place Islamic law at odds with international human rights law. Muslims' right to have such private beliefs must be respected. The situation becomes different, however, when claims that Islamic rules should supersede international human rights law are put forward with the aim of stripping other people of human rights that they aspire to enjoy and to which they are entitled under international law. Here one is not talking about personal religious beliefs but rather projects in the domains of law and politics.

In discussing Islamic human rights schemes, I have endeavored to evaluate all sources and arguments objectively, but that does not mean that I feel obligated to withhold judgment or to suppress my own opinions. My own views—with supporting reasoning—are expressed at various points in this book. On human rights questions, I do not consider that it is possible or even advisable to withhold all judgment regarding which positions are meritorious. In clarification, I would say that one can write on questions of slavery and torture in a serious and fair manner without taking a neutral stance about whether slavery and torture are benign or reprehensible institutions and without suppressing all one's moral judgments and philosophical convictions.

I believe in the normative character of the human rights principles set forth in international law and in their universality. Believing that international human rights law is universally applicable, I naturally also believe that Muslims are entitled to the full measure of human rights protections offered under international law. This inclines me to be critical of any actual or proposed rights policies that violate international human rights law, including US government actions and policies affecting the Middle East that clash with this law.

I welcome the emergence of principled human rights advocacy in Middle Eastern countries and the growing tendency to interpret Islamic sources in ways that harmonize Islamic law and international human rights law. Underlining the progressive and humanistic dimensions of contemporary Islamic thought seems particularly appropriate in an era that has seen an upsurge in vituperative, bigoted Islamophobia. The partisans of this trend refuse to distinguish Islam as a vastly complex, multifaceted religious heritage from the political uses of Islam by corrupt and thuggish regimes and by groups wedded to hate-driven ideologies and terrorist agendas, distorting Islam by portraying it as having only repressive and violent tendencies. At the same time, I recognize that I am an outside observer commenting on developments in another tradition, one in which my views can have no normative or prescriptive value. Therefore, I do not endorse any particular reading of Islamic doctrine, nor do I presume to signal which interpretations Muslims should deem authoritative.

Because the ideas of Muslims supportive of human rights are under constant attack by powerful and extremely well-financed conservative forces determined to delegitimize their programs, their beleaguered positions cannot escape being subjected to the harshest possible critical scrutiny and attacks. In reaction to this kind of imbalance, I think it appropriate to focus my critiques on projects antithetical to human rights.

At a time when Islamic themes and terminology frequently shape political discourse in Muslim societies, it can be difficult for insiders and outsiders alike to distinguish between what are properly classified as political issues and ones that should be deemed religious issues. Nonetheless, no matter how extensively Islam is invoked, analysis shows that campaigns for democracy and equality are going on in the Middle East that resemble similar campaigns by restive populations elsewhere. When antidemocratic governments are proffering Islamic rationales for familiar patterns of human rights violations, this should not immunize them from critical scrutiny.

Reacting to the unfair and often grotesque demonization of Islam in the West, some are disposed to attribute any critical perspectives on the ascendancy of political Islam and the concomitant rights violations to ugly Western prejudices. In reality, there is a big difference between studies that seek to illuminate how Islam figures in contemporary human rights controversies in the Middle East and the current efforts by Islamophobes in the West to portray Islam as a barbaric religion inherently opposed to rights and freedoms, which is an uninformed and prejudiced position. A consistent and objective application of human rights standards will show that human rights abuses can be every bit as severe in Middle Eastern countries where Islamic law is left largely in abeyance and where religious impulses are harshly suppressed as in countries where Islamic law figures, at least officially, as the legal norm. Thus, for example, the human rights records of Libya and Syria have been every bit as atrocious as the records of countries such as Iran and Saudi Arabia. However, because the purpose here is to compare Islamic human rights schemes with international human rights law, rights violations that do not take place under the rubric of applying Islamic law will receive little attention.

This book focuses on the legal dimensions of human rights problems, examining the questions within the framework of comparative law and comparative legal history. There is no intention, however, to imply that Islam is exclusively a legal tradition or that comparative legal history is the only legitimate way to approach this topic. In a more comprehensive study on the relationship of Islam and human rights, one would ideally want to include analyses of how principles of Islamic theology, philosophy, and ethics tie in with the treatment of human rights. This would carry one into areas beyond the comparative legal analyses of civil and political rights in international human rights law and in Islamic human rights schemes, which are the sole concern of this work.

For purposes of offering clarification and background, there will be excursions into topics outside comparative law. Relevant political developments in various Middle Eastern countries will be sketched. With limited space, in order to cover recent developments in the Middle East, many cuts have had to be made to the text of the earlier editions, and sections of the previous text have been significantly condensed and reorganized. The annotated bibliography will, it is hoped, somewhat compensate for the failure to delve more deeply into related issues.

Short discussions of elements of the complex jurisprudence created by Islam's learned scholars during the premodern period will be offered in order to indicate the pedigrees of various positions being put forward in Islamic human rights schemes. Some references will be made to the reformist currents in Islamic thought and to new perspectives that have surfaced over the last decades as Muslims have sought Islamic answers to the political, economic, and social challenges that confront their societies.[1] As globalization and other forces have altered Muslims' circumstances and have upended old assumptions, new trends in Islamic thought have come to the fore. One observes that reactive and reactionary reformulations of Islamic teachings are now being pitted against highly progressive readings of the Islamic sources.

Debates on Islam and human rights are being given fresh impetus by the political upheavals in the Arab world and the ascendancy of various Islamist factions, which raise the prospect of drafting new constitutions in which references to the supremacy of Islamic law and guarantees of human rights will both have their partisans. How to balance these elements is becoming an increasingly vital issue for the future of the Middle East, and this book offers an examination of what experience to date can teach us about the consequences of subordinating human rights to Islamic criteria.

Ann Elizabeth Mayer

Acknowledgments

Writing about Islam and human rights in the year 2011, I have been riveted by developments in the Middle East, hoping that the revolutions in Egypt, Libya, and Tunisia, among others, at last signal the beginning of the end of the effective imprisonment of the peoples in that region. As my writing over the last decades amply demonstrates, I have long been concerned with the deplorable human rights situation prevailing in the Middle East. In the course of years of discussions and research, I have learned a lot about the passion of Middle Easterners for human rights and democracy. I have tried to convey to a Western audience how deeply Middle Easterners yearn for freedom and how much harm is being done by corrupt despotisms that cling to power only by the use of the most egregious forms of human rights violations. I have been as distressed over the suffocating environment created by Mu'ammar al-Qadhafi's brutal dictatorship in Libya as over the savage repression meted out by Iran's ruling theocrats.

As I have acknowledged in previous editions, I owe great debts of gratitude to the people of the Middle East for what they have taught me. But for my interactions with them and their encouragement and inspiration, my scholarship would not likely ever have encompassed the domain of human rights. Because of the continuing turbulence and dangers, I think it prudent not to name names, but my indebtedness is real.

I also wish to thank Oceana Press for kindly granting me permission to reprint excerpts from their published translation of the Iranian Constitution.

A.E.M.

CHAPTER 1

Assimilating Human Rights in the Middle East

Background: Legal Hybridity in the Middle East

In the Muslim Middle East, there have been strong but mixed responses to international human rights law. These responses have included the production of what are here called Islamic human rights schemes, which borrow extensively from international human rights law while employing ideas and rules taken from the Islamic heritage.

Islamic human rights schemes can be seen as one facet of a widespread backlash against secularization of laws. In the course of the difficult modernization processes that all Middle Eastern countries have undergone since the late nineteenth century, Islamic law and institutions have been largely displaced and marginalized—with Saudi Arabia standing out as the country most resistant to such changes. The consistent movement toward secularization of legal systems left only small islands of Islamic substantive rules in such areas as family law in what were basically modern, European-style legal systems. In reaction to this secularization process, popular demands for Islamization grew in the 1970s, and several states sponsored Islamization programs—but without returning to the Islamic model of governance, which would have undermined the states' monopoly of power. The Islamic model of the *umma*, a united Islamic community of believers, is an ideal that still retains potent appeal in the abstract but has proved its impracticability in a world of states whose borders hardened and fractured political allegiances and whose leaders do not wish to cede power to a supranational entity.

The imported model of the modern nation-state is now ubiquitous in the Muslim world, along with its many accoutrements, including constitutions and modern legislative and judicial institutions. These survive Islamization, as can be seen in the Islamic Republic of Iran, where Islamic rules were imposed in such areas as criminal law and women's rights but where the state itself and related institutions remain grounded in French models that were imported before the Islamic revolution, notwithstanding the adoption of the principle of theocratic supremacy.

Living under the modern state with its great centralized power created new problems in the Middle East, where states have shown a disposition to crush civil and political rights. How to constrain such a leviathan had not been contemplated in the classical works of Islamic jurisprudence, and many Muslims naturally were prompted to appropriate rights principles that had originally been developed in the West to constrain the power of the state. At the same time, others were seeking to deploy Islamic law to shore up government power at the expense of protections for rights. In the last few decades a number of national governments and the intergovernmental Organization of Islamic Cooperation (OIC; this organization was formerly known as the Organization of the Islamic Conference before the name changed in June 2011) have been particularly assertive in promoting Islamic human rights schemes, ones that, not coincidentally, reinforce state prerogatives at the expense of the rights and freedoms of the individual. These Islamic human rights schemes impose Islamic criteria to weaken if not to nullify civil and political rights.

Such Islamic human rights schemes aim to degrade human rights at the same juncture in history when human rights awareness has flourished among Middle Easterners. Despite grave perils, activism supporting democratization and human rights has burgeoned.[1] Well before the remarkable 2011 popular uprisings against autocracies and dictatorships during the Arab Spring, long-suffering populations were seeing human rights as offering the prospect of relief from stifling Middle Eastern despotisms.

Islamic human rights schemes need to be evaluated in the context of ongoing political struggles over democratization in the Middle East, as well as in relation to Muslims' theoretical disagreements about whether Islamic law and international human rights law harmonize or conflict. An example of how Islam becomes enmeshed in conflicts over democratization could be seen in Saudi Arabia in spring 2011. Before the Saudi monarchy used a combination of brute force and payoffs to quell local protests inspired by upheavals in neighboring countries, the grand mufti of Saudi Arabia issued a *fatwa* asserting that Islam forbids street protests, a message that was echoed in Friday sermons throughout the kingdom.[2] According to this ruling, Saudis venturing onto the streets to voice demands for a more democratic and accountable government were going against Islamic law—the interests of the absolute monarchy being equated with upholding Islamic requirements.

Muslims have espoused a wide range of opinions on human rights—from the assertion that international human rights law replicates values already inherent in Islamic teachings to the claim that international human rights law should be rejected as an affront to Islam that embodies pernicious Western values. In between these extremes, one finds a range of compromise positions that in effect maintain that Islam accepts many but not all aspects of international human rights law or that it endorses human rights with significant qualifications that are allegedly required by Islamic law.

As will be seen in the following chapters, the main concern here is Islamic human rights schemes that set forth compromise positions. These purport to represent definitive Islamic countermodels of human rights, borrowing from the international formulations but reworking them in ways that circumscribe rights and superimposing Islamic qualifications on these. None of these have been ratified by a universal Islamic consensus or by anything like democratic referenda; instead, they have been promoted by undemocratic governments and various ideologues with views hostile to rights and freedoms. The focus on such compromise positions does not mean that they are more authentically Islamic than any other views on the relationship of Islam and human rights. They offer attractive subjects for investigation because they reveal the conflicting trends presently affecting what are supposedly Islamic approaches to human rights.

Comparative law is the framework for this study of contemporary controversies about how Islam relates to human rights. International human rights law is used as the standard, and Islamic human rights schemes are assessed in relation to it in order to elucidate where they coincide or diverge and also to identify where the Islamic schemes resort to vague and confusing terms that cloak the full extent of the deviations.

The opacity in the schemes will be highlighted. It correlates with the way that Middle Eastern governments have for the most part sought to maintain pretenses of respect for international human rights law even while seeking to degrade it. Wanting to have influence in the UN system, they have the incentive to try to appear friendlier to human rights than they actually are. The result is that they are disposed to put forward Islamic human rights schemes that set forth principles that in a superficial way mimic those of international human rights law even as they bear hallmarks of being customized to fit in an Islamic framework that undermines the rights that are ostensibly being provided.

The emphasis on human rights positions that states have promulgated is warranted given that states have played the central role in devising international law instruments since the inauguration of the UN human rights system. States have either approved international human rights instruments by majority votes—as in the case of the Universal Declaration of Human Rights (UDHR), which was endorsed on December 10, 1948, in the UN General Assembly—or by ratifying them in sufficient numbers and thereby bringing them into force, as in the case of subsequent covenants and conventions. Today, states from the Middle East are working in conjunction with other states hostile to rights to undermine this system.

Misperceptions About Applying International Human Rights Law as Serving Imperialism

Comparative law, the mainstay of the following analyses, is an academic field where explosive political controversies are rarely encountered. As an eminent comparatist has stated, comparative law looks at the relationships among legal systems and their rules, and ultimately it is concerned with similarities and differences in legal systems and rules in the context of historical relationships.[3] In the main, scholars can expect such studies to be of interest to specialists and can assume that any controversies they may provoke will center on issues of scholarship, not ideologically freighted political disputes. If scholars are comparing, say, German law and Japanese law, they do not expect the mere undertaking of such comparisons to be condemned by their academic peers. They have no reason to fear that their work will be denounced as politically unsound if they objectively record the similarities and differences that they have uncovered or state whether aspects of one system were historically derived from the other. Thus, if they show that Japanese law borrowed heavily from German law but that it also exhibits features that differ from German law, they will not expect to be denounced as promoting a hegemonic Western perspective or rationalizing Western imperialism in Asia. Those writing on comparative legal history are used to working in a discipline where they may express their conclusions without tailoring them to fit a prevailing ideological orthodoxy.

At a time when international consensus supports the UN system of international law, there should be no barrier to evaluating Islamic human rights schemes and Islamization measures affecting human rights by reference to the international human rights law that they borrow from and modify. Appraising Islamic human rights schemes in the light of their international precursors would not seem to entail stepping into an ideological minefield. In actuality, a Western scholar discovers that referring to international law to make critical assessments of Islamic human rights schemes often provokes hostile reactions and vitriolic attacks. Persons who are determined to delegitimize critical appraisals of Islamic human rights schemes do not hesitate to resort to grotesque distortions or to disseminate arrant falsehoods in efforts to discredit authors of such appraisals.[4] This treacherous environment may account for why such critical appraisals were slow to emerge.[5]

In light of the disinformation that has been disseminated, it is essential to lay out a preliminary response to typical attempts to discredit criticisms of Islamic human rights schemes. The hostility to critical scholarly comparisons of international human rights law and Islamic human rights schemes typically reflects unfounded preconceptions. Many Islamologists and other students of the Middle East become acculturated by their academic milieus in ways that lead them to conclude that such comparisons are inherently objectionable. They may uncritically assimilate ideas voiced by many spokespersons for Middle Eastern groups and institutions that reject the universality of human rights. They may be impressed when the latter proffer what are ostensibly culture-based objections to the UN human rights system, which they present as being imbued with Western concepts at odds with Islamic tradition. Scholars who are conscientiously seeking to understand Middle Eastern attitudes may shy away from using criteria taken from international human rights law, fearing that doing so will impede understanding Middle Eastern societies on their own terms.

There are several reasons why treating international human rights law as being inappropriate for application to issues in Muslim states is misguided, a central one being that these states have agreed to be bound by the same principles that they are now seeking to circumvent. Moreover, the regular references to international human rights concepts, even by Muslims who disagree with these, show that these concepts are already becoming part of the terminology that is employed within Muslim societies in debating laws and policies. Prominent political figures in the Middle East routinely refer to human rights in their speeches, treating them as givens in the modern international system. Since the 1980s, Muslims have produced a large literature comparing Islamic law, including the Islamic laws in force in their countries, and international human rights law.

People may react negatively to Western governments' selective criticisms of human rights abuses in the Middle East. Aiming for a balanced approach, people may reflexively classify academic discussions of Middle Eastern regimes' delinquencies as attempts to divert attention from the West's own history of egregious human rights violations—including torture, genocide, religious persecution, racism, sexism, and slavery, as well as the abusive treatment of Muslims during the colonial era. Some view criticisms of Islamic human rights schemes as being necessarily motivated by a desire to show that Western domination of the Middle East in the past was beneficial and to legitimize current Western interventions.

Many presume that there is a necessary connection between scholarship that critiques human rights deficiencies in the Middle East and the US deployment of human rights rhetoric to justify such ventures as the invasions of Afghanistan and Iraq. These invasions were preceded by US governmental professions of outrage over the human rights violations perpetrated by the Taliban and Saddam Hussein and were officially justified by US claims to be engaged in spreading democracy and human rights in the region. US claims of being motivated by concern for the human rights of the oppressed populations of Afghanistan and Iraq rang hollow at a time when US policy accommodated gross human rights abuses by governments in the region that cooperated with US foreign policy strategies, when US military actions and mismanagement were costing a staggering toll in terms of death and human suffering among the "liberated" populations, and when prisoners were subjected to shocking abuses in prison camps where they were incarcerated without even the most rudimentary rights protections. After yet another chapter in the history of the West cynically invoking human rights deficiencies in Middle Eastern countries to justify interventions in the region, observers may automatically associate all academic writing dealing with human rights deficiencies in the Middle East with White House policies.

Such associations are unwarranted. Even where the US government—like many other governments—cynically deploys human rights rhetoric, independent Western scholars should not be barred from assessing human rights issues in Middle Eastern societies if they are also applying the same standards consistently to all parties—including to the United States. After all, if scholars' study of human rights in other countries were to be disqualified simply by the fact that the foreign policies of their countries of origin evinced hypocrisy, then most such study would be barred.

The argument that private criticisms of the treatment of rights in Muslim milieus are of a piece with hypocritical governmental policy is especially weak in the case of this study, which includes criticisms of the use of Islam to deny human rights by regimes that are or were US allies. With respect to these, the United States was hypocritical not in the sense of judging their records particularly harshly but rather the reverse—it glossed over human rights abuses committed by strategically important governments that were either friendly or cooperative.

Washington has generally been reticent about publicly denouncing rights abuses committed under the rubric of applying Islamic law by Saudi Arabia, one of the most valued US allies. The United States provided the strongest military and economic support for President Muhammad Zia-ul-Haq's regime in Pakistan from his 1977 coup until his death in 1988 and winked at the rights violations perpetrated under his Islamization program. In the case of Sudan, the United States was a staunch mainstay of the Jaafar Nimeiri government in 1983–1985, when Nimeiri was pursuing his Islamization campaign, showing a readiness to tolerate its abuses. The Reagan administration even gave President Nimeiri a cordial reception in the White House in spring 1985 after Nimeiri had ordered the execution of a peaceable seventy-six-year-old Sudanese religious leader as a heretic. Islamization was resumed in 1989 when a cabal of Islamists and General Omar al-Bashir overthrew the elected government. Al-Bashir's notorious record of human rights violations earned his regime pariah status until its willingness to assist the War on Terror led to a warming of ties between the Sudanese dictatorship and the second Bush administration, which was willing to overlook retrograde Islamization measures and atrocities such as genocide and mass rapes in order to secure Sudanese cooperation.

Moreover, when Afghan factions fighting Soviet forces and aiming to establish Afghanistan as an Islamic state showed disregard for human rights, US underwriting of their campaign continued. Despite the atrocious abuses perpetrated in the guise of enforcing Islamic law by the Taliban, plans for a UNOCAL oil pipeline across Afghan territory and other strategic concerns muted US condemnations of the Taliban.[6] This changed after September 11, 2001, when the regime was accused of shielding al-Qaeda terrorists.

Such cases remind us that claims that the US government passes particularly harsh judgments on human rights violations connected to the application of Islamic law are ill-founded; US policy has often been to downplay such violations as long as the regimes involved served US interests. Thus, making consistent critical appraisals of the human rights records hardly correlates with US policies, which have responded to human rights abuses in the Middle East in a politicized manner.

Sensibilities about the linkage between critical assessments of Islamic institutions and imperialist projects have been exacerbated by the pervasive influence of Edward Said's seminal work, *Orientalism*.[7] In this book, Said argued that much of Western scholarship on the Orient, meaning the Islamic Middle East, had not been conducted in a spirit of scientific research but had been based on a racist assumption of fundamental Western superiority and Oriental inferiority. By positing ineradicable distinctions between the West and the Orient, Orientalist scholarship obscured the common humanity of people in the West and the Orient and, in Said's view, thereby dehumanized Orientals in a way that served the goals of Western imperialism.

Edward Said was not a lawyer and did not examine the extensive studies of Islamic law that Europeans carried out when European imperialism was at its zenith, but his acolytes have often tended to expand his arguments to encompass the domain of legal scholarship. Said's work does have implications for the study of law in Muslim countries—but not necessarily the implications that are commonly drawn out.[8] Although Said never pretended that all critical examinations of Islamic institutions are infected by Orientalist biases, his disciples often seem inclined to draw this inference from his book. In consequence, they may rush to condemn comparative analyses of Islamic law and international law—the latter being identified with the West—concluding that Orientalist prejudices are guiding such projects.

In reality, treating international human rights as universal implies that peoples in the West and the East do share a common humanity and that they are equally deserving of rights and freedoms. As the sharp international criticism of the US practice of extraordinary rendition and the US mistreatment of Muslims detained for suspected involvement in terrorism or insurgency has shown, international human rights law can be turned against Western powers that deny Muslims their human rights. Furthermore, to maintain that international human rights law is inherently at odds with the values of Muslim societies is to accept the quintessentially Orientalist notion that the concepts and categories employed in the West to understand societies and cultures are irrelevant and inapplicable in the East. To believe that Islam precludes "Orientals" from claiming the same rights and freedoms as people in the West is to commit oneself to perpetuating what Edward Said saw as the Orientalist tenet that Islam is a static, uniform system that dominates Oriental society, the coherence and continuity of which should not be imperiled by foreign intrusions such as democratic ideas and human rights.[9] Those who charge that comparisons of international law and Islamic law as they relate to human rights are Orientalist implicitly endorse the same elitist stance as the cultural relativists, discussed below—which is that international human rights are the sole prerogative of members of Western societies. Therefore, they are distorting Said's message that categories such as "Islam" and "Oriental" should not be allowed to obscure the common humanity of peoples in the East and in the West.[10]

Fortunately, as the years have passed, the climate that used to inhibit scholarship from treating international human rights law as applicable to Middle Eastern societies has shown improvement.[11] As Muslims have clamored in ever greater numbers for democratic freedoms and have denounced their governments for violating international human rights law, it has become harder to argue that criticizing governments' deployment of Islamic rationales for evading their obligations under international human rights law is equivalent to promoting the ideologies of Orientalism and serving the cause of Western imperialism.

Cultural Relativism

At the core of many efforts to delegitimize comparisons of Islamic and international law are convictions that such comparisons violate the canons of cultural relativism. Not all cultural relativists approach questions in an identical fashion, but in general they are inclined to endorse the idea that all values and principles are culture-bound and that there are no universal standards that apply across cultural divides. Consequently, they deny the legitimacy of using alien criteria to judge a culture and specifically reject any application of standards taken from Western culture to judge the institutions of non-Western cultures. For strong cultural relativists, evaluative comparisons of what goes on under the rubric of Islamic culture using international human rights law are deemed impermissible.

One encounters claims that international law is infected with "a strict and exclusive Western perspective."[12] Based on this kind of identification—actually a misidentification—of human rights with distinctive Western values, people may oppose the idea that international human rights law should be universal.[13] To impose principles taken from the UDHR on non-Western societies involves, according to cultural relativists, "moral chauvinism and ethnocentric bias."[14] Such views have been encouraged by the fact that many Middle Eastern governments have expressly invoked their cultural particularisms as grounds for their noncompliance with international human rights law.

Where cultural relativism leads to deference to assertions that cultural particularisms excuse noncompliance with human rights, analysis becomes confused. For one thing, cultural relativism is not a concept developed by legal specialists for application in areas where laws are being promulgated by modern states. Cultural relativism is a principle that developed within such fields as cultural anthropology and moral philosophy.[15] The warrant for extending cultural relativism to challenge international law that has been constructed with the participation of UN member states from around the globe is dubious.

People with cultural relativist proclivities might take comfort from statements such as the one made in 1984 by Iran's UN representative, Said Raja'i-Khorasani, invoking Iranian cultural particularism to shield the Islamic Republic from charges that it was violating human rights. His argument that international standards could not be used to judge Iran's human rights record was paraphrased as follows:

> The new political order was . . . in full accordance and harmony with the deepest moral and religious convictions of the people and therefore most representative of the traditional, cultural, moral and religious beliefs of Iranian society. It recognized no authority . . . apart from Islamic law . . . conventions, declarations and resolutions or decisions of international organizations, which were contrary to Islam, had no validity in the Islamic Republic of Iran. . . . The Universal Declaration of Human Rights, which represented secular understanding of the Judaeo-Christian tradition, could not be implemented by Muslims and did not accord with the system of values recognized by the Islamic Republic of Iran; his country would therefore not hesitate to violate its provisions.[16]

One observes how Raja'i-Khorasani identified the Iranian regime's position of denying the authority of international human rights law with a policy of upholding Islamic law and Iran's traditional culture and values. He spoke as if Iranians' religious convictions were at stake, when what was actually involved was state policy. Similar statements invoking cultural particularism have been made by other governmental spokespersons in international venues in attempts to defend governmental records of noncompliance with human rights, all assuming that human rights violations are placed beyond criticism if they are classed as expressions of cultural particularism.[17]

There is an audience that is receptive to claims such as those made by Raja'i-Khorasani and that is prepared to accept the notion that governmental measures carried out under the rubric of upholding Islam should not be condemned as human rights violations. An illustration can be found in a 2001 article that reproduces e-mail exchanges from an online discussion of Iran's official Islamic dress rules among people interested in the Persian Gulf region who came from a wide variety of backgrounds.[18] The debates—sharply edited in the published version—were provoked when one commentator asserted that the Iranian government promoted women's rights and argued that the government-mandated Islamic dress rules expressed a popular preference of Iranian women. This comment and many others in the exchanges ignored ample evidence that Iran's rulers are hostile to women's rights and that Islamic dress requirements are determinedly resisted by a large portion of Iranian women so that hardliners have had to resort to tough policing and harsh criminal penalties to try to deter infractions.

As the exchanges demonstrated, many professed experts on the Middle East accepted at face value the Iranian regime's claims that its forcibly imposed policies represented Islamic beliefs and Iranian culture—as if the reactions of resisting Iranian Muslim women did not count. The disposition to discount manifestations of Iranian women's rejection of the requirement that they don government-mandated uniforms whenever they left their homes correlates with a more general tendency to accord automatic deference to governmental representations of culture and to discount the aspirations of Middle Easterners to enjoy human rights on a par with other people around the globe.[19]

Observers who readily accept Iranian government claims that it has Islamic authority for its policies and its claims that the policies reflect popular beliefs fail to consider why, to enforce these policies, Iran must resort to such measures as threats, beatings, fines, jailings, torture, extrajudicial murders, and executions. Where governments must rely on harsh sanctions and violence to enforce standards, the standards involved cannot embody authentic tradition. Authentic tradition imposes itself on its own authority and is normative because it possesses authority.[20] Thus, authentic tradition is automatically accepted as such—as one sees in the Middle East, where traditional dress is voluntarily worn by many men and women as an expression of their own cultural identity. In contrast, the rules of Iran's official Islam, which depend on governmental policing to be effective, are more akin to "traditionalism" or the *ideology* of tradition.

The positions of Middle Eastern states have evolved; they have been moving away from articulating such positions as Raja'i-Khorasani's, which candidly proclaimed disdain for human rights, seeking instead to persuade the international community that their calls for respect for Islamic culture are compatible with adherence to international human rights law. At the June 1993 World Conference on Human Rights in Vienna, Iran and Saudi Arabia urged the acceptance of Islamic perspectives on human rights—but, rather than insisting on Islamic cultural particularism, they proposed a kind of vague, qualified human rights universalism.

For example, when speaking at the conference, the Saudi foreign minister maintained that Islamic law afforded "a comprehensive system for universal human rights." He professed to concur that the principles and objectives of human rights were "of a universal nature," merely adding the modest caveat that in their application it was necessary to show "consideration for the diversity of societies, taking into account their various historical, cultural, and religious backgrounds and legal systems."[21] He did not attempt to defend actual Saudi positions, which involved claims that Islam endorsed monarchical absolutism, required practices such as gender apartheid, and mandated the death penalty for practicing witchcraft.

The head of Iran's delegation at the conference also gave rhetorical support to the principle of universality and denied that religious teachings sacrificed the value of the individual for the well-being of the community. He argued that a multidimensional approach to rights—that is, one that would take into account Islamic criteria—could "provide a better background for the full realization of human rights," arguing that "drawing from the richness and experience of all cultures, and particularly those based on divine religions, would only logically serve to enrich human rights concepts."[22] Thus, the Iranian delegation claimed that the incorporation of Islamic principles would benefit human rights.

After debates over the universality of rights, the Vienna Declaration and Program of Action issued at the end of the conference asserted: "The universal nature of these rights and freedoms is beyond question." However, the declaration injected a note of ambiguity by also advising that "the significance of national and regional particularities and various historical, cultural and religious backgrounds must be borne in mind." This ambiguity in the final declaration must have pleased countries like Iran and Saudi Arabia, which had apparently decided that international human rights law had garnered so much legitimacy that, at least when faced with international audiences, they would have to mute their hostility and present Islam as complementing human rights universality. That is, believers in cultural relativism who found affirmation in Raja'i-Khorasani's 1984 hostile comments now must confront government statements that are far more nuanced.

More recently, governments seeking to use cultures as pretexts for noncompliance with international human rights law have joined in alliances in a campaign to ensure that traditional values are given more weight in the UN human rights system—but on the basis of claims that doing so will enhance human rights. The OIC, which has become increasingly assertive in promoting what are portrayed as

Islamic positions on human rights in the UN, has coordinated the positions adopted by its member states, which now typically vote as a bloc. In 2009, the OIC faction on the UN Human Rights Council supported a resolution that was introduced by Russia calling for promotion of the study of "traditional values," claiming that "a better understanding of traditional values of humankind under-pinning international human rights norms and standards can contribute to the promotion and protection of human rights and fundamental freedoms."[23]

Bearing in mind that this resolution was proposed by Russia, a country where the reinvigorated Orthodox Church has spoken critically of human rights as con-travening religious values, and that it was supported by many countries notorious for their contempt for human rights, one could predict that traditional values could be utilized against human rights. The potential dangers posed by the reso-lution were highlighted in comments by the women's human rights nongovern-mental organization (NGO) Women Living under Muslim Laws (WLUML), a group with experience and expertise in the use of Islam to deny women human rights. It observed:

> The promotion of traditional values does not necessarily mean the defense of patriarchal norms; women/human rights defenders have long sought to reclaim traditions and cultures from the purveyors of fundamentalist and reactionary ideologies. The Resolution, however, assumes that "traditional values" in-evitably make a positive contribution to human rights; there is no recognition in the resolution that "traditional values" are frequently invoked to justify hu-man rights violations.
>
> In presenting the draft resolution, Russia declined to define "traditional values" or explain what these meant. We are not alone in fearing that these "traditional values" may be invoked to excuse violations of women, sexual minorities, and other vulnerable groups. Indeed, many UN instruments and resolutions recognize that tradition and culture may be invoked to violate universal human rights.[24]

Middle Eastern states have concluded that they should try to become major players in the UN human rights system, working from the inside to manipulate it. To that end, states with deplorable human rights records, such as Iran and Saudi Arabia, have endeavored to present themselves as respectful of human rights in order to obtain seats on the UN Human Rights Council. Diplomacy was successful in the Saudi case, enabling the Saudis to win a seat and to remain on the council for years, but Iran encountered too much resistance and in April 2010 saw its bid fail. In a striking reversal of Iran's 1984 stance, in 2010 Moham-mad Larijani, secretary-general of Iran's High Council for Human Rights, told the UN Human Rights Council that Iran promoted and defended human rights and that Western criticisms of its record were groundless.[25] As the twists and turns in Iran's portrayals of how Islamic culture affects its treatment of human rights demonstrate, governmental positions on Islam and human rights turn out to be the products of states' shifting political calculations and should not be equated with culture.

Muslims Challenge Cultural Relativism

Cultural relativists tend to deprecate the positions of Muslims who support human rights universality and who protest that Islam is wrongly exploited to deprive them of rights. Meanwhile, these positions are being ever more assertively put forward, making them increasingly difficult to ignore.

As the burgeoning human rights movement in the Muslim world has demonstrated, many Muslims believe that Islam and human rights can be successfully integrated, even taking the position that Islam reinforces human rights.[26] Muslims who do not use the terminology of modern human rights often display attitudes revealing their belief in its foundational ideals, maintaining that justice, equality, and respect for human life and dignity are such central principles of Islam that a system that fails to honor these cannot be in conformity with Islamic requirements.

Human rights activists in the Middle East have been assertive in calling for adherence to international human rights law. A case in point is the Casablanca Declaration produced by the First International Conference of the Arab Human Rights Movement, which took place in Casablanca, Morocco, on April 23–25, 1999. It included a statement that is representative of the views of Middle Eastern human rights activists to the effect that "the only source of reference" is international human rights law, and it emphasized the universality of human rights. Furthermore, it specifically rejected "any attempt to use civilizational or religious specificity to contest the universality of human rights."[27]

Demands to enjoy the human rights afforded in international law were made in a 2003 conference in Beirut organized by the Cairo Institute for Human Rights Studies (CIHRS) in collaboration with the Association for the Defense of Rights and Freedoms, with a wide range of participants from Arab and international NGOs, academic and other experts, and representatives of various governmental and international entities from the Middle East and Europe. The result was the Beirut Declaration on the Regional Protection of Human Rights in the Arab World, which affirmed human rights universality and included as Principle 3 an unqualified rejection of the use of "culture" or "Islam" to restrict human rights, asserting:

> Civilization or religious particularities should not be used as a pretext to cast doubt and to question the universality of human rights. The "particularities"

that deserve celebration are those which make a citizen have a sense of dignity, equality and enrich his/her culture and life, and promote his/her participation in their own country's public affairs. Assuring the tolerant principles of Islam and religions in general should not be put in a false contradiction to human rights principles. The conference [warns against adherence to] aged interpretations of Islam that distort Islam and insult Muslims and lead to violations of human rights, particularly when excluding women and not allowing freedom of thought, belief, creative art, literature and scientific research.[28]

Similar ideas are articulated by the eminent Iranian human rights lawyer Shirin Ebadi, whose courageous work in perilous circumstances to advance human rights was crowned by a Nobel Peace Prize in 2003. In the course of an interview granted in 2004, she asserted the compatibility of Islam and human rights, explaining that her aim was to show that those governments that violated human rights in the name of Islam were misusing Islam.[29] When asked to comment on claims that international human rights law is "too Western" to win Muslims' acceptance, Ebadi answered:

> The idea of cultural relativism is nothing but an excuse to violate human rights. Human rights is the fruit of various civilizations. . . . Those who are invoking cultural relativism are really using that as an excuse for violating human rights and to put a cultural mask on the face of what they're doing. They argue that cultural relativism prevents us from implementing human rights. This is nothing but an excuse. Human rights is a universal standard. It is a component of every religion and every civilization.[30]

Views of Muslims like Ebadi who support international human rights may be dismissed by cultural relativists who brand them as excessively Westernized or, even more damning, as cultural traitors. In doing so, the cultural relativists betray their Orientalist proclivities, which, as discussed above, dispose them to view the peoples of the Orient and Occident as having inherently different natures and to consider the adoption of modern ideas and institutions by persons classified as Orientals as somehow incongruous and unnatural.[31]

The cultural relativist mindset conditions many Westerners to assume that "the natives" are content with systems that Westerners would find oppressive. As an Argentinian observer of the attitudes of cultural relativists has noted, the cultural relativists' position implies that:

> Countries that do not spring from a Western tradition may somehow be excused from complying with the international law of human rights. This elitist theory of human rights holds that human rights are good for the West but

not for much of the non-Western world. Surprisingly, the elitist theory of human rights is very popular in the democratic West, not only in conservative circles but also, and even more often, among liberal and radical groups. The right-wing version of elitism embodies the position, closely associated with colonialism, that backward peoples cannot govern themselves and that democracy only works for superior cultures. The left-wing version, often articulated by liberals who stand for civil rights in Western countries but support leftist dictatorships abroad, reflects a belief that we should be tolerant of and respect the cultural identity and political self-determination of Third World countries (although, of course, it is seldom the people who choose to have dictators; more often the dictators decide for them).

The position of relativist scholars who are human rights advocates illustrates an eloquent example of concealed elitism. Such persons find themselves in an impossible dilemma. On the one hand they are anxious to articulate an international human rights standard, while on the other they wish to respect the autonomy of individual cultures. The result is a vague warning against "ethnocentrism," and well-intentioned proposals that are deferential to tyrannical governments and insufficiently concerned with human suffering. Because the consequence of either version of elitism is that certain national or ethnic groups are somehow less entitled than others to the enjoyment of human rights, the theory is fundamentally immoral and replete with racist overtones.[32]

Where traditional values are being selectively used and manipulated for political ends by governments, Jack Donnelly's remarks deserve to be considered. He warned that "while recognizing the legitimate claims of self-determination and cultural relativism, we must be alert to cynical manipulations of a dying, lost, or mythical cultural past" and suggested that what is portrayed as "traditional" culture may actually reflect a confusing hybridity:

> In the Third World today, more often than not we see dual societies and patchwork practices that seek to accommodate seemingly irreconcilable old and new ways. Rather than the persistence of traditional culture in the face of modern intrusions, or even the development of syncretic cultures and values, we usually see instead a disruptive and incomplete westernization, cultural confusion, or the enthusiastic embrace of "modern" practices and values.[33]

This point seemed to be missed by cultural relativists, who may be imagining situations where an ethnocentric Westerner is engaged in condemning "barbaric" customs among so-called "primitive" peoples in communities clinging to ancient ways of life. In fact, the kind of cultural relativism that calls for people in developed societies to forbear casting aspersions on the cultures of rare intact traditional societies, where the latter fail to protect human rights according to modern international standards, seems justifiable. There is little reason to disturb the already jeopardized equilibrium of the few communities that have so far managed to resist the inroads of globalization and that seek to preserve their distinctive heritages. The social orders in isolated villages in the mountains or deep in jungles, the hierarchy in a remote oasis settlement, or the mores of nomadic clans struggling to survive in inhospitable conditions may not conform to UDHR ideals, but these may offer their members a more humane environment than the larger state societies surrounding them. The situation is entirely different when one is evaluating Islamic human rights schemes, where the concern is not assessing any of the few surviving intact traditional cultures but rather assessing modified versions of international human rights law that are tied to governmental policies, being designed by ruling elites to reinforce states' prerogatives at the expense of rights of individual citizens.

One way that cultural relativists may challenge the appeal of human rights is by pointing to the popular support for movements promoting Islamization in the Middle East. They may argue that this proves that Islam, not human rights, enjoys the broad-based appeal, whereas human rights are espoused by elites. In reality, both Islam and human rights have shown that they have potent popular appeal. Increasingly, human rights groups and Islamist movements compete for the loyalties of the same disaffected populations that are alienated from corrupt and despotic systems and are desperate for better lives, and sometimes their appeals to the disaffected share common themes.[34]

In many Muslim countries, proposed Islamization programs enjoy popularity precisely because Islam has become the most potent language for political protests against oppressive regimes. It should be borne in mind that popular support for groups calling for "Islamization" in situations where they stand up to hated regimes may not signal an actual intent to support the specifics of the Islamization programs that these groups intend to pursue once they come to power. As I have noted elsewhere, when proponents of Islamization are in the opposition and are still seeking to win backing for their programs, they tend to treat Islamization as a panacea for political, economic, and social ills.[35] As they seek to build up their support, Islamist groups trade on the positive connotations of Islam while eschewing detailed descriptions of their actual agendas, meaning that people can read into Islamization programs the content that they would like them to have.[36]

After regimes have carried out Islamization programs so that people learn what they entail, one has a different situation. Experience shows that Islamist regimes are not prepared to allow free elections to test whether the voters approve them after years of experience with actual Islamization measures. Witnessing the antidemocratic character of Iran's theocratic regime, Middle Easterners who aspire to enjoy rights and freedoms now fear Islamization. For example, many participants in the uprisings that toppled Zine El Abidine Ben Ali's and Hosni Mubarak's dictatorships in Tunisia and Egypt have expressed anxieties about whether in subsequent elections well-organized Islamists would manage to gain power and subsequently crush all opposition and impose repressive laws. In response, moderate Islamists in both countries endeavored to allay such anxieties and to persuade the populace that they would play by the rules of democracy and respect the human rights of all citizens. Even the head of Egypt's hard-line Islamist Nur Party took pains to convey the message that the party was dedicated to democracy, the rule of law, and human rights.[37] With the powerful showings of Islamist parties in elections in late 2011, a test of their bona fides was in the offing.

To assert that there is burgeoning support for human rights in the Middle East is not to say that if human rights were submitted to referenda, a majority of voters would endorse all features of the International Bill of Human Rights. Segments of the population might cling to Islamic rules at odds with international human rights law. In addition, the priorities expressed in different Middle Eastern countries could well diverge, even as the views of the United States and Canada diverge on many rights issues, despite the fact that the two countries are closely linked in terms of their history and legal heritage. Many overlook the fact that in the West differences in rights concepts and rights protections persist. This is true even within the European Union, which has adopted the concept of a "margin of appreciation" in order to accommodate different national approaches to human rights.[38]

Upholding international human rights law does not require that all states use identical approaches. It does require that human rights be defined and protected in a manner consonant with international principles.

Actual Human Rights Concerns in the Middle East

A deep cleft has resulted between the idealistic focus of proponents of Islamization, who tend to envisage Islamic law as the utopian solution to all problems, and the focus of Muslim human rights activists, who are concerned with overcoming obstacles to democratization, devising concrete, practical solutions that offer realistic prospects for ending rights violations. Reports of a debate between Islamists and human rights activists confirm how Islamists stress the virtues of Islamic principles in the abstract, whereas Muslim human rights activists stress the need to attend to details of reform processes and institutional frameworks.[39]

In striking contrast to the silence of Islamic human rights schemes regarding human rights abuses facing people in the Middle East, a thoughtful and exceptionally outspoken critique of the human rights situation in the Arab world was publicly issued by a group of Arab intellectuals after a meeting in Tunis in 1983. This critique, which presciently identified many of the problems that later fed the uprisings of the Arab Spring, turned out to be one of a series of critical appraisals of the ills besetting Arab societies issued by Arab intellectuals who saw all too clearly the negative consequences of the lack of freedom pervading their region. Portions of the 1983 critique, which also applies, mutatis mutandis, to the human rights predicaments in non-Arab countries in the region, are paraphrased below.

The critique asserts that under various pretexts—such as the needs of socialism, development, realization of pan-Arab unity, protecting national sovereignty, and fighting Israel—demands for democracy have been denied. It claims that freedom, aside from its social usefulness, is a value in and of itself, one that all Arabs long for and all regimes deny. Not only are Arabs prevented from free expression and from participating in the determination of their fate, but they are also constantly exposed to repression. Fear of imprisonment, murder, mass murder, and torture dominates their lives. Arab individuals are so humiliated, their spheres of personal freedom so restricted, and their voices so crushed into silence and subjugation, that they are prone to despair and become incapacitated. This critique condemns such repressive measures, as well as emergency courts and police-state tactics, and demands that trials be conducted according to law. In most Arab countries, the critique asserts, authority is based on the subjugation of citizens. The consequences are confusion in values and norms and the absence of critical thought. A monolithically structured, hermetically closed system of authority dominates the scene, leaving no room for political or intellectual pluralism or for the development of genuine culture. It calls on Arab governments to respect civil rights and to refrain from infringing personal freedoms guaranteed by the UDHR. The first priority is affirmed to be equal treatment for all citizens regardless of belief, descent, or gender. It demands guarantees for freedoms, especially freedom of belief, freedom of opinion and expression, freedom to participate, freedom of assembly, and freedom to form political organizations and unions. Guarantees for the rights of women and minorities and an independent judiciary are also demanded.[40]

This critique and others that were to follow proved that intellectuals who genuinely aspire to advance human rights in the Middle East are prepared to speak out to denounce actual patterns of human rights violations and that they do not hesitate to invoke international human rights law in their criticisms.

In 2002, Arab experts working for the UN Development Program presented a sharply critical assessment of retarded development in the Arab world. In this, the first of a series of reports, they found that the Arab region, one of seven world regions, had the lowest freedom ranking. Using indicators measuring the dimensions of the political process, civil liberties, political rights, and independence of the media, the authors depicted a gaping freedom deficit. Furthermore, the report highlighted the severe discrimination that Arab women face, ranking their political and economic participation lowest in the world.[41] The thoroughness and transparency of this critique was applauded by Arab advocates of human rights and democratization.[42] Participants in a June 2004 conference of more than one hundred Arab intellectuals and politicians issued the Doha Declaration for Democracy and Reforms, which decried the specific patterns of undemocratic governance prevailing in the Arab world and dismissed the pretexts that regimes used to defer democratic reforms.[43]

Such critiques confirm that despotic Middle Eastern regimes are not just objectionable by Western standards but also are so perceived by people within these societies. They show that people do not consider participatory democracy an exotic, Western luxury; instead, they attribute many of the problems afflicting their societies to its absence.

In striking contrast, the Islamic human rights schemes examined in this book insist on the absolute perfection of abstract Islamic ideals while ignoring altogether the grossly deficient human rights performance of Middle Eastern states. The schemes portray Islamic human rights as though such rights enjoyed unquestioned authority and automatic efficaciousness by reason of their divine provenance, owing to which no government would dare to tamper with them. For example, in its preamble, the Universal Islamic Declaration of Human Rights (UIDHR) says that "by virtue of their Divine source and sanction these rights can neither be curtailed, abrogated or disregarded by authorities, assemblies or other institutions, nor can they be surrendered or alienated."[44] In presenting the Cairo Declaration at the 1993 World Conference on Human Rights in Vienna as the authoritative statement of Islamic rights, the Saudi foreign minister insisted that in Islamic law, human rights are not mere moral exhortations but "legislative orders," containing "all the legal texts necessary for ensuring their implementation and enforcement."[45] He thereby portrayed Islamic law and the Cairo Declaration as affording efficacious rights protections. A recent study that endorses the Cairo Declaration and Islamic human rights more generally has elaborated on the Saudi position, making the argument that relying on Islamic precepts is sufficient to ensure a regime of virtue, harmony, and benevolence.[46]

Proponents of Islamic human rights schemes cannot acknowledge that Middle Eastern governments show no respect for the rule of law, including Islamic law, because doing so would require admitting that the religious pedigrees of Islamic rules do not mean that they will be respected in practice. Thus, the utopian ideals that are put forward in conjunction with Islamic human rights schemes are designed to gloss over the severe human rights problems facing Muslims in the Middle East.

The Emergence of International Human Rights Law

Proponents of international human rights espoused the idea that rights should be guaranteed not only in constitutional rights provisions but also by international law, binding on all nations. After World War II, the UN, as the preeminent international organization, took a leading role in formulating rights that had previously been left to domestic legislation. The UN Charter in 1945 called for respect for human rights and fundamental freedoms but did not undertake the difficult task of specifying what these entailed. The preamble of the UDHR, adopted by the General Assembly in 1948, called for members to seek to construct a new world order on a sounder basis, one in which "recognition of the inherent dignity and of the equal and inalienable rights of all members of the human family is the foundation of freedom, justice, and peace in the world."

One way of looking at the mentality behind this UN initiative is to see it as intimately bound to the particular situation facing the world community in the aftermath of World War II, when people around the globe contemplated the horrors of the war and proposed that respect for human rights should be ensured as a bulwark against any repetition. The wording of the preamble can thus be interpreted as spelling out "a political, sociological, and historical interpretation of the historical circumstances of world society in the aftermath of World War II."[47] That is, the UDHR may be seen as constituting UN members' responses to a shared historical experience, meaning that its inspiration was independent of any particular theological or metaphysical framework. Viewed from this perspective, international human rights law, even where it appropriates formulations taken from the Western tradition, has a different starting point, being grounded in a situated geopolitical moral rationality.[48] Their foundation is ultimately a shared vision of a better world of "freedom, justice and peace," as stated in the preamble. If one accepts this point of view, the fact that substantive UDHR provisions have antecedents that were first clearly articulated in a Western context does not mean that the new system inaugurated by the UDHR expresses principles that belong uniquely to the West.

Many instruments codifying international human rights were subsequently issued under UN auspices, vastly expanding the scope of human rights law. As UN membership grew to encompass all the countries of the Global South, many crucial declarations and conventions were produced with input from around the world, including those Middle Eastern states that had not been UN members in 1948.

Muslims' Responses to and Involvement in the UN Human Rights System

In the light of history, the efforts made by Middle Eastern governments to justify opting out of their obligations under international human rights law on the pretext of being bound by conflicting Islamic principles could seem paradoxical. Muslim states have, without exception, joined the United Nations, and in so doing they have agreed to be bound by international law. Significantly, well after they had achieved independence, Muslim states speaking as a bloc formally recommitted themselves to the UN legal system. The 1972 charter of the OIC, the international organization to which all Muslim states belong, expressly endorses the UN charter and fundamental human rights, treating them as compatible with Islamic values. In the preamble of the charter, two adjacent paragraphs assert that the members are:

> RESOLVED to preserve Islamic spiritual, ethical, social and economic values, which will remain one of the important factors of achieving progress for mankind;
>
> REAFFIRMING their commitment to the UN Charter and fundamental Human Rights, the purposes and principles of which provide the basis for fruitful cooperation amongst all people.

Muslim states contributed to the formulation of international law through their active participation in the UN and its affiliated organizations, and they participated in the drafting of international human rights instruments from the UDHR on. In a welcome development, a number of recent studies on the genesis of the international human rights system have demonstrated how constructive input from Muslim states influenced foundational UN human rights instruments. In contrast, Western states such as the United States played relatively minor roles. Of course, the personal leadership of Eleanor Roosevelt was vital in moving the human rights project forward at the UN, but the French jurist René Cassin, the Lebanese statesman Charles Malik, and the Chinese diplomat Peng Chun Chang were more influential in drafting the UDHR.[49] Far from finding human rights culturally alien, Chang, an expert on Confucianism, believed that that philosophy had laid the groundwork for human rights.[50] As Mary Ann Glendon observes, this deeply cultured man rejected stereotyping the East and the West as separate monoliths, each with a uniform culture. Chang asserted: "Culturally, there are many 'Easts' and many 'Wests' and they are by no means all necessarily irreconcilable."[51]

Interestingly, Cassin's assistant was his Iranian student Fereydoun Hoveyda, who would later become a diplomat and earn a reputation as a man of letters. From his insider's account, it seems that back in the 1940s, Muslim states were less inclined to find the UDHR religiously objectionable than to deem it problematic because of its unrealistic and utopian character. They found it hard to imagine that it could be implemented in their own countries, but they likewise did not see how one could expect Western countries to adhere to it.[52] Of course, a cynic could assert that states were prepared to endorse the exalted ideals of the UDHR precisely because the initial assumption was that they would remain nothing but words on paper.

Muslims who want to discredit international human rights law promote the notions that Muslims were excluded from the process of producing this law and that the International Bill of Human Rights—comprising the UDHR and the two major covenants that were subsequently derived from it, the International Covenant on Civil and Political Rights (ICCPR) and the International Covenant on Economic, Social and Cultural Rights (ICESCR)—expresses distinctively Western values. Susan Waltz's research establishes the inaccuracy of such notions, demonstrating that representatives of Muslim states made important substantive contributions.[53]

In the early years of the UN, it does not seem that representatives of Muslim states explicitly claimed that Islamic culture stood in the way of their accepting proposed human rights principles. Nonetheless, they occasionally did try to block or modify certain provisions where clashes with Islamic law would have been a likely basis for their objections, as in the cases of their objections to the freedom to change religion and to women's equality. A proclivity for such quibbling and disagreement was not, however, limited to one faction; other representatives also disagreed on various proposed rights provisions, both in the UDHR and in the later covenants.

In Western accounts of the genesis of the UDHR, the objections and complaints made by the Saudi Arabian representative, Jamil Baroody, are often noted, leading to generalizations about "Islamic" challenges to human rights universality or "Islamic" hostility to the UDHR.[54] In fact, the record is more complicated. As it happens, Baroody was neither a Saudi nor a Muslim but a Syrian Christian. Baroody did oppose including a phrase on the freedom to change religion that was eventually to be guaranteed in Article 18 of the UDHR, which some observers have attributed to Islam, but he did not expressly invoke Islam as a reason for his opposition. Johannes Morsink notes that Baroody's objections to Article 18 included his assessment that the language concerning the freedom to *change* religion was superfluous and that it was inconsistent to provide for the right to *change* religion as part of the freedom of religion when there were no corresponding provisions guaranteeing the right to *change* positions in the provisions on freedom of thought and conscience.[55] Some other delegations supported Baroody's objections, and not all of these were from Muslim states.[56] Thus, using Baroody's remarks to generalize about a supposed "Islamic" hostility to the UDHR is unwarranted.

Afghanistan, Egypt, Iraq, Pakistan, and Syria joined Baroody in expressing some qualms about Article 18, but as Waltz observes, at one point Sir Muhammed Zafrullah Khan, speaking for the Pakistani delegation, insisted that the Qur'an itself supported freedom of religion.[57] Significantly, no Muslim countries actually voted against Article 18 when it was finally put to a vote, suggesting that whatever objections they did have were not deemed so important that they wanted to go on the record as opposing it.

As Waltz has noted, some objections were registered regarding UDHR Article 16 of the UDHR on marriage and the family. Among other things, this article provides that spouses are to have equal rights in marriage, that it should be entered into only with the free and full consent of both spouses, and that men and women have the right to marry and found a family "without any limitation due to race, nationality or religion." Elements in the article conflicted with Islamic family laws in force in many Muslim states. Egypt, Iraq, Saudi Arabia, and Syria were among those objecting to Article 16. The Egyptian delegate argued that religious restrictions on who could marry whom should be acceptable.[58] Among Baroody's proposals was that in lieu of being accorded equal rights, women should be entitled to "the full rights as defined in the marriage laws of their country"—a proposal that prompted a strong objection by the Pakistani delegate on the grounds that Baroody's wording "would enable countries with laws discriminating against women to continue to apply them."[59] Again, Muslim states were divided. Meanwhile, not all Western states concurred with Article 16; the United States, where laws criminalizing interracial marriage were still widely in force, objected to a proposal for prohibiting limitations on marriage that were based on race, nationality, or religion.[60] Significantly, such an objection, which showed that the United States was unwilling to accommodate one of the most basic human rights ideals, has been largely ignored in accounts of the discussions leading up to the UDHR.

Baroody did make what sounded like a resentful complaint that the authors of Article 16 were, for the most part, using standards recognized by Western civilization and ignoring "more ancient civilizations," and he challenged the right of the committee to "establish uniform standards for all the countries of the world" or to proclaim "the superiority of one civilization" over others.[61] This challenge, which anticipates aspects of the Asian values debates in the 1990s, seems to have had little resonance. No Muslim states voted against Article 16, nor did any specifically object that the idea of women's equality in marital matters conflicted with Islam. That is, delegates from Muslim states seem to have steered away from complaining that Article 16 was in conflict with Islamic law.

Although Baroody was prone to quarrel with several proposals, his was not an absolute rejectionist stance. Far from insisting that the UDHR would engender an irremediable clash of cultures, Baroody proposed that, although the declaration was "frequently at variance with the patterns of culture of Eastern states, that did not mean, however, that the declaration went counter to the latter, even if it did not conform to them."[62] Moreover, the special emphasis on Baroody's carping in the secondary literature does not paint a balanced picture, because Muslim states generally supported the consensus behind the UDHR. They, along with an array of small- to medium-sized states, stayed engaged in the drafting process in the Third Committee, which worked to finalize the text. In contrast, by that stage the major powers had largely ceased their involvement.[63]

When the UDHR as a whole was submitted to the General Assembly, no Muslim state cast a vote against it, and Saudi Arabia was alone among Muslim states in abstaining, being joined only by South Africa and some Eastern Bloc countries. All in all, it is inaccurate to claim that when the foundations of the modern UN human rights system were being laid, Muslim states stood out as foes of human rights universality. Indeed, the event was lauded by the Syrian delegate at the time, who exclaimed as the UDHR was approved: "Civilization [has] progressed slowly, through centuries of persecution and tyranny, until, finally, the present declaration [has] been drawn up. . . . Now at last the peoples of the world [will] hear it proclaimed that their aim [has] been reached by the United Nations."[64] In a similar vein, the Pakistani delegate proclaimed that Pakistan fully supported the adoption of the declaration because it was imperative that the peoples of the world should recognize the existence of a code of civilized behavior that would apply not only in international relations but also in domestic affairs.[65]

As Waltz has established, after the UDHR was approved, representatives of a number of Muslim states played influential and largely constructive roles working on the Third Committee in the subsequent development of the two main covenants, the ICCPR and the ICESCR. Although there was continued quibbling on the part of some Muslim states regarding aspects of freedom to change religion and women's rights in marriage and divorce, all Muslim states on the committee voted in favor of the covenants—even Saudi Arabia. Meanwhile, the United States—immersed in a phase of isolationism and suspicion of international institutions—had bowed out of the covenant drafting process altogether and announced in 1953 its intention not to ratify either covenant.[66] Only much later, in 1992, did it ratify the ICCPR, and then only with reservations that nullified its effect.

In an era when relatively progressive nationalist ideologies were influential, several Middle Eastern states—including Iraq, Libya, Morocco, and Pakistan—sent women as UN delegates to work on human rights. One of the outstanding contributors to the formulation of the two covenants was the Iraqi delegate, Bedia Afnan, who insisted that the equality of women be unequivocally affirmed and to whose advocacy women are indebted for the strong provisions on women's equality in Article 3 of both covenants.[67] In debates over women's rights in the ICCPR, the Libyan delegate turned out to be a vigorous proponent of equality of rights for both spouses in marriage.[68] The fact that these delegates' strong support for women's equality has largely been ignored while Baroody's more problematic stances have been emphasized is another indication of how accounts of the development of the International Bill of Human Rights have tended to reinforce presuppositions about the supposed hostility of a hypostatized Islam to the values of human rights.

As one gleans from Waltz, Muslim states did not adhere to a monolithic Islamic position but rather took varying stances on human rights issues in the work producing the International Bill of Human Rights. What they had in common was a tendency to identify with the victims of human rights violations. Coming out of periods of subjugation by European powers, they were naturally enthusiastic backers of the principle of self-determination and were united in denouncing the human rights violations that European colonialism had perpetrated as well as the hypocrisy of European states that gave lip service to human rights that they were unwilling to grant to subjugated populations in their colonies.[69] Muslim states' positions on self-determination and the wrongs of colonialism were emphatically endorsed by a majority of UN members and became enshrined in many international human rights documents. In contrast, the stances of Western states did not always dovetail with a pro–human rights philosophy; they were sometimes aligned with states opposing minority rights, measures to ensure effective implementation of human rights, and bans on discrimination.[70]

Muslim states have uneven records of ratifying the major human rights conventions, with some states having ratified most conventions and others having ratified only a few, but the very unevenness and dissimilarities in the patterns of ratifications offer more reminders that, from the perspective of governments, there is no consensus on one set of Islamic human rights principles that is being followed.[71]

Despite the recent plethora of efforts to convince the world that there is a distinctive Islamic ethos that determines positions on human rights, in the years since the International Bill of Human Rights was produced, the stances of Muslim states on human rights have often dovetailed with those of various non-Muslim states that tend to adopt positions associated with upholding traditional family structures and conservative sexual mores. In this regard, Muslim states often wind up in alliances with the Vatican, states such as those in Central America with conservative Catholic orientations, and on occasion also with the United States. When under Republican leadership, the United States often joined coalitions of countries opposing rights for women, children, and homosexuals, decrying these as radical ideas offensive to religion and morality.[72]

Some Muslim states allied themselves with non-Muslim Asian states in the course of the Asian values debates that raged in the 1990s, in which claims were made that international human rights law was excessively Western and needed to be adjusted to accommodate the priorities characteristic of Asian culture. It seems implausible that in the 1990s Asian states suddenly realized that their culture stood in the way of their acceptance of the human rights principles that many of their representatives had participated in constructing. One of the possible explanations for the timing of belated attempts by states to wriggle out of commitments to international human rights law on grounds of alleged cultural particularisms could lie in their reactions to the destabilizing impact of globalization. Among the effects of globalization was the increased potency of international human rights law and attendant challenges to national sovereignty, which many states found threatening. As Karen Engle's analysis indicates, when invoked against human rights universality, "culture" could be a proxy for many different concerns, including preserving national sovereignty, prioritizing economic and social rights, protecting the right to development over civil and political rights, or opposing Western double standards in applying rights.[73] Thus, the invocations of Asian culture as a pretext for deviating from international human rights law may spring from broader concerns, and Asian culture may be little more than an umbrella label that a group of countries once agreed on as a shared rubric under which they could join to express their dissatisfaction with various international trends.

Summary

As has been discussed, the compromise positions on Islam and human rights that are embodied in Islamic human rights schemes are not definitive statements of Islamic doctrine but warrant attention because of their importance in the contemporary Middle East, where pressures for Islamization are potent and where governments espouse Islamic human rights schemes. As indicated, evaluating Islamic human rights schemes by the standards of international human rights law is a legitimate academic project, but it does mean venturing onto territory where one encounters erroneous presuppositions and the misapplication of cultural relativism, which can prompt unfounded objections that the project must be infected with Western hegemonic attitudes and serve Western imperialist goals. In hopes of avoiding misunderstandings and to clarify the basis for the comparative legal analyses that will be undertaken, aspects of the political background that impinge on discussions of this topic have been laid out. In addition, the important contributions made by Muslims to constructing the UN human rights system and evidence of Muslims' condemnation of the cultural relativism that would leave them bereft of human rights protections have been stressed. Examination reveals that governmental positions on how Islam affects human rights bear the hallmarks of political calculations and that these positions are, moreover, subject to change over the years as political calculations change. As a result, one needs to adopt a critical approach when assessing governmental representations of how the Islamic tradition bears on rights questions and investigate the politics lurking behind them.

CHAPTER 2

Human Rights in International and Middle Eastern Systems

Sources and Contexts

International Human Rights: Background

In Western thought, formulations of what we currently call human rights are relatively recent, although one can find certain antecedents in ancient times. Concepts related to human rights were spawned by trends during the Renaissance in Europe and by the associated growth of rationalist and humanistic thought, which led to an important turning point in Western intellectual history: the abandonment of the premodern doctrines of the duties of man and the adoption of the view that the rights of man should be central in political theory.[1] During the European Enlightenment, the rights of man became a preoccupation of political philosophy, laying the intellectual groundwork for modern civil and political rights.

Eighteenth-century British and French thinkers put forward the precursors of modern human rights ideas and influenced the rights provisions in the American Declaration of Independence of 1776, the Virginia Declaration of Rights of 1776, and the Bill of Rights that was added to the US Constitution in 1791. The most important model from this era was the 1789 *Déclaration des droits de l'homme et du citoyen*, developed at the time of the French Revolution. The formulations used in these models have had great historical influence.

Common to the British and French rights philosophies was the idea that the rights of the individual are paramount. In a survey of the historical evolution of rights concepts, one scholar has portrayed the significance of the concern for rights as being that "the concept of rights is individualistic in the sense that it is a from-the-bottom-up view of morality rather than one from the top down, and from the related fact that it generally expresses claims of a part against the whole."[2]

Long before international human rights law emerged, constitutionalism had been viewed as a means of securing civil and political rights, negative rights that placed limitations on the powers of government. The US Constitution and later European constitutions became influential models. Central to these constitutions are curbs on governmental power and safeguards for individual liberty, which is to be insulated from governmental intrusions. The rules establishing these curbs embody reactions to experiences of oppression and misrule and are designed to correct these ills. Recognizing that individual rights would sometimes need to be curtailed in the public interest or in extraordinary circumstances, the drafters of constitutions sought to define and restrict the justifications that states could invoke to curtail rights. Similar aims underlie international law on civil and political rights, which draws heavily from formulations first developed in the West.

Even with a focus narrowed to civil and political rights, the range of potential sources of international human rights law is too vast to be covered in this book. For the comparisons undertaken here, the International Bill of Human Rights will be central. The International Bill of Human Rights consists of the UDHR of 1948, the ICESCR of 1966, and the ICCPR, also of 1966, along with the ICCPR's Optional Protocol. The 1966 covenants entered into force in 1976. The UDHR has over time achieved the stature of customary international law and, as such, is deemed binding on states regardless of whether they have ratified any conventions.

Many countries have refused to ratify one or more of the two main covenants. Among the Middle Eastern Muslim countries that did not ratify the ICCPR and the ICESCR, one finds Saudi Arabia and the United Arab Emirates (UAE). On the other hand, such diverse countries as Afghanistan, Algeria, Egypt, Iran (here it is undoubtedly significant that the issue of Iran's ratification came up prior to the Islamic Revolution), Iraq, Jordan, Kuwait, Libya, Morocco, Pakistan, Sudan (during 1985–1989, the brief period of democracy between two military regimes committed to Islamization), Syria, and Tunisia have ratified the same covenants.[3]

Islamic Human Rights: Sources

The materials authored by Muslims purporting to define where Islam stands on human rights are so extensive that only a small fraction of the literature can be covered here. Selected provisions on civil and political rights will be reviewed, with criminal law and procedure being relegated to the margins because of space limitations. The rights provisions in several constitutions where Islam plays an important role will be considered. The treatment of human rights in constitutions is critical because international human rights law is meant to set models and relies on national laws for its implementation.[4]

The works to be examined have been composed by Muslims from both the Sunni and Shi'i traditions and from several countries. All are from the Middle East, treated here as encompassing North Africa, and from the OIC, in which Middle Eastern states play a leading role. The emphasis is on principles adopted by governments or presented by major Islamic institutions and influential figures. The exception is the work of Sultanhussein Tabandeh, who, although a relatively minor figure, is interesting because of his more candid, less diplomatically couched responses to various UDHR provisions. The range of material surveyed is, therefore, broad enough to permit some generalizations to be made.

As a preliminary matter, it should be noted that some broad distinctions will be drawn between the views of Muslims who favor and those who oppose human rights. Because the aim is to contrast the views of Muslims who fall on one or the other side of the line in disputes about human rights, for the purposes of this study, two main categories are used. Here the terms *liberal* and *conservative* are used in their dictionary senses: Liberal in this context denotes views favoring human rights and progress toward democracy—with "progressive" denoting related advocacy, whereas conservative denotes views calling for the preservation of established hierarchies and institutions at odds with human rights and precluding democratization. The terms "reactionary" or "retrograde" denote views favoring reversing progress and reinstating institutions from earlier eras. Obviously, many finer distinctions could be drawn, but they would only burden a work that is already heavily weighted down by discussions of very specific distinctions.

One of the documents assessed is *A Muslim Commentary on the Universal Declaration of Human Rights* by Sultanhussein Tabandeh (occasionally transliterated as Sultan Hussain Tabanda). This pamphlet was originally published in Persian in 1966 and appeared in an English translation in 1970. Tabandeh, who was born in northeastern Iran in 1914, inherited the leadership of the Ni'matullahi Sufi order, a mystical brotherhood affiliated with Twelver Shi'i Islam. He was educated at Tehran University and Tehran Teachers' Training College and traveled widely in the Muslim world and also in Europe. He presented his commentary on human rights to the representatives of Muslim countries who attended the 1968 Tehran International Conference on Human Rights. His purpose was to advise them of the positions they should adopt vis-à-vis various provisions in the UDHR, which he had analyzed in terms of the requirements of Islamic law. In his comments, one sees the reactions of a conservative leader of a religious order. Apparently uninhibited by political considerations, he is much more outspoken in revealing his disapproval of human rights than his fellow conservatives typically are.

A pamphlet titled *Human Rights in Islam* by the internationally prominent Sunni religious leader from the subcontinent, Abu'l A'la Mawdudi, is also assessed.

The centerpiece of the pamphlet, first published in 1976, is an English translation of a speech given by Mawdudi in 1975 in Lahore, Pakistan. In 1941, Mawdudi founded a political group, Jama'at-i-Islami, whose members are committed to the reinstatement of Islamic law and the establishment of an Islamic state in Pakistan; the group and allied factions have continued to be active in Pakistani politics over the past several decades. Before his death in 1979, Mawdudi wrote extensively on the application of Islam to contemporary problems, and his work was widely disseminated in translations. In recognition of what were said to be his outstanding services to Islam, he was accorded the King Faisal Prize by Saudi Arabia. Lacking the traditional religious education enjoyed by highly trained religious scholars, Mawdudi aimed to reach a wide popular audience, and his words resonated with Muslims who shared his bitter resentment of Western domination. He adopted a combative stance vis-à-vis the West, castigating Western society and culture for its decadence and materialism and arguing that Islamic civilization was far superior to its Western counterpart. His human rights pamphlet embodies the polemical attitudes that informed his work generally.

The 1981 Universal Islamic Declaration of Human Rights (UIDHR) is discussed as well. This document was prepared by representatives from Egypt, Pakistan, Saudi Arabia, and other countries under the auspices of the Islamic Council, a private, London-based organization affiliated with the Muslim World League, which is headquartered in Saudi Arabia. The declaration was presented with great public fanfare to the United Nations Educational, Scientific, and Cultural Organization (UNESCO) in Paris. In a casual reading, the English version of the UIDHR seems to resemble the UDHR, but many of the similarities turn out to be misleading. The English version diverges significantly from the Arabic, which states principles that diverge considerably from the UDHR. The inconsistencies in the English and Arabic versions of the UIDHR are examined here. Although the UIDHR is generally representative of conservative Muslim opinion, the confusion and equivocations in the UIDHR suggest that its authors may not have been able to achieve a consensus among themselves about the provisions.

The rights provisions in the "Draft of the Islamic Constitution" were devised by the Islamic Research Academy of Cairo, which is affiliated with al-Azhar University, the most prestigious institution of higher education in Sunni Islam and a center of conservative Islamic thought. This draft constitution, published in 1979 in Volume 51 of al-Azhar journal *Majallat al-Azhar*, represents one position on where Sunni Islam stands on human rights. Published at a juncture when the Shi'i leadership of Iran's Islamic revolution was attracting a following in the Sunni world, the al-Azhar draft may be seen as an effort to demonstrate that Sunni Islam possessed the resources to fashion a constitution for a modern government.

The rights provisions in the 1979 Iranian constitution, which, according to its preamble, "is based upon Islamic principles," are also assessed.[5] The Iranian constitution represents one attempt to state what rights belong in a constitution that establishes a theocratic regime tied to Twelver Shi'ism.

The Cairo Declaration on Human Rights in Islam was presented at the 1993 World Conference on Human Rights in Vienna by the Saudi foreign minister.[6] He asserted that it embodied the consensus of the world's Muslims on rights issues.[7] The declaration has assumed special importance because it reflected trends already established in previous Islamic human rights schemes and because it was endorsed in August 1990 by the foreign ministers of the OIC, which has subsequently treated it as the central Islamic statement on human rights. It appeared, at least superficially, to embody a more general consensus—albeit only at the governmental level—on how Islam should affect rights. In practice, the appearance of consensus was belied by the actual stances on rights taken by OIC member states and the rights formulations in their constitutions, which continued to diverge as widely after the issuance of the Cairo Declaration as they had before. The OIC announced that the Cairo Declaration would be succeeded by an OIC charter on human rights, but this proposed charter has yet to see the light of day. Meanwhile, the OIC has been assuming an active role in the UN human rights system, promoting the Cairo Declaration and seeking to persuade the UN to give weight to what are presented as Islamic concerns in the human rights domain.

The 1993 World Conference on Human Rights in Vienna provided impetus for Muslim countries to define their stance on human rights. The conflicts over whether human rights were inextricably linked to Western culture and whether they could or should be universal were central preoccupations of the conference.[8] In the period leading up to the conference, Saudi Arabia and Iran remained strong supporters of the 1990 Cairo Declaration. At one point, Iraq joined Iran in pressing the UN Commission on Human Rights for the acceptance of the Cairo Declaration as the Islamic alternative to international human rights.[9] That these regimes with their vastly diverging philosophies would promote any document on the basis of a commitment to shared Islamic values was highly improbable. Saudi Arabia's official Wahhabi Islam, which upheld the rule of an absolute monarchy and had a strong anti-Shi'i bias, was denounced by Iran. Saddam Hussein, Iraq's dictator, had been excoriated by Ayatollah Ruhollah Khomeini. A member of Iraq's Sunni minority, Saddam Hussein adhered to Ba'athism, a secular Arab nationalist ideology, and repressed and persecuted Iraq's restive Shi'i majority. However dissimilar their religious policies were, all three regimes had a common practice of denying rights and freedoms to their citizens and resorting to drastic measures to repress and eliminate their opponents and critics. All three apparently calculated that they stood to benefit from promoting an alternative to international human rights law in which Islamic criteria would be used to dilute rights. On the occasion of the OIC meeting in Tehran in December 1997, Iran and various other OIC members continued to press the idea that the existing UN human rights system was excessively Western and needed to be adjusted to accommodate the culture and religious values of Muslim countries, a view that was rejected by UN Secretary-General Kofi Annan, who insisted that human rights were universal.[10]

Also reviewed is the Basic Law of Saudi Arabia, which was issued on March 1, 1992.[11] Unlike Iran, Pakistan, or the Sudan, Saudi Arabia was not pursuing Islamization, having elected instead to retain in most areas premodern Islamic law as set forth in juristic treatises as the law of the land. Instead, Saudi Arabia was belatedly embarking on a program of tentative reforms of a kind that most nations had already undertaken by the early twentieth century. The 1992 Basic Law, although very rudimentary, was the closest thing to a constitution that Saudi Arabia had ever possessed. The provisions of the Basic Law purported to derive from Islam and to establish a government that likewise derived from Islam.[12] The disparity between the rights that the Basic Law affords and those in the Cairo Declaration, which Saudi Arabia had also publicly endorsed, reveal a lack of coherence in Saudi human rights policies.

The new Afghan and Iraqi constitutions are briefly discussed in later chapters. These documents were prepared after the previous regimes had been overthrown by US military invasions, and therefore US advisers had significant input into the constitution-drafting processes. Nevertheless, in both countries, the question of how to balance the competing claims of Islam and human rights turned out to be a central bone of contention, just as it was in several other Muslim countries. Elements of Islamization programs in Pakistan and Sudan as well as some additional publications dealing with Islam and human rights are also discussed for the purpose of comparisons.

It bears repeating that the fact that the Islamic human rights schemes presented here are referred to as "Islamic" does not imply that the principles involved represent definitive statements of where Islamic doctrine stands on rights issues, nor does it mean that all or even a majority of the world's more than 1 billion Muslims would approve them. The question of how human rights protections relate to the Islamic tradition remains an intensely contested issue throughout the Muslim world.

The Islamic human rights documents reviewed here represent in many respects compromise positions, asserting that Islam does accept human rights—as long as those human rights are subordinated to Islamic criteria. The result is a mélange—and often a very awkward one—of international law with concepts that are taken from the Islamic legal heritage or that are presented as having Islamic pedigrees.

The literature corresponding to the compromise positions provides a fascinating illustration of what happens when aspects of two dissimilar legal systems combine, producing a blend with no historical antecedent. As it happens, the compromise view that Islam accommodates human rights in some form but imposes conditions and restrictions on them is also one that has enormous political significance.

The Impact of Islamization on Constitutions and Justice

The belated emergence of Islamic human rights schemes in the Middle East ties in with the pattern of pressures for Islamization of laws. A brief review of some governmental Islamization measures affecting rights is called for. Measures to implement Islamic law and ideology in individual countries cannot realistically be severed from local politics. Thus, for example, the specifics of the Islamization programs in Iran and in its neighbor Pakistan differ widely, and these two models in turn differ from the version of Islamization that was pursued in their shared neighbor Afghanistan under the Taliban. Islamization in the chaotic war-torn Sudan has had its own particularities. However, the official Islamization programs in all countries have tended to correlate with deteriorating human rights situations and a drastic weakening of institutions that could secure the rule of law.

The autocratic regime of the late shah of Iran pursued a course of rapid Westernization and only belatedly confronted the political potency of Islam as a means of mobilizing political protest. Iran's 1979 Islamic Revolution started out as a broad-based popular revolution, but a clerical faction ultimately wrested control over the government and crushed secular and liberal forces. Iran's Islamization program, following a major revolutionary upheaval and masterminded by conservative clerics, was naturally more far-reaching and more representative of clerical attitudes than the versions of Islamization implemented elsewhere.

Iran's Islamization was theoretically designed to bring the law and the administration of justice into conformity with the standards of the *shari'a*, or Islamic law. In the course of Islamization programs, many rules taken from the premodern *shari'a*, or at least ostensibly inspired by *shari'a* principles, were enacted into law, and the previous Western standards were abandoned. Not only substantive laws but also courts and enforcement practices were altered to reflect what were officially described as Islamic requirements. The bar and judiciary, which were geared toward modern European standards, were regarded as roadblocks in the way of implementing Islamic law. Members of the bar, who had the outlook of highly trained professionals and who were influenced by liberal values that were in line with human rights, often found it difficult, if not impossible, to fulfill their professional responsibilities in the changed circumstances. Iran finally took measures in 1981–1982 to dismantle and altogether destroy Iran's bar association.[13]

One might have expected that with all the fanfare about reviving Islamic law, the postrevolutionary constitution would represent a sharp break with the past, but in reality, it expressed considerable continuity with Iran's first constitution, which was drawn up in 1906–1907. This first constitution contained both secular and Islamic elements, representing a fragile compromise between liberal and conservative factions.[14] It was heavily indebted to French influences, as was Iran's legal culture more generally, and these influences persisted even after the Islamic Revolution.

After the overthrow of the shah, a draft constitution was prepared in spring 1979, a period in which leftist and secular forces still retained influence. Like the 1906–1907 constitution, this first draft contained both secular and Islamic principles, but it showed far less deference to the ideas and wishes of conservative clerics than the constitution that was subsequently adopted. After the balance of power shifted in favor of conservative clerics and after elections that were denounced as unfair by secular political groups, a constituent assembly was chosen in August 1979, with a majority consisting of conservative Shi'i clerics. The new constitution, approved by a referendum in December 1979, reflected the consolidation of clerical control. It retained some features of the earlier draft and contained elements derived from French models but unequivocally affirmed the supremacy of Islamic law over human rights and significantly enhanced the power of the Shi'i clergy over the government and the legal system. The current Iranian constitution is, therefore, a product of decades of struggle to define what role Islamic law and the clergy should play in the legal system and government. It perpetuates rather than resolves old tensions in this regard. Significant revisions were made in July 1989 in an attempt to establish a mechanism for resolving these tensions—but without much prospect of ending them.[15]

The upheaval embodied in the Iranian revolution haunted more secular regimes. Aggressive countermeasures by dictatorial governments in countries such as Algeria, Egypt, Iraq (before the US invasion), Syria, Libya, and Tunisia stalled campaigns by opposition groups calling for Islamization. Other regimes tried to co-opt Islamization movements by making concessions to demands for reviving Islamic law. As is discussed below, in Pakistan and Sudan military dictatorships decided to follow this second course.

All in all, the systemic changes made under the rubric of Islamization in Pakistan, Iran, and Sudan did much to erode the rule of law by highly politicizing the administration of justice and compromising judicial independence. The pursuit of Islamization also coincided with shifts in the patterns of human rights violations, among other things leading to the application of certain barbaric criminal penalties, expanding discrimination against women, and fostering more aggressive persecution of minorities and religious dissidents. The significance of the overall change in human rights violations that accompanied the Islamization programs has been extensively documented by many reputable observers and by international organizations and institutions concerned with the protection of human rights.[16]

In general, regimes pursuing Islamization have reacted defensively and angrily when accused of violating human rights, even when maintaining that Islam dictates their policies. This suggests that, by and large, despite their assertions that Islamic law justifies breaching human rights, states regard international human rights law as normative and fear criticism for violating it.

When pursuing Islamization, the governments of Iran, Pakistan, and Sudan were concerned that the deteriorations in rights would lead to embarrassing constitutional challenges. As a result, various strategies were devised for obviating such challenges, including rewriting constitutional provisions so as to eviscerate rights or simply suspending them. In all three countries, Islamization has led to the dominance of philosophies antithetical to constitutionalism.

In Iran, the basic approach was to elevate Islamic law above the 1979 constitution and to add a number of vague Islamic qualifications to constitutional rights provisions. These Islamic qualifications are discussed in greater detail in Chapters 4–9. Although the addition of qualifications to rights provisions did not entirely eliminate conflicts between the government's conduct and certain provisions of the Iranian constitution, it provided sweeping justifications for infringing on rights. For example, Article 4 of the Iranian constitution set the stage for using Islamic criteria, which were left undefined, as pretexts for diluting rights. It provides: "All civil, penal, financial, economic, administrative, cultural, military, political laws and other laws or regulations, must be based on Islamic criteria. This principle applies absolutely and generally to all articles of the Constitution as well as to all other laws and regulations, and the *fuqaha* [Islamic jurists] of the Guardian Council are judges in this matter." These jurists are Islamic clerics who, according to Article 110, are to be appointed by Iran's supreme religious leader. The clerics on the council have been given the ultimate power to decide what laws are or are not in conformity with Islamic principles.

In consequence, even constitutional rights guarantees cannot have force should clerics decide that those guarantees are not compatible with Islamic principles, but what these Islamic principles consist of and how they are to affect constitutional rights have never been clarified. The clerical elite has dismantled many elements of Iran's largely French-based legal order but has not replaced them with a firm framework of legality using Islamic standards, leaving Iran in a kind of legal limbo. As one human rights report on Iran asserts, Iran's clerics have seriously undermined the rule of law in the country by monopolizing the interpretation of core ideological precepts.[17]

Rather than showing the scrupulous concern for legality that would be expected on the part of senior jurists, Iran's ruling clerics have often displayed thuggish behavior antithetical to legality. An example of their mindset was presented in 1997, when Ayatollah Mohammed-Taqi Mesbah-Yazdi, the head of Iran's judiciary, reacted to Ayatollah Hussein-Ali Montazeri's challenge to the authority of supreme jurist Ayatollah Ali Khamene'i. Montazeri, once Khomeini's chosen successor but later a bold critic of the regime's abuses, was barred from the succession and placed under house arrest. To chasten Montazeri for questioning a pillar of Iran's system of clerical rule, agents of the regime launched violent attacks on his home, and menacing demonstrations were staged by a hostile rabble. Not being sure that the violence and threats had been sufficiently intimidating, Ayatollah Yazdi thought it well to warn publicly that Montazeri would face "an even stronger response" if he did not desist from speaking out.[18] That is, in responding to critical remarks by an eminent cleric, the head of Iran's judiciary, instead of addressing the points that had been raised, spoke like the head of a criminal syndicate accustomed to threatening violence to obtain acquiescence.

Iran's theocracy has offered what should be called "political law," amounting to a system where laws—including what passes for Islamic law—and court proceedings are subordinate to politics.[19] How Iran's official Islamic ideology has shaped human rights violations is strikingly illustrated by the abuse of political prisoners and the distinctive systems of torture used in Iran's prisons.[20]

In the period before Iran's ruling clerics decided that it was diplomatic to mute their disdain for human rights, one heard them speak scornfully of these. Ayatollah Khomeini asserted, "What they call human rights is nothing but a collection of corrupt rules worked out by Zionists to destroy all true religions." Ali Khamene'i, then president of Iran and not yet elevated to the dignity of supreme jurist, stated: "When we want to find out what is right and what is wrong, we do not go to the United Nations; we go to the Holy Koran. For us the Universal Declaration of Human Rights is nothing but a collection of mumbo-jumbo by disciples of Satan."[21]

The vigorous debates about Islam and human rights in Iran have exposed how strongly Iran's clerics disagree on how Islam relates to human rights. Many of Iran's most popular and prestigious clerics have spoken out to demand expanded rights and freedoms and have denounced the official practice of using Islam to ratify tyranny—this despite the fact that the regime punishes clerical dissent with particular fury.[22]

The controversies about Islam and human rights were put to a political test in the 1997 and 2001 Iranian elections. After long excluding any prospective candidates who might pose a challenge to the establishment, Iran's clerical elite miscalculated in 1997 and permitted Mohammed Khatami, a liberal cleric, to run for president. Khatami won a broad popular mandate, a success that was repeated in the 2001 elections. His victories were achieved with promises to advance the causes of human rights, democracy, and the rule of law and to end the use of Islam to justify oppression.[23] Iranians, especially young Iranians, responded enthusiastically to Khatami's promises of liberalization, and many clerics and intellectuals were prompted to speak out in support of human rights and to denounce the conservative clergy's use of Islam to crush freedom.[24]

University Centre Library
The Hub at Blackburn College

Customer ID: ******47

Title: Islam and Human Rights; Tradition and Politics (5 ed.)
ID: BB53203
Due: Tue, 15 Nov 2016

Total items: 1
08/11/2016 09:54

Please retain this receipt for your records
Contact Tel. 01254 292165

Conservatives managed to thwart his reform efforts and even began to escalate their repression. Khatami was not up to the task of curbing the entrenched hard-liners, and when in 2004 they engineered a victory of conservative candidates for parliament, a period of tentative liberalization came to an end. Mahmoud Ahmadinejad, the mayor of Tehran and an acolyte of Ayatollah Khomeini, won the presidency in June 2005 after the Council of Guardians had drastically winnowed the candidate list to preclude the election of a charismatic reformer like Khatami. His victory led to further clampdowns on human rights in the name of Islam. When he again ran for the presidency in 2009, Ahmadinejad faced opposition not only from Iran's long-suffering populace but also from liberal clerics, who spoke out to denounce the human rights violations that had been perpetrated under his regime. When Ahmadinejad won after what were widely seen as fraudulent vote tallies, mass public protests erupted in what became known as the Green Movement that were only quelled by the regime's recourse to lethal violence. During the protests, it became clear that younger Iranians were incensed by the vote-rigging and were eager to bring the era of clerical despotism to an end.

In Sudan and Pakistan, a different approach was taken: Their constitutions were effectively suspended during most of their respective Islamization programs. The turbulent and complicated recent histories of both countries make it impossible to cover all relevant events, but some aspects of the connection between Islamization and the human rights violations perpetrated by the Sudanese and Pakistani regimes are indicated.

President Jaafar Nimeiri, who had ruled Sudan after seizing power in May 1969, decided in 1983 to try to consolidate his increasingly unpopular regime by cementing an alliance with the Sudanese contingent of the Muslim Brothers, who had long championed Islamization. He inaugurated an ambitious but haphazard Islamization program, which led to a renewed outbreak of civil war between the Arab and Muslim north and the mostly African animist or Christian South.[25] In 1984, Nimeiri sought to rewrite the Sudanese constitution to make himself the supreme political and religious leader but was thwarted by determined opposition. Instead, in order to press ahead with his Islamization program while avoiding charges that he was violating the constitution, he declared a state of emergency on April 29, 1984, insisting that it was needed to preserve Islam from its enemies.[26] Although the state of emergency was officially lifted in autumn 1984 under US diplomatic pressure, in practice, constitutional rights remained suspended until Nimeiri's overthrow the following year. Obviously, Sudanese Islamization was closely associated with the suspension of the constitution.

Upon Nimeiri's overthrow by a popular revolution in 1985, there was a period of rule by a caretaker military regime, during which the 1973 Sudanese constitution was replaced by an interim constitution.[27] Sudan reverted to a free, democratic system in April 1986. After plans were launched in spring 1989 to abrogate Nimeiri's Islamic laws, military leaders allied with Hassan al-Turabi's National Islamic Front (NIF) staged a coup, which resulted in the installation in July 1989 of a military dictatorship under General Omar al-Bashir, in which al-Turabi played the role of an éminence grise until a falling out with al-Bashir in 2001. Zealously committed to Islamization, the al-Bashir regime promptly abrogated the interim constitution and suspended all the rights and freedoms that the Sudanese had enjoyed in the brief interlude of democracy. A pattern of egregious human rights violations ensued, in which oppressive military dictatorship and systematic denials of rights and freedoms were associated with the pursuit of Islamization.[28] It was not until 1997 that the regime finally announced that a new constitution would be promulgated.[29]

Responses by Sudanese officialdom to independent human rights monitors were revealing. Reacting to the critical 1994 UN Commission on Human Rights report by Caspar Biro finding that Sudanese law, including its Islamic laws, clashed with international law, the Sudanese delegate to the commission charged that the findings constituted an attack on Islam.[30] Sudan's attorney general claimed that Biro's report was "satanic," and he castigated Biro as "an enemy of Islam" guilty of "blasphemy" for criticizing Sudan's Islamic laws.[31]

Under outside pressure, the Khartoum regime finally made a peace agreement with rebels in the South in January 2005, culminating in the adoption of a constitution signed on July 9, 2005. The new constitution retreated from endorsing the Islamization that had exacerbated tensions with the South and embraced reconstruction and reconciliation through the recognition of Sudanese racial, religious, and cultural diversity.[32] This conciliatory gesture was too little, too late. Human rights violations proliferated as the civil war continued, accompanied by genocidal massacres, which in 2009 led to the International Criminal Court issuing a warrant for the arrest of Omar al-Bashir for committing war crimes and crimes against humanity. After years of merciless oppression by Khartoum regimes wedded to Islamist ideologies, Sudanese in the South voted overwhelmingly to secede, finally achieving independence in July 2011.

There are notable similarities between Islamization in Sudan under Nimeiri and in Pakistan in the period 1977–1988, in both of which constitutionalism was enfeebled. President Muhammad Zia-ul-Haq, after overthrowing the elected government of President Zulfikar Ali Bhutto, ruled Pakistan as a military dictator until his death in a plane crash in August 1988. Zia declared martial law after seizing power, and it remained in force until December 1985. However, the formal termination of martial law in 1985 did not in practice result in a full restoration of constitutional guarantees of fundamental rights. In Pakistan, as in Nimeiri's Sudan, a project for drafting an Islamic constitution, which was to replace the existing 1973 constitution, eventually came to naught.

Zia used his pursuit of Islamization as the justification for his retention of dicta-torial powers and the suspension of constitutional rights. In a major address given in 1983, while all fundamental constitutional rights were formally suspended, Zia analogized his position as chief martial law administrator to that of a traditional prince, or emir.[33] Zia indicated that opposition would not be tolerated:

> One basic point that emerges from a study of the Quranic verses and the Prophet's sayings is that as long as the Amir or the head of State abides by the injunctions of Allah and his Prophet (PBUH) ["peace and blessings upon him"] his obedience becomes mandatory for his subjects or the people, irre-spective of the personal dislike that someone may harbor for the Amir or any of his actions. Not only in my opinion but also in the opinion of legal experts and scholars, my Government, too, is a constitutional Government, which has been acting upon the tenets of Islam. We are devout Muslims. I concede, and I am proud of it, that the present Government is a military Government.[34]

Zia borrowed from premodern Islamic thought the idea that Muslims should obey persons in authority as long as they were not being commanded to engage in conduct that was sinful. Nonetheless, Zia made the surprising assertion that his dictatorship was a "constitutional" government even though experts would be hard-pressed to cite a constitutional provision that supported Zia's position. In 1985, he had the constitution amended to ensure that he would have special immunity to escape civil and criminal liability once martial law had ended.

In that same year, Zia had the constitution amended to enhance its Islamic fea-tures by including Pakistan's Objectives Resolution, an aspirational statement that had not formerly been treated as part of the operative principles of the constitu-tion. The resolution was inserted into the text as Article 2-A, and one segment provided the basis for further Islamization measures via the assertion that Pakistan was a nation "wherein the Muslims shall be enabled to order their lives in the in-dividual and collective spheres in accordance with the teachings and requirements of Islam as set out in the Holy Quran and the Sunnah." This language was cited in the *Zaheeruddin* case, discussed in Chapters 7 and 9, and used to eviscerate the constitutional guarantee of religious freedom.

Zia tried to consolidate his alliance with friendly Islamic clerics by appointing them to serve as judges. As a result of this policy, many persons with inadequate educations were appointed as judges, leading to changes that compromised the integrity and independence of Pakistan's formerly distinguished judiciary. Is-lamization continued to have an impact well after Zia's demise.[35]

Pakistan's leading politicians, Benazir Bhutto and Nawaz Sharif, were locked in bitter struggles that precluded much benefit ensuing from the return to democracy after Zia's death. In October 1999, General Pervez Musharraf seized power and proclaimed himself "president" in June 2001, a status that was formally confirmed in a dubious election in 2002. Musharraf, effectively ruling as a military dictator, suspended the constitution for some years before restoring it in 2003. A basically secular military officer, he was preoccupied with Pakistan's difficult international relations and serious domestic unrest; for him, ending the human rights violations traceable to Zia's legacy of Islamization measures was not a high priority. Under fire from many quarters, Musharraf resigned in 2008 and was succeeded by the ill-regarded Asif Ali Zardari, elected president after the 2007 assassination of his wife Benazir Bhutto. As discontent over widespread corruption festered and incidents of intercommunal violence and urban terrorism proliferated, Pakistan seemed adrift and also lacking in leadership capable of addressing its manifold problems. With Pakistan lurching from crisis to crisis and tensions in the region growing ever more acute, predicting the future of Islamization in that country became difficult.

The Taliban Takeover of Afghanistan and Its Aftermath

Afghanistan has suffered traumas and upheavals due to ongoing conflicts since the Russian invasion of 1979, which led to a protracted and devastating civil war, which culminated in an eventual Russian pullout in 1989.[36] The 1996 conquest of most of the country by the Taliban, a Pashtun faction of Islamist zealots, led to the implementation of an extraordinarily repressive version of Islamization. The Taliban's official Islam reflected the attitudes of a brutish rabble influenced by the ideas of Deobandi Islam, a rigid, purist version of Islam that seeks to return to a supposed model of the original Islamic community and aims to reject all Western influences.

In October 1997, the Taliban renamed the country the Islamic Emirate of Afghanistan, their emir being the arch-reactionary Mullah Mohammed Omar, who ruled without the benefit of institutions of modern governance such as a constitution. Under the Taliban's Islamization program, human rights violations assumed epic proportions. After they discarded Western-style Afghan laws on the pretext of returning to the *shari'a*, the rule of law, already shaky, was further undermined. Taliban abuses included the arbitrary murders of many men, women, and children; the unacknowledged detention of thousands of persons abducted by various armed political groups; the torture of civilians; the rape of women; savage persecutions of Shi'is and non-Pashtun ethnic groups; and the routine mistreatment of persons suspected of belonging to rival political factions. Under the rubric of applying Islamic law, a highly retrograde version of gender apartheid was instituted.[37]

Although many Afghans welcomed the overthrow of the Taliban regime in late 2001 by the invading US forces, the weak central government that followed was only nominally democratic. Living in a shattered country where corruption and warlordism are rampant, Afghans remain deeply divided on crucial issues, including the acceptability of being governed by a Kabul regime answerable to the US embassy. Because of the anarchic violence and terrorism that plague the country, it is unclear whether the 2003 Afghan constitution, provisions of which could potentially be invoked to resist Islamization, will have significant impact.

Saudi Arabia Confronts Pressures for Reforms and Liberalization

Unlike countries that are pursuing Islamization, Saudi Arabia aims to resist pressures for change. The monarchy has struggled to balance competing forces; at the same time that many Saudis were demanding major reforms to advance democratization and human rights, powerful conservative forces and hardline clerics decried any loosening of Islamic strictures or relaxing of tight control by the security forces. The kingdom was unusual in that premodern Islamic jurisprudence had retained its authority, although Islamic law had been replaced by secular law in areas where commercial and economic relations had required adjustments, as had happened when the kingdom sought World Trade Organization (WTO) membership in 2005. In such important areas as family and criminal law, Islamic law remained entrenched.

Since the 1990s, Saudi Arabia has embarked on a program of modest reforms, which included promulgating the 1992 Basic Law.[38] It was adopted after both liberal and conservative sectors of Saudi society had indicated their impatience with the Saudi family's autocratic rule, the deficiencies of the legal system, and the failure to respect basic rights and freedoms.[39] The Basic Law did not improve the country's deplorable human rights situation, and it affirmed the absolute character of the Saudi monarchy, treating rule by the Saudi clan as if it were grounded in the Islamic sources.[40] King Fahd Bin Abdul Aziz appealed to "Islamic beliefs" to defend the failure to guarantee Saudis any of the rights that constitutionalism normally affords citizens. He asserted:

> The democratic system that is predominant in the world is not a suitable system for the peoples of our region. Our people's makeup and unique qualities are different from those of the rest of the world. We cannot import the methods used by people in other countries and apply them to our people. We have our Islamic beliefs that constitute a complete and fully integrated system. In my view, Western democracies may be suitable in their own countries but they do not suit other countries.[41]

The September 11, 2001, terrorist attacks on the United States and spillover violence on Saudi territory unsettled the status quo. In subsequent years, petitions calling for reforms and demanding a real constitution were circulated. The monarchy occasionally lashed out at those demanding change. The 2005 death of the ailing and inept King Fahd and the accession to the throne of King Abdullah raised the possibility that a more astute monarch might see it in the regime's interests to respond to its liberal critics. King Abdullah did initiate some modest reforms, including measures to improve the quality of the courts and allowing women to study law, but these fell far short of meeting popular demands for democratization and accountability. Restrictions on independent human rights activism remained firm, as did resistance to demands for curbing the corruption that notoriously blighted the system. The unflinching resolve of the Saudi clan to eliminate any threats to its power was manifested in 2011 in the overwhelming force deployed during the Arab Spring, initially to quell protest demonstrations on Saudi territory and subsequently to crush with even greater violence protests by members of the restive Shi'i majority in neighboring Bahrain.

Summary

As background for any discussion of Islamic human rights schemes, the consequences of Islamization programs for human rights deserve to be carefully considered. The pursuit of Islamization—or in the Saudi case, the regime's clinging to premodern Islamic jurisprudence and institutions—has correlated with patterns of disregard for human rights and with policies inimical to the rule of law. To date, one cannot find governments that are purporting to accord supremacy to Islamic law that have shown solicitude for protecting human rights as established in international law. On the contrary, as one might expect from regimes that would earn poor grades on most governance indicators, their policies have correlated with enfeebled human rights and setbacks for constitutionalism. When one bears in mind that it is regimes such as those in Iran and Saudi Arabia that have been in the forefront in promoting Islamic human rights schemes, one appreciates that the relevant political cultures mean that in these schemes, Islamic criteria will be used in ways that are inimical to human rights.

CHAPTER 3

Islamic Tradition and Muslim Reactions to Human Rights

The Premodern Islamic Heritage

One finds many concepts that prefigure human rights in the Islamic sources and in the work of premodern jurists, but, although the Islamic heritage provided the potential resources for articulating human rights, this potential long remained latent. This lag in articulating rights must be taken into account. Various factors and circumstances deterred the production of human rights within an Islamic framework, which meant that Islamic human rights schemes only came into being well after the emergence of international human rights law.

The individualism characteristic of Western civilization was a fundamental ingredient in the development of civil and political rights. In contrast, prioritizing the individual was not a characteristic feature of Muslim societies or of Islamic culture. That is not to say that individualism was totally absent, because Sufism, or mysticism, which is a major component of the Islamic tradition, does comprise elements of individualism.[1] Other features of the Islamic tradition likewise can provide grounding for an individualistic approach to rights.[2]

Islamic doctrines were historically produced in traditional societies, where one would not expect the elaboration of individualistic tenets. Nonindividualistic and even anti-individualistic attitudes are common in traditional societies, where individuals are situated in a given position in a social context and are seen as components of family or community structures rather than as autonomous, separate beings entitled to chart their own courses. Thus, to say that individualism was not prized in Islamic doctrines elaborated by Muslim thinkers in the past is to make an observation that relates more to the historical context in which these ideas were produced than to Islam as a religion. This background does not warrant assertions that Islam is inherently incapable of accommodating individualism or necessarily hostile to it. As Khaled Abou El Fadl has noted, "Premodern Muslim jurists did not assert a collectivist vision of rights, just as they did not assert an individualistic vision of rights."[3] Despite this, as many examples in this book illustrate, proponents of Islamic human rights schemes have tended to associate the defense of Islamic values with the rejection of individualism, and they have espoused principles—such as a ban on converting from Islam—that are designed to protect the collective at the expense of the individual.

Within the vast heritage of Islamic civilization, one encounters philosophical concepts, humanistic values, and moral principles that are well adapted for use in constructing human rights principles.[4] However, historical factors, such as the political ascendancy of an orthodox philosophy and theology that were hostile to humanism and rationalism—and ultimately, hostile to the liberal ideals associated with human rights—kept the exponents of such values and principles in a generally weak and defensive position. If circumstances had allowed adherents of rationalist and humanistic currents to attain greater political power and influence, such thinkers might have oriented Islamic thought in ways that would have created a much more propitious climate for the early emergence of human rights ideas. Despite their minority position, the views of rationalist and humanistic Muslim thinkers are definitely anchored in the Islamic tradition.

Some eminent Islamic philosophers, such as al-Farabi (d. 950) and Ibn Rushd ("Averroes") (d. 1198), came close to saying that reason determines what is right and true and that religion must conform to reason's dictates.[5] This was exceptional; orthodox theologians in Sunni Islam were generally mistrustful of human reason, fearing that it would lead Muslims to stray from the truth of Revelation. There was an ongoing tension between the rationalist inclinations of Islamic philosophers, many of whom were influenced by Greek philosophy, and the tenets of the dominant philosophy of ethical voluntarism. According to this influential school of thought, whatever God willed was ipso facto just. Therefore, perfect justice could be achieved if all God's creatures, both ruler and ruled, simply obeyed God's commands as expressed in Islamic law. In consequence, the orthodox view was that Muslims should unquestioningly defer to the wisdom of God as expressed in Islamic doctrines.[6] The dominance of this view made it difficult to realize an Islamic version of the Age of Reason.

One of the most important rationalist currents in Islamic thought was that of the group known as the Mu'tazila, whose members' influence in the Sunni world reached its zenith in the ninth century, after which they were largely suppressed.[7] The Mu'tazilites called for rational interpretations of the Islamic sources and claimed that Islam mandated justice in both the political and social spheres. The community was to control the government, not to defer blindly to authority, and it was free to revolt against governments that denied fundamental liberties.[8] Islamic thinkers who have adopted the Mu'tazilite approach, openly espousing the idea of the supremacy of reason over Revelation and calling for laws to conform to human notions of justice, have always risked being branded heretical by staunch adherents of the view that neither Islam nor its divine law can be evaluated by human reason.

Although rationalist thinkers have generally been marginalized in Muslim milieus since the crushing of the Mu'tazila, rationalist currents were never entirely extirpated, and in Twelver Shi'i Islam these ideas have remained influential. The cases of Nasr Hamid Abu Zaid, discussed in Chapter 9, and of Abdolkarim Soroush illustrate the continuing relevance of the controversies set in motion by the Mu'tazilites' refusal to defer meekly to established orthodoxy. Soroush, an Iranian professor of philosophy, offers visions of an Islam stripped of the restraints on freedoms that had characterized the reigning Islamic ideology, expressly endorsing Mu'tazilite positions.[9] Among other things, Soroush has dared to maintain publicly that justice preceded Islam and that Islamic law should conform to the criterion of justice. Although Iran's ruling clerics attacked him for espousing heretical views, in exalting the principle of justice, Soroush was endorsing a rationalist philosophy that had long roots in the Shi'i tradition, according to which it was legitimate for Muslims to refuse to defer unquestioningly to what they were instructed was required by Islamic doctrine and to employ reason to determine whether doctrines entailed injustice. For making bold critiques of official Iranian manipulation of Islam to circumscribe rights and freedoms, Soroush was subjected to harsh censorship and restrictions designed to silence him, and he became a target of violent physical assaults and threats, which led him to spend considerable time in overseas havens.

The ascendancy of ethical voluntarism and the relative weakness of rationalist currents in Sunni Islam had important consequences. Islamic thought tended to stress not the rights of human beings but rather their duties to obey God's perfect law, which by its nature would achieve the ideal balance in society. Today, one still finds this emphasis on duties. For example, Ayatollah Khomeini insisted that man had no natural rights and that believers were to submit to God's commands.[10]

Because the pious Muslim was simply supposed to understand and obey divine commands, demands for individual freedoms could sound distinctly subversive to the orthodox mind. Such demands might be taken to suggest that individuals did not consider themselves strictly bound to submit to the dictates of Islamic law and to the authorities charged with its execution or that they were presuming to use their own fallible human reasoning powers to challenge the supremacy of religious teachings.[11]

Scholars of Islamic law did not traditionally focus on what institutions and procedures were needed to constrain the ruler and curb oppression; rather, they tended to think in terms of scenarios in which rulers were pious Muslims eager to follow God's mandate and implement the *shari'a*.[12] In consequence, *shari'a* doctrines remained highly idealistic and were not elaborated with a view to providing institutional mechanisms that could afford legal redress when governments systematically oppressed and exploited their subjects.[13] The single exception lay in the area of property rights, where the *shari'a* did provide remedies for the individual wrongfully deprived of property by official action.[14]

These characteristics of Islamic thought inhibited the growth of concepts of individual rights that could be asserted against infringements by governments but never totally eclipsed other views more favorable to the generation of rights. One finds humanistic currents beginning in the early stages of Islamic thought and continuing to the present.[15] In addition, early Islamic thought includes precursors of the idea of political freedom.[16] Concepts of democracy very much like those in modern political systems can be found in the earliest period in Islamic history in the ideas of the Kharijite sect, which broke off from mainstream Islam in the seventh century over the community's refusal to agree to the Kharijite tenet that the successors to the Prophet Muhammad must be elected by the community.[17] Kharijites have been castigated for their unorthodox views, and their literature is not familiar to most other Muslims; but it still might be said that the Islamic tradition from the outset has included ideas that anticipated some of the democratic principles that underlie modern human rights.

When one scours the writings of premodern jurists, theologians, and philosophers for the elaboration of ideas that would either tend to accommodate human rights principles or to create obstacles to their reception in the Islamic tradition, one faces an overabundance of authority that has conflicting implications for rights. After one surveys premodern Islamic intellectual history, one realizes that there was no settled Islamic doctrine on rights or proto-rights in that period, only currents of thought that would create either a more or a less propitious foundation for the assimilation of modern human rights concepts within an Islamic framework.

Although the dominant currents in the premodern Islamic heritage did not provide a congenial setting for the early development of human rights concepts, there were from the earliest stages features that offered the potential for successful integration of the premises of modern human rights. Those who deploy Islam as a bulwark against democratization and human rights are therefore using only one aspect of the multifaceted Islamic heritage. As a former member of the Egyptian Organization of Human Rights has observed, "Authoritarian and oppressive projects draw on the wealth of authoritarian traditions, images and symbols that are present in every human culture. Liberationist projects draw on the resistance and emancipatory traditions that are equally present in every human culture."[18] Muslims who are mining their tradition for guidance on how to deal with the human rights dimensions of contemporary problems find ample ground for rejecting the authority of interpretations that construct Islam as an obstacle to progress in the human rights domain.[19]

Muslim Reactions to Western Constitutionalism

The modern system of human rights set forth in international law requires translation into rights provisions in national constitutions and laws in order to afford effective legal guarantees for those rights. Just as there is no unitary Islamic position on the merits of rationalism or humanism, so there is no unanimity on where Islam stands vis-à-vis constitutionalism, an institution closely tied to the development of legal protections for rights. The reactions of Muslims to modern constitutionalism, which clearly came to the Middle East as a legal transplant from the West, have historically run the gamut from enthusiastic endorsement to hostile rejection.[20]

Muslim elites became familiar with Western ideas of law and governance in the nineteenth century. The relative weakness of Middle Eastern countries, which proved incapable of standing up to European powers, became associated with the failure to establish and protect political freedoms. When Muslims began seeking legal means for curbing despotic rulers, they turned not to the Islamic tradition but to Europe for models. Constitutionalism in the Middle East was typically promoted by adherents of secular nationalist movements and led by educated elites and often by Western-trained lawyers.[21] Early constitutionalists moved in the direction of dismantling legally imposed inequalities among citizens, and the nation rather than the religious community became the focus of political loyalty.[22]

Muslims who advocated constitutionalism frequently found that conservative *ulama*, or learned men of religion, were among their most determined foes. Often the *ulama* fought constitutionalism in the name of preserving Islam because they were convinced that constitutional principles conflicted with *shari'a* law.[23] The historical pattern of *ulama* resistance to constitutionalism endured longest in Saudi Arabia, the Muslim country where conservative Sunni *ulama* have retained the greatest political influence. Despite decades of efforts by liberal members of the Saudi elite to win acceptance for the notion of constitutionalism, no constitution has ever been adopted. The basic law that was finally adopted in 1992 fell far short of meeting the standards of modern constitutionalism.[24]

There have also been many *ulama* who worked closely with liberal and reformist movements that promoted Western-style constitutionalism. The influential Islamic reformer Muhammad 'Abduh (d. 1905), who served as grand mufti of Egypt, is a prime example. An al-Azhar graduate and Islamic legal scholar, 'Abduh was a strong supporter of Egyptian nationalism and constitutionalism. He and other like-minded reformist clerics saw no fatal conflict between constitutionalism and fidelity to Islam.

In sum, one can say that Islamic clerics were divided and have remained so on whether constitutionalism, an institution that is of central importance for the protection of human rights, is compatible with the *shari'a*. Controversies in this area have been aggravated as contemporary Islamization programs have tended to correlate with the degradation of constitutionalism; the suspension of constitutions; or as in the case of the Taliban, a complete rejection of constitutionalism as an alien, Western idea.

The Persistence of Traditional Priorities and Values

Proponents of Islamic human rights schemes, instead of looking for elements in the Islamic heritage that complement rights, are inclined to cling to the ideas and attitudes of traditional orthodoxy, such as ethical voluntarism, the supremacy of divine Revelation, and hostility toward rationalism and humanism. They have thus elected to adhere to the same dominant intellectual framework that historically impeded the development of human rights concepts, with consequences that are delineated in analyses of rights provisions in Chapters 4–9.

Ideally, one would want to study complete expositions of the authors' philosophies of human rights appended to each of the schemes, which would enable one to correlate those philosophies directly with the provisions in each scheme. Unfortunately, the authors have not provided such expositions. In default of such, there are still some grounds for characterizing their values and priorities.

Insofar as the schemes expressly indicate their priorities, they uphold the primacy of Revelation over reason; none endorses reason as a source of law or moral guidance. In such schemes, any challenges that might be made to Islamic law on the grounds that it denies human rights guaranteed under international law are ruled out ab initio; human reason is deemed inadequate to criticize what are treated as divine orders. This affirms the traditional orthodox view that the tenets of the *shari'a* are perfect and are also just because they represent the will of the Creator, being derived from divine Revelation and the example of the divinely inspired Prophet.

For example, in the preamble to the English version of the UIDHR, one sees that it takes the position that divine Revelation has provided the "legal and moral framework within which to establish and regulate human institutions and relationships." This idea is implicit throughout the text of the Arabic version, as passages from the Qur'an and the *sunna* of the Prophet are extensively quoted. It is thus clear that for the authors of the UIDHR, sacred texts enjoy primacy as the source of law. The status of reason is correspondingly demoted. In a later passage in the preamble of the UIDHR, the authors expressly proclaim in the Arabic version that they believe that human reason (*al-'aql al-bashari*), independent of God's guidance and inspiration, is insufficient to provide the best plan for human life. In the corresponding part of the English version, after stating that "rationality by itself" cannot be "a sure guide in the affairs of mankind," they express their conviction that "the teachings of Islam represent the quintessence of Divine guidance in its final and perfect form." These attitudes contrast sharply with a foundational premise of the UDHR that is articulated in Article 1, which stresses that all human beings "are endowed with reason and conscience." In the Islamic human rights schemes proffered by Mawdudi and Tabandeh, there is similar reliance on extensive quotations from the Islamic sources, which is an indication that they follow the traditional view that the texts of Revelation and the custom of the Prophet are the definitive guides for what law should be, not human reason.

The supremacy of Islamic law in Iran is confirmed in various provisions of the 1979 Iranian constitution in addition to Article 4, which calls for all laws to be based on Islamic criteria. The primacy of Revelation is confirmed in Article 1, which calls for a government based on truth and Qur'anic justice, and in Article 2, which states that the Iranian Republic is based on belief in the acceptance of God's rule and the necessity of obeying his commands, affirming belief in "divine Revelation and its fundamental role in setting forth the laws" and the "justice of God in creation and legislation." Also according to Article 2, these aims are to be achieved by "continuous *ijtihad* [interpretation] of the *fuqaha* possessing necessary qualifications, exercised on the basis of the Qur'an and the *Sunnah* [traditions] of the *Ma'sumun* [the divinely inspired imams of Twelver Shi'ism]." The Iranian constitution, including its rights provisos, thus professes to be anchored in principles derived from divine Revelation.

In a similar vein, according to the preamble of the Cairo Declaration on Human Rights in Islam, "Fundamental rights and universal freedoms in Islam are an integral part of the Islamic religion," and they "are contained in the Revealed Books of God and were sent through the message of the last of His Prophets." That is, Revelation is theoretically central to this scheme of human rights as well. Likewise, Article 7 of the Saudi Basic Law affirms that the Qur'an and the *sunna* of the Prophet reign supreme over the Basic Law and all other laws of the state, thereby clearly subordinating rights to Islamic Revelation and the custom of the Prophet.

In the al-Azhar draft Islamic constitution, the evidence is less clear. One can, however, infer a similar emphasis on divine Revelation and conclude that a command of religious texts is deemed central to knowledge from individual provisions that incorporate Qur'anic language and concepts, from the requirements in Articles 12 and 13 that call for the memorization of the Qur'an in schools and the teaching of the custom of the Prophet, and from the provision in Article 11 stating that religious instruction should be a main subject in education.

In addition to according Revelation a central role in their Islamic human rights schemes, the authors do not seem to accept the shift from an emphasis on human duties to the emphasis on individual human rights that characterizes modern thought on rights. In a passage in the English version of the preamble to the UIDHR that has no obvious counterpart in the Arabic version, the authors indicate "that by the terms of our primeval covenant with God our duties and obligations have priority over our rights," thereby coming close to reaffirming the traditional idea that Islam prescribes the believer's duties, not individual rights. It is therefore obvious from the outset that the UIDHR will have the effect of denying rights in the guise of establishing Islamic duties. Should there be complaints about this, the ready-made defense will be that Islam aims not to secure individual rights but to ensure obedience to divine commands.

In the al-Azhar draft constitution, one sees a similar concern for the fulfillment of Islamic duties. In Article 12, the government is required to teach Muslims their duties (*al-fara'id*). In contrast, in the fourth section of the draft constitution, which deals with the individual's rights and freedoms (which turn out to be highly circumscribed), there is no mention of any need to teach Muslims about rights and freedoms.

The Cairo Declaration refers to duties and obligations and stresses the inferiority of humans vis-à-vis their Creator. For example, Article 1 provides in Section A that all human beings "are united by submission to God" and "are equal in terms of basic human dignity and basic obligations and responsibilities," and states in Section B that all human beings are God's children (*'iyal*). Similarly, having declared in Article 1 that the government is Islamic and in Article 5 that it is a monarchy vested in the Saudi family, the Saudi Basic Law in Article 6 treats the duty to obey the monarch as being religious in nature, asserting that citizens are to pay allegiance to the king, "in accordance with the Holy Qur'an and the *sunna* of the Prophet, in submission and obedience," thereby linking obedience to the king to obedience to God's commands. It is noteworthy that Section 5, titled "Rights and Duties," contains precious few rights.

A former minister of law and religious affairs in Pakistan, A. K. Brohi, has written a number of pieces on human rights in Islam and puts forth a rights philosophy similar to the ones embodied in the schemes under review here. Brohi is prominent enough in this field to be selected to give the keynote address at a major international conference on human rights in Islam. This conference was held in Kuwait in 1980 under the sponsorship of the International Commission of Jurists, Kuwait University, and the Union of Arab Lawyers.[25] Brohi's speech recapitulated points made in an earlier piece on Islam and human rights, published in the official Pakistani case law reporter in 1976—while Zulfikar Ali Bhutto, the prime minister subsequently executed by President Zia after his coup, was still in power.[26] It is significant that the same points were incorporated in an article in the official Pakistani case law reporter in 1983, when President Zia's martial law regime and Islamization programs were in full swing, showing that the regime found his perspective congenial.[27] Excerpts from the seminar and the article show how Brohi rejects the philosophical underpinnings of Western human rights, revealing attitudes prevalent among conservative Muslim authors who attempt to differentiate Islamic rights from civil and political rights as understood in the West. He depicts Islam as being inherently anti-individualistic:

> Human duties and rights have been vigorously defined and their orderly enforcement is the duty of the whole of organized communities and the task is specifically entrusted to the law enforcement organs of the state. The individual if necessary has to be sacrificed in order that the life of the organism be saved. Collectivity has a special sanctity attached to it in Islam.[28]

The Western man's perspective may by and large be called anthropocentric in the sense that there man is regarded as constituting the measure of everything since he is to be regarded as the starting point of all thinking and action. The perspective of Islam, on the other hand, is theocentric, that is, Godconsciousness, the Absolute here is paramount; man is here only to serve His Maker. . . . [In the West] rights of man are seen in a setting which has no reference to his relationship with God—they are somehow supposed to be his inalienable birthrights. . . . Each time the assertion of human rights is made, it is done only to secure their recognition from some secular authority such as the state or some such regal power.[29]

[In Islam] there are no "human rights" or "freedoms" admissible to man in the sense in which modern man's thought, belief, and practice understand them: in essence, the believer owes obligation or duties to God if only because he is called upon to obey the Divine Law and such Human Rights as he is made to acknowledge seem to stem from his primary duty to obey God.[30]

Thus, it would appear, there is a sense in which Man has no rights within a theocentric perspective; he has only duties to His Maker. But these duties in their turn, give rise to all the rights, Human Rights in the modern sense included. . . . There can, in the strict theory of the Islamic law, be no conflict between the State Authority and the individual—since both have to obey the Divine Law.[31]

Human Rights conceived from the anthropocentric perspective are treated by Western thinkers as though they were no more than an expedient mode of protecting the individual from the assaults that are likely to be made upon him by the authority of the State's coercive power—by the unjust law that may be imposed by that authority to deny man the possibility of self-development through the law-making power of the brute majorities. Islam, on the other hand, formulates, defines and protects these very rights by inducing in the believers the disposition to obey the law of God . . . and showing obedience to those "constituted authorities" within the realm who themselves are bound to obey the law of God. . . . Furthermore, affirmation of these rights is to enable man not only to secure the establishment of those conditions in terms of which the development of man as an individual on earth may be possible, but also to enable man so to conduct himself, inwardly as well as outwardly, as to be able to obey the Divine Law. . . . By accepting to live in Bondage to this Divine Law, man learns to be free.[32]

One sees that in Brohi's scheme the emphasis is on the solidarity of the community and on duties owed by the individual to the state. The need for human rights standards to protect the individual from oppression by the government is dismissed based on the same assumptions that guided the idealistic visions of premodern Islamic thinkers who assumed that ruler and ruled were united in fealty to Islam, an orientation that impeded the development of modern concepts of civil and political rights. Like the premodern theorists of Islamic government, Brohi assumes that governments will necessarily obey the dictates of the *shari'a,* making protections for individuals' rights redundant, because the *shari'a* reflects the perfect way to order society.

In Brohi's treatment of rights, one notices both a strong affirmation of the idea that the individual is bound by the duty of obedience and, withal, a carelessness regarding the issue of to whom or to what the individual owes obedience. One perceives that Brohi is sometimes speaking of subordination to God and Islamic law, which is clearly required in the Islamic tradition, but that at other times he means the subordination of the individual to organized communities, a collectivity, political authorities, or the state. Regarding the latter, there is much less in the way of unequivocal Islamic authority justifying claims that obedience is owed. Brohi does not seem to perceive that the Islamic warrant establishing the duty of a believer to obey the commands of God should not necessarily imply obligations on the part of citizens of modern states to obey submissively the commands of their governments, governments that these days tend to be both highly corrupt and brutally oppressive.

Like many other conservatives, Brohi fails to appreciate that the model of communal solidarity that one finds in traditional societies in the Muslim world is in no way distinctively Islamic but rather reflects features commonly found in societies that have not yet experienced and adjusted to the disruptions of industrialization and urbanization. Brohi apparently does not grasp that the lack of individual rights and freedoms in traditional societies did not have the same nefarious consequences that the lack of protection for individual rights has had under modern states. Brohi proceeds from a description of a past practice, the subordination of the individual to the interests of the community, to the unwarranted conclusion that Islamic doctrine requires the individual to accept such subordination in the radically different circumstances of modern state societies.[33] That there will of necessity be conflicts between the competing interests of individuals and the government of a modern nation state is rejected by Brohi. His notion that in an Islamic system one cannot separate the individual and the government reflects adherence to the premodern jurists' views that the ruler and ruled stood together, united in their duties of obedience to the *shari'a*. Where there is reliance on such anachronistic views, the reality that individual rights are being crushed by antidemocratic regimes is naturally not given weight.

Moreover, one sees that Brohi emphasizes that premodern Islamic thought was not anthropocentric. From this historical fact, he leaps to the unfounded conclusion that an anthropocentric perspective is necessarily alien to Islam and that adopting such a perspective would violate Islamic precepts, making him a foe of humanism.

Exhibiting similar views, Mawdudi's main political concern with regard to duties seems to be how to preserve the power of the state and ensure that its orders are complied with. In his book *The Islamic Law and Constitution*, Mawdudi inaccurately quotes the Prophet, who was telling Muslims to obey divine commands, as telling Muslims that "the state" (not referred to in the original account) "shall have to be obeyed, in adversity and in prosperity, and whether it is pleasant or unpleasant to do so," elaborating as follows:

> In other words, the order of the State, be it palatable or unpalatable, easy or arduous, shall have to be obeyed under all circumstances [save when this means disobedience to God]. . . . [A] person should, truly and faithfully and with all his heart, wish and work for the good, prosperity and the betterment of the State, and should not tolerate anything likely to harm its interests. . . . It is also obligatory on the citizens of the Islamic State to cooperate wholeheartedly with the government and to make sacrifices of life and property for it, so much so that if any danger threatens the State, he who willfully refrains from making a sacrifice of his life and property to ward off that danger has been called a hypocrite in the Qur'an.[34]

This is obviously an attempt to provide an Islamic rationale for total subjugation of the individual to the state—although assuming that the Prophet was referring to such modern states as the Republic of Pakistan is both inaccurate and anachronistic. One can see how Mawdudi's formulation of the individual's obligations to obey the government tracks the statement offered by President Zia in justifying his military dictatorship in Pakistan (see Chapter 2). The only excuse for disobeying the government is in cases where obeying would entail violating Islamic law, thereby constituting disobedience to a command of God. Of course, a government that purports to follow Islamic law, as President Zia's did, would not concede that it was giving the citizenry any grounds whatsoever for disobedience. In fact, many members of the political group that Mawdudi founded were among the mainstays of support for President Zia's Islamization program, accepting the loss of rights and freedoms under Zia's military dictatorship.

Such ideas betray a fundamental antipathy to human rights. If one accepts Ronald Dworkin's definition of a "right" as a claim that it would be wrong for the government to deny an individual even though it would be in the general interest to do so, one could say that it would be impossible for authors with such attitudes to embrace human rights because they consistently accord priority to the interests of the collectivity, the community, or the state. In contrast, in international law, civil and political rights accord primacy to the rights of the individual, ensuring them against infringements, particularly by governments but also by society.[35] One would expect authors wedded to worldviews so deeply at odds with rights to say that human rights cannot be accommodated within an Islamic framework where Muslims' duties are so central. Instead, one observes them trying to preserve traditional anti-individualistic, communitarian priorities and the ruler's power while paradoxically trying to present their projects as setting forth civil and political rights.

A person unfamiliar with Middle Eastern history might assume that special circumstances or unique institutions of Islamic civilization managed to compensate for the lack of formal legal safeguards for individual rights and freedoms and that this lack had less nefarious consequences for Muslims than it had in Western societies in the era before legal restraints were imposed on governments to protect the people whom they ruled from overreaching and oppression. In reality, in the Middle East the absence of legal protections for human rights has correlated with patterns of misrule, injustice, corruption, and oppression by despotic rulers that are similar to those historically experienced in the West. Anyone familiar with Middle Eastern history appreciates that the idealized schemes of Muslim ruler and Muslim ruled both acting in concert and in common obedience to the divine law were not realized in practice, and the upheavals of the Arab Spring confirm that the oppressive systems dominating the region continue to be a problem.

Although some Muslims would say that the feasibility of the Islamic model was illustrated by the harmonious collaboration of ruler and ruled in the era of the Prophet and under some of his immediate successors—to which Shi'is would add the era in which they were ruled by divinely inspired imams—these reports of saintly rulers in the earliest period of Islamic history by no means signify that the dictates of Islamic piety subsequently proved adequate to inhibit despotic tendencies and curb rulers' abuses of power. Although Muslim rulers had at their disposal the mechanisms to compel obedience, individual subjects had few ways other than the risky course of overt rebellion to challenge cruel and tyrannical misrule.

In reality, the individual and the state in the Muslim world have had conflicting interests that have most often been resolved at the expense of individual rights and freedoms. The authors of these Islamic human rights schemes must be aware that this pattern has nefarious consequences. Nonetheless, such writers are disposed to give no weight to the need to protect individuals from the state.

Consequences of Insecure Philosophical Foundations

As indicated, proposals for Islamic human rights schemes rest on idealized visions of social harmony, despite the fact that long experience has manifestly demonstrated that such visions do not correspond to how Middle Eastern societies have been governed. Because of their otherworldly focus, it is not surprising that the authors of Islamic human rights schemes deal with civil and political rights in a fashion that seems grossly inadequate by the standards of international human rights law.

Lacking a coherent human rights philosophy, authors of Islamic human rights schemes have in some instances simply appropriated ideas from texts on Islamic law and ethics, treating them as if they offered statements on human rights, irrespective of whether these ideas involve principles that could remedy actual problems or whether they deserve the status of civil and political rights. The consequence is the inclusion of many frivolous notions of entitlements, trivial or meaningless "rights" that in international law would not rise to the level of human rights. The Iranian constitution is a noteworthy exception in this respect. It appears that Iran's established tradition of constitutionalism inhibited its drafters from straying too far from the familiar categories of civil and political rights.

Elsewhere, one sees that provision is made for a "right" not to have one's corpse mutilated,[36] which seems to envisage that human rights protections should be extended to corpses, even though human rights concerns ordinarily presuppose that the rights' claimant be living, not dead.[37] Other "rights" that have been derived from Islamic sources include the right of women not to be surprised by male family members of the household walking in on them unannounced.[38] When one thinks about the implications of protecting women from surprise intrusions on the part of men living in their homes, one realizes that, far from affording protection for freedoms, it implicitly assumes restrictions on women's rights. This "right" only makes sense if the world is sexually segregated and women stay at home in seclusion from men. The segregation is presumably so extensive that even male family members stay out of women's quarters unless they first give warnings so that the women can cover themselves in a suitably modest manner. The provision implies that even in the privacy of the home, there will be female seclusion and veiling, which in turn is connected with a woman's duty to avoid indecency. Thus, the "right" is linked not with any meaningful human right but with what was seen by conservatives as women's duty to stay segregated, secluded, and veiled.

Some "rights" provisions that are included in these Islamic human rights schemes do not belong in compilations of human rights because they concern offenses by private actors better dealt with by tort or criminal law. Some inadequate formulations seem to have resulted from an author gleaning from the Islamic sources the idea that certain conduct is censured or criminalized and drawing the conclusion that human beings have "rights" not to be affected by such conduct. Thus, Islamic human rights include the "right" not to be made fun of or insulted by nicknames,[39] which is obviously taken from the Qur'an 44:11: "Let not a folk deride a folk who may be better than they . . . neither defame one another, nor insult one another by nicknames." One also encounters the "right" not to be tied up before being killed,[40] provisions that guarantee the "right" not to be burned alive,[41] and a "right" to life—which turns out in context to be a right not to be murdered.[42]

As a kind of corollary to the development of "rights" not to be subjected to behavior censured in the Islamic sources, behavior that is treated as good or proper in Islamic sources may create a related "right." "Rights" that fall within this category include "the obligation of believers to see that a deceased person's body is treated with due solemnity,"[43] affording yet another right to corpses, and the "right" to safety of life—which turns out to mean that people should come to the aid of a person in distress or danger.[44] It seems here that human rights are being confused with legal duties that might be set in criminal or tort law to deter improper handling of corpses and failures to try to rescue persons from danger or to bring succor to persons in distress. In a similar vein, the prohibition of usury, a reference to the Qur'anic ban on consuming *riba*, the meaning of which is disputed and may or may not mean that interest charges are banned, is treated as a human right.[45] Using this supposedly Islamic concept of human rights, a bank that gave loans at the market rate of interest might be charged with violating human rights.

Islamic human rights schemes may stipulate a woman's "right" to have her chastity respected and protected at all times.[46] A woman's right to have her chastity respected is a very ambiguous one because, in the context of the contemporary Middle East, the protection of women's chastity is often associated with regimes of sexual segregation and female seclusion and veiling, practices that are justified on the grounds that they are necessary to protect women's chastity. In other words, rather than offering meaningful protections for individual freedoms, such Islamic "rights" can be used to deprive women of freedoms.

A similarly insignificant "right" is the right of divorced individuals to strict confidentiality on the part of their former spouses with regard to information that could be detrimental to them.[47] This belongs to the realm of evidentiary privilege or private tort claims, which are not normally the concern of human rights law.

Another "right" stipulated is that of unbelievers—a category that by itself is problematic—to recover the corpses of their fellows who have fallen in battle against the Muslims without having to pay for the privilege.[48] The question of whether a fee could be assessed from unbelievers in these circumstances is hardly one that any serious human rights advocates in the Middle East would choose to place on an agenda of urgent human rights problems.

This category of rights that have no international counterparts also includes the "right" to cooperate (in the cause of virtue—presumably, Islamic virtue) and not to cooperate (in the cause of vice and aggression—presumably, as defined by Islam)[49] and the "right" to propagate Islam and its message.[50] These "rights" differ from international norms, where religious freedoms are protected regardless of one's religion; here it appears that only Muslims would benefit from these "rights."

After examining the idiosyncratic and confused concepts that the authors of Islamic human rights include, one appreciates that they lack a sure grasp of what the concerns of human rights really are. They include provisions that would be totally out of place in a scheme that shared common philosophical premises with those of international human rights law regarding civil and political rights.

Islamic Human Rights and Cultural Nationalism

The impetus behind the campaigns to uphold Islamic law and cast aside laws associated with the era of Western domination involves a cultural nationalist reaction, which may account for some of the confusion in Islamic human rights schemes. Campaigns to Islamize human rights are linked to the unease that is felt in the Muslim Middle East over the extent of the region's weakness and dependency on the contemporary West. Resentment of this dependency can engender efforts to assert cultural autonomy, to defend institutions associated with Muslims' cultural heritage against charges of backwardness, and to offer countermodels to Western ideas and institutions.[51] The authors also seek to appeal to sentiments of cultural nationalism in the wider population to win support for diluted human rights that claim to have an Islamic pedigree.

In contrast to the discomfiture of Islamists as they contemplate how much has been borrowed from the West and how globalization and other forces have led to the marginalization of Islamic law, the learned literature on international human rights law produced by academic specialists has traditionally shown an indifference to how this law relates to the Islamic tradition. Until recently, Islamic law was only occasionally mentioned in scholarly writing on international human rights law, and then it was treated as a marginal, exotic phenomenon. Behind this lay an assumption that international law and its associated institutions enjoyed unquestioned authority and a belief that models in conflict with international law were doomed to desuetude. The critiques offered by Muslims who object to international human rights law on religious grounds did not provoke much consternation or interest on the part of Western scholars of international law, for the latter did not feel that the legitimacy of international law was in any way jeopardized by assertions that it clashed with Islamic rules.

The relative indifference of much Western scholarship to Islamic perspectives on international human rights law reflects the reality that the foundations of that law were initially developed in the context of the unequal positions of the West and the Middle East in the aftermath of World War II, when Western power was in the ascendant. Although much has happened over the last decades to infuse international human rights law with perspectives reflecting input from around the globe, when viewed from the Middle East, the tenets of civil and political rights still retain an association with the Western culture in which they were historically first articulated. It is not therefore surprising that in an era when pressures for Islamization of law are prevalent in the Middle East, there would be a backlash against civil and political rights as a part of a more general backlash against the Westernization of laws. Islamists often express the view that civil and political rights involve the displacement of Islamic law in the interests of imperialist plots against Muslim states and the Islamic heritage. Claims by the second Bush administration that the US invasions of Afghanistan and Iraq were motivated by concerns to end the human rights abuses by the Taliban and Saddam Hussein only encourage the existing tendency in the Middle East to associate Western promotion of human rights with predatory agendas. In this connection, the very public US attempts to reduce the role of Islamic law in the post-invasion constitutions of Afghanistan and Iraq, while pressing for acceptance of a narrow human rights agenda centered on a few civil and political rights, could have the effect of strengthening the hand of Muslims who argue that human rights are tools of Western agendas to roll back Islamic law.

Cultural nationalists want to show that Islam and Middle Eastern culture possess institutions comparable to those in the West and that they are equally "advanced." But "advanced" is defined in Western terms. Thus, in the course of reacting *against* Western law, proponents of Islamization do not necessarily achieve the goal of banishing the influence of Western legal culture. This leads to cultural confusion in drawing up Islamic counterparts to Western legal models because the Islamic counterparts are constructed with constant reference to the Western models that they are designed to replace. In the process the *shari'a* is reformulated to fit borrowed Western categories, such as constitutional rights provisions.

The writings of two authors who energetically condemn the West exemplify this cultural confusion. Both Abu'l A'la Mawdudi and Sultanhussein Tabandeh have used Western examples and precedents to prop up the legitimacy of *shari'a* rules that restrict human rights. For example, when criticizing the Western model of emancipation for women and calling for its repudiation by Muslims in his book, Mawdudi relies extensively on the findings of Western "scientists," "experts," and "authorities" to establish that Western freedoms have led to social and moral disaster—with the corollary that *shari'a* rules mandating female subjugation and seclusion are sound.[52] Tabandeh, despite claiming to believe in the superiority of *shari'a* law, found a clinching argument to support his assertion that under *shari'a* rules, women should be excluded from politics in the fact that women were denied the vote in Switzerland, "one of the most civilized and most perfect societies of the world."[53] These arguments are revealing; the criticisms they fear are those that emanate from Muslims who are familiar with Western models and approaches to rights. Therefore, Mawdudi and Tabandeh felt compelled to devise rationales for *shari'a* rules based on Western science—or pseudoscience—and Western experience. However, such Western-inspired rationales are utterly irrelevant from the standpoint of Islamic jurisprudence and would play no role in any rights scheme that was actually based on Islamic sources.

Cultural nationalism also helps explain why authors of Islamic human rights schemes insist, despite the overwhelming historical evidence to the contrary, that human rights originated in Islam, asserting falsely that the Western and international principles from which they are heavily borrowing are the derivative ones. Because the sources of Islamic law date from the seventh century, and all Islamic law is in theory derived from these sources, the authors seem to have concluded that human rights must be shown to have been established from the outset of Islamic legal history. Thus, Islamic human rights principles have to be projected back into the seventh century—as they are in the preamble to the Cairo Declaration, which situates them in the Revelation to the Prophet Muhammad. There is an utter failure to deal with the historical reality that, although research in the Islamic sources may uncover ideas that have foreshadowed human rights principles, Islamic statements of human rights principles did not appear until after international human rights law was produced.

The production of Islamic human rights comes at a juncture when many Muslims call for decolonization in the legal sphere, which should in theory result in the extirpation of Western legal transplants and the reinstatement of indigenous Islamic models. The problem is that the Islamization programs rest on a false premise: They assume that there exist in all areas settled Islamic legal countermodels of the Western laws that are being repudiated. Such Islamic countermodels may be developed in the future, but in many areas they are lacking, as even Iran's ruling clerics have had to acknowledge as they pursued Islamization.[54] Authors of Islamic human rights schemes promote the idea that Islam provides a complete body of principles on human rights, but this entails denying the reality of Muslims' disagreements about what the Islamic sources mean and their extensive borrowings from international human rights formulations.

In their attempts to support the contention that human rights originated in the Islamic tradition, the authors rely on strained readings of the Qur'an or the accounts of the custom, or *sunna*, of the Prophet Muhammad to establish the ancient Islamic pedigrees of human rights. They cite passages that they claim demonstrate that from its origins, Islam possessed the equivalents of modern human rights without adequate exploration of the significance of the passages.[55] By concentrating on the era of the Prophet and projecting human rights principles back to the start of Islamic history and then jumping more than a millennium to the present, they largely avoid referring to the history of Islamic jurisprudence. This is highly problematic. If one is arguing that the Islamic tradition has a much older set of human rights principles than the West, it is important to show how Muslims have historically interpreted the Islamic sources to ascertain whether they read them as setting forth human rights.

To discover traditional Islamic views on rights and freedoms, a legal historian would turn first to juristic treatises and possibly also the writings on theology and philosophy that were produced in the premodern period of Islamic civilization—especially treatises from the ninth to the fourteenth century—and that are still widely consulted as authoritative expositions of Islamic rules. No documented Islamic authority dating from the premodern period has come to light that squarely addresses human rights issues as such or that directly anticipates modern rights formulations. Indeed, the Arabic term for human rights, *huquq al-insan*, is a recent formulation that never appears in the treatises. Islamic human rights principles are newly coined, much younger than rights principles in the West.

A desire to establish that the West is indebted to Islam for advances that the West has wrongfully claimed as its own prompted the foreword to the UIDHR to assert that "Islam gave to mankind an ideal code of human rights fourteen centuries ago," this being calculated using the Islamic lunar calendar. In the 1980 Kuwait seminar on human rights in Islam, the conclusion was drawn that "Islam was the first to recognize basic human rights and almost 14 centuries ago it set up guarantees and safeguards that have only recently been incorporated in universal declarations of human rights."[56] In the keynote address at the same seminar, it was claimed: "To the student of the Qur'an not one word, in the preamble or in the objectives of the [UN] Charter and not a single article in the text of the 'Universal Declaration of Human Rights' will seem unfamiliar. . . . [T]he 'Universal Declaration of Human Rights' must follow as a basic corollary, or an extension of the Qur'anic programme."[57] Attending a 1997 Sarajevo seminar on the Qur'an and human rights, Iran's Ayatollah Ahmad Jannati insisted that Islam had best defined all aspects of human rights and that the human rights proposed by the United Nations merely recapitulated rights propounded more than a thousand years earlier.[58] In the preamble to the Cairo Declaration, it is proclaimed that human rights are "divine commands, which are contained in the Revealed Books of Allah."

Tabandeh, for all of his professed disappointment with certain features of the UDHR, argued that Islam anticipated all the declaration's provisions and projected these back into the Islamic past, asserting that the UDHR "has not promulgated anything that was new nor inaugurated innovations. Every clause of it, indeed, every valuable regulation needed for the welfare of human society . . . already existed in a better and more perfect form in Islam."[59] Although Tabandeh's commentary on the UDHR reveals a deep philosophical antipathy toward human rights, Tabandeh obviously feels that Islam will be considered deficient unless it is seen as having anticipated the UDHR.

Mawdudi, who espoused ideas that are in fundamental conflict with international human rights law, nonetheless sought to portray Islamic law as having an earlier and more perfect version of human rights than what was offered by international law. He argued that human rights originated in Islam, while castigating Westerners for presuming to have originated human rights. In keeping with his general concern for showing that Islam and Muslim societies are wrongly accused of being culturally backward and underdeveloped, he complained that "people in the West have the habit of attributing every beneficial development in the world to themselves."[60] After presenting his own list of human rights, Mawdudi asserted:

> This is a brief sketch of those rights which 1400 years ago Islam gave to man. . . . It refreshes and strengthens our faith in Islam when we realize that even in this modern age, which makes such loud claims of progress and enlightenment, the world has not been able to produce more just and equitable laws than those given 1400 years ago. On the other hand, it is saddening to realize that Muslims nonetheless often look for guidance to the West.[61]

Mawdudi clearly meant to persuade Muslims that they should abandon all references to the allegedly derivative Western rights concepts and refer instead to the original models, which are his Islamic rights. His disappointment with Muslims who seek intellectual guidance in the West did not reflect the teachings of Islam, the doctrines of which do not set any geographic limits on where Muslims may seek wisdom and enlightenment, but instead reflects his own cultural nationalist perspective.

One sees that cultural nationalism lies behind some of the confusion in these Islamic human rights schemes. If one takes the position that Islam anticipated the most influential post–World War II human rights instruments, then Islamic human rights and constitutional rights provisions must somehow be shown to resemble those in the international documents and Western constitutions. Thus, instruments such as the UDHR effectively become the templates for presentations of the Islamic human rights that are designed to replace them, leading to the extensive borrowing from Western models and terminology. In such an endeavor, there is no room for critical examination of whether the rules and priorities of the premodern *shari'a* that the authors seek to preserve are actually compatible with human rights. Internal contradictions and inconsistencies are the inevitable result of these authors' casually appropriating the formulas and terminology of international human rights law.

Another tactic by authors of Islamic human rights schemes that indicates the influence of cultural nationalism is the frequent reference to practice in the West (from any period in the history of Western civilization) that deviated from modern human rights standards, along with a corresponding unwillingness to deal with actual rights problems in contemporary Muslim societies. Accounts of the golden age under the Prophet Muhammad and his immediate successors in the seventh century are treated as the model of how Islamic rights work in practice— as if all Muslim societies over the centuries had conformed to the perfections being ascribed to *shari'a* law in that remote period. The failure to examine critically the human rights situation in Muslim societies throughout history reflects this literature's apologetic, defensive function—to denigrate Western civilization and to exalt the heritage of Islamic civilization rather than to come to grips with the human rights problems faced by contemporary Muslims, as well as the factors that caused these.

Of course, historically, governments in both the West and the Muslim world have engaged in conduct that would constitute egregious violations of rights by the standards of the International Bill of Human Rights. However, despite many grievous lapses, Western countries since the nineteenth century have by and large been moving in the direction of affording greater protections for the civil and political rights of their citizens and imposing limits on the ability of governments to trample on these rights. Today, the rights protections afforded in the laws of Western democracies, although far from perfect, are nonetheless better developed than elsewhere, with Scandinavian countries standing out as having exemplary human rights records. In contrast, the current human rights situation in the Muslim world is generally a dismal one, even worse than it was under traditional, despotic regimes. The oppressive rule of the dictatorial, authoritarian, or totalitarian regimes that predominate in the Middle East has been stifling in its impact on freedom. The state has vastly strengthened its security apparatus, and a variety of social and economic changes have weakened the ability of societies to resist governmental power. Thus, rather than making progress in the direction of enhancing rights, with a few exceptions, Middle Eastern states have tended to move in the direction of expanding oppression. The massive explosions of popular anger and the courageous struggles waged for democracy, dignity, and freedom that the world witnessed during the 2011 Arab Spring amply demonstrated that people in the region found living under such despotic regimes intolerable. Only the extreme viciousness of the regimes and their vast security apparatus had deterred such manifestations of popular outrage from erupting years earlier.

The egregious rights violations perpetrated by Middle Eastern governments are neglected by the authors of Islamic human rights schemes. Naturally, they have no wish to address how Islamization programs have further degraded rights. Instead, where these authors do treat real human rights problems, they tend to focus on Western human rights violations in an attempt to show that Western human rights protections are inadequate and ineffectual and that Westerners who criticize human rights abuses in the Middle East are hypocritical.[62] When one considers how improbable it would be for people in a Western society to try to deflect criticism of their government's violations of human rights by pointing out that serious violations of human rights had occurred in Muslim countries, one grasps that such tactics reveal which side feels beleaguered and defensive about its poor progress in the human rights domain.

By alluding to the violations of human rights that have been perpetrated by the West, the authors seem to think they are discrediting both the Western rights models and potential Western critics of their Islamic human rights schemes. Thus, the record of rights violations in the West, which was touched on in the 1980 Kuwait seminar on Islam and human rights, was somehow deemed relevant to understanding the comparative merits of Islamic human rights.[63] In contrast, at the same seminar it was asserted that "It is unfair to judge Islamic law (Shari'a) by the political systems which prevailed in various periods of Islamic history."[64]

This last statement would be unexceptionable if it meant that one should distinguish between practice and theory and between the conduct of governments and the teachings of the Islamic religion, but it would be misguided if it suggested that the quality and efficacy of human rights guarantees could not be evaluated by the degree to which they protect rights in practice. The historical record of the centuries in which Islamic law was officially the governing standard indicates that protections for rights equivalent to the protections afforded by international human rights law were lacking. Conceding this is, however, difficult in a period when cultural nationalism is surging in response to circumstances that seem to confirm Western hegemony and arrogance.

Ambivalent Attitudes on Human Rights

One of the features that has led to the confused quality of Islamic human rights schemes is the authors' deep ambivalence about their project. The authors, even while promoting Islamic versions of human rights, seem to regard international human rights as the ultimate model against which all other rights schemes are inevitably measured, a model from which they do not want to be seen as deviating. This accounts for the defensive or apologetic tone that pervades much of the literature that puts forward distinctive Islamic schemes. On the evidence of the Islamic human rights schemes analyzed here, the authors are torn between a desire to protect and perpetuate principles linked to their preferred conservative understandings of Islamic tradition and anxiety lest that tradition be assessed as backward and deficient if Islam is not shown to possess the kinds of "advanced" institutions that have been developed in UN documents. They thus seek to accentuate the formal resemblance between their schemes and international human rights law even where that resemblance is misleading in terms of the actual level of rights protections that they intend to provide. In areas where the aim is to incorporate principles deviating from international human rights law that are prone to provoke the opprobrium of the international community, they seek to disguise and obscure this aim. As the analysis of Islamic human rights schemes shows, in such areas rights provisions may be kept at a level of idealistic abstraction and individual provisions may be formulated in a vague, equivocal, and evasive manner.

The determination to produce human rights schemes that appear to correspond to internationally accepted norms correlates with a lack of coherence in the thinking behind Islamic human rights schemes. This lack of coherence would not have arisen if the authors were actually deriving their rights schemes from Islamic models after having first identified their philosophical premises and worked out an appropriate Islamic methodology. Creating an Islamic human rights scheme in this fashion would entail the authors' having a mastery of the Islamic sciences needed for this project and also feeling genuine confidence in the sufficiency of resources within the Islamic tradition on rights questions. These authors do not in fact possess such mastery or feel such confidence.

As is illustrated by the analyses of Islamic human rights schemes in the following chapters, the authors have not bothered to work out any clear theory of what rights should mean in an Islamic context, nor have they devised methods for deriving their content from the Islamic sources in a consistent and reasoned manner. Instead, they merely assemble pastiches of ideas and terminology drawn from two very different cultures without ever determining a rationale justifying these combinations of Islamic and secular elements or devising a way to reconcile the conflicting premises underlying them. That is, the deficiencies in the substantive

Islamic human rights principles are the inevitable by-products of methodological confusion and inadequacies.

It must be emphasized that neither these methodological inadequacies nor the problematic results are inevitable consequences of working within an Islamic context. With an approach informed by methodological clarity and rigor, elaborating human rights on Islamic foundations can be fruitful. One can see, for example, in the work of Abdullahi An-Na'im the recognition that methodological questions are central to resolving the problem of where Islamic law stands on human rights. Offering a methodology that allows a fresh approach to the Islamic sources, An-Na'im has been able to develop a set of human rights principles that is, for those who accept the proposed methodology, also one grounded in Islamic principles.[65] Using a different approach, the work of Khaled Abou El Fadl has shown how a Muslim with a deep understanding of the resources in the Islamic heritage can mine these to elaborate meaningful human rights on an Islamic foundation.[66] In the Middle East, the stultifying orthodoxies that stifle the publication of original and probing studies of Islam have unfortunately forced many innovative thinkers to relocate to the West and thereby have attenuated the impact of their ideas.

The methodological shortcomings that afflict the Islamic human rights schemes are just another manifestation of problems that typify contemporary Islamic thought more generally and that have seriously hampered its ability to keep pace with modern intellectual and scientific developments. Valuable critiques of the deficient quality of contemporary Islamic thought have been provided by such intellectuals as Mohammed Arkoun and, from very different angles, by Sadiq Jalal al-'Azm and Muhammad Sa'id al-Ashmawy.[67] Seeking to remedy these deficiencies, contemporary Muslims are reviewing old methodologies with critical eyes and proposing new approaches to the Islamic sources.[68] Thus, the methodological defects decried here reflect a much bigger problem that presently preoccupies some of the most outstanding figures in the domain of Islamic thought.

Summary

Islamic human rights schemes rest on shaky foundations. Confusion is engendered by the authors' struggles to craft schemes that both exhibit distinctive Islamic features and also resemble the international instruments that they aim to supplant, which entails borrowing from international law. No serious examination of what makes these hybrid schemes Islamic is afforded. Operating without any coherent rights philosophy, the authors may incorporate random Islamic principles that do not fit in the human rights category. Moreover, one sees indications that Islamic human rights schemes are linked to a broader pattern of resistance to Western hegemony and to the unsettling transformations that Muslim societies are undergoing, factors that distract from the task of mining the Islamic heritage for guidance on human rights. The insistence that human rights were set at the outset of Islamic history in the era of the Prophet and were only much later devised in the West embodies the authors' skewed perspectives. Operating with mentalities imbued with cultural nationalism, the authors are guided more by anti-Western animus than by principled examinations of the rich and complex Islamic heritage.

CHAPTER 4

Islamic Restrictions on Human Rights

Permissible Qualifications of Rights in International Law

International law recognizes that many rights protections are not absolute and may be suspended or qualified in exceptional circumstances, such as wars, public emergencies, or even in normal circumstances in the interests of certain overriding considerations.[1] In international law, one expects these overriding considerations to fall within one of several established categories. Qualifications may be placed on human rights in the aggregate common interest and also to serve particular, specified policies.[2] The latter might include policies such as the preservation of national security, public safety, public order, morals, the rights and freedom of others, the interests of justice, and the public interest in a democratic society.[3] To ensure that accommodations and derogations are made within structures of authority and to prevent arbitrariness in decisions, the measures imposing these limitations must be taken in accordance with the law.[4]

International law therefore seeks to balance the need to protect human rights against other needs; in some cases, rights may have to defer to other priorities. It is recognized that unless the circumstances in which curbs can be placed on human rights are sharply circumscribed, rights would become illusory. Nonetheless, the extent to which curbs are permissible and exactly what grounds justify restricting rights remain contested questions in international human rights law.

The UDHR treats a number of rights as absolute or non-derogable rights, meaning that there could be no justification for curtailing them. Among these are the right to freedom and equality in dignity and rights; the right to equality before the law and to equal protection of the law; the right in full equality to a fair and public hearing by an independent and impartial tribunal; the right to marry and the right to equal rights in marriage and divorce;[5] freedom of thought, conscience, and religion, including the freedom to change one's religion;[6] and the right to work and to free choice of employment.[7] The UDHR would not accept any criteria that would deny these rights.

The UDHR includes a separate clause that defines the limits that may in general be placed on human rights. In Article 29.2, one finds the following provision: "In the exercise of his rights and freedoms, everyone shall be subject only to such limitations as are determined by law solely for the purpose of securing due recognition and respect for the rights and freedoms of others and of meeting the just requirements of morality, public order and the general welfare in a democratic society." These qualifications permitted in the general provision in Article 29.2 of the UDHR do not apply to non-derogable rights. In the drafting process of the UDHR, the Soviet delegation tried to impose a derogation clause that would nullify human rights by adding the words "and also [for the purpose of] the corresponding requirements of the democratic state," but this Soviet proposal was rejected.[8]

The limitations that could be applied to human rights were further clarified in subsequent international human rights documents, as specific qualifications were inserted in the texts of individual rights provisions. Provisions guarantee that rights that are derogable will be restricted only in specified ways. Thus, one sees rights with the following qualifications:

1. Freedom of expression: subject only to qualifications provided by law and necessary for respect of the rights and reputations of others and for the protection of national security or of public order (*ordre public*), or of public health and morals
2. The right of peaceful assembly: subject only to restrictions "imposed in conformity with the law and which are necessary in a democratic society in the interests of national security or public safety, public order (*ordre public*), the protection of public health or morals or the protection of the rights and freedoms of others"
3. Freedom of association: subject to the same qualifications as the right of peaceful assembly, above
4. The right to take part in the conduct of public affairs; to vote and be elected; and to have access, on general terms of equality, to public service "without unreasonable conditions"[9]

A number of other fundamental rights are qualified, including the right to life, which is qualified by the state's ability to impose a death penalty, but only for the most serious crimes and subject to a number of other conditions, and the right to liberty and security of person, which is qualified by the state's ability to deprive the person of these "on such grounds and in accordance with such procedure as are established by law."[10]

The International Covenant on Economic, Social, and Cultural Rights (ICESCR) has a general rule on how rights may be qualified, providing in Article 4 that governments "may subject such rights only to such limitations as are determined by law only insofar as this may be compatible with the nature of these rights and solely for the purpose of promoting the general welfare in a democratic society."

Thus, international human rights law limits the permissible reasons for curbing human rights. The formulations of the qualifications are not so airtight as to preclude all efforts by states to manipulate them at the expense of the rights of the individual, but they are designed to shore up rights by restricting the circumstances in which states may curtail them. As discussed in the following examination of Islamic human rights schemes, one of the most important differences between Islamic human rights schemes and international human rights law is that Islamic qualifications on rights have been deliberately left so vague and open-ended that they allow states vast discretion in circumscribing or nullifying rights.

Islamic Formulas Limiting Rights

The underlying thesis in all the Islamic human rights schemes is that the rights afforded in international law are too generous and only become acceptable when they are subjected to Islamic restrictions. Curiously, there is no explicit articulation of the thesis that international law has granted people excessive rights. Because invoking Islam either to eliminate or to narrow rights is such a central and distinctive feature of Islamic human rights schemes, it is also curious that exactly what these Islamic restrictions on rights entail is not precisely delineated.

The vague "Islamic" qualifications that limit rights resemble the qualifications that have been placed on human rights in the African Charter on Human and Peoples' Rights, similarly devised to dilute rights protections. These qualifications have been decried as "claw-back clauses" that allow the state "almost unbounded discretion" in using domestic legal standards to restrict internationally guaranteed human rights.[11]

International law does not accept that fundamental human rights may be restricted—much less permanently curtailed—by reference to the requirements of any particular religion.[12] International law provides no warrant for depriving Muslims of human rights by according primacy to Islamic criteria. Thus, to limit or dilute human rights by reference to the requirements of the *shari'a* is to qualify human rights established under international law by standards that are not recognized as legitimate bases for curtailing rights.

Limitations on rights that use such terms as "the *shari'a*," "Islamic precepts," or "the limits of Islam" to qualify human rights cannot be unambiguously defined by consulting the work of the premodern jurists because this work is far too diverse. Premodern Islamic law included the doctrines of several sects and many schools of law. Divergence of opinion among major law schools was historically tolerated in Islam, a situation acknowledged in the *shari'a* concept of *ikhtilaf al-madhahib*, or difference of schools of law. In fact, even within one law school, doctrines and opinions could differ significantly on the interpretation of the Islamic sources.[13] Furthermore, there were many individual jurists whose opinions differed from the views of the major schools but whose works, nonetheless, are part of the premodern *shari'a* legacy. With such a rich heritage, Muslims are faced with a large volume of conflicting views of Islamic requirements.

Despite the great diversity in Islamic legal doctrines, on certain points of premodern jurisprudence there is sufficient consensus to allow reasoned calculations of how the application of Islamic principles would likely affect rights. Reliance on rules of the premodern *shari'a* to determine the permissible scope of modern human rights could open the way to nullification of rights in areas where the *shari'a* traditionally called for restrictions on rights, such as the rules relegating women and non-Muslims to subordinate status or those prohibiting conversion from Islam. Even on these topics, there is enough complexity and diversity in the body of relevant legal doctrines to give the state considerable leeway in deciding what rules should apply.

On other topics relevant for civil and political rights, where the premodern jurisprudence is underdeveloped or the *shari'a* standards are very uncertain, resorting to Islamic criteria to qualify rights can also lead to outcomes incompatible with protecting the rights involved. Where no strong Islamic authority can be found in the doctrines of premodern jurisprudence, states enjoy wide leeway in constructing Islamic rationales to curb rights. Conservatives can always find some spokesman for Islam who will concur that the curbs that they impose have Islamic authority. The Saudi rule—ostensibly based on Islam—that women cannot drive cars is a perfect example. The rule has little basis in terms of Islamic law and is not found outside Saudi Arabia, but Saudi officials were able to find a religious figure to endorse the rule as necessary to preserve Islamic morality. States' ability to engineer religious approval for denials of rights means that the Islamic limitations can potentially be expanded indefinitely and deprive the affected rights of any substance.

Just as there is no definitive guidance in the premodern *shari'a* on rules setting forth restrictions on the kinds of human rights established in international law, if one looks at contemporary Islamic thought, there is no consensus on how to restrict such rights. The ambiguities that existed in the premodern tradition have multiplied with diverging interpretations, which are driven by new intellectual currents. By the end of the nineteenth century, reformist movements emerged that led to substantial departures from premodern Islamic thought.[14] More recently, new strains in interpretation have emerged.[15] In addition to the literature that attempts a progressive rethinking of Islamic law and theology, one sees Islam ideologized to mobilize Muslims for the reaction against the West and Western culture in writings by figures such as Ayatollah Khomeini.[16] The differences in contemporary approaches to understanding Islam have been compounded by the absence of any generally recognized central authority for resolving disputed points of *shari'a* doctrine.

It is natural that in the circumstances prevailing in the contemporary Middle East, the lack of firm rules on how Islam pertains to human rights will be exploited by the state and resolved at the expense of human rights. Thus, vague "Islamic" limitations on human rights have ominous implications.

Restrictions in the Iranian Constitution

Before examining the 1979 Iranian constitution, earlier Iranian formulations of civil and political rights provisions should be considered. Iranian constitutional history illustrates the difficulties in accommodating human rights within an Islamic framework.

Many of Iran's *ulama* were violently opposed to the adoption of Iran's 1906–1907 constitution, and one of the grounds for their objections was their opposition to the idea of freedom, which they considered dangerous and inimical to Islamic principles and values.[17] Clerical denunciations of freedom and constitutionalism as heretical were often vehement and uncompromising.[18]

Iranian nationalist sentiment and the popular determination to constrain the tyranny of Iran's Qajar shahs were ultimately strong enough to overcome clerical opposition to the proposed constitution. In addition, some clerics supported constitutionalism, believing that it was compatible with Islam. However, their support was in part attributable to the fact that they did not fully grasp the significance of constitutionalism and interpreted its concepts in ways that corresponded to *shari'a* categories and principles.[19] Thus, the first Iranian constitution emerged in an environment where the religious establishment was divided about the compatibility of constitutionalism and Islam and was not always sure what constitutions entailed.

The qualifications placed on civil and political rights in the Supplementary Constitutional Law of 1907 were largely secular, but some religious criteria were also invoked to restrict constitutional rights. Article 20 qualified freedom of publication by stating that this freedom did not apply to heretical books or materials hurtful to Islam. Article 21 qualified the freedom to form societies and gatherings by stating that it applied where such societies or gatherings did not provoke religious disorder.[20]

After the 1978–1979 Iranian Revolution, the draft constitution of June 1979, devised before the clergy had fully asserted its dominance, likewise relied primarily on secular qualifications of civil. and political rights, but there were exceptions. Article 25 of the proposed constitution on freedom of the press excluded from its protections publications that were insulting to religious belief. In an ambiguous formulation, Article 26 included the negation of "the basis of the Islamic Republic" among the reasons for denying freedom of association, which left room for religious qualifications. Article 28 qualified the freedom to choose a profession by stating that the profession should not be one opposed to Islam or to the public interest.

The draft constitution received criticism from many quarters. Among others, a group that involved the Iranian Lawyers Association and the Iranian Committee for the Defense of Freedom and Human Rights offered proposals for rewriting the draft. The concerns of this group included ensuring the independence of the judiciary and protecting individual rights and the rights of women. It proposed that the UDHR be incorporated in the constitution and that international human rights organizations and lawyers be enabled to intervene in Iranian courts on behalf of Iranian nationals.[21] The proposals, had they been accepted, would have meant that international human rights law would have been treated as part of Iran's domestic law and that international human rights advocates would have had the capacity to defend Iranian nationals against their own government. This implied a mistrust of the ability of Iran's domestic legal institutions to afford adequate protection for human rights.

The draft constitution was challenged by a coalition of clerics and Islamic organizations demanding that it be rewritten in a way that would give it a more Islamic character.[22] Ayatollah Khomeini said that he wanted the draft reviewed from an Islamic perspective so that it would result in an Islamic constitution, not one made by foreign-influenced intellectuals who had no faith in Islam.[23] Ultimately, the rewriting of the draft was entrusted to an assembly of experts in which clerics had a large majority. The draft was finalized in December 1979 after a major political shift that followed the occupation of the US embassy in November 1979 and the taking of the diplomatic staff as hostages. Not only were the proposals to adopt the UDHR as part of Iran's law rejected, but Islamic qualifications were added to the rights provisions in the draft constitution. Nonetheless, the prestige enjoyed by human rights meant that, even with the ascendancy of a clerical faction opposed to human rights, references to human rights were not excised from the constitution. They appear in the preamble and in Articles 14 and 20, and individual rights are mentioned in Article 3.14.

To make human rights palatable to conservative clerics, they had to be expressly subordinated to Islamic criteria. Significantly, Article 4 provided that Islamic principles should prevail over those in the constitution and all other laws and regulations, indicating that the constitution itself ranked below Islamic law. In similar fashion, Article 20 provides: "All citizens of the country, both men and women, equally enjoy the protection of the law [*qanun*, or secular law] and enjoy human, political, economic, social and cultural rights, *in conformity with Islamic criteria [mavazin-e eslami].*" This equal protection article is discussed later in greater detail, but at this point one observes that Article 20 expressly states that Islamic criteria govern human rights.

A brief clarification of the term *qanun* used in Article 20 and elsewhere needs to be offered at this point. In Islamic milieus, *qanun*, derived from the Greek *kanon*, is normally used to refer to secular laws as opposed to laws based on Islamic sources in the *shari'a*. Given the principles set forth in Article 4 and the Article 20 provision that rights are enjoyed in Iran "in conformity with Islamic criteria," references to *qanun* in articles of the constitution imply not that secular law determines the applicable standards but only that secular law will provide the legal framework for implementing principles that are subject to overriding Islamic criteria, the latter being ultimately controlling in the area of human rights.

Other rights provisions similarly provide that Islamic standards determine rights, using qualifications that in the following quotations are italicized for emphasis.

Article 21

"The government must ensure the rights of women in all respects *in conformity with Islamic criteria [mavazin-e eslami].*"

Like Article 20, this article indicates that Islamic criteria are controlling, and therefore it might be considered redundant. In reality, the specification that women's rights are determined by Islamic standards is significant because in Iran the application of secular law has been associated with women's emancipation and the application of *shari'a* law with the relegation of women to a subordinate status. In this context, it is significant that there is no provision subordinating men's rights to Islamic standards. By including a separate provision stipulating that women's rights must conform to Islamic criteria, the government was indicating its intention to reinstate discriminatory *shari'a* rules that had been reformed under the shah. The consequences of this for women's rights are addressed in Chapter 6.

Article 24

"Publications and the press have freedom of expression *except when it is detrimental to the fundamental principles of Islam [mabani-ye eslam]* or the rights of the public. The details of this exception will be specified by law [*qanun*]."

Article 26

"The formation of parties, societies, political or professional associations, as well as religious societies, whether Islamic or pertaining to one of the recognized religious minorities, is permitted, provided they do not violate principles of independence, freedom, and national unity, or *the criteria of Islam [mavazin-e eslami] or the basis of the Islamic Republic.*"

The status of minorities is discussed in greater detail in Chapters 7 and 8, but it is worth stating here that this provision not only waters down protection for freedom of association by making it subject to Islamic criteria but also allows the government to deny minority religious groups even these fragile freedoms simply by refusing to accord them the status of "recognized" minority religious associations.

Article 27

"Public gatherings and marches may be freely held, provided arms are not carried and that *they are not detrimental to the fundamental principles of Islam [mabani-ye eslam].*"

Article 28

"Everyone has the right to choose any occupation he wishes, *if it is not contrary to Islam [mokhalef-e eslam . . . nist]*, to the public interests, and does not infringe the rights of others."

Article 168

"Political and press offences will be tried openly and in the presence of a jury, in courts of justice. The manner of selection of the jury, its powers, and the definition of political offences will be determined by law *[qanun] in accordance with Islamic criteria [bar asas-e qavanin-e eslami].*"[24]

Because Article 168 provides that it will be Islamic criteria that determine what constitutes a political crime, it thereby places religious restraints on political freedom.

In the above provisions, rights terms have been borrowed from Western constitutions and international law. Some include both secular and Islamic qualifications, but others have only Islamic qualifications. As these examples demonstrate, in the Iranian constitution, Islam is not envisaged as the basis for protecting human rights but is used solely as the basis for limiting or denying them.

One might object to this conclusion by questioning the idea that the Islamic qualifications placed on these rights would necessarily restrict them more than secular qualifications would. Although in the abstract this question might seem justified, both the regime's conduct and its statements show that Iranian official-dom treats Islam as justifying curbing and denying human rights, not as protecting human rights.

The unlimited scope of Iran's Islamic restrictions on rights might be contrasted with the limitations on the qualifications that may be placed on rights in the US Bill of Rights, such as the freedom of speech guarantee in the First Amendment. When individuals assert in US courts that the government has unconstitutionally infringed freedom of speech, they can rely on an elaborate array of precedents and principles that have been developed by independent courts and that sharply inhibit the ability of the government to curtail freedom of speech. If the government does not abide by the limits that the courts have set, it will be deemed to have violated the Constitution, and the speech in question will be protected by such measures as injunctions or nullifications of relevant laws. US freedom of speech guarantees are strong in part because of the framework of legal rules that define narrowly and specifically the grounds on which this right can be restricted or denied, but also because of the respect for laws and legal institutions that has constrained government actions.

In contrast, in Iran there are no firmly ingrained precedents set by an independent judiciary that narrowly limit the circumstances in which Islamic principles can be invoked to justify restricting or denying rights. Iranian courts cannot offer a neutral forum that could build up a jurisprudence protective of human rights. On the contrary, the Iranian judiciary is politicized and subservient to the government, meaning that the Islamic qualifications on rights provisions will have whatever content that the government chooses to ascribe to them without there being any prospect of successful legal challenges by Iranians deprived of rights. Of course, the ability of the government to rely on Islam to insulate its conduct from effective judicial review is linked to the deterioration in the rule of law.[25]

Relevant in this connection is the fact that in Iran Islam is not only the state religion but also the state ideology, an ideology that the ruling theocrats insist embodies God's divine plan for human society. Because the government professes to be carrying out this divine plan, there is a built-in tendency toward absolutism, intolerance, and harsh repression of dissent. A symptom of the inherent repressiveness of the official Islamic ideology can be seen in the scope and vigor of the persecutions and prosecutions of dissident Shi'i clerics, many of whom have experienced severe retaliation after questioning the official Islamic ideology.[26]

As a point of clarification, no claims are being made here that adding the Islamic qualifications to rights provisions in the constitution by itself caused the infringement of human rights or that the regime always relied on Islamic criteria when undertaking measures aimed at curbing rights. Instead, the connection appears to have been a more subtle one. The addition of the Islamic criteria, which effectively gave the theocracy carte blanche to curb human rights, signaled a general disposition not to be bound by the standards such as those in the UDHR. In addition, the Islamic qualifications were representative of the fundamental antipathy towards human rights on the part of Ayatollah Khomeini and supporters of the theocratic system.

Significantly, the conduct of the regime revealed that it did not lay great store by principles of legality, irrespective of whether these were religious or secular, and that it was quite prepared to engage in public violations of basic tenets of Islamic law when those legal principles stood in the way of its political objectives.[27] That is, the Iranian state was in practice treated as being above Islamic law. The Expediency Council was set up via the 1989 constitutional amendments in Article 112 to establish an entity to mediate when legislation in the public interest, which actually translated into the regime's interest, was deemed to be in conflict with Islamic law. It was a sign that the regime was looking for a mechanism to get out of the awkward situations that had been caused by the Council of Guardians blocking politically desirable legislation on the grounds that it conflicted with Islamic law.[28] That is, the Expediency Council could give its stamp of approval to laws that Iran's rulers wanted to enact regardless of whether they conflicted with Islamic law. This amendment was one of many signs that Iran's theocracy was not a regime that fastidiously adhered to Islamic law. Since the clerical takeover, the regime has acted based on its own notions of political expediency, as if it were unconstrained by Islamic law, resorting to whatever measures were deemed essential to maintain the stranglehold on power. In this, of course, it acted exactly like the many secular regimes in the Middle East that pay lip service to official ideologies of nationalism or socialism, which on closer inspection turn out to be mere window dressing for policies dictated by the elites' desire to monopolize power to pursue their own selfish agendas.

In summary, it is inaccurate to say that the Islamic qualifications on constitutional rights provisions by themselves created the human rights violations that ensued in Iran. Nonetheless, there is an important correlation between the rights violations and the official view that human rights could be restricted or denied in the name of upholding Islamic criteria.

Restrictions in the UIDHR

The Universal Islamic Declaration of Human Rights (UIDHR) relies more extensively and explicitly than the Iranian constitution on Islamic criteria to limit rights. This pattern of pervasive reliance on the *shari'a* to qualify rights is much less obvious in the English version than it is in the Arabic version. The explanatory notes section accompanying the English version of the UIDHR states that the Arabic text is "the original," which suggests that it should be treated as definitive. The relationship between the Arabic and English versions is a very problematic one, as there are significant inconsistencies between the two as well as vagueness and ambiguities in the Arabic version.[29]

The explanatory notes section includes the following assurance: "In the exercise and enjoyment of the rights referred to above every person shall be subject only to such limitations as are enjoined by the Law for the purpose of securing the due recognition of, and respect for, the rights and the freedom of others and of meeting the just requirements of morality, public order and the general welfare of the Community (Ummah)." Reading the English version, one could get the impression that many of the UIDHR provisions are subject to qualifications imposed by secular laws because the wording of the qualifications is consistently "according to the Law." Although the authors have obviously tried to mislead the readers of the English version by disguising the centrality of Islamic qualifications, in reality there is no similarity between the qualifications placed on rights in the UIDHR and those found in international law. After scrutiny, it turns out that in the UIDHR the *shari'a* is the law that qualifies rights when the term "according to the Law" is used.

It will not be immediately obvious to the average reader of the English version that "the Law" in the UIDHR means the *shari'a*. The explanatory notes section states that the term *Law* in the text means the *shari'a*, which is defined as "the totality of ordinances derived from the Qur'an and Sunnah [the reports of what the Prophet Muhammad said and did] and any other laws that are deduced from these two sources by methods considered valid in Islamic jurisprudence."[30] As the foregoing has indicated, a definition such as this does not by any means settle how this term should be understood or what qualifications would thereby be placed on rights. At a minimum, "the *shari'a*" would encompass the premodern jurisprudence and, depending on what methods are "considered valid in Islamic jurisprudence," this term might or might not also include many more recent interpretations as well. That is, given the enormous literature that this definition potentially encompasses, the legal standards comprised in the qualification are open-ended.

Consider some examples of how the *shari'a* is used in the UIDHR to qualify basic rights. In the English version of the declaration, Section 12 of the preamble includes the guarantee that "no one shall be deprived of the rights assured to him by the Law except by its authority and to the extent permitted by it." Unless one bears in mind the fact that "Law" means the *shari'a*, one might not appreciate the implications of this provision; that is, *shari'a* requirements determine what rights people ultimately have. Essentially, this implies that the *shari'a* both ensures rights and takes them away. The wording of Section 12 of the preamble in the Arabic version states a similar precept, providing that "each person is guaranteed security, freedom, dignity, and justice according to the dictates of what the *shari'a* of God has decreed in the way of rights for people."

In the specific provisions of the UIDHR (English), one finds that the *shari'a* (the Law) determines the scope of the following rights:

1. The right to inflict injury or death, in Article 1.a
2. The right to liberty, in Article 2.a
3. The right to justice, in Article 4.a
4. The right to assume public office, in Article 11.a
5. The right of expression, in Article 12.a
6. The right "to protest and strive," in Article 12.c
7. The right to disseminate information (also qualified by considerations of the security of the society or the state), in Article 12.d
8. The right to earn a living, in Article 15.b
9. The right to pursue given economic activities (also qualified by considerations of the interests of the community), in Article 15.g
10. The rights of spouses in marriage, in Article 19.a
11. A wife's right to divorce, in Article 20.c, and her right to inherit, in Article 20.d

An example of a problematic article is Article 14. In English, it appears to guarantee a kind of right to freedom of association, with distinctive Islamic qualifications—associations being accepted where they command what is good and forbid what is evil. There is, however, no provision corresponding to this in the Arabic original, so its status is open to doubt.[31] Article 11 provides for a right to participate in public life, but the provision is qualified in a way that ensures that it will have discriminatory impact on non-Muslims, as is discussed in Chapter 5.

To evaluate the strength of the human rights provisions in the UIDHR, one should put oneself in the position of a person being denied rights by the Iranian government in the name of Islam. Could one use the UIDHR to prove that Iran's rights violations constitute violations of Islamic human rights? It seems not. The UIDHR accepts the idea that all rights may be qualified by the *shari'a*, but it effectively leaves it to the authorities to determine the scope of Islamic qualifications of rights; that is, it defines the *shari'a* so broadly that governments can freely choose what "Islamic" principles circumscribe rights. Thus, if the UIDHR standards were applicable in Iran, they would permit the Iranian government to do exactly as it has done: consistently interpret Islamic law to legitimize curbs on rights. In contrast, a person being denied civil or political rights in Iran could use international human rights law to establish that the Iranian government was violating his or her human rights.

Restrictions in Other Islamic Human Rights Schemes

Other Islamic human rights schemes impose analogous Islamic limitations on human rights. Some examples are discussed in this section, and others that specifically affect women, minorities, and religious freedom are treated in greater detail in later chapters.

The al-Azhar draft Islamic constitution should be examined in both the Arabic version, which one presumes was the original, and the often awkward English translation that accompanies it. The al-Azhar draft constitution relies especially heavily on vague Islamic restrictions on rights. Article 29 guarantees freedom of religious and intellectual belief, freedom to work, freedom of expression, freedom to form and join associations and unions, personal freedom (*al-hurriya al-shakhsiya*), freedom to travel,[32] and freedom to hold meetings, all within *shari'a* limits (*hudud al-shari'a al-islamiya*). Article 37 guarantees the right to work and gain a living within *shari'a* precepts (*ahkam al-shari'a al-islamiya*). Article 43 states that rights are enjoyed according to the objectives of the *shari'a* (*wafqan li maqasid al-shari'a*). With the exception of Article 42, which places additional secular conditions on rights, Islamic law is treated as the sole basis for restricting or denying rights.

Although all of these qualifications are left indefinite, one might be particularly curious as to what Islamic restrictions on the freedom of travel would entail. In international law, Article 13 of the UDHR guarantees everyone the freedom of movement within the borders of each state and the right to leave and return to one's own country without any qualifications. The religious criteria invoked in Article 13 to qualify the exercise of this freedom must refer to the views of Islamic conservatives that women should not leave their homes save in case of necessity, and that if they do leave their homes, they should be chaperoned by a male relative.[33] Moreover, some archconservative Muslims believe that it is "un-Islamic" for women to be allowed to drive cars. The general treatment of women in the al-Azhar constitution, which is examined later, warrants the inference that its "*shari'a* limits" on freedom of travel are intended to justify restrictions on women's mobility.

In the work of Sultanhussein Tabandeh, one finds similar religious qualifications placed on human rights. However, Tabandeh coupled Islamic qualifications with others that indicate a bias in favor of preserving social order and harmony and enforcing respect for authority. In international law, Article 3 of the UDHR guarantees the general right to life, liberty, and security of person without qualification, but according to Tabandeh, those rights should be qualified by the requirement that they not be "contrary to the regulations of Islam [or] molest the peace of others."[34] It is striking to see that in Tabandeh's view, even the right to life itself is qualified by Islamic criteria. Apparently, he would allow the subjective reactions of persons who felt that their peace had been molested to deny another person the right to live. These standards deviate sharply from Article 6 of the International Covenant on Civil and Political Rights (ICCPR), which says that the right to life should be protected by law and that no one should be arbitrarily deprived of life. With regard to freedom of opinion and expression, Tabandeh said that freedom in these areas ceases to be a right where "it threatens public order or grows contumacious against government and religion."[35] This view betokens a mentality light-years removed from the philosophy of international human rights law, which does not accept limitations that treat speech critical of government or religion as being subject to banning under such open-ended criteria.

As has already been noted, Mawdudi's discussion of Islamic human rights is sketchy and uneven and leaves the impression that he was avoiding a number of difficult problems. His presentation of Islamic qualifications on human rights is correspondingly short and incomplete. In his scheme, he did limit freedom of expression and association by imposing the condition that such freedoms must conform to the Qur'anic command in 3:104 to order what is good and forbid that which is evil.[36] This indicates that Islamic standards of virtue would be used to determine what could be expressed and what associations would be allowed, but without giving the exact meaning of this qualification. There is more evidence that he supported the use of Islamic law to deny rights in other areas, as discussed in Chapters 6–8.

The pattern of imposing vague Islamic limitations on rights continues in the Cairo Declaration, Article 24 of which provides that "all the rights and freedoms stipulated in this Declaration are subject to the Islamic *shari'a*." Article 25 follows with a circular and unhelpful indication of what these limits would entail, providing that "the Islamic *shari'a* is the only source of reference for the explanation or clarification of any of the articles of this Declaration."

In the Cairo Declaration promoted by the Organization of Islamic Cooperation (OIC), one finds various vague Islamic restrictions placed on specific provisions. Several of the provisions relevant for civil and political rights are mentioned in this chapter, with others to be discussed subsequently. Article 16 establishes the right to enjoy the fruit of one's scientific, literary, artistic, or technical production and the right to the interests therefrom, except where such production is contrary to the principles of the *shari'a*. Article 22 invites extensive censorship based on vague Islamic criteria and Islamic morality. Article 22(a) provides that there is a right to express opinions freely—but only in a manner not contrary to the principles of the *shari'a*. Article 22(b), reflecting the directive in the Qur'an (3:104) to order what is good and forbid what is evil, provides that everyone shall have the right to advocate what is right and propagate what is good and warn against what is wrong and evil according to the norms of the Islamic *shari'a*. In Article 22(c), the declaration provides that information "may not be exploited or misused in such a way as may violate the sanctities and the dignity of prophets, undermine moral and ethical values or disintegrate, corrupt, or harm society or weaken its faith." As will be discussed in Chapter 9, the idea that international human rights law should be altered by including prohibitions of expression that violates religious sanctities or the dignity of the Prophet Muhammad has been vigorously promoted in the UN by the OIC.

The Saudi Basic Law, which had already provided in Article 7 that the Qur'an and *sunna* of the Prophet were the supreme law and thereby placed them above the Basic Law, also provides in Article 26 that the state will protect human rights according to the Islamic *shari'a* (*wafqa 'l-shari'a al-islamiya*), with no further definition of what restraints this could entail. It is intriguing that, although the OIC has many close connections to Saudi Arabia, in drafting its basic law, Saudi Arabia declined to copy the Cairo Declaration formulations of civil and political rights. The Saudi clan had the special need to set up a system in which Islam ratified absolute monarchy, a system where civil and political rights could hardly fit. Article 6 orders citizens to make the traditional oath recognizing the rule of the king in accordance with the Qur'an and *sunna* and in submission and obedience, essentially asserting that Islam requires Saudi citizens to accept being mere subjects. Furthermore, Article 23 asserts that the state shall respect and apply the Islamic *shari'a*, ordering the good and forbidding the evil, thereby providing an additional basis for using Islamic law and Islamic values to shape the scope of rights.

Under the Omar al-Bashir dictatorship, Sudan likewise explicitly subordinated rights to Islamic principles. A document on human rights in Sudan published in Khartoum on July 17, 1993, proclaimed that the principles of Sudanese philosophy protected the dignity and rights of individuals in accordance with Islamic law.[37]

Islam and Human Rights in the New Constitutions of Afghanistan and Iraq

The controversial relationship between Islam and human rights was dramatically illustrated by the intense wrangling over their respective roles in the Afghan and Iraqi constitutions, which were drafted in the aftermath of the US invasions. Both Afghanistan and Iraq comprised Muslims adhering to various sects and also having differing perspectives on how Islam pertained to rights. Tensions among religious groups and disputes about the role of Islam in government were explosive in both countries. As a result, any constitutional references to Islam were sure to provoke controversy. In both countries, there are fervid proponents of Islamization—predominantly Sunni in Afghanistan and predominantly Shi'i in Iraq—who face off against proponents of more secular systems.

Not surprisingly, as both countries neighbor Iran, where Islam has been converted into a rationale for denying and circumscribing rights, the assumption was made by supporters of human rights that the greater the role accorded to Islam in the constitution, the more enfeebled rights would be. That is, Islam and human rights tended to be treated as if they were two conflicting value systems.

Both countries are politically volatile, and both have records of appalling human rights violations. Afghanistan has been wracked by competition among rival warlords seeking control of the capital and provinces; in Iraq, the policies of the brutal dictator Saddam Hussein aggravated tensions between the Kurdish north, the Sunni center, and the Shi'i south. In Afghanistan, women were brutally oppressed under the Taliban, with feminist activists fighting back and demanding protections for women's rights; in Iraq, the relatively secular Ba'athist regime had offered expanded opportunities to women and imposed a reformed version of Islamic law that enhanced women's rights—and alienated religious conservatives, who wanted to see Islamic strictures reimposed. Women's rights were hotly contested in both countries.

As one might expect given this background, the constitution-drafting process was highly fractious. US officials in Kabul and Baghdad pressed the contending factions to reach agreement and influenced the crafting of the substantive provisions. They often advocated their positions publicly, trying to counterbalance the forces calling for the supremacy of Islamic law.

Resolving how to treat the respective roles of human rights and Islam was a central problem in the work leading up to the November 2003 Constitution of the Islamic Republic of Afghanistan and the March 2004 Iraqi Transitional Administrative Law, or TAL. The tortuous formulations of the relevant constitutional provisions indicated that disagreements were not resolved on how to weight the respective concerns of Islam and human rights, necessitating recourse to awkward compromise language.

In the Afghan constitution, the preamble opens with statements that effectively establish Islam and the UDHR as pillars of the new system.[38] The first line proclaims that the constitution is written "with firm faith in God Almighty and relying on His mercy, and Believing in the Sacred religion of Islam." Four lines below, one finds: "Observing the United Nations Charter and respecting the Universal Declaration." In Section 8 of the preamble, human rights are stipulated as being among the goals of Afghan society—without any mention of Islamic qualifications. Article 7.1 reiterates the commitment to the UDHR, stipulating that the state shall abide by the UN Charter, international treaties, international conventions that Afghanistan has signed, and the UDHR.

In addition to referring to the UDHR, the Afghan constitution in Article 3 also provides that no law shall contravene the beliefs and principles of the sacred religion of Islam. This provision seemingly establishes Islam as the criterion of legality, but it leaves this criterion undefined, there being no objective way of ascertaining what a category like Islamic "beliefs and principles" means. In any event, the door was opened to using conservative interpretations at odds with human rights.

The 2004 Iraqi TAL was merely an interim document.[39] It asserted that the Iraqi people were "affirming today their respect for international law, especially having been amongst the founders of the United Nations, working to reclaim their legitimate place among nations."[40] Islam's privileged status was affirmed in Article 7.A, but in a manner that was confusing. Islam was to be considered *a* source—not *the* source—of legislation. No law that contradicted the universally agreed tenets of Islam, the principles of democracy, or the rights provisions of the TAL could be enacted. Thus, proposed laws had to be acceptable under Islamic criteria while also conforming to provisions on rights and democracy—without any ranking of these criteria. This was tantamount to requiring that laws meet two sets of potentially conflicting criteria.

As work progressed during 2005 on the permanent Iraqi constitution, the US Commission on International Religious Freedom (USCIRF) protested that the drafters were moving away from the TAL model. Provisions under consideration at that juncture would have allowed Islamic law to override human rights. The USCIRF announced that it wanted the constitution to afford unqualified guarantees of the right to freedom of thought, conscience, and religion or belief; equality and nondiscrimination for members of all groups, including women; and stipulation that no law should be contrary to the rights guaranteed in the bill of rights in the Iraqi constitution and international human rights law.[41]

As the Iraqi drafters complained that irreconcilable differences precluded them from completing their work, the United States increased pressure on the drafters to finalize the constitution.[42] A final draft was somehow patched together, and it was eventually approved in October 2005.[43] Unable to devise a coherent statement of the relationship between Islam and human rights, the drafters opted for a scheme resembling the one in the TAL, listing an amalgam of potentially conflicting principles in Article 2 without indicating which should have priority. On the one hand, it established Islam as *a main* source—as opposed to *a* source or *the main* source—of legislation and provided that no law could violate the established rules of Islam. On the other hand, it provided that no law could violate the principles of democracy or the rights and basic freedoms outlined in the constitution—without making any reference to international human rights law. The impact of Article 2 will ultimately be decided by those interpreting what the rules of Islam require. Article 90 gives the Supreme Federal Court the task of interpreting the constitution, and Article 89 provides that the court is to be composed of judges and experts in Islamic law—leaving it to parliament to decide their numbers and the method of selection. If powerful Shi'i conservatives come to dominate the new system, any ambiguities will be resolved as they have been in Iran: Islamic law will override guarantees of democracy and human rights. The US ambassador, Zalmay Khalilzad, called the constitution a balance between forces demanding Islamic laws and those calling for universal human rights.[44] In reality, it offers no stable balance; it represents another example of unresolved tensions between Islam and human rights.

It is significant that in the Afghan and Iraqi situations, where one actually had debates between contending factions over the respective places of Islam and human rights in the constitutions, the result was a stalemate—despite strong pressures from the United States to elevate the position of human rights. Islam and human rights were juxtaposed in ways that left it uncertain which would be accorded priority. This contrasts with the superior position accorded to Islamic law in all of the Islamic human rights schemes that have been discussed.

Summary

Imposing Islamic qualifications on rights sets the stage not only for the diminution of these rights but potentially for denying them altogether. As the foregoing discussion illustrates, those who impose vague Islamic criteria circumscribing human rights do not see the relationship of the individual and the state as being an adversarial one in which the weaker party, the individual, needs ironclad guarantees of civil and political rights to offset the tendencies of modern governments to assert their powers at the expense of the individual. Furthermore, they seem to believe that where the rights of the individual and religious rules are in conflict, it is the former that should give way. Because the *shari'a* criteria that are employed to restrict rights are so left so uncertain, they set no line beyond which curtailments of rights would be deemed impermissible. That is, with these open-ended Islamic criteria in place, Islamic human rights schemes offer no protections against laws and policies violating international human rights law.

CHAPTER 5

Discrimination Against
Women and Non-Muslims

Equality in the Islamic Legal Tradition

Accommodating the principle of equality in an Islamic human rights scheme involves dealing with two basic strains in the Islamic heritage, one egalitarian and the other hierarchical.[1] Much depends on which of these is taken to be more truly representative of Islamic values.

There is much in the sources of Islamic law that indicates a fundamentally egalitarian philosophy. For example, it is an important tenet of Islam that the best person is the person who is most pious. The accounts of the earliest rulers of the Islamic community, including stories of the life of the Prophet, are full of incidents indicating the rulers' humility, their egalitarian spirit, and their humane concern for the rights and welfare of all of their subjects.

Other passages in the Islamic sources can provide a warrant for upholding privilege and discrimination. The sources do distinguish in a number of areas between the rights of Muslims and non-Muslims, men and women, and free persons and slaves. Premodern jurisprudence ranking men above women, Muslims above non-Muslims, and free persons above slaves became an ingrained feature of *shari'a* law.[2] Going beyond these distinctions, some of the early shapers of Islamic doctrine endorsed hierarchical features of local social structures, treating them as if they were mandated by Islamic law. The implications of these distinctions for today's societies are sharply debated. Although few would uphold the merits of slavery in current circumstances, in other areas contemporary Muslims sharply differ on whether laws should respect the old juristic categories or reflect the idea that Islam was ultimately meant to afford equality to all human beings.

When it comes to deciding whether the principle of equality is compatible with Islam, one can distinguish between two different approaches on the part of those Muslims who wish to retain the premodern *shari'a* rules affecting women and non-Muslims. One is to affirm that the principle of equality violates *shari'a* law. Conservative Muslim clerics in the past have been outspoken in their condemnation of the principle of equality on the grounds that it makes equal those who under the *shari'a* must be treated differently.[3] The other approach is to pretend to accept equality but to offer reasons why the principle of equality is not violated by the retention of the discriminatory rules of the premodern *shari'a* assigning subordinate status to women and non-Muslims. Today, the second approach is the prevalent one.

In seeking to understand the position of Muslims who assert that the retention of discriminatory rules of the premodern *shari'a* does not violate the principle of equality, one should bear in mind that "equality" may have a different connotation for many Muslims than it has for people who have grown up with the idea of the absolute equality of all human beings. Social conditioning plays a crucial role in how people think about the principle of equality, as is clear from the history of this principle in the United States. Although egalitarianism was a fundamental tenet of the political and legal order envisaged by the 1776 Declaration of Independence, many white men in the era of the Founding Fathers thought that the principle of equality was compatible with denying equality to women and to black slaves, who were assumed to be created unequal. Thus, it was possible to affirm equality while at the same time supporting a regime of laws that discriminated based on sex and race. Not until the 1960s was the contradiction between the principle of equality and toleration of de jure discrimination effectively tackled by civil rights legislation, which prohibited discrimination based on sex and race.

Because of the cultural conditioning that prevails in the Middle East, it is easy for conservative Muslims to assume that the distinctions made between different groups of persons in Islamic law are part of the natural order of things and to believe that the retention of premodern Islamic rules does not in any way contravene the principle of equality. Thus, one finds Muslims who argue that Islam recognizes the principle of equality even while they uphold rules relegating women and non-Muslims to an inferior status. From their perspective, *shari'a*-based discrimination is compatible with the principle of equality. Such Muslims have a problem, however, when they confront international human rights standards, which clearly state that the principle of equality is not compatible with discrimination based on sex and religion.

Equality in Islamic Human Rights Schemes

The authors of Islamic human rights schemes are reluctant to go on the record as denying equality, electing to use formulations that are designed to disguise the extent to which their schemes accommodate discrimination. To evade the issue of equality in rights, one tactic is to write around the topic. For example, the Saudi Basic Law avoids dealing with equality in rights, thereby obviating the need to stipulate the kinds of inequalities and discriminatory treatment that the authors planned to retain. Another tactic is the use of misleading language and the omission of categories of persons to be affected by Islamic provisions. Although Abu'l A'la Mawdudi included "the equality of human beings" in his list of Islamic human rights,[4] a probe reveals that this is a restricted equality. He goes on to assert that Islam outlaws discrimination among "men"—not among "men and women"—based on color, race, nationality, or place of birth.[5] In his comments on the principle of equality before the law in Islam, he states that Islam also outlaws discrimination based on class.[6] Completely absent is any reference to discrimination based on sex and religion, the topics where discriminatory rules are stipulated in Islamic law.

In any social context, a critical measure of the human rights protections that are afforded by the laws is the extent to which the laws aim at redressing ingrained patterns of discrimination. Where laws have traditionally discriminated against certain categories, it is essential that provisions on equality mandate an end to such discrimination. Therefore, it would have been hypocritical for the United States to have outlawed discrimination based, say, on caste while ignoring discrimination based on race, just as it would be meaningless in a Hindu environment to outlaw discrimination based on race while ignoring discrimination based on caste. In each instance, the actual patterns of discrimination in the local culture would have been ignored. In a scheme like Mawdudi's, it is disingenuous to talk about equality without addressing the problems posed by discriminatory *shari'a* rules denying women and non-Muslims the rights enjoyed by Muslim men.

Article 19 of the Iranian constitution uses a similarly evasive formula to deal with the principle of equality: "All people of Iran, whatever the ethnic group or tribe to which they belong, enjoy equal rights; and color, race, language, and the like, do not bestow any privilege."[7] Significantly, Article 19 does not address the issue of whether equality can be denied on the basis of sex or religion. The extensive discrimination practiced against women and non-Muslims in postrevolutionary Iran indicates that the omission of these categories was deliberate.

The Iranian constitution also has an equality provision that echoes one in the draft constitution. The draft constitution had provided in Article 22, the very first principle in the chapter on rights, that "all members of the people, both women and men, are equal before the law." In the section of the 1979 constitution setting forth the aims of the Islamic Republic, one finds in Article 3.14 that these aims include "securing the multifarious rights of all citizens, both women and men, and providing legal protection for all, as well as the equality of all before the law [*qanun*]." The fact that this liberal provision was retained, even though it

expressed a philosophy of equality that was radically at odds with the actual policies of the emerging theocratic regime and inconsistent with other provisions in
the constitution, shows how much normative force international human rights
concepts still possessed, at least in the immediate aftermath of the revolution.

Article l(a) of the Cairo Declaration avoids stipulating that people are entitled
to equal rights, stating instead that all human beings "are equal in terms of basic
human dignity and basic obligations and responsibilities, without any discrimination on the grounds of race, color, language, sex, religious belief, political affiliation, social status, or other considerations." Given the evasiveness typically found
in the wording of Islamic human rights schemes, one is alerted to the fact that the
failure to stipulate equality in "rights" is not accidental and that the equality in
"dignity" and "obligations" is not intended to signify equality in "rights." The
declaration further provides in Article 19(a): "All individuals are equal before the
law, without distinction between the ruler and the ruled." Viewed in isolation,
this might seem to be an affirmation of equality, but in the context of a document
that carefully avoids guaranteeing women and non-Muslims equal rights or equal
protection of the law, it should be read as meaning only that the law applies
equally to rulers and ruled—that is, that rulers are not above the law. Similarly,
Article l(b) states that the persons most loved by God are those who are most useful to the rest of his subjects, and no one has superiority over another except on
the basis of piety and good deeds. This last statement should, in context, be taken
as an indication of how people are evaluated by God, which is not the same as affording a legal guarantee of equality and protection against discrimination. These
weak provisions are not necessarily an advance over the Saudi Basic Law, which
makes no provision whatsoever regarding equality in rights.

Sultanhussein Tabandeh expressed approval of Article 1 of the UDHR, which
says that all human beings are born free and equal in dignity and rights, and declared that the UDHR reflects ideas in the Qur'an.[8] In discussing equality, however, he talked of prohibiting class-based or racially-based discrimination only,
omitting any mention of sex discrimination. He explicitly claimed that differences
are recognized based on "religion, faith, or conviction," seemingly in the belief—
unfounded—that the UDHR Article 1 equality provision allows such religious
discrimination.[9]

In his discussion of Article 2, the general provision of the UDHR prohibiting discrimination, Tabandeh again avoided addressing the issue of sex discrimination but did indicate his approval of Islamic rules according Muslims a higher
status than non-Muslims and according free persons a higher status than slaves.[10]
He concluded that Islam could not accept certain parts of Article 2, "for it cannot deny the difference between Muslim and non-Muslim."[11] One gathers from
Tabandeh's failure to mention the status of women in connection with these arti-

cles that the idea of female equality struck him as so far-fetched that he did not need to bother explaining that it was unacceptable under the *shari'a.*

The al-Azhar draft constitution circumvents the issue of equality by avoiding any specific discussion of categories on the basis of which it is impermissible to discriminate. Article 28 does say that justice and equality are the basis of rule, but this vague provision is far from a stipulation that all persons are guaranteed equality in rights.

One sees in the contrasting treatment of equality in the al-Azhar draft constitution and the Iranian constitution the impact of the very different circumstances in which the two documents were produced. The Iranian model is an actual constitution, unlike the al-Azhar draft, which was no more than a hypothetical agenda of rights formulations produced by Islamic conservatives who did not have to deal with the arguments of Muslims who wanted to follow modern rights models. At the time when the constitution was being drafted in Iran, conservatives had to engage in a dialogue with liberals because the latter had not yet been suppressed. Iran's clerics also had to cope with a political reality in which spelling out their rejection of human rights concepts would have been unpopular. It is significant that in this real-world conflict involving differing views on human rights, conservative Muslims agreed to accommodate—at least at the formal level—a number of fundamental human rights principles, such as equality and equal protection, that they would otherwise have preferred to exclude.

In contrast, Islamic rights schemes that lack any endorsement of equality or equal protection emerge from contexts where the authors did not have to respond either to popular pressures for such provisions or to the arguments of liberal jurists on behalf of established norms of constitutionalism. This is yet another reason for questioning whether the Islamic human rights schemes discussed here are representative of where Muslim opinion generally stands on rights issues.

Equal Protection in US and International Law

The principle of equality before the law is closely related to the principle of equal protection of the law. The most influential formulation of the principle of equal protection of the law was set forth in the 1868 Fourteenth Amendment to the US Constitution, which stipulates that "no State shall . . . deny to any person within its jurisdiction the equal protection of the laws."

The purpose of the US equal protection clause in the aftermath of the Civil War was to end the legal regime of discrimination against blacks in the South.[12] Its original reach has been extended by judicial interpretation to end discrimination on bases other than race. In general, one could say that classifications violate equal protection when they are made for the purpose of placing certain groups at a disadvantage, as happened when laws in the South barred people from voting based on their nonwhite racial classification. Such classifications can reflect the idea that one group is inherently inferior to another group or stereotypical views of classes of people who are traditional victims of societal discrimination. The US principle of equal protection provides a basis for correcting actual patterns of discrimination that result in persons who are similarly situated being treated differently.

Although many features of US equal protection jurisprudence necessarily reflect the peculiarities of US history, the basic concept has been emulated in other laws, and the idea of equal protection of the law is also endorsed in international law. Article 7 of the UDHR stipulates: "All are equal before the law and are entitled without any discrimination to equal protection of the law. All are entitled to equal protection against any discrimination in violation of this Declaration and against any incitement to such discrimination."

One sees in Article 7 of the UDHR unequivocal endorsement of equality and equal protection, and Article 2 of the UDHR delineates the relevant categories, providing that it is impermissible to discriminate based on sex or religion, race, color, language, political or other opinion, national or social origin, property, or birth or other status. The UDHR envisages equal protection under a neutral law, a law that does not deny rights to members of weaker or disfavored categories but accords all people equal treatment.

Equal Protection in Islamic Human Rights Schemes

Although in Islamic law one can discern elements that in some ways anticipate modern notions of equality, one does not find any counterpart of the principle of equal protection under the law. For those trained in Islamic law rather than Western law, the meaning of equal protection may be obscure. In the past, when Muslims were first attempting to come to grips with the constitutional principles of equality, some tended to assume that the principle of equality was not violated as long as *shari'a* law, with its discriminatory features intact, was applied equally to persons within the separate categories that it established.[13] That is, where differences in religion were at issue, they took the position that equality before the law meant that all Muslims should be treated equally under the *shari'a* and that all non-Muslims should also be treated equally under the *shari'a*—not that Muslims and non-Muslims should be treated alike or accorded the same rights under the law.[14] This original confusion about the meaning of the principle of equality carries over, it seems, to equal protection of the law.

It comes as no surprise that the al-Azhar draft constitution, the Cairo Declaration, and the Saudi Basic Law offer no guarantee of equal protection of the law, nor does it come as a surprise that, when equal protection of the law is included in one of the Islamic human rights schemes examined here, it does not have the same significance that it does under international law. As will be seen, the idea of equal protection is modified to accommodate forms of discrimination mandated by tradition and by premodern rules of Islamic law. In other words, the assumption is made that it is possible to have equal protection under a law that itself mandates unequal treatment.

In the English version of the UIDHR, Article 3.a provides that "all persons are equal before the Law and are entitled to equal opportunities and protection of the Law," which, if taken at face value, could leave the impression that the authors of the UIDHR wanted to end the discrimination required by *shariʿa* law in the treatment of women and non-Muslims. Although the uninitiated Western reader might think that the authors had espoused the principle of equal protection of the law, this is not the case.

To understand the significance of the terminology, one needs to consult the Arabic version of Article 3.a of the UIDHR, which states that people are equal before the *shariʿa* and that no distinction is made in its application to them or in their protection under it. That is, people are not being guaranteed the equal protection of a neutral law but rather "equal protection" under a law that in its premodern formulations is inherently discriminatory and thereby in violation of international law.[15] The misleading formulation of the English version of Article 3.a, which tends to obscure this difference, is only one of many aspects of the UIDHR suggesting that the authors are seeking to disguise how far their rules deviate from international law.

As will be shown, the Arabic version includes indications that the authors do not believe that the principle of equal protection is violated when the discrimination is based on sex or religion. According to this way of thinking, it is as legitimate to use the *shariʿa* to deny women and religious minorities the rights granted to Muslim men as it is, say, in Western legal systems that uphold equal protection to treat noncitizens differently from citizens.

In the UIDHR, one finds the categories on the basis of which it is impermissible to discriminate in the Arabic version of Article 3.a. Following the statement that all persons enjoy equal protection of the *shariʿa*, in the Arabic text of Article 3.a, there are quotations from the Prophet and the caliph Abu Bakr, his first successor. These quotations support the notion that there should be no discrimination based on ethnic background, color, social standing, and political connections.[16] These are, in fact, categories on the basis of which *shariʿa* rules do not ordinarily discriminate. There is no mention of sex or religion.

Some clarification of the actual positions of the authors of the UIDHR can be obtained by comparing provisions of various articles. Such internal comparisons reinforce the conclusion that the guarantee of equality and equal protection in Article 3.a does not extend to discrimination based on sex and religion because such discrimination is endorsed in other provisions. Some of these provisions are examined in Chapters 6 and 7, but a few are presented here to illustrate the failure to protect the rights of women and religious minorities.

Article 11 of the UIDHR provides for a right to participate in public life. Conservative Muslims generally claim that the *shari'a* excludes women and non-Muslims from most, if not all, governmental positions. The Arabic version of Article 11 appears to confirm this position by qualifying the right, providing that all members of the *umma*, or community of believers in Islam, who are possessed of the requisite *shari'a* qualifications are eligible to serve in public employment and public office. Although the Arabic version specifically provides that race and class cannot be used as a basis for excluding people from such positions, the possibility is left open that discriminatory *shari'a* rules may exclude women and non-Muslims from public office and employment on the grounds that they are lacking "requisite qualifications." Moreover, by its terms the article seems to exclude all non-Muslims from its protections because they are not members of the *umma*.

Dealing with the specifics of equality seems to have presented great problems for the authors of the UIDHR, leading to the production of extremely convoluted and ambiguous formulations. Because it is very easy, if one actually endorses full equality, to provide for it using the international standards, the obscurity of the UIDHR provisions on equality suggests that the authors had difficulty in finding formulations that would offer token recognition of the principle while restricting equality to domains that would not threaten the privileges enjoyed by Muslim men.

Turning to Article 3.c of the UIDHR, one finds that in the English version under the rubric "Right to Equality and Prohibition Against Impermissible Discrimination," there is the following guarantee: "No person shall be denied the opportunity to work or be discriminated against in any manner or exposed to greater physical risk by reason of religious belief, color, race, origin, sex or language."

This differs from the wording of the corresponding Arabic provision, which, with no regard for consistency, eliminates any reference to discrimination in work. In the Arabic version under the rubric "Right of Equality," the corresponding section, in Article 3.b, says that all people are equal in terms of their human value (*al-qaima al-insaniya*); that they are distinguished in merit (in the afterlife by God) according to their works (*bi hasab 'amalihim*); that no one is to be exposed to greater danger or harm than others are; and that any thought, law, or rule (*wad'*) that permits discrimination between people on the basis of *jins* (which can mean nation, race, or sex), *'irq* (race or descent), color, language, or religion is in direct violation of this general Islamic principle (*hadha 'l-mabda al-islami al-'amm*). One notes that the order of the categories changes from the English version and wonders why.

As a result of the stark difference between the English and Arabic texts and the ambiguity in the Arabic, one cannot tell whether the intent was to abolish discrimination based on sex in the areas covered.[17] Given the pattern of evasiveness in the UIDHR, one has reason to assume that the wording here has been deliberately made opaque. The English version in Article 3.b does seem to bar discrimination in work opportunities, but there is no corresponding provision in the Arabic version of Article 3. The Arabic version does not say that no one should be discriminated against "in any manner" based on the categories mentioned. Instead, this convoluted provision appears to be more of an endorsement of the proposition that people should not be discriminated against in the sense of being exposed to greater danger or harm based on those categories. It is not obvious what kind of discrimination this greater exposure to danger or harm would involve, but it seems certain that the discrimination covered would have a narrower range than is indicated in the English version.

The Arabic version of Article 3.b does not correspond to any tenet of international human rights law, and providing that different categories of people should not be exposed to greater danger or harm than others does not address the major problems of discrimination in the Middle East. The real issues lie elsewhere. Women and non-Muslims complain that they suffer discrimination in such areas as education, employment, and political participation. They object that where Islamic law covers rules of evidence and criminal law, they are relegated to inferior status. Feminists condemn patterns of sex discrimination in personal status law, whereas non-Muslims protest the favored status accorded to Islam and restrictions on their religious freedoms.

Not only do the protections offered in Article 3.b seem quite trivial, but other provisions of the UIDHR indicate that discriminatory rules are being retained. The initial stipulation that all persons have the same human value therefore turns out to be a moral abstraction, not one designed to establish full equality before the law.

Given the disparity between the English and the Arabic versions of Article 3 of the UIDHR, it is noteworthy that the English, not the Arabic, version of Article 3 was invoked in a court case in Pakistan.[18] In the case, the petitioner charged that the appointment of women as judges in Pakistan was un-Islamic. Although the petitioner was unable to adduce any support from the Qur'an or *sunna* for his argument, he did manage to cite prestigious jurists who had ruled that women could not be judges. The attorney general of Pakistan in turn found a jurist who held the contrary view and also argued that the other jurists had drawn an overly broad conclusion from a statement by the Prophet on women's capacity to rule. Although the decision did not turn on the UIDHR, the court did refer to Article 3 of the English version to support its ruling that Islamic law did not prohibit women from serving as judges, saying: "It deals with the equality before Law, entitlement to equal opportunities and protection of the Law [and] also provides firstly that all persons shall be entitled to equal wage for equal work and secondly that no person shall be denied the opportunity to work or be discriminated against in any manner or exposed to greater physical risk by reason of religious belief, color, race, origin, sex, or language."[19] Obviously, had the court examined the Arabic version of the same article, it would have had much greater difficulty finding support for the proposition that under Islamic law women should not be discriminated against in employment or excluded from serving as judges. Women aspirants to the bench were fortunate that in Pakistan competence in the Arabic language was not more widespread.

It is not only in Islamic human rights provisions that deal expressly with equality or discrimination that one sees accommodation of discriminatory Islamic rules, but careful scrutiny may be needed to identify discriminatory biases in measures dealing with other rights issues. A number of seemingly neutral provisions with discriminatory implications are discussed in the next two chapters, but one example is afforded here.

One might get the impression from a reading of the English version of Article 14 of the UIDHR, headed the "Right of Free Association," that it endorses a right to freedom of association. In fact, on closer reading, it does not. In the English version, Article 14.a stipulates: "Every person is entitled to participate individually and collectively in the religious, social, cultural and political life of his community and to establish institutions and agencies meant to enjoin what is right (*ma'roof*) and to prevent what is wrong (*munkar*)." This provision relates to the command to Muslims in the Qur'an (3:104) to enjoin the good and prohibit the evil. Although its full implications are unclear, it could limit the freedom to participate in institutions or agencies—which presumably mean "associations" in this context—to ones that promote Islamic virtues and forestall what Islam deems sinful. No protection is afforded for the right to participate in associations of other kinds, which means that the right involved is minimalist. (This same Qur'anic command is included in Article 6 of the al-Azhar draft constitution and Article 8 of the Iranian constitution, but without any connection being made between it and a right of association.)

The heading of the Arabic version of Article 14 is completely different, indicating that the concern is *haqq al-da'wa wa'l-balagh*, or the right to propagate Islam and to disseminate the Islamic message. Among the Qur'anic passages cited in the Arabic version of Article 14 is part of 12:108: "Say, this is my way. I call on Allah with sure knowledge, I and whosoever follows me." From the Arabic version, one learns that only activities connected with spreading Islam are protected; no broader freedom of association is being established. No right to spread religions other than Islam or to disseminate works tinged with secularism or atheism is being protected. The Arabic Article 14 therefore opens the way to curbing freedom of expression and potentially associational freedoms.[20]

The drafters of the Iranian constitution, as noted in Chapter 4, included an equal protection provision in Article 20, in which the first sentence provided for equal protection under the *qanun*, or secular law. This makes Iranian equal protection resemble the international standard set forth in Article 7 of the UDHR. The intent is not, however, ultimately to guarantee equality to all persons under a secular law. As already indicated, the critical second sentence of Article 20 provides that all human rights are determined by Islamic principles, and Article 4 provides that Islamic principles in general prevail over constitutional principles. These provisions indicate that discriminatory *shari'a* principles would override the secular equal protection principle.

The inclusion of an equal protection clause in Article 20 suggests the enduring influence that Western and international ideas of equal protection have had. Today, an equal protection clause seems to have become a customary part of constitutions, so it may be included even where the philosophical premises on which the concept of equal protection rests are rejected—as they are in the Iranian constitution. In any event, the incongruous inclusion of an equal protection clause in the Iranian constitution is perfectly emblematic of its hybridity and its awkward blend of Islamic principles and dissimilar and imperfectly integrated elements of international human rights.

The question remains: How do the authors of the Iranian constitution rationalize the conflicting provisions that they have included in the text? In this regard, it is interesting to consider the treatment of equality in an article by a Shi'i cleric and strong supporter of Ayatollah Khomeini, Ayatollah Yahya Nuri, who played a prominent and active role in the postrevolutionary regime.[21] Nuri attempted to adjust the idea of equality so that it could fit within a framework of premodern *shari'a* rules mandating inequality. He argued that the principle of equality is the basis of Islam and that Islam shuns the violation of human rights and grants freedom to all under the law.[22] However, in listing impermissible bases for discrimination, he enumerated only the categories of race, color, social class, "weakness," and poverty.[23] This pattern of omitting the critical categories, sex and religion, is by now familiar.

Ayatollah Nuri elaborated on his philosophy of equality. He said that Islam supports the idea that all men (here the omission of women is probably not accidental) should have equal political and social rights, but with the qualification that "equality must be established by the law and it must not transgress the law."[24] For Nuri, the law, by which he means the *shari'a*, serves as a necessary corrective to the principle of equality, which, if not adequately curbed, would have undesirable effects on society, whence his formula "equality must be established by the law" but "must not transgress the law." By holding that equality should be confined within legal limits so that excessive equality can be avoided, Nuri is effectively saying that some inequalities should be imposed by law. Nuri's formula, which is designed to enforce legal inequality at the same time that it proclaims support for the ideal of equality, is essentially a cousin of the conceit of the elite pigs in George Orwell's *Animal Farm*, according to which all animals were equal but some were more equal than others.[25]

A comparison of Nuri's formula and the treatment of equality in the Islamic human rights schemes shows that they share a common assumption—that the right to equality is acceptable as long as people who should not be made equal are kept in their proper place by the retention of the relevant Islamic rules. In contrast, international law, as embodied in the UDHR, assumes that there can be no legitimate societal or governmental interest in mandating inequality.

Equality in the New Afghan and Iraqi Constitutions

In the same way as the authors of the new Afghan and Iraqi constitutions had to struggle with the disputes on how Islamic law affects rights, they faced competing views about the idea of equality in rights. Article 22 of Afghanistan's 2003 constitution bars any kind of discrimination or privilege among the citizens of Afghanistan and provides also that citizens, whether men or women, have equal rights and duties before the law. However, as noted in Chapter 4, Article 3 of the Afghan constitution provides that no law shall contravene the beliefs and principles of the sacred religion of Islam. Thus, the equality provision is qualified by Islamic law, making its parameters uncertain. It might be upheld according to the references to international human rights law in the preamble and Article 7, but it could be cancelled by reference to Islamic law. Iraq's 2005 constitution afforded a strong equality guarantee in Article 14, which asserted that "Iraqis are equal before the law without discrimination based on gender, race, ethnicity, origin, color, religion, creed, belief or opinion, or economic and social status." However, as noted in Chapter 4, provisions on Islam elsewhere in the constitution, such as those in Article 2, provided a potential basis for superimposing Islamic criteria on human rights. Thus, one is left to speculate whether these guarantees, which are potentially qualified by Islamic criteria, will be interpreted in a manner that will give them real substance.

Summary

One can say that the al-Azhar draft constitution, the Cairo Declaration, the Saudi Basic Law, and the models endorsed by Mawdudi and Tabandeh—all of which fail to endorse unequivocally the principles that all persons are equal and that discrimination based on religion or sex is impermissible—are less internally inconsistent than the Iranian constitution. The latter amounts to an admixture of human rights principles concerning equality and conflicting assertions of the supremacy of Islamic law, and similar features are found in the new Afghan and Iraqi constitutions. It is more difficult to characterize the treatment of equality in the UIDHR because of the sloppy draftsmanship and numerous ambiguities and inconsistencies in the provisions regarding equality and equal protection.

Taken together, these schemes reveal the profound ambivalence that conservative Muslims feel about the principle of equality, a principle that they are reluctant to condemn openly but that they seek to circumvent or subvert by a variety of subterfuges. As these examples show, the principles of equality and equal protection of the law as mandated in international human rights law wind up being compromised in Islamic human rights schemes, whose authors seek to uphold conflicting Islamic criteria.

CHAPTER 6

Restrictions on the Rights of Women

Background

With the rise of dynamic Islamic feminist currents and the simultaneous rise of reactionary factions deploying Islamic rationales for curbing women's rights, what Islam says about women's rights is hotly contested. Faced with this contestation, Islamic human rights schemes have elected to use Islamic criteria to neutralize or restrict women's human rights, endorsing views that reflect older sociocultural milieus that were imbued with the patriarchal values that have been common in societies around the globe. Their philosophy fits with trends in Islamization programs that aim to demote women to second-class citizenship, invoking calcified versions of Islamic tradition and sex stereotyping to justify this. At the same time, in implicit tribute to the normative force of the principle of equality, conservatives such as the ones behind Islamic human rights schemes are increasingly trying to avoid advertising their aims to deploy Islam against women's rights, resorting to equivocations, obfuscations, and hypocrisy—all of these constituting an implicit tribute to the authority of women's equality as set forth in international human rights law. As it turns out, when speaking in an international forum, even a country such as Saudi Arabia prefers to be seen as supporting women's equality, not as a sponsor of gender apartheid.

Islamic Law and Women's Rights

Over the last decades, one of the most striking developments in Islamic thought has been the production of critiques of the premodern jurists' views on the status of women, turning away from them in favor of mining the original sources of Islam, the Qur'an and the example of the Prophet as set forth in the *sunna*, for insights into what Islam originally envisaged as women's role. Basic Islamic rules affecting women's rights need to be outlined to provide the background for these critiques. Because of space limitations, some generalizations must be resorted to, but it should be recalled that even within one single school of law, variations in juristic interpretations were frequent.

Against the background of a highly patriarchal social order in pre-Islamic Arabia, Qur'anic innovations tended in the direction of enhancing women's rights and elevating their status and dignity. In an environment where women were so devalued that female infanticide was a common and tolerated practice, the Qur'an introduced reforms that prohibited female infanticide, permitted women to inherit, restricted the practice of polygamy, curbed abuses of divorce by husbands, and gave women the ownership of the dower, the bride price that had previously been paid to the bride's father.[1] As the thrust of the Qur'anic reforms in women's status is an ameliorative one, there are grounds to conclude, as did the eminent liberal scholar Fazlur Rahman, that "the principal aim of the Qur'an was the removal of certain abuses to which women were subjected."[2]

Islam conferred rights on women in the seventh century that women in the West were unable to obtain until relatively recent times. For example, Muslim women enjoyed full legal personality; could own and manage property; and according to some interpretations of the Qur'an, enjoyed the right to divorce on very liberal grounds. The historical accounts regarding the status of women in the first decades of the Islamic community under the Prophet Muhammad suggest that women were originally accorded considerable freedom, that within the family they used the rights given them by Islam to defend their interests, and that they participated in public and religious affairs on a footing of approximate equality with men.[3]

Given this background, supporters of women's rights are naturally skeptical when assured that Islam, which initially aimed to remove the disabilities women had suffered in pre-Islamic Arabia, calls for keeping women in a subjugated, inferior status. They criticize the premodern jurists, who developed elaborate rules in their treatises that endorsed patriarchy and often severely circumscribed women's rights, decrying what they see as distortions of the original Islamic message and influences from local cultures that ultimately obscured Qur'anic ideals.[4] In an analysis echoed today by many others, Rahman concluded that the influence of social conditions and the interpenetration of many diverse cultural traditions led to the inferior status of women being written into Islamic law.[5]

For centuries, juristic treatises were viewed as authoritative statements of Islamic doctrine, a doctrine that endorsed male privilege and power. The premodern jurists generally treated women as needing male tutelage and control, imposing many disabilities on women, putting them in a distinctly subordinate role vis-à-vis men within the family, and largely envisaging them as being enclosed in secluded domesticity. Jurists condoned the practice of young girls being married off against their will by male marriage guardians—typically their fathers. According to the jurists, women were required to be monogamous, whereas men could have up to four wives at a time. Wives owed obedience to their husbands, who were entitled to keep them at home and to beat them and withhold maintenance for disobedience. Husbands could terminate marriages at their discretion simply by uttering a divorce formula, whereas wives, according to many jurists, needed to overcome difficult hurdles to obtain a divorce over their husbands' objections. Men enjoyed great power as the guardians of minors, and after a divorce, men got custody of children once they passed the stage of infancy. In the scheme of succession, women got one-half the share of males who inherited in a similar capacity, meaning that they stood in the same relationship to the deceased.[6]

Many questions about women's rights and freedoms were hard for the jurists to answer conclusively by reference to the Qur'an, where there was little guidance on topics outside family law and inheritance. Women were commanded to dress modestly, but what modesty entailed was disputed. In domains such as access to education, employment, and participation in public life, relevant textual authority was conflicting or scant. Furthermore, there were unresolved questions about how to reconcile the rights granted to women, such as the right to manage their own property and to conduct business, with other rules that seemed to be in direct conflict with them, such as rules barring women from contact with men outside the family and allowing the husband to control his wife's activities and to keep her at home, isolated from all but close family members.

Since the late nineteenth century, members of the elites in Muslim societies have been gradually won over to the idea that the premodern *shari'a* rules need to be reformed. Except for Saudi Arabia, Middle Eastern countries have introduced reforms to improve women's status and to remove many of the disabilities formerly imposed under the *shari'a*.[7] Until the forces of Islamization became so powerful that they were able to reverse this trend, it seemed that changes in the legal status of women were moving in the direction of their achieving greater equality.

Political, economic, and social changes and expanded access to education have expanded horizons for women. As women joined the salaried workforce and feminist ideas circulated through urban milieus, conservatives rallied to denounce women's expanded freedoms and autonomy.[8] The case of Afghanistan, discussed below, is an example of how clashes between the emancipation of women in more cosmopolitan urban communities and the archconservative mores prevailing elsewhere can spur the adoption of retrograde interpretations of Islam that call for women to be demoted to the status of chattel. Indeed, in their reactive and reactionary formulations, such groups as Saudi clerics or the Taliban have often inflated Islamic rationales for depriving women of rights to cover areas where the Islamic warrants for doing so are dubious. Islamic rationales have been concocted for forbidding women to drive cars, to wear white socks, and to sing or dance. Conservatives have argued that Islam limits or precludes the use of contraceptives and forbids abortion, thereby disregarding the established views of Islamic jurists, who generally accepted contraceptive measures and approved of abortions in the early months of pregnancy.[9] With the adoption of modern political institutions, new questions about women's political role have been raised, prompting conservatives to argue that "Islam" bars women from participation in politics and precludes them from voting. As salaried employment outside the home has become common and even necessary for many urban women, conservatives have asserted that "Islam" mandates that women not work outside the home or that any employment should be limited to jobs dealing with women and children. With the growth of public education, questions have arisen about the degree to which women should have access to schooling and opportunities for advanced study. Conservatives who do allow women access to education argue that "Islam" calls for sexual segregation in schools and that it limits women to the study of subjects suitable for females, which tend to be ones that prepare women for a life oriented toward the home and family or that train women to provide services to other women.

Meanwhile, other Muslims have critically reappraised the basis for rules restricting women and concluded that true Islam supports reforms designed to ensure women's equality. The kinds of constraints that conservative Muslims wish to impose on women's lives tend to be dismissed by Islamic feminists as representing nothing more than male biases and outmoded patriarchal values disguised as religious precepts. Fatima Mernissi, a Moroccan sociology professor who was one of the founding members of the Moroccan Organization for Human Rights, offers a prominent example of a feminist who has reexamined the original sources and concluded that Islam calls for women's equality.[10] Just as feminists' perspectives have challenged the gender biases in Christian and Jewish theology, so Islamic feminists are challenging the theological justifications that have been offered for denying Muslim women rights.[11]

Muslims who advocate equality for women are commonly attacked for being servile imitators of the West. Feminists are condemned as agents of Western cultural imperialism who aim to destroy sound customs and morality and to deviate from *shari'a* principles.[12] Thus, Abu'l A'la Mawdudi sneers at "Oriental Occidentals," his pejorative epithet for Muslim women who espouse Western-style philosophy, moral concepts, and social principles.[13] Mawdudi complains that in the works of Muslims who support feminist interpretations of the Islamic sources, "the limited and conditional freedom that women had been allowed by Islam in matters other than home science is being used as argument to encourage the Muslim women to abandon home life and its responsibilities like the European women and make their lives miserable by running after political, economic, social and other activities shoulder to shoulder with men."[14] Thus, he cloaks his determination to curb women's rights in the garb of an ostensible concern for safe-guarding women's happiness.

One also encounters Muslims who may not believe that full equality is compatible with Islamic doctrine but who are nonetheless critical of conservatives' insistence that Islam requires that women be kept utterly subordinated and secluded. A substantial portion of the Muslim community seems to espouse views on women's status that constitute a middle-ground position.[15]

Given the intense and unresolved controversies that have developed regarding women's rights in Islam, Muslims can no longer rely on settled doctrine in this area but must decide which of the great variety of competing views they find most persuasive. The authors of the Islamic human rights schemes examined here have opted for conservative positions at odds with international law. The details of their rights schemes and related policies—or in Mawdudi's case, the principles set forth in writings on women outside his human rights pamphlet—amply demonstrate that they want to retain discriminatory rules. It is noteworthy that, with the exception of Sultanhussein Tabandeh, they deploy formulations that attempt to minimize or disguise their opposition to women's equality. Thus, lack of candor in the authors' formulations effectively confirms that they acknowledge the authority of women's international human rights law even as they seek to uphold substantive rules that conflict with it.

Muslim Countries' Reactions to the Women's Convention

The Convention on the Elimination of all Forms of Discrimination Against Women (CEDAW), also known as the Women's Convention, entered into force in 1981. Measured by the standards of this convention, the treatment of women in Islamic human rights schemes and related policies in national laws in the Middle East seems particularly deficient. Article 1 defines discrimination as including "any distinction, exclusion or restriction made on the basis of sex which has the effect or purpose of impairing or nullifying the recognition, enjoyment, or exercise by women, irrespective of their marital status, on a basis of equality of men and women, of human rights and fundamental freedoms in the political, economic, social, cultural, civil, or any other field." Article 2.f of the convention calls on states to take all measures necessary to eliminate all laws, regulations, customs, and practices discriminating against women. CEDAW lists many specific kinds of sex discrimination that are to be eliminated. For example, Article 16 requires eliminating all discrimination between men and women in the family and ensuring that men and women have the same rights and responsibilities during marriage and at its dissolution.

Many Muslim states have ratified CEDAW without reservation—implying that they found its principles unexceptionable. A few have not ratified it at all, including Iran and Sudan. Muslim states have commonly ratified CEDAW subject to significant reservations that have qualified their adherence. Many non-Muslim states also have entered reservations in ratifying CEDAW, but often these reservations deal with relatively peripheral matters. Muslim states stand out in that so many of their reservations amount to refusals to be bound by the most central CEDAW provisions, such as Articles 2 and 16, and that many of them specifically invoke Islamic law as the reason for making these reservations.[16]

By qualifying their adherence to CEDAW through imposing Islamic reservations, Muslim states are following the practice in Islamic human rights schemes of placing Islamic law above international law. In effect, they treat Islamic law as if it were a binding supranational religious law that was beyond their powers to alter. In practice, however, the Islamic law that is of concern where CEDAW reservations are being made consists of laws in various national legal systems. These rules exist in the form of widely varying, inconsistent rules enacted by individual national governments and amended at will. Occasionally, these are supplemented by judgments rendered in national courts. That there is no supranational Islamic law that is being referred to is demonstrated by the fact that Muslim countries enter Islamic reservations to different provisions of CEDAW, indicating that they have dissimilar opinions regarding which CEDAW articles conflict with Islamic law. Furthermore, Muslim countries may subsequently decide to change the "Islamic" rules in their domestic laws and withdraw their reservations to CEDAW.[17] Faced with pressures to withdraw their reservations, governments confront decisions that are more anchored in local politics than they are reflective of Islamic doctrine. For example, in 2004 Egypt's Ministry of Foreign Affairs considered withdrawing several CEDAW reservations but abandoned its plans when it encountered resistance from al-Azhar, which has consistently opposed women's international human rights and which the ministry was reluctant to antagonize.[18]

Moreover, many CEDAW reservations have been entered by Muslim states on the basis of discriminatory domestic laws that have no connection to Islamic law—such as rules on the acquisition of citizenship, showing that they are disposed to uphold existing patterns of sex discrimination regardless of whether these are grounded in Islamic tradition.[19] That is, Muslim countries' responses to CEDAW provide evidence that factors other than the rules of Islamic law per se are what define Muslim countries' positions on women's international human rights.

Tabandeh's Ideas

Sultanhussein Tabandeh is exceptional in his forthright assertion that Islam opposes the idea of male/female equality. His candor on this point may be a by-product of his general lack of political sophistication. He himself concedes: "I have never taken part in politics, and know nothing of any political aspects or implications which the Declaration [the UDHR] may have. It is only from the religious angle, and in particular the relation to the sacred theology of Islam and of Shi'a beliefs, that I shall discuss the matter."[20] Tabandeh proposes that, where Islamic law diverged from the UDHR, it was the UDHR that should be rewritten to make it conform to Islam.[21] That is, unlike the typical authors of Islamic human rights schemes, he has unshaken confidence in the definitive and binding character of Islamic law and does not hesitate to say where he sees conflicts with international law.

Tabandeh professes his opposition to the notion of male/female equality embodied in UDHR Article 16 if it means "that a natural equality exists between men and women, fitting them to undertake identical tasks and to make equal decisions."[22] He says that a wife must obey her husband, consult his wishes, not go out of the house without his permission, take due care of the property, look after the household equipment, invite a guest only with the husband's agreement, uphold the family's good name, and maintain her husband's good standing whether he is present or absent.[23] In addition, Tabandeh states that Islam forbids women from "interference in politics."[24]

Tabandeh's mindset is typical of Muslim conservatives. It is assumed that all women will marry, so the primary determinant of an adult woman's life is her relationship with her husband. In this relationship, she is considered to be a dependent who is required to submit to her husband's authority. It is expected that her life will be passed at home fulfilling domestic duties. There is no concern for protecting women's needs to develop as individual persons with distinct identities and abilities; to become educated in ways that fit their specific talents; to be able to sustain themselves; or to play a part in the social, economic, or political institutions that shape their destinies. Although other authors are less forthcoming than Tabandeh, when one scratches the surface, one finds similar philosophies.

Mawdudi's Ideas

Abu'l A'la Mawdudi avoids the subject of women's rights in his human rights pamphlet. Unlike Tabandeh, Mawdudi was a canny politician who seems to have appreciated the damage it would do to the credibility of his human rights scheme if he admitted that he aimed to deny fundamental rights to one-half of the population. Like the authors of the Saudi Basic Law, who deliberately avoided any mention of women, he prefers to avoid outlining the restrictions on women's rights that he aims to retain. However, Mawdudi's views on women are on record in his other writings, and they are similar to Tabandeh's, with the exception that Mawdudi believes that women should be able to sue for divorce on liberal grounds.[25]

In his book defending purdah, the custom of keeping women veiled and se-cluded, Mawdudi points to Western degeneracy as the proof that purdah was re-quired. He lists as tenets of Western society the principles of male/female equality, economic independence of women, and "free intermingling of the sexes."[26] He then describes his abhorrence of these principles and argues that they lead to the undermining of the family, lower birthrates, immorality, promiscuity, perversion, and social decay.[27] According to Mawdudi, people in the West "perpetually re-main in a feverish condition on account of nude pictures, cheap literature, excit-ing songs, emotionally erotic dances, romantic films, highly disturbing scenes of obscenity and ever-present chances of encountering members of the opposite sex."[28] He accuses Muslims who advocate "Western" rights for women of aban-doning "the sense of honor, chastity, moral purity, matrimonial loyalty, undefiled lineage, and the like virtues."[29]

Perhaps realizing that it would seem strange if he failed to provide any rights for women in his human rights pamphlet, Mawdudi does list as one of his "basic human rights" respect for the chastity of women.[30] As has been amply demon-strated in many Middle Eastern countries, the obsession with preserving women's chastity can justify a policy of locking women up in their homes, and Mawdudi indicates that he associates preserving chastity with confining women at home. Thus, the only "right" Mawdudi stipulates for women, respect for their chastity, is a principle used to restrict women's freedoms. Determined to denigrate the West, Mawdudi tries to implicate the West in patterns of crimes against women's chastity:

> This concept of the sanctity of chastity and the protection of women can be found nowhere else except in Islam. The armies of the Western powers need the daughters of their own nations to satisfy their carnal appetites even in their own countries, and if they happen to occupy another country, the fate of its womenfolk can be better imagined than described.
>
> But the history of the Muslims, apart from individual lapses, has been free from this crime against womanhood. It has never happened that after the con-quest of a foreign country, the Muslim army has gone about raping the women of the conquered people, or, in their own country, the government has arranged to provide prostitutes for them.[31]

Mawdudi's resentment of the West seems to have impelled him to make the patently false charge that no legal systems other than the *shari'a* protect a woman from sexual molestation and assault or rape.[32] Moreover, contrary to his boasts, there is no evidence that Muslim armies have historically acquitted themselves any better in their treatment of vulnerable women than have their counterparts in other societies. One is prompted to inquire why this curious, contrary-to-fact assertion was included in Mawdudi's human rights pamphlet.

Mawdudi's comments came after a notorious mass rape that was carried out by the Pakistani army in the course of the 1971 civil war fought in East Pakistan, which culminated in the breakup of the country and independence for Bangladesh.[33] In this context, Mawdudi's insistence that a Muslim army had never raped women served at least two functions. It was designed to comfort members of his audience who were still smarting from the international condemnation following the Bengali mass rapes by denying that rape by Muslim armies was even possible.[34] It was also designed to put the West on the defensive by accusing it of systematic sexual exploitation and mistreatment of women in wartime. This correlates with general themes in Mawdudi's writings on Islamic law, which are infused with a polemical, anti-Western spirit.

Given Mawdudi's mentality, he could not be expected to acknowledge how rhetoric about Islamic values and protecting women's chastity could not only co-exist with but even encourage a tolerance of rape in Pakistan. In reality, however, in the wake of Zia's Islamization, rapes have often been committed with impunity in Pakistan, sometimes even being employed systematically as a device to subordinate women and to reinforce the subjugation of disadvantaged groups.[35]

In any event, Mawdudi's stance raises doubts about whether he understands that international civil and political rights are addressed to presumptively law-abiding officials and governmental institutions. International human rights law is no more designed to protect chastity against violations such as rape than it is to protect people from robbery, murder, or fraud. (Of course, international law may become concerned with criminal issues in the event of mass rapes when these are perpetrated as instruments of state policy, such as when they are used as a tool of ethnic cleansing.) Thus, Mawdudi's chastity right deals with a problem outside the realm of human rights.

The UIDHR

Aiming to present Islamic human rights diplomatically, the Universal Islamic Declaration of Human Rights (UIDHR) deliberately obscures crucial issues. Many of the provisions assigning women to a subordinate role do so only indirectly and are written in such a convoluted style that their significance may not be obvious to readers—and especially not to readers of the English version of the document.

For example, in Article 19.a of the English version, a provision begins as follows: "Every person is entitled to marry, to found a family, and to bring up children in conformity with his religion, tradition and culture." This should be compared carefully with the wording of its international counterpart in the UDHR, Article 16.1: "Men and women of full age, without any limitation due to race, nationality or religion, have the right to marry and to found a family."

In international law, the freedom to marry is unqualified. In contrast, UIDHR Article 19.a qualifies the entitlement to marry; the qualification "in conformity with his religion" means that rules of the *shari'a* can impose restrictions, including the bar on Muslim women marrying non-Muslims.[36] Furthermore, a Muslim man is allowed to marry only a woman who is either a Muslim or a member of the people of the book. In addition, other Islamic rules could prohibit marriages, say, between persons related by suckling or between Muslims and apostates.[37] Therefore, this UIDHR provision runs directly counter to the principle in the UDHR that men and women should be allowed, without any religious restrictions, to choose their own spouses.

Article 19.a of the English version of the UIDHR continues: "Every spouse is entitled to such rights and privileges and carries such obligations as are stipulated by the Law." This language should be contrasted with the international rule in the UDHR, Article 16.1: "They are entitled to equal rights as to marriage, during marriage and at its dissolution." There is no mention of equal rights in the English version in the UIDHR—only rights "stipulated by the Law." In the UIDHR, "the Law" means the *shari'a*; thus all the discriminatory rules of the premodern *shari'a* can be upheld. Qur'anic verses referred to in the English version of Article 19.a are identified in the fine print of the references section in the back of the document, where Islamic sources are noted, but the texts of those verses are not reproduced anywhere in the document.[38]

In the Arabic version of UIDHR Article 19.a, the implications for rights in marriage and divorce are much clearer because the Islamic sources are incorporated into the text. One of the cited Qur'anic verses implies that the inequality of the sexes is an underlying assumption of the UIDHR. The verse, 2:228, states that "[women] have rights similar to those [of men] over them in kindness, and men are a degree above them." This is one of the texts that is traditionally interpreted by conservatives to confirm that male superiority is mandated by Islam.[39]

The English and Arabic versions of Article 19.h convey different impressions. The English provision runs: "Within the family, men and women are to share in their obligations and responsibilities according to their sex, their natural endowments, talents and inclinations, bearing in mind their common responsibilities toward their progeny and their relatives." This English version suggests that men and women share family obligations and responsibilities, although it qualifies this sharing in problematic ways. Depending on what is read into these qualifications, the English-language provision might or might not be taken to mean that a fairly equal division of duties in the home between husband and wife is intended, particularly because factors other than sex are listed as determinants of the spouses' obligations and responsibilities.

The Arabic version of Article 19.h, presumably the authoritative one, deals with a different subject. It says that the responsibility for the family is a partnership (*sharika*) among its members, each contributing according to his capacity and the nature of his character, and that this responsibility goes beyond the circle of parents and children and extends to close relatives and distant kinsmen (*al-aqarib wa dhawi'l-arham*). In contrast to the English version of the article, the Arabic version establishes a right to collect support from members of one's extended family—a right not recognized in international law. The article potentially places binding support obligations on persons only distantly related to each other in accordance with the system of mutual obligations among members of the extended family that was set in premodern *shari'a* rules.[40]

The stark disparity between the English and Arabic versions suggests that the English version was redrafted to make it more attractive to the audience in the West, where nuclear families are the norm and where the financial burden of maintaining distant relatives would be onerous and unwelcome. For such an audience, the principle stated in the Arabic Article 19.h would have little appeal.

The UIDHR contemplates retaining the premodern *shari'a* rules that impose disabilities on women. The one major exception is the provision in Article 19.i, providing that no one may be married against his or her will. Rules developed by some jurists, especially in the Maliki school of law, allowed a girl's marriage guardian to marry her off at any age and without her consent.[41] Customs in Muslim societies also allowed girls to be forced into marriages as soon as they reached puberty. Parents continue to compel their daughters to marry while still very young in many parts of the Middle East today, endangering the girls' health and causing heartbreak for young women compelled to wed men whom they dislike—and who are often decades older than they are—and to give up their hopes of pursuing their studies and realizing their aspirations for careers.

Many Muslims consider the premodern rules of *jabr* or *ijbar*, or forced marriage, outdated and incompatible with the ideal of marriage as a union freely consented to by both parties, and legal reforms in most Middle Eastern countries have officially eliminated the marriage guardian's traditional right to compel his ward to marry.[42] Still, some Muslims remain convinced that forced marriages of young girls enjoy an Islamic warrant. Because the practice of forced marriage has not ceased, the UIDHR is performing a service by going on the record as saying that no one should be compelled to enter a marriage. This is a rare instance in the literature under discussion in which a real human rights problem in the Middle East is confronted, the premodern jurisprudence is rejected, and an enlightened interpretation of Islamic requirements is offered.

Meanwhile, victims are rebelling against the injustices and harms occasioned by forced marriages. In 2008 in Yemen, a ten-year-old girl went to court to demand a divorce after being forcibly married off, followed by another girl who challenged her marriage after being forcibly married off at age eight. These acts were hailed by human rights advocates, whereas conservative forces denounced the idea that a girl child could challenge the validity of such a marriage.[43]

The most extensive UIDHR provision dealing with women is Article 20. The rubric for Article 20 in the English version of the UIDHR is "Rights of Married Women." It is significant that no provisions in the document are made for the rights of unmarried women—just as there is no provision on the rights of married men or unmarried men. Given the nature of the document, one can hypothesize several reasons for this: All Muslim men are expected to marry, so the status of a single man is not significant. Married men presumably enjoy the husband's rights and privileges, which are counterparts of the wife's duty to obey and serve the husband. Given the apologetic nature of this exercise, it is understandable that the authors would not have wanted to include a separate article detailing the rights of the Muslim husband. To do so would make it all too obvious that they were endorsing a traditional, patriarchal system in which the law supports men's power in matters of marriage and divorce. For example, if the authors catalogued as rights of the husband his entitlements to beat his disobedient wife, to have four wives at a time, and to have sexual intercourse regardless of his wife's wishes unless she has religiously acceptable grounds for refusing him, this would give their whole scheme the retrograde appearance that they were seeking to avoid.

The existence of autonomous adult women who are not answerable to male authority is not envisaged in this scheme, so there is no need to specify the rights of unmarried women. By speaking exclusively of the rights of married women, the authors of the UIDHR reveal that they do not envisage a system where women ever escape male tutelage.

It is important to note the significant disparity here. In international human rights schemes, the focus is on the rights of individuals, irrespective of their marital status. Because spouses enjoy equal rights in international law, although there are specific rights provisions dealing with marriage, marital status cannot be a prime determinant of human rights in the way it appears to be in the UIDHR.

What are the "Rights of Married Women" granted by the English version of the UIDHR? Article 20 provides that every married woman is entitled to:

A. live in the house in which her husband lives;
B. receive the means necessary for maintaining a standard of living which is not inferior to that of her spouse, and in the event of divorce, receive during the statutory period of waiting (Iddah) means of maintenance

commensurate with her husband's resources, for herself as well as for the children she nurses or keeps, irrespective of her own financial status, earnings, or property that she may hold in her own right;

C. seek and obtain dissolution of marriage (*Khul'a*) in accordance with the terms of the Law. This right is in addition to her right to seek divorce through the courts;

D. inherit from her husband, her parents, her children, and other relatives according to the Law;

E. strict confidentiality from her spouse, or ex-spouse if divorced, with regard to any information that he may have obtained about her, the disclosure of which could prove detrimental to her interests. A similar responsibility rests upon her in respect of her spouse or ex-spouse.

This scheme reinforces women's disadvantages. The English version of Article 20.b actually limits a divorced wife's ability to claim support. During the *'idda*, or waiting period, following divorce (either three months or, if the divorcée turned out to be pregnant, until the birth of the child), premodern jurists held that the husband had to maintain the divorced wife, but that the obligation ceased at the end of the *'idda*. In an era when extended family networks were strong, the expectation was that she would be supported by her relations or by a subsequent husband.

In contemporary circumstances, this cutoff of support obligations can leave a divorced woman destitute. The economic predicament of divorced women who are not independently wealthy or gainfully employed has often become dire now that urbanization and economic changes have undermined the extended family and diminished divorced women's ability to secure support from relatives. In order to rescue such women from destitution, family law reforms in many Middle Eastern countries have extended the husband's support obligations beyond what they were in the premodern *shari'a*. It is therefore noteworthy that the UIDHR fails to address the financial hardships of the indigent divorced woman while limiting the husband's financial obligations to the period of the *'idda*. In context, this constitutes a rejection of the reformist position, showing indifference to the financial distress suffered by many divorcees.

The English version of Article 20.b makes no mention of the Qur'anic verse 4:34, which is cited in the Arabic version of the same article. The cited verse connects male control over women to the maintenance that men pay for women: "Men are in charge of women, because Allah has made the one of them to excel the other, and because they [the men] spend of their property [for the support of women]." This verse is invoked by Muslim conservatives to justify according men superior rights.[44] It is significant that this very verse is quoted in the text of the Arabic version of Article 20.b, a subsection of an article purportedly concerned with the rights of married women. Its quotation in this context reinforces the idea that male superiority comes from the fact that men support women economically. Women's financial dependence on men is in turn the consequence of other *shari'a* rules that keep women housebound. With the inclusion of this Qur'anic verse in the Arabic text, it conveys a significantly different impression than the English version does.

Similarly, Article 20.d seems innocuous in its English version, stating that a married woman has a right to inherit from her husband and other relatives in accordance with the law. However, this law is *shari'a* inheritance law, which discriminates against women generally, allowing them to take only half the share that males inheriting in the same capacity do, and is particularly hard on widows. In the Arabic version of this article, the impact of the *shari'a* on a woman's ability to inherit is more obvious. The Qur'an 4:12, quoted in the text, assigns the widow (a maximum of) one-quarter of her husband's estate if there are no children and (a maximum of) one-eighth of the estate if there are children. These Qur'anic shares constitute the legal maximum that the widow may take because, according to prevailing opinion, Islamic law does not allow the spouse relict (widow or widower) to inherit more than the Qur'anic share.[45] Moreover, the *shari'a* allows the Muslim husband to have up to four wives simultaneously, and if the husband dies and leaves more than one widow, the widows have to divide the one-quarter or one-eighth share that would go to a sole wife, in which case their shares will be very much reduced. Meanwhile, a widowed husband takes one-half of the estate in the absence of children and one-fourth if there are children, a portion that he does not have to share with any other heir. Thus, in incorporating the Qur'anic standards for inheritance by the spouse relict, Article 20.d reaffirms discriminatory *shari'a* inheritance rules and restricts a wife's right to inherit from her husband in a way that is very much to her disadvantage. This article does not afford protection for any human right as understood in international law, nor does it make an attempt to adjust the inheritance scheme to take into account the erosion of the extended family network that the original Qur'anic scheme assumed would ensure a widow's livelihood if her share of her husband's estate was minimal.

Regarding divorce, the reader of the English version of Article 20.c, cited above, might interpret the language to mean that a woman who wanted to terminate her marriage could claim a divorce as a right. The article provides that the wife "is entitled to seek *and obtain* dissolution of marriage" (emphasis added), an entitlement that is said to be "in addition to her right to seek divorce through the courts." This suggests that women are being guaranteed a right to divorce, which is not actually the case. When one consults the authoritative Arabic version of Article 20.c, one sees that no such right is being offered. The Arabic version says that a woman may *ask* her husband to agree to dissolve their union through a consensual termination of marriage, known as a *khul'*, or may *ask* a judge for a dissolution within the scope of *shari'a* rules (*fi nitaq ahkam al-shari'a*). When one considers the implications of this wording, one appreciates that it is not much of a "right" for a wife to be allowed to *ask* her husband to agree to terminate a marriage or to *ask* a court for a *shari'a* dissolution. According to the *shari'a*, the husband is under no obligation whatsoever to grant her request, and except in the doctrines of the Maliki school of law, a woman must meet difficult requirements before she can obtain a divorce from a judge over her husband's objections. The provisions in the Arabic version of the UIDHR were meant to reassure a largely Muslim audience that the *shari'a* regime of male privilege was being maintained, whereas the English version was devised to hide the discriminatory rules restricting women's right to divorce.

The remaining "rights" that are provided to married women in Article 20 are simply frivolous or meaningless. For example, in Article 20.a, a woman is given the right to live in the house in which her husband lives. This would appear to be a solution to a nonexistent problem under present circumstances in the Middle East, particularly in the urban areas that have grown so quickly in the past few decades. Few men today can afford to maintain separate residences for their wives, even if they might wish to live separately from them. In countries such as Egypt, where the population pressure is enormous and the stock of urban housing is woefully inadequate, it would be virtually impossible for the average husband to find and afford two residences so that he could house his wife separately. Indeed, so serious is the shortage of housing in some urban areas that even couples who are divorced may have to continue to live together in the same dwelling because neither ex-spouse can find affordable alternative housing. Moreover, because the UIDHR does not abolish polygamy, this "right" might be interpreted to mean that co-wives could not demand that the husband provide separate residences, as they could under the premodern *shari'a* rules, but would have to live together in their common husband's home. The beneficiary of this "right" would be the husband, who would be spared the expense of maintaining his co-wives in separate residences.

Article 20.e purports to give a woman a right to have any potentially damaging information that her husband may have about her kept confidential, but it accords the same right to the husband regarding any confidential information that his wife may have about him. Thus, listing this right with the rights of married women is misleading. Here, there is no significant difference between the Arabic and the English versions, but in neither case does the principle embodied in the provision rise to the stature of a human right. A puzzling aspect of this article is that no Islamic legal rule prevents spouses from disclosing detrimental information about each other; on the contrary, the husband may need to do so to annul a marriage, and the wife may need to do so to obtain an annulment or a divorce.

Depending on circumstances, the ability to disclose evidence about her husband's defects, failings, and misconduct may be the only means a Muslim woman has at her disposal to terminate a marriage.[46] Therefore, such a rule could conceivably inhibit a woman's ability to terminate a marriage over her husband's objections by barring her testimony about relevant evidence, such as her husband's disease or his impotence. Because this provision offers no significant rights for married women, its inclusion may amount to an effort to pad the very limited list of rights afforded to women in the UIDHR scheme.

Islamization in Iran and the Iranian Constitution

The 1979 Iranian constitution does not expressly relegate women to second-class status, and it contains provisions that, taken in isolation, might indicate that it endorses equal rights for women. A section of the preamble titled "Women and the Constitution" portrays the revolution as being sympathetic to women's rights, saying that after the overthrow of the shah, people will regain their original identities and human rights (*hoquq-e ensani*) and that, in consequence, women "should benefit from a particularly large augmentation of their rights."[47] Article 3.14 includes in a listing of the goals of the Islamic Republic: "securing the multifarious rights of all citizens, both women and men, and providing . . . the equality of all before the law [*qanun*]." Article 21.1 calls for the creation of "a favorable environment for the growth of women's personality and the restoration of her rights, both material and intellectual."

One also sees provisions of a very different sort, ones that are much more in keeping with the Islamic human rights schemes that are under discussion here. It has already been noted that the Iranian constitution in Articles 20 and 21 provides that citizens' rights are qualified by Islamic standards and that women's rights in particular are so qualified. The negative implications of such qualifications are by now familiar.

The section of the preamble on women and the constitution indicates that women's function is primarily to bear children committed to the regime's ideology. The preamble states, in part:

> The family is the fundamental unit of society and the main centre for the growth and edification of human beings. . . . It is the duty of the Islamic government to provide the necessary facilities for the attainment of this goal. This view of the family unit delivers woman from being regarded as an object or as an instrument in the service of promoting consumerism and exploitation. Not only does woman recover thereby her momentous and precious function of motherhood, rearing of ideologically committed human beings [*ensanha-ye maktabi*], she also assumes a pioneering social role and becomes

the fellow struggler of man in all vital areas of life. Given the weighty responsibilities that woman thus assumes, she is accorded in Islam great value and nobility.

In context, the emphasis on the family and women's role in raising children was a code indicating that the aim was to return Iranian women to a domestic role after decades in which they had made progress in the areas of education, employment and the professions, and government service. This family theme is repeated in Article 10, along with a claim that Islamic law and morality must govern: "Since the family is the fundamental unit of Islamic society, all laws, regulations, and pertinent programs must tend to facilitate the formation of a family, and to safeguard its sanctity and the stability of family relations on the basis of the law and the ethics of Islam [*hoquq va akhlaq-e eslami*]."

What this meant was indicated in one of the first measures that Ayatollah Khomeini took in February 1979, setting aside the Iranian Family Protection Act of 1967 as amended in 1975. The Family Protection Act was one of the two most progressive reforms of Islamic personal status law (the other being the Tunisian Code of Personal Status of 1956) enacted in the Middle East in the latter half of the twentieth century. The act included rules requiring that all divorce actions be brought before a court (thereby eliminating the husband's right of extrajudicial divorce by uttering a divorce formula); significantly broadening the grounds on which women could seek divorce; assigning custody based on the best interests of the child (instead of automatically giving custody to the father after age two for boys and age seven for girls); and requiring a married man to get a court's permission before taking a second wife, which would only be granted if he convinced the court of his ability to provide justly for both wives.[48] Claiming that these reforms violated *shari'a* law, Khomeini and other clerics condemned the Family Protection Act. In another revelation of their attitudes, they also promoted the peculiar Twelver Shi'i institution of temporary marriage, in which a man may contract for a woman's sexual services for a limited period of time.[49] This institution has been widely condemned by Iranian feminists as degrading to women and is regarded by most Sunni Muslims as a form of prostitution.

One might wonder how the idea in Article 10 of exalting women's role in the family fits with Article 28, which provides in part: "Everyone has the right to choose any occupation he wishes, if it is not contrary to Islam [*mokhalef-e eslam . . . nist*] and the public interest, and does not infringe the rights of others." To better understand the provisions of Articles 10 and 28, it is helpful to examine the record, which indicates that postrevolutionary Iran tried hard to push women back into a domestic role. To lock women into maternal duties at the earliest opportunity, the regime encouraged early marriages for girls by lowering the minimum age for marriage from eighteen to nine.[50] Of course, having girls marry so young meant cutting many women off from any chance to continue their education and to prepare for careers, thereby diminishing their prospects to be self-supporting.

Pursuant to the goal of keeping women housebound, in the years following the revolution, women's educational opportunities were restricted by a variety of measures, women were fired and excluded from a wide spectrum of prestigious jobs and displaced from employment in the media and the entertainment industry, and women were practically eliminated from the world of politics and government. Women were banned from serving as attorneys in court and as judges—and thus were excluded from having a say in the legal order that was seeking to demote them.[51]

In another effort to lock women in the domestic sphere, the regime adopted vigorous pro-natalist policies. Distressed by its inability to cope with the soaring population growth that ensued, the regime subsequently reversed course, relaxing many restrictions on women's participation in the workforce and energetically promoting birth control.[52]

Islamic standards as applied to Iranian women have eliminated their right to choose how to dress. Iran's clerical rulers have aggressively, albeit unevenly, enforced their rules on Islamic dress, which are ostensibly needed to uphold morality. Women have been pressured to wear all-enveloping chadors or similar covering in dark, dull colors and have been subjected to harsh criminal penalties for minor contraventions of the dress rules. Iranian women have resisted compliance, trying to get away with more revealing head coverings and injecting some variety and color in their attire—at the risk of being arrested and flogged for their acts of defiance.[53] Angered by women's resistance to *hejab* rules, the regime expanded the punishments for noncompliance in 1996, adding imprisonment and fines as penalties for women caught in "un-Islamic" attire.[54]

Morality police also engage in systematic intimidation and harassment designed to discourage women from appearing in public with unrelated men. In addition, women's ability to participate in sports has been drastically curtailed by rules mandating that women not engage in athletic activities in places where men could observe them and that when in public, women must wear cumbersome, baggy, concealing clothing—even while swimming or skiing.

Having instituted these reactionary policies, Iran nonetheless took care to convey a more progressive image when in the international spotlight. After years of barring Iranian women from participating in the Olympic games and sending all-male teams, which had refused to march into Olympic stadiums behind women from the host country carrying the placards with Iran's name, Iran allowed a few women athletes to attend the 1996 Olympic games in Atlanta. Although Iran's women athletes could compete only in events where they could wear their cumbersome and concealing Islamic dress, an Iranian woman athlete dressed in a smart white coverall carried the flag and led the team into the stadium. The purpose of this display, Iran announced, was "to neutralize poisonous propaganda on the status of women in Iran."[55] That is, even while cracking down domestically, the ruling clerics decided that the hallowed rules of Islamic dress could be significantly compromised in situations where forcing women to stay enshrouded could expose Iran to international criticism and ridicule.

The zigs and zags in policies on women's rights in Iran in the few decades since the revolution have shown that even a theocratic government can shift its interpretations of Islamic law in response to political calculations. For example, after the revival of premodern *shari'a* rules limiting the husband's support obligations resulted in financial misery for divorced women, which provoked adverse publicity, the government overrode the Islamic rules to give divorced women enhanced ability to claim support from their ex-husbands.[56] This showed that, despite their reactionary attitudes, at least some in the theocracy were sufficiently pragmatic to consider adjusting premodern rules that made the regime appear especially backward or insensitive to the needs of the poor.

Far from being confident that its Islamic rationales excuse its noncompliance with international law, Iran has often shown acute embarrassment over being exposed as a violator of women's rights, and the Iranian leadership has proffered strained arguments asserting that its policies on women's rights are consonant with international law.[57] Iran's theocratic rulers detested the Taliban, who were virulently anti-Shi'i. Iran eagerly exploited the contrast between its relatively lenient policies on women and the extraordinarily retrograde policies of the Taliban in neighboring Afghanistan. In 1996, Ayatollah Jannati publicly denounced the Taliban: "What could be worse than committing violence, narrow-mindedness and limiting women's rights [thereby] defaming Islam?"[58] At the same time that it denounced the backward policies of the Taliban, the regime continued to impose Islamic restrictions on women that reflected its reactionary ideology. As ruling *faqih*, Ayatollah Khamene'i admonished Iranian women not to embrace Western feminist ideas, insisting that these ideas brought sexual promiscuity and that Iranian women had to follow "Islamic models" of sexual equality.[59]

Significantly, after Iran's parliament voted to ratify the Women's Convention, the proposed ratification was overridden on August 12, 2003, by a ruling of the Council of Guardians asserting that ratification would violate both Islamic law and the Iranian constitution. Thus, an attempt by the elected representatives of the Iranian people to endorse women's international human rights law was thwarted by clerics using constitutional provisions upholding the primacy of Islamic law, making it clear that the Islamic qualifications on women's rights in the constitution precluded equality for women. In the aftermath, Iranian women's rights activists mobilized to demand changes in the constitution, charging that its terms presented the major obstacle to improving women's rights.[60]

The regime's antagonism toward women's international human rights was exemplified by the persecution and prosecution of Mehrangiz Kar, who with fellow attorney Shirin Ebadi—later to become a Nobel laureate—was one of Iran's most prominent advocates of women's rights as set forth in international law. Kar was arrested in 2000 and tried in proceedings characterized by the usual absence of due process on a host of charges, including spreading anti-regime propaganda, rejecting the commands of the *shari'a*, and violating Iran's Islamic dress rules. She was eventually convicted in 2001.[61] Kar was able to obtain permission to leave Iran to obtain urgently needed cancer treatment and decided to stay in exile, where she has written that separation of religion and state is a prerequisite for Iranian women to achieve equality.[62] The severity of the regime's retaliation against Kar was significant; an attorney exposing the disparity between the rights afforded women in Iran's Islamic laws and those in international law was seen as a dire threat by a regime that simultaneously wanted to discriminate against women and to maintain the fiction that its policies on women were progressive.

The pitiless repression directed at activists in the One Million Signature Campaign, which was launched in 2006, expressed the fury of Iran's rulers at having to confront a large grassroots campaign aimed at overturning laws denying women equality. In this campaign, women's rights activists had sought to educate the public about Iran's discriminatory laws and to collect one million signatures from Iranians from all walks of life on a petition calling for women's equality. Treating their efforts to mobilize public support for women's equality as heinous crimes, the regime sought to suffocate the movement by extensive arrests and imprisonments of activists.[63]

As an outgrowth of its policies of relegating women to second-class status, the Islamic Republic has banned them from sitting in stadiums to watch sporting events. Iranian women have repeatedly challenged the ban. In the first week of March 2006, two incidents indicated a clampdown. In one, security officers forcibly removed several hundred women spectators from a Tehran stadium where they were watching athletes performing in the 2006 Gymnastics World Cup Tournament. In the second, dozens of young women who had bought tickets to attend an international football match pitting Iran against Costa Rica were barred from entering Tehran's Azadi Stadium. The women held a protest demonstration after being denied entry, which prompted the authorities to threaten the demonstrators that they would be arrested and sent to Tehran's notorious Evin prison if they did not disband.[64] *Offside*, a touching and humorous 2006 film, was made about girls desperately trying to get in a stadium to watch a World Cup qualifying match. Censored in Iran, it was directed by the internationally renowned Jafar Panahi and distributed outside the country. For making this and other films that struck Iran's theocrats as subversive, Panahi was eventually sentenced to six years' imprisonment in December 2010 and also barred for twenty years from directing movies, writing screenplays, conducting interviews, and leaving Iran.[65]

After decades of harshly restricting women's opportunities to participate in sports, the regime responded angrily when in June 2011 the Fédération Internationale de Football Association (FIFA) barred the Iranian women's soccer team from an Olympic qualifier for wearing a style of Islamic dress that breached explicit FIFA rules on athletes' attire. FIFA had made adjustments allowing special head coverings to accommodate Muslim women athletes, but Iran sent a team wearing hoods, not the approved head coverings. President Ahmadinejad blasted the FIFA officials as "dictators and colonialists who want to impose their lifestyle on others."[66] Of course, because his regime punished any Iranian women, including athletes, who failed to dress according to rules dictated by the theocracy, Ahmadinejad's protest involved stark double standards. Moreover, if the regime saw FIFA as imposing a lifestyle linked to Western colonialism, it hardly made sense for Iran to insist that its women's team be included in a FIFA competition, a competition that also involved playing a game that came from Great Britain, the colonialist power par excellence. The gross inconsistencies and confusion in Iran's rhetoric correlate with its difficulties in reconciling its ambitions to be treated as a respectable country participating in international activities on a par with other countries while at the same time clinging to retrograde rules mandating women's subjugation and corresponding onerous dress restrictions.

In April 2010, a sign of Iran's determination to gain a prominent role in the field of women's human rights in the UN occurred when it managed to engineer Asian backing for its bid to serve on the new UN Commission on the Status of Women, known as UN Women, an entity that is supposed to set standards for the advancement of women's equality. Obviously, Iran aspired to this UN role to enhance its stature at the same time that it was crushing advocacy of women's rights on the domestic scene. Because of strong opposition, Iran eventually lost out in November 2010 in the voting for countries to represent Asia on the commission.[67] Nonetheless, Iran's ambitions to be a player in the UN entities concerned with women's human rights persist, which constitutes a sign that hypocrisy has replaced its former aggressive insistence on its right to uphold Islamic particularism at the expense of human rights.

The al-Azhar Draft Constitution

The al-Azhar draft constitution has some features that resemble those found in the Iranian constitution, although the former is a far briefer document. Article 7 in the section on rules governing "Islamic Society" provides that the family is the basis of society and that the family's foundations are religion and morality (*al-din wa 'l-akhlaq*), and Article 8 states that safeguarding the family is a state duty. As has been noted, "protecting the family" is a code phrase used by conservative Muslims to denote a system requiring the subordination of women to men and their confinement to the domestic sphere.

In the al-Azhar draft, Article 8 provides that the state should encourage early marriage and provide "the means according to which the wife would obey her husband and look after her children and consider keeping the family the first of her tasks." This shows how in these schemes, the state winds up as the enforcer of supposedly traditional values at a time when social and economic changes have unsettled the traditional family. It reflects al-Azhar sheikhs' abhorrence of contemporary Egyptian reality, where many women are educated and work in full-time jobs, thereby gaining autonomy and escaping the confines of the home. Women's earning power has weakened the control that their husbands formerly enjoyed as the sole providers, which does not fit with the assumptions underlying Islamic family law. The al-Azhar draft therefore envisages governmental initiatives aimed at reversing these changes and ensuring that the wife will accord primacy to her duties as mother and housewife and defer to her husband.

In addition to a provision offering a general guarantee of the right to work in Article 37 of the al-Azhar constitution, there is a separate provision in Article 38 that states that women have the right to work within the limits of the precepts of the *shari'a* (*hudud ahkam al-shari'a al-islamiya*). It is significant in this regard that there are no Islamic qualifications imposed on men's right to work—implying that there is no possibility that a man's choice of work could infringe *shari'a* principles. Extrapolating from other cases, one can presume that women would need their husbands' permission to work, and that they would be allowed to work in only a limited range of jobs deemed suitable for women and that did not bring them into inappropriate proximity to men.

The most distinctive provision in the al-Azhar draft constitution is Article 14, which in the English version provides: "Bedizement [bedizenment, or gaudy dress] is forbidden and observing others' feelings is a duty. The government is to pass the laws and decisions to preserve the feelings of the public against profligacy according to the rules of the Islamic Sharia." This English translation of Article 14 seems disingenuous. The reader of the article may not realize that this prohibition of bedizenment is a call for governments to take measures to force women to veil themselves in public and to discourage them from leaving their homes or associating with men from outside the family circle. The use of the term "profligacy" is misleading in this context because it gives the impression that the concern is for the curbing of dissipation generally, when in reality it is only "shameless" conduct by women that is targeted.

In the Arabic version of Article 14, the word corresponding to what should be "bedizenment" in the English version is *tabarruj*. The reference is to the command in the Qur'an 33:33, which in an English translation that favors archaisms reads: "Bedizen not yourselves with the bedizenment of the Time of Ignorance."[68] The verse is widely interpreted to mean that women must avoid immodest or provocative clothing and ornaments and by Islamic conservatives to mean that heavy veiling and no makeup are de rigueur for women whenever they are exposed to the sight of men outside their family circles.[69] Their enshrinement of the ban on female "bedizenment" in the early fundamental provisions of the al-Azhar draft constitution reveals the authors' mentality, their social priorities, and their attitudes toward women's rights.

In the Arabic version of Article 14, the ban on bedizenment is followed by statements that preserving female honor is a duty (*al-tasawun wajib*). This could be interpreted as justifying the retention of Arab concepts of honor, which traditionally have been used to justify keeping women segregated and secluded and imposing harsh penalties on women (not men) for violating sexual taboos.[70] The al-Azhar draft also provides that the state must issue laws to prevent offenses to the public sense of decency according to the principles of the *shari'a* (*ahkam al-shari'a al-islamiya*). In the light of experience, one assumes that such laws might include penalties against women for going about without male chaperones or for failing to veil.

The Cairo Declaration and the Saudi Basic Law

As has been noted, the Cairo Declaration is carefully drafted so as to avoid providing for equality in rights for women—as one would expect in a document endorsed by Saudi Arabia, where sex-based discrimination is state policy. In an evasive formulation, Article 6 provides that women are equal to men in "human dignity"—saying nothing about equality in rights. However, the term "rights" is used later in the same article, when it is stipulated that a woman "has rights to enjoy as well as duties to perform." The duties are left unspecified, and only three rights are enumerated as such: a woman's right to legal personality, to own and manage her property, and "to retain her name and lineage." The first two were among the important improvements in women's rights provided by Islam more than a millennium ago, but they are less significant today, as such minimal rights are now taken for granted. The third "right" does not advance women's position in Middle Eastern societies, where women have traditionally kept their family names after marriage. Article 6 also imposes on the husband the duty to pay his wife maintenance and to care for the family, thereby perpetuating the traditional spousal relationship in which the husband is treated as both master and provider with the wife bound to show him obedience.

Furthermore, it seems that the Cairo Declaration envisages using Islamic criteria to restrict women's freedom of movement and their employment. Article

12 provides that everyone shall have the right, within the framework of the *shari'a* (*fi utur al-shari'a*), to freedom of movement. If reference were made to traditional *shari'a* rules, this seemingly neutral provision would accommodate restrictions on women's mobility, preventing women from leaving the home except with their husband's permission and from traveling except when accompanied by a male relative. Although Article 13 provides that men and women are entitled to fair wages for work without discrimination—a positive step—it does not prohibit restricting the fields in which women are permitted to work. Instead, it provides that everyone "shall be free to choose the work that suits him best and which serves his interests and those of society," and that a person "may not be assigned work beyond his capacity." These conditions would permit authorities to exclude women from work on the grounds that it was unsuitable for them, that the demands were beyond their capacity, or that the interests of society dictated such exclusion. This is in violation of UDHR Article 23.1, which guarantees that everyone has the right to work and to free choice of employment. Article 23 of the Cairo Declaration stipulates that the *shari'a* determines the right to assume public office, which could be exploited by conservatives opposed to women's participation in government.

The Cairo Declaration affords no guarantee for the right to marry the partner of one's choice, providing in Article 5 only that the right to marry should not have "restrictions stemming from race, color, or nationality," thereby leaving intact the old *shari'a* rules barring Muslim women from marrying non-Muslims. One is far, indeed, from the standards of the UDHR, which in Article 16.1 guarantees that both men and women have the right to marry without any limitations because of religion.

The Saudi Basic Law has no provision directly addressing women's rights. However, in Article 10 it provides that the state is to "aspire to strengthen family ties" and to maintain "Arab and Islamic values." There are also stipulations in Article 9 that members of the family shall be inculcated with the Islamic faith and with obedience to God, the Prophet, and those possessing authority—which in context would be the ruling Saudi clan—and also with respect for the law and love of country. Taken together, these suggest that the regime will resort to appeals to Islamic family values, Arab tradition, and Saudi patriotism in order to maintain the traditional patriarchal family structure and to keep women subordinated and cloistered within its confines. In other words, the Basic Law accommodates the Saudi system of gender apartheid. Not surprisingly, Saudi Arabia was one of only three nations willing to have full diplomatic relations with the Taliban government in Afghanistan, a regime that nearly all states refused to recognize because of its appalling rights abuses, especially its gender apartheid.[71]

Paradoxically, Saudi Arabia decided in 2000 to ratify the Women's Convention, albeit with reservations indicating that the Saudi version of Islamic law would override the convention, stating, "In case of contradiction between any term of the Convention and the norms of islamic law [*sic*], the Kingdom is not under obligation to observe the contradictory terms of the Convention."[72] Of course, Islamic law as enforced in Saudi Arabia locks women into a system of rigid segregation and subordination that is utterly incompatible with women's equality. As would have been expected by those familiar with the official Saudi mentality, after ratification of the convention, the reactionary Saudi laws enforcing women's subordinate status and upholding patriarchal controls over their lives remained in force.[73] Feeble measures, such as the 2006 appointment of a few women as advisers to the toothless Consultative Council and plans to allow women to vote in municipal elections in 2015, exemplified Saudi minimalism.

Like Iran, Saudi Arabia has decided that it should try to play a powerful role in the UN human rights system, and its enormous wealth and political influence have enabled it to gain positions that no country with its human rights record would be deemed qualified to hold if UN elections were based on the candidates' merits. Having won and held a place on the UN Human Rights Council, Saudi Arabia later campaigned successfully to win a seat on the board of UN Women, where to the dismay of women's human rights advocates it gained a position where it could influence the UN agenda affecting women.

As part of its campaign to gain influence in the UN human rights system, Saudi Arabia decided to pose as a country supportive of international human rights law and respectful of women's human rights. Saudi Arabia's 2007 report to the CEDAW committee resorted to gross misrepresentations, containing startling assertions that Saudi laws and policies ensured women's equality in rights and were in full compliance with CEDAW.[74] The report, the reasoning of which was far from coherent and in which elements of gender stereotyping surfaced at various points, spoke as if Saudi jurists had embraced the most advanced tenets of Islamic feminism. This was a shocking misrepresentation from a country that the 2010 *World Economic Forum Global Gender Gap Report* ranked 129 out of 134 countries and that was the only country to score a zero for female political empowerment.[75] By recourse to such egregious misrepresentations of how it treated Saudi women, the kingdom effectively acknowledged the authority of the human rights principle of equality for women and the utter indefensibility of ingrained Saudi patterns of denying women even the most basic rights and freedoms.

Saudi Arabia has had to struggle to defend the reservation that it entered to CEDAW when ratifying back in 2000. In their 2007 dialogues with the CEDAW committee, Saudi representatives insisted that the reservation did not mean that Islamic law conflicted with CEDAW or that the kingdom would be violating its CEDAW obligations in order to uphold Islamic law. Feeling under siege, Saudi representatives eventually resorted to a far-fetched excuse for entering the reservation, claiming that it had been entered primarily as a precautionary measure against possible future interpretations of CEDAW that might contradict Saudi laws.[76] That the Saudi regime felt obliged to offer a feeble and convoluted defense of its CEDAW reservation illustrates the difficulties currently facing governments that prefer to keep women subjugated while simultaneously seeking to pretend that they uphold women's international human rights.

An interesting exchange occurred after the CEDAW Committee observed that the Saudi report was silent on the ban on women driving. With striking disingenuousness, the Saudi response was: "There is no legal provision banning women from driving cars."[77] If one took "legal provision" to mean statutory law, this statement could be said to be technically correct because the ban was essentially a customary one that had been reinforced by a *fatwa* issued after a women's driving protest carried out in 1990 during the first Gulf War. But, of course, this denial amounted to deviousness on the part of the Saudi delegation because Saudi women who were apprehended while driving were subject to arrest and punishment, the problem persisting because women's rights activists continued to flout the ban on driving.[78]

In the heady days of the 2011 Arab Spring, Saudi women decided to mount a challenge to the driving ban. One of the main organizers of the campaign, Manal al-Sharif, was imprisoned in May 2011 after publicizing her own driving, the punishment seemingly being designed to deter other women from participating in a mass driving protest that had been set for June 17, 2011. She was held for nine days and only released after she agreed to issue a contrite statement saying that she was abandoning the campaign.[79] It was clear that in practice Saudi authorities still regarded a woman driving a car as a criminal offense—regardless of the grossly misleading statements that had been given to the CEDAW committee. The lack of candor on this point was emblematic of a basic quality of Islamic human rights schemes, which on a regular basis resort to evasiveness and obfuscations in attempts to disguise how they are designed to accommodate denials of women's international human rights.

Women's Rights in Pakistan

The enormously complicated situation in Pakistan defies easy characterization. Although Pakistan is one of the rare Muslim countries to have elected a woman as prime minister, powerful Islamist factions agitate constantly for restrictions on women's rights, and many support the Taliban model of subjugating women. Pakistan's assertive feminists, including the distinguished human rights lawyers Asma Jahangir and Hina Gilani, mobilize and litigate, seeking to thwart proposals for more Islamization and to roll back discriminatory rules and practices. At the same time, the authorities have a record of condoning rape, tolerating egregious incidents of domestic violence, abusing women held in detention, and failing to punish perpetrators of honor killings. It is important, however, to note that many of the most notorious incidents of violence against women in Pakistan have no connection to Islam, stemming instead from retrograde local customs and mentalities imbued with primitive sexism.

Not surprisingly, there were contentious debates about whether Pakistan should ratify the Women's Convention. Ultimately, a compromise was made; the 1995 ratification was said to be "subject to the provisions of the Constitution of Pakistan." Because, as previously noted, the constitution called for Muslims to be enabled to live in "accordance with the teachings and requirements of Islam," what appeared to be a "constitutional" reservation was potentially the equivalent of the Islamic reservations that had been entered by other Muslim countries.

In a striking departure from the typical pattern of using Islamic law to curb rights and freedoms since the inauguration of Pakistan's Islamization program, in 2006 Pakistan's Federal Shariat Court referred both to the Islamic sources and international law in an opinion declaring section 10 of the Pakistani Citizenship Act, 1951, to be discriminatory against women.[80] The citizenship rules allowed a foreign woman marrying a Pakistani man to obtain Pakistani citizenship but not a foreign man marrying a Pakistani woman. When the rules were challenged, the government took the position that there was a threat of men from other countries misusing the opportunity to gain Pakistani citizenship through marriage, especially Afghan refugees and illegal Bengali and other South Asian immigrants. It warned that if women could obtain Pakistani citizenship for their foreign husbands, such undesirables could marry Pakistani women and after getting citizenship divorce them.[81] The court was not impressed and said of the section that it was:

> discriminatory, negates gender equality and is in violation of Articles 2-A (Objective Resolution) and 25 (equality of citizens) of the Constitution, also against international commitments of Pakistan and, most importantly, is repugnant to the Holy Quran and Sunnah.[82]

Among other comments, the court asserted: "The last sermon of Holy Prophet is the first Charter of Human Rights wherein all human beings are equal."[83] That is, in this unusual and progressive court opinion, the Shariat Court offered a different way of thinking about Islam and human rights, treating the Islamic sources as supporting international law and upholding women's equality, thereby reminding Pakistanis that Islam did not have to be treated as mandating an inferior status for women. Here Islam was used as a tool to discredit a discriminatory secular law. The court requested the President to amend the law within six months. Regrettably, years later, the change in the law had still not gone through.[84]

The New Afghan and Iraqi Constitutions

In the drafting of the most recent constitutions of Afghanistan and Iraq, pressures for Islamization have been countered by demands for protecting women's rights. In the postinvasion era, the influence of US officials in both countries added an extra factor to the resistance to Islamization. Nonetheless, Islamic elements were included in both documents that could be exploited to curb women's rights.

In the turbulent, war-torn years just before the Taliban takeover, various factions competed for supremacy in Afghanistan. During this period, women suffered from abduction, displacement, abuse, torture, rape, and slaughter.[85] All this was but a prelude to the even harsher crackdowns and more extensive abuses perpetrated under the Taliban, who succeeded in extending their domination over most of the country in 1996. They unleashed fierce enforcers of their retrograde version of Islamic morality to terrorize the population into submission. Ironically, their Islamic dress rules were less clearly discriminatory than many others because men, like women, were required to don approved Islamic dress. Women had to be completely swathed in the enveloping *burqa* when in public, and their mobility was sharply curbed because they were not allowed go out without a male relative to escort them. The Taliban's policies amounted to a regime of gender apartheid, barring women from all education and virtually all employment outside the home and even blocking women's access to health care.[86]

Seemingly chastened by the international chorus of condemnation and the refusal of most states to recognize their regime, Taliban officials denied charges that they were trampling on women's human rights.[87] Their denial proved that the prestige of human rights had grown to the point where even regimes pursuing the most retrograde Islamization programs felt obliged to deflect charges of violations.

Afghan women struggled against the Taliban's program and mobilized to support the opposition.[88] Many celebrated the Taliban's 2001 downfall and the adoption by the new government of policies more supportive of women's rights. Women pressed hard to have protections for their rights written into the 2003 Afghan constitution, but they came out of the difficult drafting process with only limited victories; the constitution has both worrisome and positive features. It advises in Article 3 that no law should contravene the beliefs and principles of the sacred religion of Islam, which could be used to bar laws advancing women's rights. At the same time, Article 22 provides that citizens, whether men or women, have equal rights and duties before the law, which could ban discrimination against women if "the law" being referred to were not itself discriminatory. Moreover, the post-Taliban government ratified the Women's

Convention in 2003 without imposing any Islamic reservations, which seemed a positive step.

Meanwhile, Afghan women in the aftermath of the US invasion were forced to cope with turmoil and violence, as a weak central government struggled un-successfully to assert control beyond the capital and to uproot vestiges of the Tal-iban in the war-ravaged, economically prostrate country.[89] By 2011, Afghanistan ranked in one survey as the most dangerous country for women, more dangerous even than Congo or Somalia.[90] In these circumstances, the promise of eliminating discrimination against women and improving their lives seemed little more than an idealistic illusion, and boasts about the US mission of "saving" Afghan women could be viewed as the hypocritical rhetoric of "the new colonial feminism."[91]

The situation in Iraq was similarly chaotic. Although the ravages of Saddam Hussein's despotism affected all Iraqis, women fared relatively well under his dic-tatorship when compared with their sisters in Iran and Afghanistan. A reformed version of Islamic law prevailed in the area of personal status, and many oppor-tunities were open to women. The US invasion displaced Saddam's Ba'athist rul-ing clique and enabled long-suppressed Shi'i forces to assume power, creating a situation where Islamist extremists could exert pressures on women to veil them-selves and retire to the domestic sphere. Various Shi'i and Sunni factions, as well as more secular groups and Kurds, struggled bitterly but inconclusively to realize conflicting agendas. The huge increase in crime and terrorist violence in the chaos that ensued created such perils for women that many felt compelled to stay locked inside their homes or to seek refuge in other countries.

The United States publicly pressed the drafters of the Iraqi constitution to include an express guarantee of equality for women.[92] (In part because of US pressures, the 2004 Iraqi Transitional Law, in Article 12, had already barred dis-crimination "on the basis of gender.") Nevertheless, ambiguous provisions in the 2005 Iraqi constitution left women's rights in doubt. Article 14 provides that all Iraqis are equal before the law without discrimination because of gender, race, ethnicity, origin, color, religion, creed, belief or opinion, or economic and social status, and Article 20 gives male and female citizens political rights, including the right to vote and run for office. A different impression is created by provi-sions in Article 2 that state that no law may contradict the undisputed rules of Islam and that Islamic law is to be a main source of legislation. These provisions open the door to the application of Islamic criteria in conflict with women's rights. Furthermore, Article 39 contains a vague provision allowing Iraqis to be governed by religious law in matters of personal status. This would allow men to ask the courts to impose premodern Islamic jurisprudence with all its patriarchal features, an outcome that troubled Iraqi feminists. Taken together, these provi-sions suggest that the constitution left room for deploying Islamic rules at the expense of Iraqi women's rights, especially in personal status matters.

The Influence of Sex Stereotyping

CEDAW recognizes that sex stereotyping constitutes an obstacle to realizing full equality for women and calls on governments to attack the attitudes and practices that stereotype women as inferior beings whose nature disqualifies them from enjoying freedoms on a par with men. Article 5.a binds the parties "to modify the social and cultural patterns of conduct of men and women, with a view to achieving the elimination of prejudices and customary and all other practices which are based on the idea of the inferiority or the superiority of either of the sexes or on stereotyped roles for men and women."

One sees no concern for transcending or eliminating sex stereotyping in the Islamic human rights schemes reviewed here; on the contrary, such stereotyping is a central feature of the schemes, if sometimes only an implied one. The belief that men and women have inherently different natures and thus have distinct rights and obligations is reflected in the formal reservations to CEDAW expressed by several Muslim countries, which combine references to Islam and assumptions that women and men must play different, complementary roles.[93] According to proponents of the complementarity thesis, the goal should be equity that recognizes differences between men and women, not equality in rights that disregards such differences.

Sultanhussein Tabandeh freely expresses his stereotypical views of women in the course of explaining why the human rights accorded to women in the UDHR are incompatible with Islam. Women, according to Tabandeh, are touchy and hasty, volatile and imprudent. They are generally more gullible and credulous than men. Their sexual desire makes them easy prey for the blandishments of salacious individuals.[94] In Tabandeh's opinion, women were designed for "cooking, laundering, shopping, and washing up," as well as for taking care of children. Men, in contrast, were created for field work, warfare, and earning a living.[95] Women are deficient in the intelligence needed for "tackling big and important matters"; they are prone to making mistakes and lack long-term perspective. For this reason, he said, they must be excluded from politics.[96] Women cannot fight in war because they are "timorous-hearted," limited by physical weakness, and may become frightened and run away.[97]

Abu'l A'la Mawdudi takes a similar line, although not in his publication on human rights. In his book on purdah, he argues that nature has designed men and women for different roles, treating menstruation, pregnancy, and nursing as incapacitating disabilities.[98] Women, he asserts, are created to bear and rear children. They are tender, unusually sensitive, soft, submissive, impressionable, and timid. They lack firmness, authority, "cold-temperedness," strong willpower, and the ability to render unbiased, objective judgment.[99] Men have coarseness, vehemence, and aggressiveness, which make them suited to assume roles as generals, statesmen, and administrators. The education of men should, therefore, aim at training them so that they can support and protect the family, whereas a woman should be educated to bring up children, look after domestic affairs, and make home life "sweet, pleasant, and peaceful."[100]

Similar observations were made by Ayatollah Javad Bahonar, a cleric who briefly served as Iran's prime minister before being assassinated. Bahonar was one of Khomeini's closest aides, and his thinking may be taken as representative of many of the leading clerics in Khomeini's regime. In an article on Islam and women's rights in an English-language journal distributed in the West by the Iranian regime, Bahonar said that men are bigger and stronger and have larger brains, with a larger proportion of the brain "dealing with thought and deliberation."[101] A relatively larger proportion of the smaller female brain is "related to emotions," and women have more in the way of the affection and deep tender sentiments that suit them for child care and nursing. Women's sentiments and emotions make them ill equipped to cope with earning a livelihood, which calls for farsightedness, perseverance, strength, tolerance, coolness, planning ability, hard-heartedness, connivance, and the like—characteristics that women lack. Men are designed by nature to deal with "the tumult of life," to fight on the battlefield, and to manage the affairs of government and society.[102] A note at the end of the article offers some statistics on female physical inferiority, including the comment that "a man's brain weighs 100 grams more than a woman's." Bahonar summed up his evidence by saying that the "differences in physical structure are reflected in the mental capacities of the two sexes."[103]

Notwithstanding this recital of women's natural deficiencies and infirmities, Bahonar sought to maintain the fiction that Iran's official Islam supported women's rights, asserting that "Islam considers men and women equal as far as the basic human rights are concerned."[104] Although Bahonar cited many ways that men and women share equal religious and moral duties—both are required to pray, to be faithful and obedient believers, to command the good and prohibit the evil, to keep their looks cast down, and to accept punishment for crimes—Bahonar cited only two rights that the two sexes share on an equal basis: the right to own and use property and the right to inherit.[105] On the latter, he neglected to mention that although women have a right to inherit, they take only one-half the share of men inheriting in the same capacity.

A 2003 study of more recent sex stereotyping in religious discourse in Iran notes that it assumes that men and women have opposite characteristics. Among other things, men are described as logical and disciplined, women as confused and lacking in discipline; men as courageous, women as fragile; men as authoritarian and independent, women as obedient and in need of protection; and men as not tolerating physical suffering, women as managing to endure physical abuse from their husbands.[106]

Because the Islamic legal tradition developed in traditional, patriarchal milieus and because the authoritative works on the legal status of women in Islam have been exclusively written by men, it is not surprising that men's stereotypes of women were incorporated and that they have been retained as part of Islamic rights schemes. In contrast, one finds little in the original Islamic sources that supports these stereotypes, and there is, moreover, nothing distinctively Islamic about the self-interested and biased appraisals of women's inherent traits that they offer. In fact, the sex stereotyping that one sees in the Islamic tradition resembles stereotypes found in other cultural and religious contexts. For example, the Saudi prohibition against women driving, which is associated with conservative Islamic precepts, has a historical counterpart in the United States of the early twentieth century, when sex stereotyping was used to justify prohibiting women from driving cars.[107]

The Catholic Church is only one of many denominations where sex stereotyping has been used to support the view of church clergy—all men—that women must be kept subjugated because of their "natural" inferiority to men. Among the characteristics that the church fathers attributed to women were fickleness, shallowness, garrulousness, weakness, slowness of understanding, and instability of mind.[108] Saint Augustine asserted that compared to men, women were small of intellect.[109] In a 1966 book designed to persuade Catholic women that because of their gender, their "entire psychology is founded upon the primordial tendency to love," two priests asserted that a woman's brain "is generally lighter and simpler than man's."[110]

Pope Pius XII, speaking to an audience of women in 1945, described "the sensibility and delicacy of feeling peculiar to woman, which might tempt her to be swayed by emotions and thus blur the clearness and breadth of her view and be detrimental to the calm consideration of future consequences."[111] He maintained that as a result of their characteristics, women were suited for tasks in life that called for "tact, delicate feelings, and maternal instinct, rather than administrative rigidity."[112]

As a major feminist critic of Catholic doctrine has pointed out, the sex stereotypes upheld by men in the church hierarchy became closely intertwined with the Catholic teachings calling for the subordination of women: "The very emancipation which would prove that women were not 'naturally' defective was denied them in the name of that defectiveness which was claimed to be natural and divinely ordained."[113]

One can see the same presuppositions about inherent female characteristics in both the Islamic and Christian traditions. The question that remains is whether the sex stereotypes associated with religious doctrine are actually supported by the original sources or whether they are simply being read into religious teachings by male interpreters with patriarchal biases.

Summary

The failure to accord women equality in rights turns out to be one of the ways that Islamic human rights schemes deviate most dramatically from international human rights law. The intention to accommodate discriminatory rules is cloaked by vague Islamic conditions placed on women's rights that may look harmless to a casual observer but that, depending on how they are interpreted, have the potential to nullify women's rights. In the wake of the upheavals of the Arab Spring, a number of countries will be wrestling with formulating rights provisions in their new constitutions. With the dramatic rise of Islamist political forces, it is entirely possible that women who fought and sacrificed alongside men in the dangerous struggles to defeat dictatorships will have to mobilize to combat projects aimed at restricting their rights under the rubric of upholding Islamic law. Knowing how Islamic conditions on women's rights in documents such as the Iranian constitution have correlated with official efforts to demote women to second-class status, they will be alert to the implications of constitutional provisions that accord priority to upholding Islamic law. It is sobering to observe that, after many decades of campaigning to secure their equality, women in the Middle East may have reason to worry lest they see a repetition of the loss of freedoms that Iranian women endured in the wake of a revolution that many had hoped would usher in a new dawn of freedom.

CHAPTER 7

Islamic Human Rights Schemes and Religious Minorities

The Historical Background of Current Issues Facing Religious Minorities

The issue of the rights of non-Muslim minorities in the Middle East has a peculiar historical background that casts a shadow over any discussion by a Western observer. Critical assessments of discriminatory treatment of non-Muslims tend to be linked in people's minds with the pursuit of Western imperialist and neo-imperialist agendas. The US reconstruction projects in postinvasion Afghanistan and Iraq, which included buttressing protections for religious minorities and for religious freedom, tend to reinforce this link. Aspects of the historical background are summarized here to distinguish the heyday of European imperialism, when grand strategies sought to extend domination of the Middle East by exploiting the issue of their treatment of non-Muslim minorities, from today's calls by international human rights NGOs and other independent observers for consistent and evenhanded application of international human rights law. The latter have—or should have—different connotations. These critiques of mistreatment of religious minorities can be contrasted with the selective and self-serving invocations of human rights made by Western states to justify their interventions in the Middle East.

For centuries, the status of non-Muslims in the Middle East was determined by *shari'a* law, which relegated them to subordinate status. In the nineteenth century, European powers with imperialist ambitions intervened to advance the rights of non-Muslims, wielding allegations that non-Muslims were being oppressed as pretexts for interfering in Middle Eastern politics. In response to European pressures, the Ottoman sultans promulgated special edicts in 1839 and 1856 that formally granted equality to their non-Muslim Ottoman subjects.[1]

When Europeans came to control most of the Middle East, they inevitably favored non-Muslim minorities and invoked the need to protect non-Muslims from oppression by the Muslim majorities as rationales for their rule.[2] In an important development, Great Britain used its mandate over Palestine to foster the creation of a Jewish homeland.[3] When Muslim Middle Easterners demonstrated their aspirations to enjoy self-determination, Europeans showed themselves unsympathetic so that their expressions of solicitude for non-Muslims naturally became associated with double standards. Christian missionary activities in the Middle East, which flourished when the region was under European domination, suggested that there was a plot to draw Muslims into the European orbit by converting them to Christianity.

Eventually, Middle Eastern countries became independent of European control, generally in the wake of World War II. Although many members of non-Muslim minorities emigrated from the newly independent states, some of the old Christian communities of Egypt and the Fertile Crescent remained largely intact. Overall, the proportion of non-Muslims in the Middle East dwindled, leaving a reduced population that today is affected by *shari'a* rules governing the treatment of non-Muslims.

Events since World War II, especially the strong Western support for Israel, have tended to exacerbate Muslim resentment and suspicion of Western policies concerning non-Muslim minorities. Muslims were outraged that Great Britain and France ignored the right of self-determination of the native Palestinian population in order to accommodate the political goals of a Jewish community long persecuted by European Christians. Palestinian self-determination has become a central concern in the politics of human rights in the region, which is reflected in the text of the 1999 Casablanca Declaration adopted by the First International Conference of the Arab Human Rights Movement:

> The Conference declares its full support for the right of the Palestinian people to self-determination. . . . The rights of the Palestinian people are the proper standard to measure the consistency of international positions towards a just peace and human rights. The Arab human rights movement will apply this standard in its relations with the different international organizations and actors.[4]

The ongoing US support for the human rights of religious minorities is commonly seen as linked to US support for Israel in a context where US indifference to the plight of Palestinians occasions anger. Thus, religious minorities are seen by many in the region as pawns in a cynical US strategy to achieve domination of the Middle East, one aspect of which involves dismantling Islamic law.[5]

Muslims tend to view any discussion of the status of non-Muslims in the contemporary Middle East in relation to this particular historical background. Muslim resentment has been exacerbated by the callous indifference shown by the West to the fate of Muslims during the disintegration of Yugoslavia. Muslims were outraged to witness Europe standing by as Serbians decimated Bosnia's Muslim population. Given this background, Westerners' complaints about the treatment of non-Muslim minorities in the Middle East tend to be viewed as cynical.

The tendency to associate such critical evaluations with neo-imperialist designs has also been aggravated by recent US political initiatives, including the passing of the US International Religious Freedom Act of 1998 and the establishment of the US Commission on International Religious Freedom (USCIRF), which is entrusted with the task of dealing with religious freedom around the world.[6] The commission publishes annually a *Report on International Religious Freedom*, which is available online. The annual reports present detailed information on religious freedom and religious minorities in countries around the world, and the sections on the Middle East can be referred to, amplifying the short discussion offered here.

These US initiatives did not come out of a concern for religious freedom in the abstract; they were spearheaded by a coalition of politicians and lobbyists apparently seeking to win support from Christian Evangelicals. Although the scope of the legislation was later widened to encompass such minorities as Baha'is and Buddhists—apparently with the aim of avoiding charges of sectarian bias—the original focus was on assisting Christians and converts to Christianity.[7] Under the International Religious Freedom Act, violations of the rights of religious minorities could trigger US sanctions against offending countries. Persons knowledgeable about the Middle East who were genuinely concerned for the well-being of beleaguered Christians and other religious minorities in the Middle East understood that associating calls for improvement in the status of religious minorities with aggressive US intervention on their behalf would only heighten Muslims' inclination to view religious minorities as pawns of Western interests.

Given this background, one appreciates that when appraising the rights accorded to non-Muslims in Islamic human rights schemes, one must confront issues that have been politicized by US policies, even though objective analyses using international human rights law do not fall in the same category.

Today, the rules for the treatment of religious minorities are relevant not only for persons who are avowedly non-Muslim but also for persons within the Muslim community who may suffer discrimination and abuse because of their sectarian affiliations. In this regard, the disposition to treat Islam as the state ideology has tended to exacerbate intolerance of dissenting Muslim opinion and has ominous consequences for Muslim religious minorities. This was appreciated by members of Iraq's Sunni minority as they witnessed the ascendancy of Shi'i clerics after the 2003 overthrow of Saddam's secular Ba'athist regime and the displacement of the Sunni ruling elite, which had savagely persecuted Shi'is under Saddam. Throughout the constitution drafting process, Sunnis determinedly fought plans by the Shi'i majority for enshrining the central role of Shi'ism and Shi'i clerics in the new constitution. They had only to look at the discriminatory treatment of Sunnis in neighboring Iran to be reminded how the combination of Islamization and Shi'i clerical rule had correlated with oppression of a Sunni minority. Meanwhile, sectarian tensions in Iraq had been brought to a boiling point by lethal violence and counterviolence between the Sunni and Shi'i communities. This replicated the experience of Pakistan under Islamization, with the difference that in the Pakistani case Shi'is were in the minority and were the ones exposed to the worst abuses and persecutions as Islamization took hold. Given the fact that minority rights for members of Muslim sects are of growing importance, it is time to stop automatically associating all critiques of *shari'a* rules affecting religious minorities with neo-imperialist objectives and attempts to secure privileges for non-Muslims.

International Standards Prohibiting Religious Discrimination

Under international human rights law, it is not permissible to discriminate based on religion. This principle is enshrined in Article 2 of the UDHR and Articles 2 and 26 of the International Covenant on Civil and Political Rights (ICCPR). The Declaration on the Elimination of All Forms of Intolerance and of Discrimination Based on Religion or Belief, proclaimed by the UN General Assembly on November 25, 1981, reaffirmed this principle in Article 2, elaborating on it in Article 2.2 to define impermissible discrimination as "any distinction, exclusion, restriction or preference based on religion or belief and having as its purpose or as its effect nullification or impairment of the recognition, enjoyment or exercise of human rights or fundamental freedoms on an equal basis." Article 4.1 requires all states to take effective measures to prevent and eliminate discrimination on the grounds of religion. Article 4.2 calls on governments to take affirmative steps to dismantle patterns of discrimination and eliminate religious prejudice: "All States shall make all efforts to enact or rescind legislation where necessary to prohibit any such discrimination, and to take all appropriate measures to combat intolerance on the grounds of religion or belief in this matter."

Shari'a Law and the Rights of Non-Muslims

The premodern *shari'a* rules affecting the status of non-Muslims were formulated by Islamic jurists at an early stage of the history of the Islamic community and reflect the circumstances of that era. The nascent community was weak and beleaguered, faced with the difficult task of absorbing non-Muslim communities in newly won territories while having to meet the military threat of powerful non-Muslim foes.[8] The *jihad*, or Islamic holy war, was undertaken both to expand the territory subject to Muslim control and to spread the Islamic religion.[9] Contrary to Western images of Muslim conquerors presenting the conquered peoples with a choice of conversion to Islam or the sword, conquered Christians and Jews, known as *ahl al-kitab*, or people of the book, were allowed to persist in their beliefs. In Islam, these faiths are regarded as being based on earlier divine revelations, which were deemed to have culminated in God's final revelation to the Prophet Muhammad.

Although the premodern doctrines of *jihad* remain part of the Islamic cultural legacy and *jihad* may be proclaimed in a variety of military and political contexts by contemporary leaders—much as "crusade" is invoked by leaders of Western countries in time of war or conflict—governments of Muslim countries appreciate that, under international law, they cannot invoke religious doctrines to justify military campaigns to conquer the non-Muslim world. In practice, many of the premodern doctrines regarding *jihad* and treatment of non-Muslims have been discarded, having been recognized as anachronisms in present circumstances, in which the Muslim community has burgeoned to well over a billion adherents and its existence is no longer threatened.[10] Of course, Islamist zealots who seek to mobilize Muslims for what they proclaim is an epochal battle against the West may freely invoke the idea of *jihad*, but rubrics deployed by extremists are not the concern here.

Some *shari'a* rules remain relevant for the status of non-Muslims today. In the early Islamic conquests, Muslim rulers had to decide how to treat the Christians and Jews who persisted in their old beliefs.[11] Jews and Christians ruled by Muslims were accorded the status of *dhimmis*, or those accorded toleration in return for submitting to Muslim rule and accepting a number of conditions.[12] *Dhimmis* had to pay a special capitation tax, known as the *jizya*, and were excluded from serving in the military because, as non-Muslims, they could not be expected to fight in wars on behalf of Islam. Depending on the jurists' opinions, *dhimmis* were either excluded from serving in government altogether or excluded from high government positions. Although they were generally subject to *shari'a* law, *dhimmis* were allowed to follow their own rules of personal status except in cases where persons from more than one religion were involved.

Despite discrimination and incidents of mistreatment of non-Muslims, it is fair to say that Muslim rulers, when judged by the standards of the day, generally showed far greater tolerance and humanity in their treatment of religious minorities than European rulers did.[13] In particular, the treatment of the Jewish minority in Muslim societies stands out as fair and enlightened when compared with the dismal record of European Christian persecution of Jews over the centuries.[14]

With the rise of secular nationalism in the Muslim world in the nineteenth century, it seemed that the significance of distinctions between Muslim and non-Muslim was destined to diminish.[15] Although the *shari'a* prohibitions affecting intermarriage persisted and most Muslim countries retained the legal requirement that the chief of state had to be Muslim, with the adoption of modern concepts of national citizenship, in many respects non-Muslims gained the status of citizens of the nation on a par with Muslims.

Today, as the influence of secular nationalism has waned and the influence of Islam as a political ideology is mounting, issues surrounding the status of non-Muslims, which had seemed settled, have recently been reopened. Some proponents of Islamization have been openly calling for reinstating rules on *dhimmi* status in contemporary Middle Eastern societies. In Egypt, the ascendancy of Islamist political parties at the end of 2011 left members of the Coptic minority deeply apprehensive about their prospects for enjoying equal citizenship.[16] Spokesmen for the Salafists, the hard-line Islamist faction, sought to reassure Copts that no harm would come to them in the wake of Islamization.[17] Nonetheless, reviewing the past manifestations of Islamist animus toward the Coptic minority, which included calls for subjugating Christians and attacks on their churches, many Copts saw ample grounds for fearing the worst.[18]

The kind of robust human rights advocacy that one finds in the promotion of Islamic feminism today is less frequently matched in Muslims' discussions of equal rights for non-Muslims. Still, one finds Muslims representing a variety of currents of Islamic thought who have taken the position that Islam accommodates equal treatment for non-Muslims. For example, the Lebanese scholar Subhi Mahmassani argued in his work on Islam and human rights that there can be no discrimination based on religion in an Islamic system.[19] His approach essentially assumes that there must be harmony between Islam and international law, which entails tacitly suppressing or discarding any features of the *shari'a* that would be incompatible with international human rights. Mahmassani places great emphasis on aspects of the original sources and examples from early Islamic history that demonstrate the tolerant and egalitarian strains that have from the beginning constituted important components of the Islamic tradition.[20]

The conviction that there must be a natural affinity between Islam and the tenets of international human rights law has led other Muslims as well to endorse full equality for all citizens as compatible with Islam.[21] The Egyptian thinker Tariq al-Bishri, concerned with the status of Egypt's Copts and insisting that they should enjoy equality, called on specialists to reconcile this equality with Islamic law, expressing confidence that in a tradition as flexible and egalitarian as the Islamic one, this should present no great problem.[22] Al-Bishri also noted that the nature of the modern state is so different from the kind of government envisioned by medieval Islamic theorists that the *shari'a* restrictions on non-Muslims holding high political office no longer logically apply.[23]

Abdullahi An-Na'im, using the ideas of Mahmud Muhammad Taha, distinguishes verses that were meant to govern the early Islamic community from those that were meant to have enduring validity, proposing Islamic principles that abolish the status of *dhimmis* and mandate an end to all discrimination on a religious basis.[24]

In contrast, even where the Islamic human rights schemes reviewed here do not expressly relegate non-Muslims to an inferior position, they have been deliberately drafted to accommodate the continued application of discriminatory rules from the premodern *shari'a*. Whereas Islamic human rights schemes envisage that non-Muslims will be governed by the *shari'a*, international human rights law assumes that a neutral, nondiscriminatory law will be applied to all citizens of a country, not accepting that a person's rights can be denied by reason of discriminatory religious laws.[25] With the exception of Tabandeh, the authors of these human rights schemes are less than candid about their objectives. They formulate their provisions regarding non-Muslims in such a manner that their intention to accommodate discrimination against non-Muslims is not obvious. That is, as with their evasive treatments of the status of women, the authors are reluctant to state forthrightly how far their ideas deviate from the principle of equality as understood in international law.

Tabandeh's Ideas

Sultanhussein Tabandeh candidly admits that in his view the *shari'a* precludes equality between Muslims and non-Muslims. In commenting on the UDHR, Article 1, guarantee of equality, Tabandeh insists that the principle of equality does not apply when it comes to differences of religion, faith, or conviction. This is because "nobility, excellence and virtue consist in true worship of the One God and obedience to the commandments of Heaven." According to Tabandeh, the *ahl al-kitab* deserve respect because of their belief, but "since their faith has not reached the highest level of spirituality . . . therefore [the *shari'a*] makes certain difference between them and Muslims, treating them as not on the same level."[26]

For those who have not accepted the one God, Tabandeh has only contempt; they are "outside the pale of humanity."[27] This fits with the premodern *shari'a*, which took the view that other than the *ahl al-kitab*, non-Muslims were not entitled to the status of legal persons. It sharply conflicts with the ICCPR, which stipulates in Article 16 that everyone has a right to recognition everywhere as a person before the law.

Tabandeh endorses premodern *shari'a* rules that absolutely prohibit Muslims from marrying polytheists.[28] He likewise endorses the premodern *shari'a* rule that prevents a Muslim woman from marrying a Christian or Jew while allowing a Muslim man to marry a woman from those faiths.[29] It is at this point in Tabandeh's argument that one sees how for Muslim conservatives, the inferior status of women and the inferior status of non-Muslims are linked. Tabandeh argues:

> The scripture says: "Men are guardians of women and guarantors of their rights" [Qur'an 4:34]. The wife must obey her husband. But, if she weds a non-Muslim husband it means that she as a Muslim is subordinating herself: and Islam never allows a Muslim to come under the authority of a non-Muslim in any circumstance at all, as is made perfectly plain in "God will never make a way for infidels (to exercise lordship) over believers" [Qur'an 4:41]: and therefore He never granted permission that Muslims should by marriage voluntarily subordinate themselves to non-Muslims. . . . In Islam every distinction is abolished except the distinction of religion and faith; whence it follows that Islam and its peoples must be above infidels, and never permit non-Muslims to acquire lordship over them.[30]

Tabandeh is indifferent to the rights of the individual man and woman who wish to marry despite religious differences. Instead of the concern that one finds in international human rights law for the freedom of the individuals involved, the concern is for the prestige of the Muslim community, the honor of which is deemed sullied if one of its members is subordinated to a member of the inferior group, the non-Muslims. The assumption is that, just as Muslims are placed above non-Muslims, so men are placed above women—so that the Muslim woman who marries a *dhimmi* violates the rules of status set for the respective groups.

Tabandeh rejects rights to participate in government and freedom of expression for non-Muslims, rights that are guaranteed to all persons regardless of religion by international law. Non-Muslims, he says, must be entirely excluded from the judiciary, the legislature, and the cabinet.[31] Furthermore, no "propaganda" for any non-Muslim religion may be allowed.[32]

The UIDHR

The authors of the UIDHR are not forthright in spelling out specifics where discriminatory rules affecting non-Muslims are concerned. The UIDHR addresses the situation of non-Muslims in Article 10, failing to guarantee equality for religious minorities. Article 10.a states that the religious rights of non-Muslim minorities are governed by the principle that there is no compulsion in religion, which is based on the Qur'an 2:256. A traditional interpretation of this verse is that *dhimmis* should not be forced to convert to Islam, which is far from saying that any discrimination against *dhimmis* or other non-Muslims is prohibited.

What the UIDHR envisages is the *millet* system that flourished under the Ottoman Empire. Under this system, members of the various non-Muslim communities were governed by their own religious laws in internal matters and lawsuits involving members of the same faith, but they were subject to the *shari'a* in mixed cases and in all other matters. In most Muslim countries today, remnants of this system persist.

In the English version of Article 10.b, "religious minorities" are given the right to be governed either by Islamic law or by their own laws in personal status or civil matters. Although the English version of Article 10.b seems to apply to all non-Muslims, the Arabic version of the same provision resurrects the old distinction between Christians and Jews on the one hand and other non-Muslims on the other, suggesting that only members of the *ahl al-kitab* enjoy this right. In a peculiar formulation, the Arabic version of Article 10.b provides that non-Muslims may appeal to Muslims for judgment, but that if they do not do so, they must follow their own laws, provided that they (seemingly, the non-Muslims) believe that those laws are of divine origin. This would seem to mean that where non-Muslims did not elect to be governed by the *shari'a*, their subjective convictions that the laws of their own communities were divinely inspired would lead to their laws being controlling. However, the references in the same provision to the Qur'an 5:47, dealing with people of the Gospel, and 5:42, dealing with the followers of the Torah, give reason to believe that this right of religious minorities to follow their own religious rules actually pertains only to Christian and Jewish minorities. That is, as in the premodern *shari'a*, no provision is made allowing non-Muslims who are not Christians or Jews to follow their own religious law in civil and personal status matters. This leaves open the question regarding what status the UIDHR assumes will be accorded to non-Muslims who stand outside the category of *dhimmis*, who might be classed as nonpersons.

In another article, the UIDHR echoes an idea put forth by Mawdudi in his human rights pamphlet. Mawdudi states that Islam does not allow Muslims to use abusive language that may injure the religious feelings of non-Muslims.[33] The UIDHR states in Article 12.e that no one shall hold in contempt or ridicule the religious beliefs of others. Both of these principles seem to be broad ethico-moral injunctions as opposed to rules setting forth enforceable legal rights. Again, Islamic human rights schemes turn away from actual laws or governmental actions, which in the Middle East often relegate non-Muslims to second-class status, addressing instead the conduct of private individuals, which is likely to have less far-reaching impact on the lives of non-Muslims.

Article 12.e of the UIDHR elaborates on this idea, stating that "people" should not incite hostility toward non-Muslims. This is a laudable ethico-moral precept, and a commendable step by the Islamic Council. However, for this broad principle to have teeth—and legal force—further specification of what constitutes such impermissible incitement is necessary. Article 12.a, which provides that all speech is allowed within the limits of the *shari'a*—a standard that is vague and open-ended—is not helpful in clarifying this.

The Iranian Constitution

The article of the Iranian constitution dealing with religious minorities seems to contemplate a model similar to the *millet* system, where there are two categories of persons, Muslims and the *ahl al-kitab*, which, reflecting local tradition, Iran deems should also include Zoroastrians. Article 13 provides: "Zoroastrian, Jewish, and Christian Iranians are the only recognized religious minorities, who, within the limits of the law [*dar hodud-e qanun*], are free to perform their religious rites and ceremonies, and to act according to their own canon in matters of personal affairs and religious education."[34] That is, aside from acts of religious observance and education and personal status matters, the *ahl al-kitab* are to be governed by Iranian law. As has already been discussed, under Article 4 of the constitution, all Iranian laws are subordinate to Islamic law. This means that the *ahl al-kitab* are subject to discriminatory Islamic rules. The nonrecognition of religious minorities other than the *ahl al-kitab* in this *shari'a*-based system excludes them from any constitutional protections.

The disabilities imposed on non-Muslims under the postrevolutionary regime have been severe, in many instances going beyond those that would be called for under the premodern *shari'a*. This is not surprising given the bigoted mentality of the less enlightened members of Iran's clergy. For example, in November 2005, Ayatollah Ahmad Jannati, a close associate of Ayatollah Ali Khamene'i, remarked in a speech that non-Muslims were not human beings but merely animals roaming the Earth and engaging in corruption, indicating that clerical animus toward non-Muslims has not diminished over the years.[35] Of course, Iran's representatives eschew making such invidious characterizations of non-Muslims when seeking to win support for their human rights positions at the UN.

Because in postrevolutionary Iran Twelver Shi'ism is interpreted to be an ideology, the fact that non-Muslims are persons who by definition do not subscribe to the official Iranian ideology has provided additional grounds for discriminating against them. Iran has imposed tests of ideological purity on applicants for public employment that effectively exclude non-Muslims.[36] Moreover, Muslims who subscribe to sects other than the peculiar ideologized version of Islam that is sponsored by the regime have also been excluded.

An example of the consequences of Iran's ideologization of Islam can be seen in the test imposed on those who wish to serve in the Iranian military. A close reading of Article 144 reveals that non-Muslims are excluded from the military, just as *dhimmis* were in premodern Islamic civilization. The article provides: "The Army of the Islamic Republic of Iran must be an Islamic Army, i.e., committed to Islamic ideology and the people, and must recruit into its service individuals who have faith in the objectives of the Islamic Revolution and are devoted to the cause of realizing its goals." Obviously, Iran's non-Muslim minorities have no place in an Islamic army set up under these criteria.[37]

In this connection, one should bring up Mawdudi, who also believed that Islam must be the official ideology in Muslim states and has indicated that he considers discrimination against persons who do not share that ideology to be perfectly reasonable.[38] Nonetheless, as a committed Sunni, Mawdudi would hardly have been pleased by the consequences of Iran's ideologization of Shi'ism, which has led to a pattern of discrimination and even persecution directed at Sunni Muslims. Members of Iran's ethnic minorities are in large measure Sunnis, which means that they may suffer discrimination and abuse on both ethnic and religious grounds. Since the revolution, Iran has been castigated for mistreating its religious and ethnic minorities, and several prominent Sunni figures have been executed or have died in suspicious circumstances.[39]

This pattern turns out to be a mirror image of trends in neighboring Pakistan in the wake of the official Islamization program, which had a strong pro-Sunni bias. Pakistan's large Shi'i minority has become increasingly beleaguered and subjected to threats and assaults, and lethal sectarian violence has frequently exploded. A militant Sunni group has campaigned for laws that would stigmatize Shi'is and has called for declaring Pakistan a Sunni state, just as Iran has been declared a Shi'i state.[40] This recent history demonstrates that when a state imposes an ideologized version of Islam, it will have a sectarian bias, and Muslims who dissent from this ideology may wind up being treated as members of a despised minority and exposed to persecution.

Article 14 of the Iranian constitution provides in part: "The government of the Islamic Republic of Iran and all Muslims are duty-bound to treat non-Muslims in conformity with ethical norms and the principles of Islamic justice and equity, and to respect their human rights [*hoquq-e ensani*]." Here, "Islamic justice" means that non-Muslims' rights are shaped by *shari'a* law. Far from granting non-Muslims protections for the rights to which they are entitled under international law, the constitution reinforces the principle that their human rights are subject to Islamic criteria.

Other lines in Article 14 reveal that the drafters presumed that non-Muslims are inclined to act against Islam and are disposed to be disloyal to Iran's Islamic Republic. Of course, given the Islamic bias in the system, such opposition would only be natural. Having promised Islamic justice to non-Muslims, Article 14 goes on to say: "This principle applies to all who refrain from engaging in conspiracy or activity against Islam and the Islamic Republic of Iran." In other words, the limited human rights that non-Muslims enjoy are to be forfeited where conspiracies against the state are involved—a vague standard affording a broad range of potential justifications for curbing their rights. Significantly, this article provides special grounds for depriving non-Muslims of human rights in addition to the curbs that are provided in Article 26, which enables the government to curb the activities of groups, including "minority religious associations," if they are "contrary to the principles of Islam or the Islamic Republic." Together, Articles 14 and 26 set up the basis for depriving minorities of rights and freedoms for being against the principles of Islam and the Islamic Republic.

Although Iran denies recognized minorities many rights and subjects them to discrimination and persecution, they are distinctly better off than other non-Muslims who do not qualify as *ahl al-kitab*. The exclusion from the status of recognized minorities in Article 13 was particularly ominous for Iran's Baha'is.

The Baha'i religion, sometimes called Babism, originated in Iran in the nineteenth century. It is named after Baha'ullah, who in 1863 announced that he was a messenger from God and espoused liberal and ecumenical teachings. Baha'ism teaches veneration for the founders of all the major world religions and insists on the brotherhood and equality of all persons, stressing that men and women are meant to be equal. Baha'ism denies that clerics are needed as intermediaries in understanding religion, calling instead for universal education so that individuals can pursue the path of enlightenment. It also supports the idea of a world government and world peace.[41] Baha'i doctrines appealed to many of Iran's Muslims and led them to convert from Islam to the new faith, thereby violating the rule banning conversion from Islam.

Baha'is are subject to harsh discrimination in many Muslim countries. In Iran, the position of the Baha'i community, by far the largest in the Middle East, has always been precarious, and its members have suffered from periodic waves of persecution. From the beginning, Baha'ism has been perceived as a threat by Shi'i clerics, who have supported attempts to eliminate Baha'ism from Iran through massacre, torture, intimidation, and discrimination.[42] This clerical animus was based on several grounds: Baha'ism challenged the doctrine of the finality of God's Revelation to the Prophet Muhammad; it tried to win converts from Islam, in violation of the *shari'a* ban on conversions; its egalitarian doctrines challenged the hierarchy of privilege mandated by the *shari'a*, according to which men are superior to women and Muslims superior to non-Muslims; and its members showed no inclination to defer to the views of Iran's clerics.

Given this long history of animosity toward the Baha'i community, which by the time of the Iranian Revolution may have numbered 200,000–300,000, it was natural that when Shi'i clerics achieved political dominance, they would seek to eliminate Baha'ism once and for all. The government, sometimes acting directly and at other times indirectly through allied groups, has carried out a fierce campaign of terror against Baha'is, who have been slaughtered in large numbers. Hundreds of Baha'is were arrested, imprisoned, and subjected to brutal torture, and Baha'i leaders were executed on a variety of trumped-up charges. In addition, their shrines and houses of worship were destroyed and desecrated, and all of their associations were forcibly disbanded. They were fired from jobs, their property was confiscated, and their homes were subject to invasion at any time by persons bent on harassment and plunder in the guise of investigating "crimes." The savage persecution of the Baha'is has been extensively documented by neutral observers and international human rights organizations.[43]

Embarrassed by the bad publicity that Iran's discriminatory and cruel treatment of religious minorities has received, Iranian officials have made intermittent attempts to improve the country's image. For example, in 1999, a foreign ministry spokesman claimed that, following Islam and its constitution, Iran accorded full freedom to followers of all divine religions.[44] This is another sign of Iran's official hypocrisy; being aware of how far the government's policies affecting religious minorities diverge from international human rights law, Iran's representatives when speaking to international audiences seek to draw a cloak over their abuses and persuade outsiders that its system is respectful of human rights. Of course, those who knew that Iran's constitution did not recognize Baha'ism as a religion would appreciate that in the eyes of Iranian officialdom, there would be no reason to accord freedom to its adherents.

Mawdudi and Pakistan's Ahmadi Minority

Abu'l A'la Mawdudi's vague, ambiguous position on equality merits further examination in connection with his views on the rights of non-Muslims. Just as Mawdudi avoids detailing his views on women's rights in his human rights pamphlet, he also steers clear of any specifics on how the *shari'a* affects non-Muslims. He merely mentioned *dhimmis* in passing, saying that their lives and properties are as "sacred" as those of Muslims.[45]

Mawdudi's views on this subject are on record in other publications, where he advocates discrimination against non-Muslims and according Muslims superiority. He favors reinstating the *jizya* tax,[46] excluding them from military service,[47] and eliminating them from high positions in government.[48] He asserts that Islam "does not permit them to meddle with the affairs of the State."[49] Because Mawdudi believes that Islamic law should control personal status cases where at least one party is a Muslim,[50] he believes that the *shari'a* prohibitions regarding intermarriage should be retained. Thus, Mawdudi's publications prove that he shared Tabandeh's views.

Mawdudi's Jama'at-i-Islami party was among the instigators of the Pakistani campaigns against Pakistan's Ahmadi minority, whose rights were undermined by President Zia's Islamization program. The experience of the Ahmadi minority, amounting to about one million in Pakistan, provides an illustration of how, when governments adopt official Islamic ideologies, Muslims who adhere to minority sects may be demoted by governmental policy to the category of non-Muslims and punished if they dare to protest that they are Muslims.

Although Ahmadis fervently believe that they are Muslims, they are considered heretics by many other Muslims. The Ahmadi sect was founded by Mirza Ghulam Ahmad (d. 1908) in India. Ahmadis, their opponents charge, treat their founder as a prophet, thereby violating the Islamic doctrine of the finality of the prophethood of Muhammad. Mawdudi and his followers in the Jama'at-i-Islami became bitter foes of the Ahmadis, and the Jama'at was implicated in the serious disturbances that resulted from their anti-Ahmadi agitation in the Punjab in 1953.[51] Mawdudi was incarcerated after being convicted of playing a leading role in anti-Ahmadi agitation.

In a concession to anti-Ahmadi sentiment, Prime Minister Zulfikar Ali Bhutto amended the constitution in 1974 to define Ahmadis as non-Muslims. President Zia, who was allied with the Jama'at, went further and in 1984 issued a decree, the "Anti-Islamic Activities of the Quadiani Group, Lahori Group and Ahmadis (Prohibition and Punishment) Ordinance XX of 1984," forbidding Ahmadis to "pose" as Muslims or to call their religion Islam, to use Islamic terminology, to use the Islamic call to prayer, to call their houses of worship mosques, or to preach or propagate their version of the faith—all prohibitions under sanction of criminal law.[52] Extensive criminal prosecutions of Ahmadis ensued.

There have been various challenges to Ordinance XX, the most important of which resulted in it being affirmed in 1993 in *Zaheeruddin v. State*, when the Supreme Court rejected the Ahmadis' claim that the ordinance violated the constitutional guarantee of freedom of religion.[53] The ruling in this case set a precedent that had ominous implications for rights and freedoms more generally. A 1991 bill, the Enforcement of Shari'ah Act, had already proclaimed that the Qur'an and *sunna* were the supreme law of Pakistan and that law should be interpreted in the light of the *shari'a*, but the Supreme Court had initially resisted applying this principle to restrict fundamental rights.[54] In *Zaheeruddin*, the court decided that the reference to "the Injunctions of Islam" that had previously been incorporated in the text of the constitution implied that the constitution itself was subordinated to Islamic criteria, including its provisions on fundamental rights.[55] However, the court never troubled to define how "the Injunctions of Islam" affected rights protections, leaving this vague term open to being construed so broadly that rights could be essentially nullified. That is, in this ruling the court adopted the same position that is set forth in Iran's constitution in Articles 4 and 20, that human rights could be overridden by Islamic criteria. Breaking with precedents that had upheld the supremacy of the constitution and safeguarded fundamental rights, the court proceeded to rule that under Islamic law, Ordinance XX did not violate the constitutional guarantee of freedom of religion. That is, according to the court, freedom of religion as modified by superimposed Islamic criteria allowed the persecution of a beleaguered religious minority whose members refused to accept that Pakistani law could render them non-Muslims.

The Cairo Declaration, the Saudi Basic Law, and the al-Azhar Draft Constitution

Against the background of the prior Islamic human rights schemes, one would expect that the Cairo Declaration, which duplicates so many of the flaws of its precursors, would also fail to ensure equality for non-Muslims. As has been noted, there is no provision for equality in rights in the Cairo Declaration, even though it guarantees equality in "basic human dignity" in Article l(a), which is not paired with any stipulation of equality in rights and freedoms like the one in the UDHR. Dignity in the Cairo Declaration significantly deviates from the concept of dignity as set forth in the UDHR. Whereas in the UDHR, dignity is presumed to constitute an inherent trait of all human beings, Article 1(a) of the Cairo Declaration concludes: "True faith is the guarantee for enhancing such dignity along the path to human perfection," indicating that dignity is a feature that is affected by true faith. Because the entire declaration has a pronounced Islamic bias, with Article 10 positing that "Islam is the religion of unspoiled nature," the natural inference is that belief in Islam constitutes the "true faith" that enhances human dignity—with the implication that Muslims have advanced further along "the path to human perfection" than have others. This in turn correlates with the idea expressed in the first lines of the preamble of the Cairo Declaration, in which the authors assert that they are: "Reaffirming the civilizing and historical role of the Islamic Ummah which God made the best nation." Article 1(a) therefore can be fairly read to say that non-Muslims possess an inferior level of dignity, a concept that could in turn accommodate discrimination against them.

The Cairo Declaration does not protect the rights of religious minorities any more than it protected women from being denied rights established in international law, which is predictable in a system where all rights and freedoms are subject to the *shari'a*. There is a vague provision in Article 18(a) to the effect that everyone shall have the right to live in security for himself and his religion, his dependents, his honor, and his property. This is clearly not designed to block discrimination against religious minorities, as can be seen in Article 23(b), which imposes *shari'a* restrictions on the right to serve in public office, in effect allowing the use of religious criteria to exclude non-Muslims.

The al-Azhar draft constitution avoids dealing with the status of non-Muslims. In the context of a document that seems to support the general applicability of premodern *shari'a* rules, the failure to address the issue suggests that the intent was to retain discriminatory rules governing the status of non-Muslims. Egypt's large Coptic community feels oppressed and has protested for decades over the restrictions that are imposed on Christians' rights, which has caused frictions with Muslims. Therefore, Azharites had to be familiar with controversies concerning the treatment of Christians, but they preferred to sweep them under the rug.

Virtually all Saudi citizens are Muslim, and Article 34 of the Basic Law provides that the defense of the Islamic faith is a duty imposed on every citizen. The Saudi Basic Law offers no protections whatsoever for the rights of non-Muslims, but this does not mean that Saudi Muslims are necessarily better off. According to Saudi officialdom, Islam is Wahhabism, a rigid creed deeply hostile to Shi'ism. In Saudi Arabia, the Shi'i faith is vilified by clerics associated with the monarchy, and members of the large Shi'i minority, including the Isma'ili sub-branch, are commonly designated as heretics and are exposed to persecution.[56]

Non-Muslims, who are largely expatriates and who face discriminatory treatment on the basis of alienage, continue to be bereft of legal protections. They can be subjected to police harassment for such acts as worship in private. The large contingent of migrant laborers working in menial jobs, many of whom are non-Muslims, suffers from severe abuses and brutal exploitation.[57] It can be hard to ascertain whether expatriates are actually being targeted for persecution and prosecution based on their alienage as opposed to their religious affiliations. Because of the broad pattern of Saudi human rights abuses affecting various vulnerable minorities, including Muslim minorities, singling out violations of the religious rights of non-Muslims as if these had to be the overriding concern will get in the way of achieving an accurate understanding of the overall political context, in which violations of the rights of minorities are bound to occur.

Since the late 1990s, when pressures from Christian activists led to the establishment of the USCIRF, discussed above, Saudi deficiencies in the areas of religious tolerance and respect for the rights of religious minorities have been spotlighted. In 2004, Saudi Arabia was placed on the list of egregious human rights violators called the "Countries of Particular Concern," or CPCs.[58] There is little evidence, however, that US demands for enhanced protections for the rights of religious minorities have ameliorated their situation.[59]

US Policies on Religious Minorities and Developments in Afghanistan and Iraq

The US invasions of Afghanistan and Iraq were supposed to culminate in the establishment of vibrant democracies. Following their own priorities, US officials pressed those drafting the new constitutions to ensure the rights of religious minorities—in this regard repeating the patterns of former European colonial powers in the Middle East. Islamic law was conceived of as creating problems in this connection, and curtailing the scope of Islamic law became a natural part of the US agenda.

Article 2 in the postinvasion Afghan constitution, which establishes Islam as the state religion, guarantees that followers of other religions are free to exercise their faith and perform their religious rites within the limits of the provisions of law. However, it is not specified what law, secular or Islamic, applies in this provision. Because Article 3 advises that no law shall contravene the beliefs and principles of the sacred religion of Islam, there was room for applying traditional Islamic rules. The USCIRF expressed its disappointment with the outcome in its 2011 Report:

> Conditions for religious freedom remain exceedingly poor for minority religious communities and dissenting members of the majority faith, despite the presence of U.S. armed forces in Afghanistan for almost 10 years. . . . The 2004 Afghan constitution has effectively established Islamic law as the law of the land. Afghan jurists and government officials do not view the guarantees to [*sic*] human rights that come later in the document as taking precedence. Individuals lack protection to dissent from state-imposed orthodoxy, debate the role and content of religion in law and society, advocate for the human rights of women and members of religious minorities, or question interpretations of Islamic precepts.[60]

The United States was heavily involved in shaping the 2005 Iraqi constitution, which in Article 14 provided for equality before the law without discrimination because of religion, creed, belief, or opinion. Article 2 guaranteed "full religious rights of all individuals to freedom of religious belief and practice"—mentioning Christians, Yazidis, and Sabeans, which was in addition to the Article 41 provision declaring that the state guaranteed freedom of worship. Given that Article 2 also provided that Islam was the state religion and was a basic source of legislation, the rights of religious minorities might be customized to fit Islamic criteria. In the meantime, the sectarian polarization and Islamist fervor that had been stirred up by the US invasion and occupation intensified intercommunal antagonisms. Local Christians were terrorized, leading them to flee in large numbers, potentially portending the decimation of some of the world's most ancient Christian communities. In its 2011 report, the USCIRF found little to celebrate:

> Members of the country's smallest religious minorities suffer from targeted violence, threats, and intimidation, against which the government does not

provide effective protection. Perpetrators are rarely identified, investigated, or punished, creating a climate of impunity. The smallest minorities also experience a pattern of official discrimination, marginalization, and neglect. . . . In addition, sectarian attacks continue between Shi'a and Sunni Iraqis.[61]

The provisions on Islamic law in the Afghan and Iraqi constitutions left the door open to discriminating against religious minorities, but the central problems facing such minorities in both countries had much more to do with their tortured recent histories and deep resentments born of past conflicts, clashes of warring factions and unconstrained violence, the unbridgeable gaps separating the mentalities of educated elites wedded to secular nationalist visions and groups beholden to retrograde Islamist ideologies, and the fact that US policies on religion and minorities exacerbated many tensions. In such circumstances, the precise wording of the constitutional text could turn out to be of little relevance.[62]

Summary

Islamic human rights schemes do not respect the requirements of international law regarding protections for the rights of religious minorities. In fact, to the extent that they do deal with religious minorities, they seem designed to accommodate premodern *shari'a* rules that call for non-Muslims to be relegated to an inferior status if they qualify as members of the *ahl al-kitab* and for them to be treated as nonpersons if they do not qualify for such inclusion.

Not only does the record of the treatment of religious minorities in Middle Eastern states reveal laws and policies that relegate religious minorities to second-class status, but it also establishes that regimes are in some instances ready to engage in active campaigns of religious persecution directed at non-Muslims and Muslims who belong to disfavored minority sects or who refuse to defer meekly to official versions of Islamic orthodoxy. Authors of Islamic human rights schemes deliberately choose not to address these serious problems.

The Organization of Islamic Cooperation and Muslim States Resist Human Rights for Sexual Minorities

Background

The UN human rights system only belatedly came around to addressing problems related to sexual orientation and gender identity. Those terms are the ones currently favored in UN parlance, a usage reinforced by the influence of the 2006 Yogyakarta Principles on the Application of International Human Rights Law in Relation to Sexual Orientation and Gender Identity.[1] These principles were the result of a project proposed by a coalition of human rights NGOs that was intended to map the rights violations that people suffered based on their sexual orientation and/or gender identity, to outline how international human rights law applied to these cases, and to define the nature of states' obligations in this area. The principles were developed in response to reports of a wide range of discrimination affecting people on the grounds of their sexual orientation or gender identity, cases where they were denied freedom of speech and assembly, and abuses suffered by them—such as rape, torture, extrajudicial executions, and medical abuse. After extensive preparatory consultation and work, in November 2006 twenty-nine experts from around the world convened on Java in Indonesia to finalize the principles, which were presented in 2007 to the UN Human Rights Council in Geneva and to the UN in New York. The UN High Commissioner for Human Rights, Louise Arbour, issued a statement that the Yogyakarta Principles affirmed the basic human rights tenet of equality in rights. She warned that appeals to culture could not justify noncompliance with these principles, admonishing that in her view "respect for cultural diversity is insufficient to justify the existence of laws that violate the fundamental right to life, security and privacy by criminalizing harmless private relations between consenting adults."[2] Although they were not formulated via the usual UN treaty-making processes and do not possess the force of a ratified convention, the principles are now widely regarded as offering a kind of soft law, authoritative even though not legally binding statements of the relevant human rights principles.[3] A central concept of the Yogyakarta Principles lies in Principle 3, which provides that "Each person's self-defined sexual orientation and gender identity is integral to their personality and is one of the most basic aspects of self-determination, dignity and freedom." This point of view continues to be strongly resisted by conservatives.

One confronts philosophical disputes and terminological confusion in the literature on this subject, and any choice of nomenclature will be problematic. Debates swirl about the merits and drawbacks of various sets of nomenclature, with no one set being supported by general consensus and with claims that terms that make sense in one society may not fit well in dissimilar social and cultural contexts.[4] Recognizing that more refined definitions can be made, this discussion assumes that sexual orientation classifications indicate individuals' erotic or emotional attraction to the same and/or opposite gender, whereas gender identity classifications refer to individuals' psychological identification as male or female, which may or may not be the same as their classification based on their physical characteristics or biological makeup. Other terms will surface when they seem to fit better in a particular geographic and cultural context. One is "homosexual," a term that can potentially have a pejorative connotation but is the rubric most often used to designate men having sex with men in the Middle East. Another is "gay," which has various connotations but is here used for those attracted to persons of the same sex in settings where the concepts of gay rights and equality for sexual minorities have gained traction.

In other chapters, the main comparisons have been between well-established provisions of international human rights law and related provisions in Islamic human rights schemes. To date, such comparisons are not possible regarding sexual minorities, which has delayed coverage of this topic in previous editions of this study. International human rights law is in the process of developing principles on sexual minorities, but there is as yet no convention addressing their rights. Moreover, Islamic human rights schemes do not expressly address issues of sexual orientation and sexual identity, although the implications of the Islamic qualifications that these schemes place on human rights can be inferred from the negative responses of the OIC and Muslim states to emerging proposals for new UN human rights principles on sexual orientation and gender identity.

When confronting such principles, the Organization of Islamic Cooperation (OIC) and Muslim states are in a situation very different from the one that they confront when clinging to laws discriminating against women. Where women are concerned, some Muslim states stand out in terms of their particularly retrograde views, which are clearly out of synchrony with the consensus that discrimination against women is wrong—a theoretical consensus that is not, one realizes, necessarily matched by effective actions on the ground to eliminate discrimination. Embarrassed by having laws and policies that make them look backward by international standards, states such as Iran and Saudi Arabia now feel obliged to lie to the international community and to pretend that they respect women's international human rights. In contrast, where principles upholding equality regardless of sexual orientation and gender identity are concerned, the OIC and its member states are comfortable candidly proclaiming their unequivocal opposition, having confidence that they will have broad backing from many other states.

Sexual Minorities in the Middle East

Given their poor overall human rights records, Middle Eastern states could hardly be expected to treat vulnerable sexual minorities well. Indeed, governments and public figures may find it politically rewarding to lambaste and persecute people whom the public views as sexual deviants and perverts because they can thereby both pander to popular prejudices and position themselves as champions of Islamic morality.[5]

As it happens, in the Middle East the overwhelming emphasis of authorities has been on punishing men who have sex with men, which will be the main focus here. Far less attention is paid to instances of lesbianism. In the Middle East, people involved in subtler cases of sexual nonconformity, such as discreet bisexuality, are far less likely to be prosecuted.[6]

Those who condemn homosexuality in the Middle East, like their counterparts in other regions, tend to reject the scientific evidence that same-sex attraction is inborn. Disregarding or overlooking the findings of modern research, many cling to the notion that people who live as homosexuals have freely chosen to flout divine commandments by willfully engaging in immoral and perverted sexual practices rather than putatively "normal" ones. People laboring under such misconceptions believe that punishing homosexual conduct between consenting adults is no harder to justify than punishing other moral offenses that are regularly criminalized, such as engaging in prostitution or purveying pornography.

Not only do Middle Eastern states figure on the lists of states that criminalize consensual same-sex relations among adults, but some impose the death penalty for such relations, including Iran, Mauritania, Saudi Arabia, Sudan, and Yemen. Despite their shared Islamic heritage, their laws relating to same-sex conduct define the crimes involved in widely disparate fashions, and the punishments vary considerably.

In some criminal codes, various physical acts are described in great detail with specific penalties being listed for each of the acts, but in other countries, homosexuals may be prosecuted under broad provisions criminalizing breaches of morality that allow for a range of punishments.[7] Saudi Arabia applies its uncodified Islamic jurists' law to punish homosexuals, which has allowed prosecutions on various charges with differing penalties.[8] Leaving aside the penalties actually stipulated in laws, in the Middle East homosexuals are also exposed to murder, especially sadistic forms of torture, and arbitrary detentions. In Iraq, the criminal code does not penalize homosexual acts, but in the climate of insecurity and lawlessness that has prevailed since the US invasion, extrajudicial murders and savage tortures of homosexuals are carried out with impunity, abuses that have been blessed by a 2005 ruling by the prominent Shi'i cleric Ayatollah Sistani, who called for those engaging in homosexual acts to be killed in the most severe way.[9]

The preoccupation with punishing homosexual conduct does not seem surprising given the prevalence in the Middle East of patriarchal systems where sex roles are rigidly defined and where women are deemed inferior creatures who are meant to be kept in subjugation. In such settings, a man perceived to be assuming the subordinate role that nature has assigned to women causes particular scandal, with the corollary that forcibly sodomizing a man makes him like a woman—the ultimate humiliation. In Egypt under Mubarak's dictatorship, the police exploited the stigma that attached to any man who was forcibly sodomized to instill fear—as illustrated by the notorious January 2006 case when the police violently attacked Imad al-Kabir, a microbus driver who had stood up to them. A videotape showed the Cairo police savagely abusing al-Kabir after he had dared to challenge them by intervening in a dispute between a policeman and his cousin. Because the police chose to make a videotape of this incident with a mobile phone and then disseminate it, Egyptians had clear proof of how the police used the threat of forcible sodomy to intimidate men. Al-Kabir was taped being beaten and then being sadistically sodomized with a broom as he writhed and screamed out in agony. Thinking that publicizing this attack would cow other drivers, the police forwarded the videotape to the cell phones of microbus drivers to convey a warning that they needed to show humble deference to the police or risk humiliation by the dissemination of videotapes showing them being treated as if they were no better than women.[10]

Mubarak's regime was more concerned with punishing consensual sodomy than stopping forcible sodomy as a police torture technique. The notorious Queen Boat prosecutions in Cairo in 2001 are illustrative of the perils facing homosexuals in Egypt.[11] At a time when the Mubarak dictatorship was nervous about Islamist challenges and eager to distract the citizenry from bad economic conditions, the regime launched a crackdown on homosexuals that went on for years and resulted in the suppression of manifestations of their existence, eliminating their websites, organizations, and bars and clubs. Those initially arrested were patrons of a floating night club on the Nile called the Queen Boat that was popular with men seeking sex with men. Treating them as threats to national security, the regime had them criminally prosecuted with great fanfare and publicity in the state security court. Lurid reports of the defendants' alleged sexual perversions were published.

Not content with leveling such accusations, the prosecutorial authorities demonstrated their inventiveness in portraying the accused as being engaged in crimes against Islam, such as devil worship, false interpretations of the Qur'an, and contempt for heavenly religions. Speaking to the court in one of the cases during this crackdown, the prosecutor made an assertion that illustrated how Egyptian officialdom liked to depict homosexuals as morally depraved, stating that they "submitted to vice, until they became its servants with no conscience, have hurried towards all that God has prohibited, ridding themselves of all morals. They strayed from the straight path that God has drawn for man."[12]

In keeping with a pattern that is common in the Middle East of associating tolerance of homosexual conduct with Western values that offend the local morality, the Egyptian government sought to portray the case as part of a bigger culture war, praising the prosecution for defending authentic culture against sexual perverts who were in conspiracies with foreign forces that threatened national security.[13] A government spokesman, who in 2003 was defending Egypt's criminalization of homosexual conduct to the *New York Times*, made the point that "allowing homosexuality" was not accepted in Egypt, adding "what is good for America or for Europe may not be good for another place."[14]

Iran is notorious for its fierce persecution of people who do not conform to the rigid gender binary envisaged in the official Islamist ideology, according to which there are only stereotypically defined men and women, and only sex between a man and a woman can be licit. In the years immediately following the Islamic revolution, Iran criminalized all forms of gender transgressions. Men whose appearance was effeminate and women who appeared masculine, homosexuals, bisexuals, cross-dressers, and transsexuals were all exposed to the regime's wrath. Because transsexual and transgender individuals were treated as perverts who deserved to be classed with homosexuals, they were subjected to similar forms of intimidation, persecution, arrest, torture, and such brutal punishments as floggings and executions.[15] Later, a door was opened for what were called "gender troubled" individuals to escape their predicament by submitting to intensive psychotherapy, hormone therapy, and genital surgery, which in the regime's view could cure their sexual perversion and render them normal by moving them into either the male or female category.[16] Some contemporary Islamic jurists have shown themselves prepared to consider the psychological dimensions of gender identity and to propose that it is licit to use medical technology to alter the body to fit a person's gender identity.[17] Iran's clerics have endorsed this position.

In September 2007, President Ahmadinejad informed a startled New York audience that in his country there were no homosexuals, maintaining "in Iran we do not have this phenomenon."[18] In reality, unlike members of the gay community in New York, Iran's homosexuals have been forced so deep underground that they have become largely invisible. Facing the threat of execution, they have a potential escape route in the form of sex-reassignment surgery, but it turns out that this route is not necessarily being voluntarily chosen.

The Iranian regime likes to present itself as progressive, treating its willingness to accept sex reassignment surgery for persons whose bodies are at odds with their subjective sexual orientation as a hallmark of Iran's openness to scientific approaches. Indeed, given that most Muslim states outlaw sex reassignment surgery, Iran's approach could initially seem relatively enlightened. In reality, Iranian men who self-define as men who are attracted to other men may feel compelled to submit to sex reassignment surgery in order to avoid criminal prosecution and death sentences for homosexual conduct.[19] A 2008 documentary film, *Be Like Others*, explores the feelings of Iranians awaiting sex reassignment surgery and those who have already undergone the surgery. Some of those interviewed say they did not want to be surgically altered but were compelled to submit to surgery because there is otherwise no place for them in Iran.[20] Thus, fearing that his life may be in danger, a man in a same-sex relationship who has no desire whatsoever to have his body surgically altered to make him look like a woman may nonetheless decide that such an operation is essential for him to survive.

This kind of coercive environment—one in which to escape the punishment that menaces anyone who transgresses the rules of heteronormativity, people feel forced to submit to what they perceive as physical mutilation—has nothing in common with what human rights advocates have in mind when they support Yogyakarta Principle 17.G, which calls for states to "facilitate access by those seeking body modifications related to gender reassignment to competent, non-discriminatory treatment, care and support." A state respectful of human rights would be expected to adhere to the provision in Principle 3, which provides that "no one shall be forced to undergo medical procedures, including sex reassignment surgery, sterilisation or hormonal therapy, as a requirement for legal recognition of their gender identity." Therefore, one sees that Iran's policies punishing homosexual conduct are not only violative of human rights principles covering sexual orientation but also lead to violations of human rights principles covering gender identity.

In the Persian Gulf region, where rapid socioeconomic change and the presence of large contingents of expatriates and migrant workers has had an unsettling impact on the status quo, states have manifested a growing obsession with curbing gender-transgressive appearance and behavior in public. One particular concern has been suppressing challenges to the local gender binary by women who adopt a masculine appearance and openly defy traditional concepts of femininity. Known as *boyat*, the English word "boy" with the Arabic feminine plural appended, such woman have been vilified as being sick and needing treatment to cure and correct their inclinations. The media in the Gulf region have decried the emergence of *boyat* and "the third sex," comprising both effeminate men and transgender women. In Dubai, the threat of the masculinization of women led the government in 2009 to adopt a public awareness campaign designed to halt the phenomenon and to reinforce girls' femininity.[21]

Proceeding from a very different starting point than Iran does, Kuwait, which is a far more open and democratic country, one where Islamists play a role in politics but do not always get their way, has shown increasing intolerance of failures to respect conventional gender classifications. Unlike Iran, however, Kuwait does not offer the option of having sex reassignment surgery. In December 2007, the National Assembly approved an amendment to Article 198 of the criminal code that stipulated that "any person committing an indecent act in a public place, or imitating the appearance of a member of the opposite sex, shall be subject to imprisonment for a period not exceeding one year or a fine not exceeding one thousand dinars." This was immediately followed by a tough crackdown by the police, with many arrests and jailings. Detainees, who were denied access to lawyers, reported mistreatment that included beatings, insults, and having their heads shaved.[22] Observing this crackdown, Human Rights Watch objected that:

Dress codes based solely on gender stereotypes restrict both freedom of expression and personal autonomy. . . . Kuwait allows transgender people neither to change their legal identity to match the gender in which they live, nor to adapt their physical appearance through gender reassignment surgery. The new law . . . aims at further restricting their rights and completely eliminating their public presence.[23]

Assessing the human rights violations involved, Human Rights Watch observed that:

Arbitrary and intrusive gender-based codes for acceptable demeanor and dress violate the rights to privacy and to free expression protected under international law. The beatings and ill-treatment to which authorities reportedly subjected the prisoners violate internationally recognized prohibitions against torture or cruel, inhuman or degrading treatment or punishment.[24]

It also pointed out that Yogyakarta Principle 19.C called upon states to take all necessary measures "to ensure the full enjoyment of the right to express identity or personhood, including through speech, deportment, dress, bodily characteristics, choice of name or any other means."[25]

In an intriguing step, in 2009 the Pakistan Supreme Court ruled that national identity cards should include a third category for transgendered persons, in this case the subclass of men often called *hijras*, who identify as women and dress in women's attire.[26] It is worth pondering why Pakistan would undertake this measure at a time when others in the region were harshly suppressing manifestations of a third sex. It seems that because the category of *hijras* had long been a feature of the culture of the subcontinent and had showed itself compatible with a stable social order, the decision to accord its members official recognition did not threaten any disruption of the status quo. Moreover, recognition of such a traditional category could not be attributed to corrupting Western influences, which likely made this step much easier. A study of such transgender models in Asia proposes that this kind of "third sex" category shows that Western categories may not adequately address such models.[27]

A recent development in Turkey may encourage Middle Easterners who aspire to win acceptance for the notion of equal rights regardless of sexual orientation and gender identity. In the wake of the Arab Spring, Turkey is commonly looked to as a model. Straddling Europe and Asia and having deep historical ties to the Arab world because of the long period of Ottoman suzerainty, Turkey is respected as a Muslim country that has achieved rapid economic development under a democratic system. Although Turkish homosexuals suffer discrimination and persecution, gay rights activists enjoy the freedom to organize to promote their cause and to demonstrate publicly on behalf of their goals—and even to stage such events as an annual gay pride march in Istanbul. The large march staged in June 2011, a time when revisions of the constitution were being planned, included a press release that explicitly demanded that the equality provision of the constitution be amended to include the category of "sexual orientation and identity."[28] Although the battle for extending the equality provision is not close to being won in Turkey, it has at least begun and serves as a reminder that it is not only in the non-Muslim West that people can conceive of equality provisions as covering all persons regardless of their sexual orientation and gender identity.

Contested Islamic Authority

The question naturally arises whether the widespread belief among Muslims that Islam requires punishing men having sex with men, even imposing the death penalty for such conduct, is actually well grounded in the Islamic sources. In keeping with the general trend of Muslims offering fresh insights into how the Islamic heritage can be meshed with human rights, this belief is being challenged.[29] Muslims engaged in this project confront many of the same difficulties that faced their Jewish and Christian counterparts, who broke new ground in offering innovative analyses designed to provoke their coreligionists to reconsider conventional views on sexual minorities. Like their counterparts, Muslims are engaged in challenging traditional interpretations of their scripture that have encouraged the belief that all same-sex relations between consenting adults are intrinsically immoral and violate religious commands.

Scott Siraj al-Haqq Kugle, who explores many angles beyond those briefly adumbrated here, points out that the Qur'an addresses the heterosexual majority, only referring obliquely to homosexuals and not dealing with them as a minority social group. In his assessment, the relevant scriptural passages condemn same-sex acts only in those cases where they are exploitative or violent.[30] This leaves open the possibility that acts between same-sex partners that are consensual and not exploitative were not intended to be criminalized.

There are not many lines in the Qur'an that bear on sexual orientation or gender identity, and the implications of the passages that do treat these subjects can be debated. Qur'anic verses being reexamined include those concerning the story of Lot and the destruction of Sodom and Gomorrah. Plausible new readings have been put forward that point out problems in the traditional interpretations and propose that it was not homosexuality but other vices that provoked God's wrath and the destruction of the cities.[31]

One of the issues being reexamined is whether same-sex relations are rightly classified as *zina*. *Zina*, or sexual intercourse between parties not married to each other, figures among the *hadd* crimes, ones that are regarded as particularly heinous, because the Qur'an stipulates the crime and the penalty to be applied. A question arises whether *zina*, which in the Qur'an seems only to cover intercourse between a man and a woman, should have been extended by analogy to cover same-sex acts, with the result that the latter were also classed as *hadd* crimes. There has long been diversity of opinion on the topic, many eminent premodern jurists having declined to classify same-sex relations as falling in the category of *zina* and therefore having recommended imposing lighter penalties for such relations.[32] Such views were common among jurists of the large and influential Hanafi school of law.

In the context of the Qur'an, there is an obvious reason to impose extremely harsh penalties to deter extramarital sex between men and women that would not apply to same-sex conduct. The text of the Qur'an comprises extended passages setting forth elaborate rules of succession based on people's blood tie to the deceased. Because the bulk of an estate had to be distributed to blood relatives of the deceased according to the complex Qur'anic scheme, a woman bearing children by anyone other than her husband would potentially lead to illegitimate progeny, with no right to inherit, taking shares that should have gone to those actually related by blood to the deceased. Thus, illicit sex between a man and a woman threatens the integrity of the scheme of succession. Given that same-sex relations posed no threat of producing offspring who could diminish the portions of those entitled share in the estate, there is a reasonable basis for questioning whether they logically should incur equivalent penalties.

The process of scholarly reexamination of what Islam says about sexual orientation, which has only been cursorily sketched here, is a work in progress, but it already affords grounds for arguments that the Islamic sources have the potential to be understood in ways that do not support the kind of harsh criminalization of homosexual conduct that is commonly found in the Middle East and that is casually attributed to Islamic authority.

Tensions with the West over the Treatment of Sexual Minorities

In the Middle East, conflicts over human rights in the area of sexual orientation and gender identity are regularly presented in terms of Westerners promoting human rights that clash with the culture of the region.[33] Europe, which has advanced human rights law by setting high standards in the European Convention of Human Rights, was the first region to recognize and protect human rights regardless of sexual orientation. In the landmark 1981 case *Dudgeon v. United Kingdom*, the ruling that criminal prosecutions of consensual sex between men in private was a violation of the right to privacy was the first in a series of rulings dismantling criminal laws affecting same-sex activity.[34] Progress toward dismantling laws discriminating against gays has been slower and more uneven in the United States, but an important breakthrough was made by the Supreme Court in 2003 when it ruled in *Lawrence v. Texas* that criminally prosecuting private sexual conduct between consenting adults entailed a violation of the liberty interest protected by the due process clause of the Fourteenth Amendment. One is reminded that it is only quite recently that the West has moved to repudiate older laws that reflected the deeply ingrained idea that same-sex relations should be criminalized.

Not only are laws in the West currently far more liberal than they are in the Middle East, but contemporary campaigns to advance the human rights of persons regardless of their sexual orientation and gender identity tend to be spearheaded by Western states and by human rights NGOs based there. Amnesty International and Human Rights Watch, both headquartered in the West, have been prominent in criticizing human rights violations affecting people on the basis of their sexual orientation or gender identity. In these circumstances, it is not hard to see why many in the Middle East equate advocacy of gay rights with

promoting Western ideas. Moreover, many Muslims living in the West have supported advocacy organizations concerned with the human rights of lesbian, gay,
bisexual, or transgender people who live in Muslim countries.[35] More than a few
of these Muslims will have fled to the West to claim asylum based on their past
exposure to persecution on the basis of their sexual orientation or gender identity in the Middle East.[36]

Of course, it is not surprising that such advocacy is displaced to the West, because human rights NGOs operating in the Middle East have tended to shy
away from such campaigns for various reasons, among them the facts that such
advocacy is in itself dangerous and that their being associated with "gay rights"
would make it easier for their critics to brand them as agents of Western hegemonic projects and could undermine their work in other areas. The Egyptian
human rights advocate Hossam Bahgat has been unusual in his insistence on
pursuing such advocacy in difficult circumstances, being convinced that ensuring protections for personal autonomy, bodily integrity, and privacy are vital for
human rights.[37]

Identifying equality in rights regardless of sexual orientation with Western
culture is an oversimplification. Western attitudes have been far from uniform,
and Western criminal laws were until recently shaped by homophobic attitudes.
As late as the 1950s in Great Britain, homosexual conduct was being aggressively
prosecuted and harshly punished.[38] Ironically, when European colonialism dominated the Middle East, Europeans were prone to speak disparagingly about what
they saw as the peculiar licentiousness and the homosexual proclivities of "Orientals."[39] Moreover, during the colonial era, Western governments planted the
seeds of modern homophobia in parts of the Middle East. Premodern Islamic jurists had supported penalties for sex acts between men, but it has been proposed
that it was from European colonial powers that the Middle East absorbed the notion that that there was a class of humans to be designated as "homosexuals" who
should be condemned as deviants because of their same-sex orientations. After
Europeans implanted laws criminalizing homosexuality in the Middle East that
reflected then-dominant European values, these Western transplants, facets of
the hybridity characteristic of contemporary Middle Eastern legal systems, were
subsequently construed as reflecting Islamic values.[40]

Muslim States' Objections to New UN Initiatives

Issues such as discrimination and persecution based on sexual orientation were
not explicitly addressed at the outset of the UN human rights system. Nonetheless, the general language on all human beings being born "free and equal in dignity and rights" in Article 1 of the UDHR and the provision in Article 2 ensuring
everyone all the rights and freedoms set forth in the UDHR "without distinction

of any kind" had the potential to be understood as ensuring rights regardless of sexual orientation and gender identity. It took until 1994 for the UN Human Rights Committee, the UN treaty body monitoring the implementation of the International Covenant on Civil and Political Rights (ICCPR), to affirm that discrimination based on sexual orientation violated human rights in *Toonen v. Australia*.[41] In *Toonen*, a challenge was raised to Tasmanian laws criminalizing consensual sexual relations between adult men in private. The committee ruled that such laws clashed with the right of privacy in the ICCPR and also that discrimination on the basis of sexual orientation fits within the ICCPR prohibition of discrimination on the basis of sex. The committee also rejected Tasmania's defenses that men having sex with men presented a threat to the moral standards of Tasmanian society and that moral considerations had to be taken into account when dealing with the right to privacy.

Only a few of the milestones in the tortuous history of efforts within the UN system to promote equality in rights and freedoms regardless of sexual orientation or gender identity can be catalogued here.[42] In a breakthrough initiative in 2003, Brazil attempted to win support in the former UN Commission on Human Rights, which in 2006 was reorganized and renamed the Human Rights Council, for a resolution asserting that human rights should not be hindered in any way on the grounds of sexual orientation, only to be defeated by strong opposition. In March 2011, a "Joint Statement on Ending Acts of Violence and Related Human Rights Violations Based on Sexual Orientation and Gender Identity" was delivered to the Human Rights Council on behalf of eighty-five states. It called on states to end violence, criminal sanctions, and human rights violations tied to sexual orientation and gender identity and urged the council to address related human rights issues. The statement built on similar language in a statement that had been delivered in 2006 to the council by Norway, this one being the first such statement to make an explicit reference to gender identity, and on another statement that had been presented by Argentina in 2008 to the UN General Assembly. The Argentinian statement had won support from sixty-six states, but it was countered by an alternative text promoted by the OIC that had won the backing of sixty states. The OIC text affirmed "principles of non-discrimination and equality," but claimed that universal human rights did not include "the attempt to focus on the rights of certain persons."[43] That is, the OIC attempted to present the Argentinian statement as distorting the principles of universal human rights, implying that it was wrong to single out subgroups for special protections. The OIC objection made no sense in the light of the history of the UN human rights system, which had started out with the general principles in the UDHR but which was subsequently greatly amplified by rules affording more specific rights protections for subgroups of humanity. Thus, UN member states have overwhelmingly approved later human rights conventions and declarations concerning subgroups whose needs and circumstances call for special protections, such as children, indigenous peoples, women, migrant workers, refugees, and persons with disabilities.

On June 15, 2011, the Human Rights Council adopted by a vote of twenty-three in favor, nineteen against, and three abstentions, a landmark resolution on human rights, sexual orientation, and gender identity that had been presented by South Africa. Countries voting against were Angola, Bahrain, Bangladesh, Cameroon, Djibouti, Gabon, Ghana, Jordan, Malaysia, Maldives, Mauritania, Nigeria, Pakistan, Qatar, Republic of Moldova, Russian Federation, Saudi Arabia, Senegal, and Uganda. The resolution called for a study of discriminatory laws and practices and acts of violence against individuals based on their sexual orientation and gender identity and for a study of how international human rights law can be used to end violence and related human rights violations based on sexual orientation and gender identity.[44] When the report was issued in December 2011, Navi Pillay, the UN High Commissioner for Human Rights, called for, among other things, countries to repeal laws criminalizing homosexuality and to enact comprehensive antidiscrimination laws. The report detailed "a pattern of human rights violations" that needed to be addressed, including homophobic and transphobic violence.[45]

Thus, despite the fact that no human rights convention has appeared specifically covering the rights of sexual minorities, the pattern in UN initiatives is signaling that significant progress is being made toward eliminating this gap.

All initiatives of this kind have encountered intense criticisms and vigorous resistance, with the OIC and its members figuring in the forefront of the coalition opposing them. Although the OIC and its members do often refer to Islam in rejecting these UN initiatives, there is also a range of other objections that they offer to justify their opposition. In a remarkable turnaround, instead of invoking Islam to justify noncompliance with international human rights law, the OIC and Muslim states have regularly repositioned themselves as states that are defending international human rights law from those who, they claim, would distort it by making inappropriate changes. Moreover, when referring to cultural grounds for objecting, they often mention that the declaration issued by the 1993 Vienna Human Rights Conference, discussed in Chapter 1, called for national, regional, and cultural specificities to be taken into account. That is, rather than invoking Islamic particularism, they base their cultural defense on a principle that was articulated within the UN human rights system.

Some examples of their statements are offered here, which illustrate that Islam is only one of various grounds being deployed. One of the themes in such responses is embodied in the 2004 OIC letter distributed by Pakistan on behalf of the OIC to states attending a meeting in Geneva asserting that "sexual orientation is not a human rights issue."[46] This tough, uncompromising, rejectionist stance was one that the OIC could expect to enjoy widespread backing.

In a book that seeks to minimize the degree to which OIC states deviate from international human rights law, it is proposed that OIC members should be given leeway to define their positions in this area, viewed as an area where moral questions are involved, in accordance with the margin of appreciation doctrine.[47] This doctrine merely intends, however, to allow states a level of discretion in interpreting how to apply human rights principles, and it constrains states' discretion by various criteria. It does not afford states the prerogative of refusing altogether to recognize certain human rights, as the OIC has done in insisting that there is absolutely no basis for protecting the human rights of sexual minorities.

In response to the 2008 statement presented by Argentina, referred to above, the OIC produced a statement that was delivered by Syria on behalf of fifty-seven states, only twelve of which were not OIC members. In speaking scornfully of "the so-called notions" of sexual orientation and gender identity, Syria maintained that there were "no legal foundations in any international human rights instruments" for Argentina's statement, and professed to be "disturbed at the attempt to focus on certain persons on the grounds of their sexual interests and behaviors" at the expense of other forms of intolerance and discrimination. It also complained that Argentina's statement "delves into matters which fall essentially within the domestic jurisdiction of States," thereby failing to respect national sovereignty. It further warned that the notion of sexual orientation "spans a wide range of personal choices" that could be expanded, thereby "ushering in the social normalization and possibly the legitimization of many deplorable acts, including pedophilia." Echoing other OIC responses, Syria complained: "We note with concern the attempts to create 'new rights' or 'new standards' by misinterpreting the Universal Declaration and international treaties to include such notions that were never articulated nor agreed by the general membership."[48]

Again, one encounters the common themes that sexual orientation is a matter of personal choice and that provisions on sexual orientation and gender identity do not belong in the UN human rights system, with the additional complaint that establishing human rights in these areas interferes with national sovereignty. The Syrian warning that the ideas in the 2008 Argentinian statement could result in legitimizing sexual perversions embodies a familiar tactic employed by those defending the criminalization of sexual conduct that does not conform to the rules of heteronormativity. For example, US Supreme Court Justice Antonin Scalia in his dissent in the *Lawrence v. Texas* decision asserted that the logic behind the constitutional ruling calling for the decriminalization of same-sex conduct among consenting adults would imply that states could not constitutionally criminalize such conduct as bigamy, same-sex marriage, adult incest, prostitution, masturbation, adultery, fornication, bestiality, and obscenity.[49]

With the OIC's encouragement, in November 2010, the UN General Assembly's Third Committee voted seventy-nine to seventy (with seventeen abstentions and twenty-six absent) to approve the removal of the words "sexual orientation" from a resolution protecting persons from extrajudicial, summary, or arbitrary executions—a modification that, however, was eventually reversed. At the time of the vote, Morocco, speaking on behalf of the OIC, provided the following reasons for excising the reference to sexual orientation, explaining that what it called "the Group" was:

> seriously concerned by controversial and undefined notions that had no foundation in international human rights instruments. Intolerance and discrimination existed in cases of colour, race, gender and religion, to mention only a few. Selectivity intended to accommodate certain interests over others had to be avoided by the international community. Such selectivity would set a precedent that would change the human rights paradigm in order to suit the interests of particular groups. An attempt to create new rights was a matter of concern for the Group. All Member States were urged to continue to devote special attention to the protection of the family as the natural and fundamental unit of society.[50]

Notably, this OIC statement characterized the inclusion of wording aimed at protecting people from extrajudicial, summary, or arbitrary execution on grounds of their sexual orientation as involving "selectivity" and as being designed to serve the interests of "particular groups"—as if this would entail a distortion of human rights. As already noted, given the range of human rights conventions and declarations on subgroups of human beings, the idea that adding new rights concerning "particular groups" necessarily distorts international law has no foundation. The real grounds for objecting instead must have related to hostility to enhancing the rights of sexual minorities. One notes that the statement also complained that the wording was embracing new, undefined notions that were controversial and problematic. Of course, adding "sexual orientation" to the categories covered in the resolution might raise some definitional questions, but lack of definitional precision was not likely to have been the real concern of the OIC, given that its Cairo Declaration was rife with vague and ambiguous terms that were casually deployed to qualify human rights—as if definitional precision was of no consequence whatsoever.

The objections made by representatives of several Muslim countries to the aforementioned June 15, 2011, resolution in the Human Rights Council exemplify themes commonly encountered in statements by the OIC and its members.

Speaking on behalf of the OIC, Pakistan claimed that the resolution had no basis in international legal and human rights standards and that the OIC was objecting to attempts to create new standards, again invoking the previously discussed language on culture from the declaration from the 1993 Vienna Human Rights Conference. Saudi Arabia complained that the resolution imposed values without consideration of how these clashed with Islamic law and with other religions, but to this it appended the objection that the resolution was not in line with internationally agreed human rights principles. Bahrain condemned the attempt to make the council deal with such controversial issues as gender identity and protested that the resolution was an attempt to create new human rights based on personal decisions that were not fundamental human rights, also charging that the resolution was misinterpreting the existing international human rights standards. Qatar stressed the need to respect cultural diversity and also indicated that the resolution went against Islam.[51]

As one observes, objections grounded in Islam were buried in a mixture of other objections that were secular in character. Many objections centered on the states' ostensible disapproval of adding new, controversial principles that were supposedly not in line with international human rights law and that were also at odds with respecting cultural diversity. The objectors continue to insist that homosexuality is voluntarily elected, not an innate characteristic of a large segment of humanity. All in all, the OIC clearly tried to downplay Islam as the basis for its positions as part of a strategy to build a cross-cultural coalition that would resist efforts at the UN to protect the human rights of all people regardless of their sexual orientation or gender identity, a clear illustration of the opportunism that lies behind the selective invocations of Islam to restrict human rights.

Summary

The firm opposition of the OIC and its members to proposed UN principles that would expand human rights protections to cover matters involving sexual orientation and gender identity stands in sharp contrast to the largely constructive engagement of Muslim states in drafting human rights principles at the outset of the UN human rights system. Their obstructionist positions have won them many allies among non-Muslim states that are similarly undemocratic and antagonistic toward the philosophy of international human rights law. The wish to form such alliances accounts for the fact that, although Islam is occasionally invoked as the reason for resisting the new principles protecting sexual minorities, other rubrics with broader appeal are more frequently offered.

One observes that when and how Islam is deployed as a pretext for state policies denying human rights is strictly a matter of political calculations. Thus, although they have in the past repeatedly and expressly invoked Islam as a basis for refusing to adhere to international human rights law, the OIC and its members now prefer to take the route of hypocrisy, presenting themselves not as advocates of Islamic cultural particularism at odds with human rights but as states engaged in defending the integrity of international human rights law and as resisting the addition of new principles that they maintain will distort it.

The positions being taken by the OIC and Muslim countries have direct implications for Islamic human rights schemes. As noted, in all instances such schemes subordinate human rights to Islamic criteria. Because the OIC and Muslim countries have so consistently denounced the idea of equality in rights regardless of sexual orientation and gender identity, one can project that the Islamic qualifications on rights in Islamic human rights schemes would be interpreted to block such equality.

Meanwhile, liberal Muslims are embracing ideas such as those afforded by the Yogyakarta Principles and are offering critiques of the way that Islam is invoked to mandate criminalizing consensual adult sexual activity not fitting within the confines of heteronormativity. Promoting these critiques will not quickly solve the problems of human rights abuses in the Middle East based on sexual orientation and gender identity. Nonetheless, they should go some way toward opening the door to reconsidering the merits of relevant criminal laws and policies, which presume an Islamic authority that now can be shown to be less solid than was previously assumed.

CHAPTER 9

Freedom of Religion in Islamic Human Rights Schemes

Controversies Regarding the *Shari'a* Rule on Apostasy

Freedom of religion is a topic where Islamic human rights schemes clash directly with international human rights law. Because such states as Iran and Saudi Arabia, which are notorious for their violations of the right to freedom of religion, have assumed leading roles in formulating such schemes, it is not surprising that these schemes offer no protection whatsoever for freedom of religion. They are written to accommodate the premodern jurists' rule that bars conversion from Islam, and they accommodate states' prerogative to decree that any people whom they wish to so designate are apostates. The authors of Islamic human rights schemes are disposed to ignore the fact that there is ample authority in the Islamic heritage supporting respect for freedom of religion.

Many Muslims question the rules prohibiting and punishing conversion from Islam set forth by the premodern jurists. The latter tended to say that apostates were to be given an opportunity to repent and return to Islam, but if they refused, they were to be executed if they were men or imprisoned until they changed their minds if they were women. Premodern *shari'a* rules also provided that apostasy constituted civil death, meaning, among other things, that the apostate's marriage would be dissolved, and the apostate would become incapable of inheriting. Naturally, the *shari'a* imposed no penalty on conversion to Islam from other faiths.

Progressive thinkers have stressed that there are plausible interpretations of the Islamic sources that accommodate religious freedom.[1] Muslims who oppose criminalizing apostasy point out that the death penalty for apostasy is not called for in the Qur'an.[2] Indeed, in the Qur'an 2:26, one reads a specific admonition that there must be no compulsion in religion, and various passages speak as if belief or unbelief is a personal choice.[3] A Tunisian scholar understands the Qur'an to say that God wants submission to Islam "in full consciousness and freedom," indicating that religious liberty is fundamental to respect for God's plan for humanity. This plan includes the mysterious privilege of rejecting Islam's message of salvation, a privilege that precludes recourse to compulsion or killing in matters of faith.[4]

Contemporary scholars often observe that the premodern jurists' rules on apostasy were extrapolated from incidents in the Prophet's life and from historical events after his death that are open to a variety of constructions and that do not necessarily provide justification for executing apostates, as in cases where the penalty was actually for treason.[5] The Lebanese scholar Subhi Mahmassani asserts that the circumstances in which the penalty was meant to apply were intended to be narrow ones. He points out that the Prophet never killed anyone merely for apostasy and that the death penalty was applied when the act of apostasy was linked to an act of political betrayal of the community. This being the case, Mahmassani argues that the death penalty was not meant to apply to a simple change of faith but to punish such acts as treason, joining forces with the enemy, and sedition.[6]

Muslim Countries Confront Freedom of Religion

International human rights law allows no constraints on a person's religious beliefs: Freedom of religion is an unqualified freedom. One of the most influential statements of this freedom is in Article 18 of the UDHR. Article 18 states: "Everyone has the right to freedom of thought, conscience and religion; this right includes freedom to change his religion or belief, and freedom, either alone or in community with others and in public or private, to manifest his religion or belief in teaching, practice, worship and observance." Freedom of religion is unqualified in the ICCPR, Article 18.1. Although the wording is similar to UDHR Article 18, the ICCPR provision does not specifically mention the freedom to change religion.

It is historically significant that the phrase guaranteeing the right to change religion was added to the UDHR at the behest of the delegate from Lebanon, who was a Christian. Lebanon in the 1940s and 1950s was an oasis of religious pluralism and toleration, where large communities of Christians, Muslims, and Druze coexisted and where it seemed incongruous that Christians could convert to Islam but that Muslims were barred from converting to Christianity. Not surprisingly, when the Lebanese representative Charles Malik proposed that this language be added, he faced objections from some Muslim countries, as discussed in Chapter 1.

Objections were later raised in other contexts. Iran, in discussions of the 1981 Declaration on the Elimination of All Forms of Intolerance, asserted that Muslims were not allowed to convert from their religion and were to be executed if they did so.[7] The Convention on the Rights of the Child (CRC), the most widely ratified of all the human rights conventions, guarantees in Article 14 a child's freedom of religion. Although some Muslim countries ratified the CRC without reservation, others ratified it subject to qualifications. Whereas some expressly invoked Islamic law in reserving, others resorted to circumlocutions, invoking their constitutions, which incorporated Islamic principles that could provide the basis for barring conversions. Afghanistan, Iran, and Saudi Arabia entered sweeping reservations when ratifying the CRC, indicating that they would not be bound by provisions contravening Islamic law, potentially encompassing Article 14. In the Middle Eastern region, Algeria, Iraq, Jordan, Kuwait, Morocco, Oman, Pakistan, Qatar, Syria, and the United Arab Emirates entered specific reservations to Article 14. Perhaps these countries were more willing to register openly their nonacceptance of freedom of religion in a context where paternal control over children was at issue. After all, in Middle Eastern countries, family solidarity and paternal authority are sacrosanct, and it is assumed that children must adhere to the religion of their father. These public statements indicated their continued estrangement from the principle of freedom of religion.

The Contemporary Significance of Apostasy

Because Islam is the world's fastest-growing religion and attempts to convert from Islam are uncommon, one might find the zeal to punish apostasy puzzling. It seems fair to assume that the number of persons affected by the *shari'a* ban on apostasy would be minimal. In reality, the ban on conversion from Islam has broad ramifications and potentially limits the rights of a much larger segment of the populations of Muslim countries than one might initially surmise.

As interpreted, the ban can apply to people who are born into a non-Muslim religion but whose parents, grandparents, or even more distant ancestors converted from Islam. The notion that Baha'is started as renegades from Islam has been one basis for their persecution in Iran since the revolution. Although the targeted individuals had not changed their religion, the record shows that Iranian Baha'is may be punished and persecuted as apostates by virtue of their ancestors' defections from Islam.

The ban can also affect Muslims who adhere to doctrines that are out of keeping with whatever standard of orthodoxy is currently being espoused by locally powerful Islamic institutions or by governments. Although premodern Islamic culture was generally tolerant of diverging views on questions of Islamic theology and law, when contemporary Middle Eastern governments have espoused one official Islam or adopted Islamization programs, they have shown intolerance, labeling Muslims who do not accept the officially approved Islam heretics and apostates. The circumstances under which the Ahmadi minority in Pakistan was legally demoted to "non-Muslim" status under the official Islamization program have already been discussed. Likewise, the Sudanese Republicans officially became "apostates" from Islam under Nimeiri, even though they never repudiated Islam. Thus, the ban on apostasy has become a means to criminalize what are deemed as heretical views, acting as a curb on the freedom of Muslims to follow a locally disfavored version of Islamic teachings.

The notorious 1994–1996 case of the Cairo University professor Nasr Hamid Abu Zaid showed that Egypt's courts were prepared to penalize progressive Islamic thought by classifying it as apostasy.[8] Among other things, the Abu Zaid case proves that the quarrel of Sunni orthodoxy with Mu'tazilite ideas, which are discussed in Chapter 3, is far from over because many of Abu Zaid's controversial positions were closely linked to the rationalist approach to Islam advocated by the Mu'tazilites.[9] Abu Zaid took stances at odds with the notion, popular among contemporary proponents of Islam as an ideology, that the Qur'an possesses a univocal meaning, emphasizing the diversity in interpretations.[10] Moreover, he disputed the tenet that Islam covers all domains, arguing that areas such as human rights are based on developments outside the sphere of religion.[11] Like the Iranian philosopher Abdolkarim Soroush, who has been persecuted for uttering similar views, Abu Zaid critically appraised the consequences of the monopoly over Qur'anic interpretation exercised by state theologians, claiming that their dependency on the state leads to repressing new interpretations and stifling critical analysis.[12] As if anticipating his own fate, he charged that the ideological exploitation of the Qur'an legitimizes the status quo and leads to branding Muslims who raise challenges as unbelievers, atheists, and heretics.[13]

Egypt's personal status laws allow recourse to Islamic law in default of an applicable code provision, meaning that judges can use the works of the jurists of the locally dominant Hanafi school of law. A third party, totally unrelated to Abu Zaid, was allowed to bring a claim asserting that, according to Hanafi jurisprudence, Abu Zaid's marriage to his Muslim wife had to be dissolved because his writings showed that he was an apostate. The courts reviewed Abu Zaid's writings, which called for revising conventional approaches to Qur'an interpretation, and agreed that his theories made him an apostate. On this basis, the courts declared his marriage dissolved. They referred to the constitutional protection for freedom of religion but, as had happened in the *Zaheeruddin* case in Pakistan, they interpreted it in the light of overriding Islamic criteria. That is, the courts decided that Islamic qualifications on religious freedom were implied and concluded that the forcible divorce of a couple on the grounds of the husband's allegedly heretical religious beliefs did not conflict with freedom of religion as set forth in Egypt's constitution.[14] The judges did not want to acknowledge that they were denying the human right to religious freedom even though they were flouting it by accepting Islamic qualifications that nullified it.

The Abu Zaid case provides an illustration of how the human rights issues of religious freedom and women's status are interlinked. The upholders of the premodern *shari'a* insist that the wife must be subordinate to her husband, which makes it intolerable for her, if she is a Muslim, to be married to a non-Muslim because Islam—the Muslim woman being seen as a marker for Islam—must not be subordinated to another faith. They also reject the principle that both men and women should be allowed freely to choose their spouses, without any hindrances based on religion. The outcome of the Abu Zaid case could be as readily attributed to Egypt's failure to accord women equality as to Egypt's failure to uphold religious freedom.

Although the implementation of the divorce ruling was ultimately stayed and Egypt subsequently changed its laws to prevent private parties from bringing such suits, these belated responses did not protect Abu Zaid and his wife from the religious zealots who were ready to enforce their own version of Islamic justice. They threatened to kill him for his supposed apostasy or to kill them both for living together in sin after they had been forcibly divorced. The couple was obliged to seek asylum in Europe. This outcome is a reminder that in the climate of intolerance prevailing in many Muslim countries, it is not necessary for the state itself to impose a death penalty for an "apostate" to be severely penalized.

This apostasy case shows why it is an oversimplification to ascribe such rulings to Islamic law. After all, the objectives of the premodern jurists were to punish Muslims who abandoned their faith and to deter defections from the early Islamic community. Abu Zaid, a professing Muslim who had been a member in good standing of the Muslim community and who wished to revitalize Islamic scholarship through his study of the Qur'an, was cast out of the community against his wishes and on the flimsy basis of a decision by a secular court that happened to find his challenges to received opinions offensive. From punishment for a willful act of abandonment of the faith, "apostasy" had been converted into an arbitrary sanction that courts serving national governments could mete out to believing Muslims who elected to take different paths to understanding scripture. In consequence of the "apostasy" ruling, two Muslims became outcasts and were forced to uproot themselves from their Muslim homeland and move for their own safety to live as exiles on non-Muslim territory.

Abu Zaid's arguments on behalf of a reformed understanding of the Islamic sources had made him vulnerable to the same kinds of attacks that have forced many of Islam's distinguished thinkers into exile. As one author who has written about the Abu Zaid case laments, it is precisely the most creative, the brightest, and the most courageous spirits in the Muslim world who are slandered, attacked, persecuted, and killed by members of their own cultures—this for trying to take up the challenge of renewing and preserving their culture.[15] One should bear this reality in mind when Islam is portrayed as a reactionary and oppressive religion: Muslims who could transform Islam into a more open system and who offer enlightened views on their faith are all too often deterred from challenging orthodoxy because of the risk of sharing the kind of fate that befell Abu Zaid and others like him, resulting in a sterile religious climate in the Middle East.

As is so often the case, human rights violations that seem at first blush to be tied to the application of the *shari'a* turned out upon closer inspection to be intertwined with local politics. Abu Zaid himself claimed that he was targeted for persecution as an apostate as retaliation for his criticisms of an Islamic investment scheme in which a powerful personage had an interest. In any event, this grim case illustrates why protecting freedom of religion is at least as important for Muslims as it is for the non-Muslim populations in the Middle East. It is, of course, an illusion to think that a system that persecutes members of the Muslim majority for their religious ideas can protect the religious freedom of non-Muslim minorities.

In the climate of intolerance that has been fostered by official Islamization campaigns and Islamist activism, sectarian tensions have grown, and charges of apostasy have multiplied. This trend has grown so destructive that in July 2005, a meeting of high-ranking Islamic clerics was convened in Jordan to produce a declaration denouncing the practice of one group of Muslims calling others apostates, asserting that this was an affront to Islamic values. Although the declaration affirmed that both Sunnis and Shi'is are true Muslims, it failed to make any explicit call for an end to the persecutions of other sects.[16]

The prohibition of conversions from Islam can also limit the freedom of Muslim women, preventing them from escaping *shari'a* law. The choice-of-law rules that are in force in most Middle Eastern countries mean that religious affiliation decides which law is applicable to personal status issues. Except in rare countries, such as Turkey and Tunisia, where far-reaching reforms have been enacted so that one national standard applies to all citizens, Muslims find that in issues like marriage and divorce, they are governed by *shari'a* law.

In such systems, if there were no ban on conversion, a Muslim woman could change the personal status law applicable to her simply by abandoning Islam. In the Middle East, conversions from one religion to another—and sometimes switches from one Islamic sect or school of law to another—have long been used to change the applicable law in personal status issues. These conversions are the equivalent of forum shopping in the United States, where litigants, by changing their domicile from one state to another, can alter the law applicable to their family law issues—"shopping" for the forum that has a more favorable law.

Conversions potentially enable parties to accomplish objectives impossible to achieve under their original personal status law. For example, in a Middle Eastern country, a Roman Catholic woman married to a Catholic man would be barred from divorcing, but she could sever her marital tie by converting to Islam. Her marriage would thereby become void, for she would gain the benefit of the *shari'a* rule that a Muslim woman cannot be validly married to a non-Muslim. A non-Muslim man might also convert to Islam to gain the benefit of a more favorable personal status law, such as a lenient divorce rule. Penalizing conversion from Islam can be used to deter "conversions" undertaken out of expediency by preventing such opportunists from converting back to their original faiths after they get a legal ruling that was made possible by their temporary status as Muslims.

Because the apostate incurs civil death, apostasy offers an escape route for Muslim women who seek divorces but encounter legal obstacles. Thus, the Muslim woman who is willing to incur civil death can escape the applicability of *shari'a* law by abandoning Islam. In the past, many informal social and cultural factors inhibited Muslim women from taking such a radical course, but these inhibitions are crumbling under the impact of major social changes. Improved educational opportunities, exposure to different social models through the media, a more skeptical attitude toward the traditional subordination of women, and other factors may lead women to chafe under an onerous marital tie that formerly might have been tolerated. In these changed circumstances, the prospect of achieving freedom through apostasy may be alluring.

Thus, there is a connection between the refusal of Islamic human rights schemes to allow freedom to change religion and their authors' determination to ensure that Muslim women remain governed by *shari'a* rules. Where *shari'a* rules are seen as a scheme for controlling women, it becomes essential to block conversions as a means by which women can manipulate choice-of-law rules.

In Kuwait, where a Muslim woman's ability to opt out of the *shari'a* system has been perceived as a threat, a different legal solution was found. There, a law was enacted discarding the premodern *shari'a* rule that a Muslim woman's marriage would be automatically dissolved by her apostasy. The reason for this change was offered in an explanatory memorandum accompanying the reform: "Complaints have shown that the Devil makes the route of apostasy attractive to the Muslim woman so that she can break a conjugal tie that does not please her. For this reason, it was decided that apostasy would not lead to the dissolution of the marriage in order to close this dangerous door."[17] One sees that in Kuwait, fidelity to the *shari'a* takes second place to concerns for preserving the patriarchal order; the *shari'a* rule on civil death for the apostate has been abandoned because of worries that this penalty is insufficient to deter women from having recourse to apostasy to terminate their marriages. With the change in the law, Muslim women in Kuwait can no longer open "this dangerous door."

Until recently, the progressive Westernization of Middle Eastern legal systems seemed to promise that the practical importance of *shari'a* restrictions on religious freedom would diminish. In the wake of nineteenth- and twentieth-century reforms in the area of criminal law, the application of the *shari'a* death penalty for apostasy from Islam became a rarity. Moves for the Islamization of Middle Eastern law have reversed this trend and have produced serious breaches of international human rights law.

In Egypt since the 1970s, there have been insistent demands for a revival of the death penalty for apostasy from Islam.[18] These demands have met energetic opposition on the part of Egypt's large Coptic population and have also been opposed by liberal and secular forces. Although the Egyptian government in 1980 changed the constitution to make the *shari'a* the main source of legislation, it resisted attempts to have the death penalty for apostasy from Islam incorporated in its criminal law. However, many instances of harassment and intimidation of Egyptian Muslims who convert from Islam have been reported.

Even where no rule mandating execution of apostates from Islam has been incorporated in the criminal code, governments that have undertaken Islamization programs may nonetheless execute people for apostasy from Islam—as if the *shari'a* rules were binding even in the absence of corresponding provisions in the criminal code. At the same time, governments that execute apostates often act reluctant to proclaim publicly that they kill people for their religious beliefs or to enact laws that confirm that conversions from Islam incur the death penalty.

Tabandeh's Ideas

Not surprisingly, Sultanhussein Tabandeh is the most candid of the authors in calling for the retention of premodern Islamic rules restricting religious freedom. He concedes that *dhimmis* do enjoy the right to practice their own religions, but this right is not extended to others. Members of the Baha'i faith are considered by Tabandeh to be defectors from Islam who must be forced to recant and return to the fold. Tabandeh asserts that "followers of a religion of which the basis is contrary to Islam" could have no freedom of religion under an Islamic government, analogizing them to adherents of political parties that were "contrary to the ideology of the regime."[19] Tabandeh assumes that Islam is effectively ideologized, treating it like the official Marxist line in a communist country that allows no dissent.[20]

Tabandeh is unyielding in his insistence that conversion from Islam should not be tolerated.[21] The reasons why a person might desert Islam, according to a speech by the Egyptian UN representative cited by Tabandeh, include duress, bribes, and a woman's desire "to exploit easier conditions for divorce obtaining under some other religions."[22] As other possible inducements to abandon Islam, Tabandeh lists false promises by another religion, spite on the part of a Muslim who has been injured by another Muslim, and being led astray by carnal lusts that Islam forbids.[23] A Muslim who abjures Islam must be killed as a person who is "diseased . . . gangrenous, incurable, fit only for amputation."[24] To illustrate the solicitude of Islam for women's welfare, Tabandeh proposes that the female apostate is not to be killed but is to be offered a more lenient fate, being condemned "to life imprisonment with hard labor."[25] In contrast, Tabandeh noted that "a person who gives up some religion other than Islam to accept Islam's sound faith is received and respected."[26] Seemingly unaware how widely his views diverge from international law, he apparently presumes that, once those who make international law are made to understand the reasons why Islam forbids conversion, international law will likewise decree that conversions from Islam should be banned.[27]

It is worth considering how Tabandeh's arguments for banning conversion from Islam contrast with a central premise of international human rights law. International human rights law is based on the assumption that allowing individuals the freedom to make fundamental choices affecting their lives is part of what is involved in being human and in achieving dignity and self-respect.[28] In contrast, Tabandeh absolutely rejects the right of individuals freely to follow their consciences in matters of faith.

The UIDHR

The Universal Islamic Declaration of Human Rights (UIDHR) purports to treat the "Right to Freedom of Belief, Thought and Speech" in Article 12.a, but again, it uses formulations in the English and Arabic versions that convey very different impressions. In the English, Article 12.a states: "Every person has the right to express his thoughts and beliefs so long as he remains within the limits prescribed by the Law. No one, however, is entitled to disseminate falsehood or to circulate reports that may outrage public decency, or to indulge in slander, innuendo, or to cast defamatory aspersions on other persons."

At first glance this provision appears to impose neutral, secular restraints on freedom of expression, while sidestepping the issue of freedom of belief. The idea that slanderous, defamatory speech can be curbed by law seems unobjectionable. It is when one recalls that "the Law" refers to Islamic law that one appreciates that the restrictions on freedom of expression are sufficiently broad to allow for governments to negate the right.

The Arabic version of Article 12.a conveys a very different message because it expressly indicates that Islamic criteria limit freedom of expression. As has already been pointed out, using criteria taken from one religion to set limits on rights is unacceptable under international human rights law. Article 12.a states: "Everyone may think, believe and express his ideas and beliefs without interference or opposition from anyone as long as he obeys the limits [*hudud*] set by the *shari'a*. It is not permitted to spread falsehood [*al-batil*] or disseminate that which involves encouraging abomination [*al-fahisha*] or forsaking the Islamic community [*takhdhil li'l-umma*]."[29] Thus, *shari'a* rules set limits not just on freedom of expression but also on the freedoms of thought and belief.

Based on past experience, one can make some surmises about what *shari'a* rules would likely be employed to curtail these rights. Among other things, people would be prohibited from attempting to convert Muslims to other faiths and would be forbidden to speak disparagingly of the Prophet. The significance of the second sentence is difficult to ascertain. The English version suggests that defamation and slander are categories of expression that are not protected, but the Arabic version appears to deny protection to quite different categories of expression. Spreading falsehood, the encouragement of abomination, or the forsaking of the Islamic community are vague, value-laden terms that have no settled meanings as they apply to limiting human rights. It is conceivable that any speech that might challenge or threaten to diminish loyalty to the local version of Islamic orthodoxy could be banned. The provision also seems to allow broad censorship in order to protect morality. Here, as in other instances, the open-ended nature of the qualifications has the potential to emasculate the very freedoms that the UIDHR makes a pretense of granting.

"Right to Freedom of Religion" is the (misleading) rubric for Article 13 of the UIDHR. This article states in the English version that everyone has the right to freedom of conscience and worship in accordance with his religious beliefs. The wording is different from the wording of comparable international human rights principles, but the difference is a relatively subtle one.[30]

The significance of the difference between Article 13 and the relevant international standards is more readily ascertained if one consults the Arabic version, which states that everyone has freedom of belief and freedom of worship according to the principle, "you have your religion, I have mine." This line is taken from the Qur'anic sura "*al-kafirun*," 109:6. *Al-kafirun* can mean "unbelievers," "infidels," or "atheists"; in any case, it has strong negative connotations. The complete sura runs as follows, in Marmaduke Pickthall's flowery translation: "Say: O disbelievers [*al-kafirun*] I worship not that which ye worship; Nor worship ye that which I worship. And I shall not worship that which ye worship. Nor will ye worship that which I worship. Unto you your religion, and unto me my religion."[31] The sura contemplates a division between Islam and "unbelief." It lays the groundwork for coexistence but does not attempt to establish any principle of freedom of religion comparable to that found in international human rights documents. If there is a right implied in this provision, it is the right to follow one's own religion, which in a *shari'a*-based system would be a right accorded only to Muslims and, within limits, to the *ahl al-kitab*. As a consequence of being obliged to follow their own religion, Muslims would be bound by *shari'a* rules, meaning that they would not be allowed to convert from Islam.

The Arabic version of Section 7 of the Preamble of the UIDHR displays the religious bias underlying this document. The English version of this section seems neutral and innocuous, calling for a society in which "all worldly power shall be considered as a sacred trust, to be exercised within the limits prescribed by the Law and in a manner approved by it, and with due regard for the priorities fixed by it." In sharp contrast, the same section in the Arabic version is an expression of a commitment to a society where all people believe that Allah alone is the master of all creation. This is tantamount to a commitment to converting the world's population to Islam, a commitment that is not compatible with the attitudes that shaped the international human rights norms regarding freedom of religion but that fits well in a scheme where conversions from Islam are barred.

The al-Azhar Draft Constitution

The al-Azhar draft of an Islamic constitution states in the English version of Article 29 that "within the limits of the Islamic *shari'a*, the Government provides for the natural basic rights of religious and intellectual beliefs." In this obscure formulation, there is no mention of any freedom of religion. Given this omission, the article could provide the same kind of "right" to follow one's own religion—without granting any right for Muslims to change religion—that was set forth in Article 13 of the UIDHR. In contrast, the same article of the al-Azhar draft constitution expressly mentions "freedoms" of labor and expression and personal "freedom." The omission of the "freedom" (*hurriya*) of religion is unlikely to be accidental, particularly given the fact that "the natural basic rights" set forth in the article are offered only "within the limits of the Islamic *shari'a*." Any doubts about whether the application of these limits is intended to restrict the freedom of religion in accordance with premodern *shari'a* rules are removed by Article 71 of the draft constitution, which provides for the application of the death penalty for apostasy. Because the *shari'a* sets the governing standards, this penalty can only apply to apostasy from Islam.

The relative candor of the al-Azhar draft with respect to the death penalty for apostasy from Islam is in striking contrast to the evasiveness one normally encounters in Islamic human rights schemes. The willingness of al-Azhar to call openly for the execution of persons who abandon Islam is probably the result of several factors. Al-Azhar University is the most prestigious center for training in Sunni Islam, where emphasis is placed on the study of premodern jurisprudence, not international human rights law. Furthermore, it is located in Cairo, where the question of whether to execute apostates has been a hotly contested issue for decades. Given the intensity of the controversies, it would have been difficult for an institution such as al-Azhar to sidestep the issue of punishment for apostasy. Furthermore, the draft was merely a proposal for what Azharites would ideally like to see incorporated in a constitution. Because their exercise was an academic one, the authors were not forced to accede to political compromises with disaffected Egyptian Copts, nor did the drafters have to accommodate those politicians and jurists who were abreast of modern trends in constitutionalism and would consider putting the death penalty for apostasy in the constitution inappropriate.

The Iranian Constitution

The 1979 Iranian constitution does not address the issue of religious freedom as such. It is significant that a constitution that in many respects copies the French model should have eliminated any protection for religious freedom from its list of rights. True, Article 23 does forbid interrogating or attacking people because of their beliefs, a provision that might be interpreted as meaning that religious persecutions should be outlawed. Whatever the original intent or hopes of the drafters of this article may have been, in practice it has not inhibited the Iranian government from violating related rights. The conduct of the Iranian government serves as a gloss on the meaning of the protections afforded by Article 23. The extensive persecutions of Iran's Baha'is unequivocally establish that the Iranian government does not believe that Article 23 prevents interrogating or attacking members of disfavored religious minorities because of their religious beliefs.[32] Baha'is have been put under enormous pressure to recant their beliefs and return to Islam. It is well established that Baha'is are persecuted on the basis of their religious beliefs because trumped-up criminal charges leveled against them have been dropped when Baha'is have repented and proclaimed their adherence to Islam.[33] Being deemed apostates, Baha'is are treated as persons who have incurred civil death, and all Baha'i marriages have been declared invalid; sexual intercourse between the former spouses has been treated as fornication (punishable by death); and the children of the dissolved marriages have been declared illegitimate, thereby depriving their parents of any claim to them.[34]

Despite the extensive evidence that the persecution of the Baha'is is religiously motivated, in communications designed for international audiences, the Iranian government has gone to great lengths to justify executions of Baha'is on the grounds that those executed had committed crimes such as treason. Executed Baha'is are routinely alleged to be guilty of spying for Israel or the CIA. Reclassifying Baha'is as "traitors," "spies," and "conspirators" enables Iran to pretend that its criminal justice system follows a more conventional model than it actually does. In international forums, the regime insists that Iran does not persecute Baha'is for religious reasons.[35] Iran has stressed that apostasy is not listed as a crime in its codified laws, which is true, and in 1995 it falsely assured a UN rapporteur that "conversion was not a crime and no one had been punished for converting."[36] Thus, not only do Iran's ruling theocrats avoid stipulating in law that apostates are to be executed, but they also lie about their practice of killing Baha'is as apostates.

In trying to convince international audiences that the prosecution of Baha'is is political rather than religious, the Iranian government has pretended that a distinction is made in Iran between political and religious crimes. This is a distinction that by the terms of Article 168 of the Iranian constitution cannot, in fact, exist. The second sentence in Article 168 reads: "The definition of a political crime, the manner in which the jury will be selected, their qualifications and the limits of their authority shall be determined by law, based upon Islamic principles [*mavazin-e eslami*]."[37] One sees in this article that it is not the secular law that defines political crimes but law based on Islamic principles. As befits a theocracy following a religious ideology, religious categories and rules determine the definitions of political crimes; thus, political crimes are ultimately also religious crimes.

The lack of candor on the part of the Iranian government about the religious nature of its prosecutions of Baha'is correlates with the patterns of ambivalence and evasiveness that one sees in Islamic human rights schemes generally. Given the fact that the Iranian constitution stipulates that Islamic principles are the supreme law of the land, one might have expected that Iran would publicly defend its policy of killing apostates and that the government would confidently cite *shari'a* rules in response to any criticisms of its actions. After all, in the al-Azhar draft constitution, one reads a forthright endorsement of the rule that apostates are to be killed. But in actuality the Iranian government realizes that its persecutions and executions of Baha'is are egregious violations of international human rights law, and it lacks faith that appeals to Islamic law can suffice to justify these. Iran's dissimulations reveal that it implicitly recognizes the authoritative, universal character of international human rights law.

One notes the irony of Iran's theocratic government whose supreme head is an Islamic jurist trying to disguise its religious persecutions as secular political cases, whereas in the far more secular political order in Pakistan, laws expressly target the Ahmadi religious minority for criminal prosecution. Pakistani officials are trying to convince their domestic constituency, which includes Islamists, that they are committed to defending Islam, whereas Iran's theocratic rulers are trying to deflect charges by international entities that their Islamic system is backward and primitive. Obviously, strategic calculations tied to the interests of governmental elites play a major role in shaping how different regimes decide whether to assert openly that Islamic law requires the prosecution of people for religious crimes.

Iran's ruling clerics also wield "apostasy" as a strategic tool to stifle dissent within the clerical establishment. One example could be seen in August 2000, when Iran's hard-liners decided to prosecute a liberal, pro-reform cleric, Hojjatoleslam Hassan Youssefi Eshkevari.[38] He faced a variety of charges, which included apostasy and propaganda against the regime.[39] Hard-liners were motivated to punish Eshkevari for his vigorous advocacy of the principle that Islam is compatible with democracy—thereby challenging absolute clerical authority. Eshkevari was prosecuted in closed proceedings by the special court established after the revolution for the specific purpose of trying clerics—and stifling clerical dissent. Although he was convicted and sentenced to death, the death sentence was revoked on appeal, and he was sent to prison instead—another sign of the regime's nervousness about being seen to execute people for their beliefs.

Even high-ranking officials did not enjoy impunity from accusations of religious deviance. In spring 2011, as political tensions mounted between circles around Ayatollah Khamene'i and President Ahmadinejad, accusations flowed from Khamene'i's camp that close associates of Ahmadinejad were engaged in sorcery. Moreover, Ayatollah Mesbah-Yazdi, a close ally of Ayatollah Khamene'i, issued a warning that seemed aimed at Ahmadinejad, admonishing that disobeying the supreme jurist was equivalent to "apostasy from God."[40] This implied that Iran's supreme jurist was a kind of divinity, tantamount to God.

Sudan Under Islamization

Except for brief democratic interludes in Sudan, it has been the site of atrocious violations of human rights under particularly savage dictatorships since the 1980s. It should be borne in mind that human rights violations tied to the application of Islamic law are merely one facet of a broader pattern of egregious rights abuses, which have included genocide and mass rapes.

In 1985, Mahmud Muhammad Taha, the leader of the Sudanese Republican movement, was executed as a heretic and apostate from Islam. Too little attention was originally paid to the Taha case, an apostasy case that presaged others as Islamization increased the pressures for ideological conformity.

Taha had led a liberal school of thought in Sudan known variously as the Republicans or the Republican Brothers. The Republicans viewed Islam as establishing an egalitarian order compatible with human rights, holding that Islam, correctly interpreted, supported complete equality between men and women and Muslims and non-Muslims.[41] Taha offered a controversial interpretation of the history and aims of the Revelation of the Qur'anic verses, according to which much of what had come to be regarded as timeless *shari'a* law was actually legislation that had been intended only to guide the early Muslim community in Medina. Taha's liberal, reformist views were anathema to many Muslim conservatives—so much so that, in 1976, al-Azhar officially declared him to be an apostate.[42] In Sudan his views were also attacked by the Ikhwan, a locally powerful Islamist movement, one faction of which closely collaborated with the military dictatorships of Nimeiri and al-Bashir.

The Republicans criticized the human rights violations that were propagated as a result of Nimeiri's Islamization campaign of 1983–1985 and brought several unsuccessful suits claiming that the imposition of the premodern *shari'a* rules violated the constitution by discriminating against non-Muslims and women.[43] Taha was arrested along with a group of his followers and tried in January 1985. Declarations by al-Azhar and the Muslim World League to the effect that Taha was an apostate were cited in the ruling, which relied on such secondhand evidence in proceedings lacking any semblance of due process.[44] There was not even a Sudanese law in force in 1985 establishing that apostasy from Islam constituted a crime. Nimeiri maintained that Taha was being executed for his "slander of God and his insolence towards Him [God]."[45] In reality, of course, Nimeiri wanted him killed for criticizing the human rights abuses caused by Nimeiri's Islamization campaign.

Taha was publicly hanged on January 18, 1985, in a prison courtyard in Khartoum. According to reports, he conducted himself in his last moments with the utmost dignity and calm while surrounded by a taunting mob of members of the Ikhwan and other supporters of Nimeiri, who hailed his execution as a great victory for Islam. The regime calculated that Taha's execution would bring it credit, but this calculation turned out to be a serious error in terms of the reaction of the average Sudanese. The revulsion over the execution of the peaceable, elderly religious leader provided a strong impetus for mobilizing the popular coalition against Nimeiri, which succeeded in toppling him on April 6, 1985. Killing Taha as a heretic converted him into a martyr for the cause of freedom. Arab human rights activists selected the anniversary of Taha's execution as the day on which Arab Human Rights Day is to be annually commemorated—a sign that in his opposition to human rights violations perpetrated in the name of Islam, Taha did not stand alone.

Mawdudi and Pakistani Law Affecting Religious Freedom

Knowing that his position is in conflict with human rights, Abu'l A'la Mawdudi avoids mentioning in his human rights pamphlet that he supports killing those who converted from Islam, but his support for executing apostates is on the record elsewhere.[46] In addition, the anti-Ahmadi campaign that he and his followers waged showed his disdain for freedom of religion. The Pakistani Ordinance XX, discussed in Chapter 7, which provided a legal warrant for persecuting Ahmadis, can be seen as the culmination of his campaign.

There are various permutations of crimes related to apostasy from Islam.[47] In Pakistan, the risk of prosecution for "blasphemy" has turned out to be the major threat. Under President Zia ul-Haq, the existing blasphemy laws, which had originally been implanted during British rule, were modified several times to expand the grounds for prosecution and to increase the severity of the penalties so as to include the death penalty. Because the courts have not curbed the arbitrariness of blasphemy prosecutions, Muslims who write or say anything on religious topics that causes offense to other Muslims' religious sentiments can potentially be charged with and convicted of blasphemy. Moreover, the record shows that the blasphemy laws have been exploited to initiate prosecutions that are politically motivated or the result of personal grudges and that courts are disposed to find defendants guilty even where the evidence is disputed and flimsy. The consequences for Ahmadis and Christians, who have been disproportionately targeted, have been particularly harsh, meaning that the laws not only set back religious freedom but also exacerbate the sufferings of Pakistan's beleaguered religious minorities.[48] The death penalty for blasphemy has not so far actually been carried out, but a mere accusation of blasphemy has often sufficed as a pretext for zealots bent on carrying out vigilante justice to murder the accused.

The sharp deterioration in the rule of law in Pakistan and the aggravation of intercommunal tensions was illustrated by the case of Asia Bibi, an illiterate Christian peasant in a Punjab village. A dispute erupted between her and Muslim women at a well, leading to charges that she had defamed the Prophet Muhammad, charges that she consistently denied. In November 2010, she was condemned to death for blasphemy, an outcome that was widely denounced as unjust. The governor of Punjab, Salman Taseer, a prominent liberal politician, espoused her cause and denounced the blasphemy laws, only to be assassinated in January 2011 by one of his bodyguards, who had been outraged by the governor's support for this Christian defendant and by his criticisms of the blasphemy laws. The assassin was acclaimed as a hero by many, with more secular Pakistanis being deeply shocked and grieved by the assassination.[49] Shortly thereafter, in March 2011, Minority Affairs Minister Shahbaz Bhatti, the only Christian in the cabinet, was assassinated for criticizing the blasphemy laws and championing the rights of Pakistan's religious minorities.[50] The fact that the much-criticized blasphemy laws, which have been so blatantly abused to serve personal and political agendas and to persecute minorities, remain on the books is a reminder of how difficult it is to cancel Islamization measures.

Pakistan has been lurching from crisis to crisis for many years, and in this context, burgeoning sectarian extremism and religiously motivated violence adds to the country's miseries. Inept and corrupt governments have failed to take adequate measures either to protect members of the Sunni majority from religiously based criminality or to shield religious minorities from abusive treatment and terrorism. As might be expected, religious freedom has withered in these circumstances.

The Cairo Declaration and the Saudi Basic Law

Not surprisingly, neither the Cairo Declaration nor the Saudi Basic Law offers any guarantee of freedom of religion, and both documents declare that the state should propagate Islam. Article 10 of the Cairo Declaration provides that Islam is "the religion of unspoiled nature," prohibiting any form of compulsion or exploitation of a person's poverty or ignorance in order to convert him to another religion or to atheism. Given the biases in the declaration, one assumes that all conversions from Islam would be deemed to have resulted from "compulsion" or "exploitation," whereas presumably any technique that was applied to convert people *to* Islam would be acceptable.

Article 23 of the Saudi Basic Law calls on the state to propagate the faith, which in context means Wahhabism, the puritanical strain of Sunni Islam endorsed by the Saudi monarchy. As in other Muslim countries where there is no protection for freedom of religion and where the state endorses one version of Islamic orthodoxy, both non-Muslims and Muslim minorities were exposed to religious persecution in Saudi Arabia.[51] A further complication lies in the fact that in Saudi Arabia, personal vendettas may play a role in who is charged with religious offenses. As a sign of how far Saudi justice deviates from upholding religious freedom, prosecutions for witchcraft and sorcery, crimes for which the death penalty may be applied, have increased.[52]

The Afghan and Iraqi Constitutions

Although it was prepared under US supervision, the 2003 Afghan constitution did not deal squarely with freedom of religion. Article 2 establishes Islam as the state religion, while providing that followers of other religions are free to exercise their faith and to perform their religious rites within the limits of the provisions of law. This offers some protection for freedom of worship for non-Muslims but falls short of guaranteeing freedom of religion.

In an ominous development, a prosecution for apostasy soon surfaced. In October 2005, Ali Mohaqiq Nasab, a liberal Afghan from the Hazara minority who edited a women's rights magazine, was convicted of "disrespecting Islamic law," after the prosecutor charged that he had committed apostasy. As often happens, the apostasy prosecution was not based on the accused having intentionally abjured Islam. Nasab's crime had been publishing articles supporting Islamic feminist ideas and opposing the notion that Islam treated apostasy as a crime.[53]

On these grounds, outraged conservatives called for him to be executed as an apostate. Probably because of Western diplomatic intervention, Nasab was released from prison in December 2005 after agreeing to apologize publicly for his controversial writings.[54]

As a result of US pressure, Article 2 of the 2005 Iraqi constitution offered a guarantee of "the full religious rights of all individuals to freedom of religious belief and practice," which was in addition to provisions on freedom of worship in Article 41. Article 35 afforded a guarantee of protection from "religious coercion." Nonetheless, given that Article 2 also barred laws violating established Islamic rules and made Islam a main source of legislation, the stage was set for religious freedoms being limited by recourse to Islamic criteria.

Because US officials pressed the drafters of the Iraqi constitution to roll back proposed Islamic provisions and to buttress religious freedom, religious freedom has become associated with the US political agenda. The stage was thereby set for a potential nationalist backlash in favor of upholding Islamic criteria at the expense of religious freedom, creating a worrisome situation for any Iraqis not supporting the Shiʻi factions that gained power after the December 2005 elections.

US Interventions in the Domain of Religious Freedom

The USCIRF, mentioned in Chapters 4 and 7, is ostensibly concerned with religious freedom around the world, but certain features suggest a central preoccupation with religious freedom in Muslim countries. For example, a particularly detailed report on the treatment of religious freedom in the constitutions of Muslim countries has been compiled and made available in both English and Arabic.[55] Not surprisingly, Muslim countries figure prominently in the annual lists of "Countries of Particular Concern," or CPCs, the classification of countries where the governments are deemed to engage in or tolerate particularly severe violations of religious freedom and countries with bad records that warrant close monitoring.[56]

In theory, the commission's activities promote respect for rights as set forth in the UDHR and ICCPR, but in fact, it reflects a US policy of privileging religious freedom over other human rights, a distortion of the international human rights system.[57] The unilateral US initiative to expand religious freedom in the Middle East coincides with a period of heightened anger over US intervention in the region and over the ongoing US failure to address grievances linked to Palestinians' thwarted demands for self-determination, that being a cause particularly dear to the people of the Middle East.[58]

In these circumstances, US initiatives that are intended to advance the cause of religious freedom in the Middle East could play into the hands of those portraying this human rights agenda as a weapon of Western imperialism. The more that demands for respect for religious freedom and protection for minority religions are identified with US strategies, the easier it becomes to discredit US proposals as ones aiming to undermine the solidarity of Muslim societies and the sovereignty of Middle Eastern states.

Expanding the Reach of Laws Criminalizing Insults to Islam: From the Rushdie Affair to the Danish Cartoons Controversy

Today, there is a sharp divide separating the strict regimes of censorship that stifle discussion of sensitive religious topics in the Middle East and the far more open climate that accommodates freedom of expression in the West. Prior to globalization, this situation would not have created acute tensions and conflicts, but today it does. Not content to suppress religious freedom by harsh censorship on their own territories, Middle Eastern governments in conjunction with the OIC have been working at the UN to get international law to incorporate the duty to exert the kind of religious censorship that they engage in. This involves adopting a new rule establishing a duty to combat what they call "defamation of Islam," a rule that will be inimical both to freedom of expression and to religious freedom. This concerted campaign targets the West with a view to pressuring Western states to criminalize and punish defamation of Islam. Middle Eastern states see this as a means to stifle inconvenient discussions of their own repressive religious policies, to place the West on the defensive when it fails to censor publications offensive to Islam, and to curry favor with Muslim opinion, which is sensitive to any Western slights directed at Islam.

Middle Eastern regimes are frustrated when discussions of what they consider subversive ideas and embarrassing topics move offshore to the West, which has become a haven for airing views on controversial topics involving Islam and politics. Liberated from the harsh regimes of censorship that constrain expression in the Middle East, Muslims who have moved to the West have engaged in innovative critiques of stale Islamic orthodoxies and have also challenged the Islamic rationales that governments wield to justify their human rights abuses. Accustomed to enforcing conformity and using Islam as a cloak for their repressive policies, Middle Eastern governments bridle at such challenges.

In addition to critical discussions of Islam and politics carried out in the West by serious thinkers seeking to explore and illuminate issues that are ruled off-limits in the Middle East, there has been a big accumulation of crude Islamophobic books, tracts, films, websites, and programs. These have proliferated in the West as Islamophobic trends have gained momentum. Lethal terrorist attacks that were carried out by Muslim extremists in London, Madrid, and New York have provided fodder for hate-mongers eager to identify Islam with terrorist violence, backwardness, and security threats to the West. The burgeoning Islamophobic literature has naturally caused grave offense to Muslims generally, including to the large Muslim minorities now living in the West, a situation that Middle Eastern regimes have sought to exploit to their advantage. When they campaign for establishing a duty to combat defamation of Islam, they seek to associate their campaign with concerns for the harms that Islamophobic speech can cause to Muslims in the West, even though their resolutions are not narrowly tailored to address such concerns, being designed to have a far more sweeping reach.

Today, because the world is being knitted ever more closely together and the media can quickly convey stories around the globe, Muslims living in the Middle East may feel that discussions of Islam in the West are practically taking place on their own doorsteps and become shocked when hearing about insults to Islam and the Prophet that take place in distant countries. Thus, for example, after the 2005 publication of the Danish cartoons, an incident discussed below, violent protests erupted in places as remote as Afghanistan, Indonesia, Iran, Somalia, and Syria.[59] Such protests are deliberately stirred up by the machinations of demagogues and agents of Middle Eastern regimes who see political benefits in directing popular ire at the West. Unpopular regimes can hope to harvest a windfall of approval among their restive citizenries if they pose as defenders of Islam and the Prophet in denouncing aspersions that are being cast on Islamic sanctities in the West, identifying themselves with a cause that has popular support.

On the question of what is often called hate speech, US and European standards diverge. Regardless of the quality of the expressive activity involved, it is usually difficult to find legal grounds for censorship in the United States, where First Amendment protections for freedom of expression are strong. The prevailing US view has been that in order to allow valuable ideas to come to the fore, there must be an openness to a wide range of expressive activities, including ones that reflect deeply bigoted and hate-filled attitudes. In contrast, law in Europe has tended to take the position that certain speech falling in the category that is often called hate speech should be barred.[60] This stance roughly correlates with the principle in ICCPR Article 20/2, which stipulates: "Any advocacy of national, racial or religious hatred that constitutes incitement to discrimination, hostility or violence shall be prohibited by law." In the eyes of many Muslims, the pattern of punishing hate speech in Europe has been selective, one where the significance of Muslims' concerns is downgraded while anti-Semitic speech incurs tough sanctions.

As will be discussed, the OIC has been seeking to expand the concept of religious hatred beyond the parameters set in ICCPR Article 20/2 so that expression that insults religions and prophets will be prohibited. The OIC has demanded that international law be altered to incorporate this principle and to establish a universally binding rule that all states must criminalize and punish expression that in UN discussions it calls "defamation of religions" but where the actual concern is "defamation of Islam," a term that the OIC also employs. In mobilizing support for rewriting international law, since 1999 the OIC has promoted measures in the UN that are designed to present the duty to criminalize defamation of Islam as a valid and necessary principle for securing respect for the human rights already enshrined in the UN system. This OIC campaign has been consistently focused on the West. By making it clear that the intent is to target the West for its failure to clamp down on defamation of Islam, the OIC has been able to win the support of countries such as China and Russia, which have records of severely mistreating their Muslim minorities but which feel confident that the OIC will not be attacking them.

To understand the current campaign to have international law incorporate a rule requiring criminalizing defamation of Islam, it is helpful to review some history, which shows that it is an extension of positions taken by Iran and the OIC in the famous Rushdie affair, which erupted after the British novelist Salman Rushdie published *The Satanic Verses*.[61] The controversy mushroomed due to Ayatollah Khomeini's wish to buttress his faltering prestige as the leader of militant Islam. In 1989, he had reason to worry that his stature had been tarnished by his acceptance of a UN plan to end the Iran-Iraq War, a war that he had earlier sworn to pursue until a final victory was achieved. He could observe how agitators were able to incite mobs to riot in many Muslim countries by making inflammatory assertions, such as proclaiming that Rushdie was directing insults at the Prophet Muhammad and that Rushdie was denying the divine inspiration of the Qur'an. The responses included bans on the book in Bangladesh, India, Pakistan, and South Africa. The Grand Sheikh of al-Azhar called for banning the novel in Egypt. In this he espied an opportunity. Khomeini adopted a tactic often employed by politicians in the Middle East, seeking to buttress his legitimacy by positioning himself as the defender of Islamic sanctities. On February 14, 1989, he issued a death edict that stated: "I inform the proud Muslim people of the world that the author of 'The Satanic Verses,' a book which is against Islam, the prophet and the Koran, and all those involved in its publication who were aware of its content, are hereby sentenced to death."[62]

Khomeini's death edict reflected the strain of opportunism that lurks behind many of the demands for censorship in the name of protecting Islam. What occasions regimes select for making calls for punishing speech that allegedly offends Islam has a great deal to do with their calculations of their political interests rather than reflecting well-grounded tenets of Islamic law. Like so many others who called for killing Rushdie, Khomeini left unexplained the central question of precisely what Rushdie's crime had been. There was not even the most cursory attempt to justify the edict in terms of applicable standards of Islamic law. In Khomeini's edict, Rushdie and others involved in publishing *The Satanic Verses* were simply classified as being "against Islam" and on this slim basis were ordered to be killed.

One was left to wonder on what basis Khomeini had concluded that a capital crime had been committed by Rushdie in his complex novel. A main thread in the novel is a fictional account of the misadventures of two maladjusted Indian expatriates living in Great Britain who miraculously survive after their hijacked airplane explodes twenty-nine thousand feet in the sky and they fall down to earth. One of these, Gibreel Farishta, confused and delusional, imagines that he is the archangel Gabriel, who in Islamic belief transmitted the Qur'an to the Prophet Muhammad. Gibreel has dreams in which various Islamic themes surface and figures appear, such as one who is called "Mahound" and who seems loosely modeled on the Prophet. In the course of receiving revelations, this fictional prophet confronts certain verses that may not have been of divine origin.

Early accounts of Islamic history mention a related episode in the life of the Prophet Muhammad, who belatedly realized that some verses that had come to him were not divine revelation but "Satanic verses" and therefore needed to be rejected. That is, to the extent this fictional account could indirectly suggest that there had been doubts about whether every line received by the Prophet was of divine origin, Rushdie was merely touching on an issue that early historians of Islam had already confronted. In any case, because the relevant passages purport to describe the dreams of a delusional individual, any echoes of episodes in early Islamic history are hardly designed to be taken as offering truth claims about Islam.

One observed that Khomeini did not hesitate to issue a death edict in direct contravention of articles in Iran's own constitution, which is supposedly based on Islamic principles. It includes in Article 36 the requirement that criminal punishment must only be by the decision of a competent court and by virtue of the law, and in Article 37 the provision that innocence is basic and that no one can be considered guilty except after guilt has been established by a competent court.

Significantly, in issuing his edict, Khomeini acted as if Islamic criminal law—or, more accurately, what amounted to his own subjective version of Islamic law—had extraterritorial reach and could define criminality in the West, prefiguring the OIC's subsequent attempts to make international law incorporate Islamic criteria for censorship. No rationale was offered to explain how any conduct in Britain could be deemed to fall under the jurisdiction of an Islamic cleric in Iran or why Rushdie, who had not maintained any affiliation with Islam even though he was of Muslim ancestry, was obligated to follow Islamic law. Khomeini also ignored sectarian barriers; he did not limit the edict to his fellow Shi'is, acting as if a cleric of the minority Shi'i sect had the authority to speak for the world's Muslims. Although many zealots applauded the death edict, few personages with any claim to eminence in Islamic scholarship approved Khomeini's edict, realizing that it strayed far from the rules of Islamic law. Muslims' responses to Khomeini's death edict, which ranged from enthusiastic plaudits to outspoken condemnations, proved that they were deeply divided on whether Islamic law supported this death edict.[63] Despite the grave risks, courageous Muslims publicly protested the calls for killing Rushdie.[64]

Retreating for many years into a cocoon of elaborate security, Rushdie was able to escape assassination, but a translator of his novel was killed in Japan and another was wounded in Italy. A Norwegian publisher of his novel barely survived an assassination attempt. Many bookstores in the West were too frightened of terrorist attacks to stock the novel.

Iran unsuccessfully sought to obtain the OIC's formal endorsement of Khomeini's death edict. Although the OIC was not prepared to go on the record as calling for assassins to hunt down Rushdie and those involved in publishing his novel, a March 1989 meeting of OIC foreign ministers that was convened in Riyadh issued a statement declaring that Rushdie was an apostate and urged that *The Satanic Verses* be withdrawn.[65] That is, as early as 1989, the OIC deemed itself entitled to call on Western countries to take measures to censor literature published in the West that it deemed offensive. It also showed that the OIC assumed that unarticulated "Islamic" principles could be invoked by Muslim governments to accuse a Western writer of a capital crime. Like Ayatollah Khomeini, the OIC did not bother to present any evidence or any reasoned arguments to support its contention that Rushdie had committed apostasy. Instead, the OIC acted as if whether a British citizen of Indian Muslim ancestry had in fact abjured Islam could be confidently determined in his absence by a group of foreign ministers from Muslim countries meeting in Saudi Arabia. Thus, the OIC proceeded to make this momentous determination without offering Rushdie even a minimal opportunity to defend himself. In so doing, the OIC was conducting itself in the same manner as many of its member states did, when they regularly acted as if they were entitled to castigate and punish Muslims who did not meekly toe their ideological lines as "apostates," "heretics," or "blasphemers."

Although OIC members apparently realized that it was not prudent to go on the record as specifically endorsing Khomeini's death edict, the OIC did not condemn it, nor did it challenge the basic premise of the death edict, that a Middle Eastern government claiming to be defending Islam should have a free hand to order the killings of people in the West. Moreover, by issuing a public statement declaring that Rushdie was guilty of apostasy, the OIC indicated its lack of concern for how its statement could be used by zealots bent on carrying out vigilante justice who could cite the OIC's statement as a warrant for murdering Rushdie.

The OIC's conviction that it was entitled to pronounce Rushdie guilty of apostasy offered a clear indication that for the OIC, questions of momentous importance relating to freedom of religion could be decided with reference to crude political calculations. It illustrated that the OIC felt entitled to charge people in the West with crimes against Islam without any concern for basic principles of the rule of law. In its actions in the Rushdie affair, it also showed utter disregard for the Western tradition of freedom of expression. Article 22 of the Cairo Declaration, already discussed in Chapter 4, retroactively provided cover for the Rushdie death edict, prohibiting in 22/c the violation of sanctities and the dignity of Prophets.

Significantly, Iran's clerical leadership seemed subsequently to back away from saying that Rushdie should be assassinated on the basis that his novel was "against Islam." Efforts were made to portray Rushdie, in actuality a leftist supporter of Third World causes, as an antirevolutionary agent of the forces of capitalism and Zionism, serving both the CIA and its Israeli counterpart, the Mossad, and as a participant in a British imperialist plot to destroy Islam. That is, as time went on, instead of delineating exactly what in the novel constituted a capital crime against Islam, the Iranian regime decided to characterize Rushdie's offense as a political one, speaking as if he had been caught conspiring with governments hostile to the interests of Muslim countries. The change suggested that the regime had belatedly realized that it was hard to identify principles of Islamic law that proved that the novel had warranted the death edict.

Khomeini's bold flouting of international law in issuing the Rushdie death edict was an exception to the more typical Iranian insistence that all accusations that Iran grossly violated the principle of freedom of religion were baseless.[66] After Khomeini's death in 1989, it appeared that some in Iran's officialdom were open to rescinding the Rushdie death edict, and Iranian factions have subsequently quarreled over whether Iran remained religiously bound to carry out Khomeini's order.[67] In an apparent effort to disassociate the Iranian regime from the practice of killing people on religious grounds, Iranian officials argued that it is essential to differentiate between the responsibilities of the Iranian government and a religious ruling[68]—a claim that is particularly strange coming from a government committed to the indivisibility of religion and state.

Iran subsequently tried to turn the tables on its critics, arguing that Rushdie was an offender under international law and that European countries were violating international law in praising and welcoming Rushdie.[69] These claims that international law required Europe to adhere to Iran's stance that Rushdie had engaged in criminal conduct foreshadowed the theory behind the subsequent defamation of religions resolutions.

In the years since the Rushdie affair, the OIC has honed its diplomatic skills and has radically changed the way that it represents its human rights positions, making strained attempts to convince the international community that it does respect freedom of religion and freedom of expression. Nonetheless, careful examination of its UN resolutions on the duty to combat defamation of religions reveal that these continue to embody the same mentality that the OIC exhibited in the Rushdie affair, an attitude that human rights should be sacrificed where preserving Islamic sanctities is concerned. This is consistent with the basic premise of Islamic human rights schemes, that Islam must be treated as the overriding concern.

Since 1999, the OIC has repeatedly sponsored resolutions on combating defamation of religions in the UN Human Rights Council and General Assembly and has tried to convince the international community to accept the idea that all governments are bound to punish such defamation.[70] Seeking to win international backing, the OIC has had to adjust to speaking of defamation of "religions," but it is obvious that its concern is shielding Islam from insults. This is indicated by the references to Islam in the resolutions; the OIC's repeated complaints about Islamophobia and the plight of Muslim minorities in the West that have been made in conjunction with these resolutions; and in the OIC's revised 2008 charter, which proclaims in Article 1(12) that it aims to "protect and defend the true image of Islam, to combat defamation of Islam."

The fact that in votes in the General Assembly and the Human Rights Council these resolutions have repeatedly won majority support is emboldening the OIC to claim that its position has now become part of international law. A sample Human Rights Council resolution from 2009 is reproduced in Appendix C. A review of it and others in the series reveals that they are replete with references to international human rights instruments, resolutions, declarations, and reports. They also invoke principles like freedom of religion, freedom of expression, and protecting the rights of minorities, and they condemn phenomena like racism, racial discrimination, and discrimination based on religion or ethnicity. Such verbiage gives them the superficial appearance of belonging in the UN human rights system. On closer inspection, however, like Islamic human rights schemes, the resolutions on the duty to combat defamation of religions turn out to be designed to promote incongruous principles that will be nefarious for human rights, a fact that has led credible human rights NGOs and most democratic states to condemn them in the strongest terms.

The fact that the OIC now intends to try to work within the UN human rights system to achieve its objectives is shown in the OIC ten-year program of action announced in 2005, which in Article VII.3 records the OIC's plan to "endeavor to have the United Nations adopt an international resolution to counter Islamophobia, and call upon all States to enact laws to counter it."[71] A resolution from the 2007 OIC foreign ministers' conference makes clear that the OIC intends to insert its positions that defamation of religions must be criminalized into international law. Among other things, in section 6 one reads that it: "Calls upon the Human Rights Council to adopt a universal declaration to incriminate the defamation of religions and Expresses [*sic*] the need to effectively combat defamation of religions through the adoption of an international convention in this regard."[72] The resolution in paragraph 4 indicates that all states will be expected to criminalize "defamation of Islam," calling on them "to take appropriate measures, inter alia, by enacting necessary laws to render all acts whatsoever defaming Islam as 'offensive acts' and subject to punishment."[73]

Among the aspects of the resolutions on combating defamation of religions that have prompted sharp criticisms by human rights advocates is the fact that elevating defamation of religions to the status of a human rights violation injects an incongruous element in the UN human rights system. International human rights law, which aims to protect the rights of individuals and occasionally those of groups, has never had within its mandate protecting an institution such as a religion, and injecting a requirement to protect religion inevitably distorts it. On these grounds, objections were registered in 2008 to the resolutions on combating defamation of religion by two prominent human rights groups, ARTICLE 19 and the Cairo Institute for Human Rights Studies (CIHRS):

> A key problem with the resolutions is that they seek to protect not only individuals or communities which adhere to a given religion but also the religion itself, as such. . . . As the Special Rapporteurs on freedom of religion or belief (Asma Jahangir) and on contemporary forms of racism, racial discrimination, xenophobia and related intolerance (Doudou Diène) have noted: "The right to freedom of religion or belief protects primarily the individual and, to some extent, the collective rights of the community concerned but it does not protect religions or beliefs per se."[74]

Critics have also recognized that the OIC resolutions on combating defamation of religions potentially clash with guarantees of freedom of thought and conscience by adopting the stance that people must have a positive attitude toward religion. For example, in their 2008 statement, ARTICLE 19 and the CIHRS pointed out that:

> the resolutions suggest that the appropriate standard is respect for religions. Para. 10 of the most recent resolution, for example, claims that respect for religions is essential for the exercise of the right to freedom of religion. It is perfectly possible to disagree, even vehemently, with a particular religious tenet, while respecting the right of others to believe.[75]

In summing up their reasons for opposing the 2008 resolution, they concluded that it was "not in accordance with international human rights law on the right to freedom of expression and freedom of religion, will not be effective in promoting equality in practice and has not been carefully tailored so as to limit the possibility of abuse."[76]

One of the many features in this series of resolutions that is troubling to human rights advocates can be seen in paragraph 7 of the 2009 resolution, which expresses "deep concern . . . that Islam is frequently and wrongly associated with human rights violations." Because so many human right violations in the Middle East are carried out under the rubric of enforcing Islamic law, this provision would seem to justify labeling critiques of such human rights violations "defamatory" on the grounds that any association of Islam with human rights violations is necessarily false and insulting to Islam.

In 2007, the human rights NGO Women Living Under Muslim Laws (WLUML), which had long monitored human rights violations in the Middle East and was familiar with the patterns of stifling critical opinion and penalizing dissent on religious grounds, denounced the 2007 resolution on defamation of religions. It warned that the principle that there was a duty to criminalize such defamation could be used "to silence and intimidate human rights defenders, religious minorities and dissenters, and other independent voices. In effect this resolution has the potential to dramatically restrict the freedoms of expression, speech, religion and belief."[77]

One tactic that the OIC and its members have used to try to convince others that their resolutions do belong in the human rights system is to posit a causal relationship between defamation of Islam and harms to Muslim minorities who live in the West in an era when Islamophobia is widespread. Concern about the impact of Islamophobia is legitimate; Islamophobia and anti-Muslim bigotry in various Western countries have culminated in threats, violence, assaults, and even in killings.[78] Whether importing Pakistan-style blasphemy laws would remedy the problem was, however, highly dubious. Like other mainstream human rights NGOS, WLUML challenged the notion that censoring speech deemed offensive to Islam was the right tool for protecting minorities. Instead, it saw the potential for using such censorship to stifle a range of important freedoms:

> This Resolution will do nothing to counter the racism towards and singling out of Muslims. Those supporting this Resolution are using the very real discrimination faced by minorities due to their religious and ethnic identities to gravely jeopardize the rights of minority and majority communities alike to the freedoms of expression and belief or non-belief, the right to reinterpretation of religious texts and laws, and the freedom to express their sexuality, which they are entitled to under national and international laws, without fear of repression and punishment.[79]

In challenging the OIC position, the human rights NGO ARTICLE 19 and the CIHRS noted that the censorship presaged in the resolutions could actually be turned against minorities:

> Discrimination and hostility against adherents of minority religions by both State and non-State actors is an extremely serious problem, as recent reports by the Special Rapporteur on freedom of religion or belief have disclosed. . . . The resolutions do little to address this problem and, in particular, fail to address situations where different religions hold strong contrasting views on a particular matter. In such situations, the resolutions may be used to justify the stifling of religious dissent and the oppression of minority religions.[80]

They also cited the Special Rapporteur for freedom of religion, who had warned that "there are worrying trends towards applying [domestic blasphemy laws] in a discriminatory manner and they often disproportionately punish members of religious minorities, dissenting believers and non-theists or atheists."[81]

The OIC has felt compelled to answer critics who have charged that accepting the duty to combat defamation of religions would result in eroding the level of freedom of expression that is guaranteed in international human rights law. In response, the OIC has attempted to convey the impression that the resolutions do not aim to dismantle existing protections for freedom of expression. The OIC's efforts to persuade the world that it does respect the right to freedom of expression would be more convincing if OIC members did not routinely trample on that right and if the OIC's own Cairo Declaration were not so seriously deficient in affording adequate protections for that right.

The OIC's claims to be respectful of freedom of expression were often belied by its conduct. A dramatic example came in March 2008, when the OIC successfully campaigned to have the mandate of the UN Special Rapporteur on the promotion and protection of the right to freedom of opinion and expression changed. The Special Rapporteur after the change was charged with investigating abuses of the right of freedom of expression. In a world where the right to freedom of expression is imperiled in most places and is consistently denied in many, this expansion of the rapporteur's mandate was shocking. It meant that a crucial UN office would henceforth be operating on the assumption that the problems of abuses of the right to freedom of expression were as deserving of attention as the extensive violations of the right. Of course, having such tasks as part of its expanded mandate would mean that the office of the Special Rapporteur would have less time to investigate the kinds of draconian censorship imposed by OIC members. The media freedom group Reporters Without Borders (often called RSF) vigorously protested the changed mandate, saying: "It is not the rapporteur on free expression's job to do this. It is like asking the rapporteur on freedom of religion to investigate human rights abuses committed in the name of religion. Such reasoning is absurd."[82]

A speech exposing the attitudes of OIC officialdom was made by an adviser to the OIC secretary-general Saad Eddine Taib in December 2008 at an OIC forum in Geneva. He asserted that in Europe "Islamophobia has become an overwhelming wave of aversion and hatred targeting Muslims," complaining that the situation had worsened and that Muslims living in the West had become "victims of discriminating bigotry, harassment and mental and physical abuse."[83] Claiming to find this "a blatant affront to human rights," he decried the fact that "many circles in the West still cast doubt on the relationship between the concept of human rights and the notion of the defamation of religion." He scoffed at Western claims to be concerned with protecting freedom of expression and claimed that "the freedom of expression enjoyed by hate mongers inflicts a deep psychological damage to Muslims," lamenting that Islamophobia and hatred were seeking to destroy Islamic cultures and civilization. Muslims' dignity and human rights were thereby harmed, but, he complained, one still heard voices "claiming that defamation of religion or culture has nothing to do with human rights."[84]

The OIC excoriated the Danish cartoons as an example of the kind of Islamophobic publications in the West that, according to its claims, promote intolerance and lead to discrimination against Muslim minorities living there. Cartoon depictions of the Prophet Muhammad were published in September 2005 in *Jyllands-Posten*, a Danish-language newspaper with a circulation of only 200,000. The cartoons can be found on Internet sites, including the cartoon that caused the greatest offense, which was a drawing by Kurt Westergaard of the head of the Prophet with a bomb poking out of his black turban. The announced objective of the newspaper in publishing the cartoons was to assert the principle of freedom of speech in the face of mounting pressures for self-censorship that some argued had to be practiced in order to avoid offending Muslims. The paper indicated that it wanted to break with the political correctness that did not allow treating Muslims like any other religious group.[85] Of course, because there was a wave of strong anti-immigrant sentiment in Denmark that often involved hostility to Muslims, many saw the cartoons as being connected to these anti-Muslim prejudices. Although it was easy to understand why Muslims in Denmark would find the drawings offensive, it would have been a stretch to establish that the caricatures of the Prophet fell within the ICCPR Article 20/2 category of "advocacy of national, racial or religious hatred that constitutes incitement to discrimination, hostility or violence."

Some Muslims in Denmark launched a campaign to stir up international outrage over the cartoons, which entailed disseminating the very cartoons that they claimed should have been suppressed.[86] Delegations of Danish Muslims went to Egypt, Lebanon, and Syria with a view to mobilizing Muslim opinion against

Denmark.[87] They presented a dossier that included pictures that were far more inflammatory than the original set of cartoons—without indicating that they had added items to the set published by *Jyllands-Posten*.[88] Their conduct suggested that the set of cartoons that had actually been published in *Jyllands-Posten* were deemed insufficiently offensive for their purposes. For example, an image from a French pig-squealing contest was included as if it had figured among the cartoons, creating the false impression that the Prophet had been depicted as a pig.[89] Of course, this was sure to add fuel to the flames and incite more protests and rioting over the cartoons.

Many Muslims decry the Danish cartoons as epitomes of the insults that are hurled at their religion in the West. As in the Rushdie case, however, it needs to be borne in mind that the impact was enormously inflated as a result of deliberate attempts by agitators to aggravate tensions. Rushdie's challenging novel had been intended to be savored by London's literati, and Westergaard's cartoon was meant for Danish readers of a local newspaper. Neither would ever have attracted attention in Muslim countries or have ignited a global firestorm of Muslim indignation but for the machinations of ambitious provocateurs and leaders of Muslim countries who believed that they could harvest a political windfall by whipping up public outrage. In such circumstances, Europeans who want to portray Muslims and Islam as threats to national security and to the values of Western civilization wind up being pitted against Muslims who exploit the sensitivities of their coreligionists to perceived insults in efforts to incite outrage and inflame hostility toward the West. The cartoons controversy and the accompanying calls for boycotts and killings promoted polarization and aggravated the tensions between the Muslim minority community in Denmark and the majority non-Muslim population, while enhancing the influence of demagogues on both sides of the debates about multiculturalism and pluralism.

Among the states eager to profit from the controversy by leading protests against the cartoons was Egypt, which took steps in October 2005 to convert the incident into an international cause célèbre.[90] There were distinct parallels between how eager Egypt was in 2005 to present itself as being in the vanguard of Muslims' protests against the insults to the Prophet in the Danish cartoons and how eager it was in 2009 to present itself as standing up for Egypt's dignity after a particularly bitter, humiliating defeat of the Egyptian soccer team in a crucial contest with its Algerian rival.[91] In both instances, one saw an intensely hated dictatorial regime rushing to exploit rare opportunities to link its policies to causes that would have resonance among its alienated citizenry.

The OIC undertook to mobilize worldwide Muslim opinion against the cartoons.[92] Exhibiting the attitudes that are prevalent among OIC governments, in 2005, ten ambassadors of Muslim countries wrote to the Danish prime minister, calling on the Danish government "to take all those responsible to task" and advising him that the Danish press "should not be allowed to abuse Islam in the name of democracy, freedom of expression and human rights, the values that we share."[93] The ambassadors might elect to portray themselves as supporters of "democracy, freedom of expression and human rights," but the records of such countries as Iran, Libya, and Saudi Arabia, which were in the group sending the letter, were egregiously deficient in respect for such values.

Because the OIC member governments involved control and strictly censor all speech on their territories, the concept of a government feeling bound to respect the right of freedom of expression exercised by an independent press lay beyond their grasp. They assumed that the same type of draconian censorship that they exercised was—or at least should be—the norm everywhere. The inconsistencies in the stances of Muslim countries demanding that the Danish government take steps to punish those responsible for cartoons deemed offensive to Islam published in an independent newspaper and the claims by these same countries to be engaged in supporting human rights is not unusual. In their calls at the UN for censoring defamation of Islam, Muslim countries commonly insist that they are committed to freedom of expression and freedom of religion.

These demands for censorship and punishment for those behind the cartoons were rebuffed by the Danish government, which prompted objections in February 2006 by the OIC Secretary-General Ekmeleddin Ihsanoglu. He revealed the kind of tough governmental repression of independent media that the OIC envisaged as appropriate when he complained of European backing for Denmark's failure to prosecute *Jyllands-Posten* and protested the decision by the Danish court system to dismiss a defamation lawsuit brought by Muslims who tried to sue the paper:

> We expected from the European Governments . . . to take a political and ethical stand against uncivilized transgressions in the name of freedom of expression. To our dismay, what we found in return was an official common European position in support of the stance of the Danish government who refrained for a long time to take any political or ethical responsibility on the grounds that the laws of the country guarantee the freedom of the press and that there is no government authority or responsibility over this matter as it is completely up to the court to determine if what was published was within the boundaries of law or not. However, Danish public prosecutors, both at local and federal levels later ruled that the act was not illegal and the cases of the offended Muslim citizens of Denmark were either dismissed or filed away.[94]

The OIC raised its voice in the chorus of those lambasting Denmark, a country that has a particularly fine human rights record, claiming that the Danish government had violated international human rights law when it failed to carry out what the OIC claimed was a binding obligation to censor the cartoons and to punish those involved in their publication. In January 2006, the OIC espoused the cause of the Muslims condemning the Danish cartoons at the UN and asked the UN for a binding resolution "banning contempt for religious beliefs and providing for sanctions to be imposed on contravening countries or institutions."[95]

As Muslims called for killing the Danish cartoonists and as awards were promised in Pakistan and India for anyone who killed them, in February 2006, the OIC Secretary-General belatedly stepped in to try to calm things down. Ihsanoglu's comments included a statement that showed the superior public relations skills that the OIC had acquired since the Rushdie affair, when it had refused to condemn Khomeini's death edict. Realizing that it would be disadvantageous to be associated with assassinations, he said: "This is a very serious matter and nobody has the authority to issue a ruling to kill people." Ihsanoglu asserted that the calls for killings were un-Islamic, and even the Iranian Foreign Minister said that the situation should be calmed down.[96]

At the same time, Ihsanoglu rejected the view that the cartoons could be justified by the principle of freedom of expression, demanding that Europeans defer to Muslims' sensitivities. He added a warning that if Europeans failed to do so, it would mean "a problem of universality of European values."[97] By this he seemed to mean that Europe would be inappropriately asserting a cultural particularism that gave excessive weight to freedom of expression. As the OIC had been winning majority support in UN votes for its campaign to get the duty to combat defamation of religions accepted as a universally binding principle, it seemed that as of 2006, Ihsanoglu felt confident that he could speak as if the OIC position had been endorsed in international human rights law. On this basis, he deemed that he was entitled to accuse Europeans of accommodating insults to Islam by upholding a peculiarly broad concept of freedom of expression and thereby failing to respect international human rights law.

Reflecting the way that the OIC has moved away from asserting Islamic particularism, in a 2008 interview with *Jyllands-Posten*, Secretary-General Ihsanoglu presented the OIC as the proponent of human rights universality, speaking as if in asserting that all states were bound to combat defamation of religions, the OIC was aligned with the consensus of the international community and international legitimacy, referencing UN support for OIC resolutions:

It is not only OIC or OIC member states and myself who are expressing this understanding . . . the international community have given their frank endorsement to this opinion, through resolutions adopted by the United Nations General Assembly and the United Nations Human Rights Council, by large majority. This is tantamount to say [*sic*] that this opinion is the opinion of the international community and the international legitimacy.[98]

Meanwhile, the threat of terrorist attacks on publications in the West was having a chilling impact. In an act of self-censorship, Yale University Press eliminated the cartoons from Jytte Klausen's *The Cartoons That Shook the World*, a 2009 book about the Danish cartoons controversy. In 2010, the cartoonist Kurt Westergaard, who had been forced drastically to circumscribe his activity because of threats to his life, only narrowly escaped an assassination attempt by a Somali man with links to Islamist militants.[99] In another sign of the OIC's eagerness to avoid association with terrorist attacks, it promptly condemned the assassination attempt as being "totally against the teachings and values of Islam."[100] Again, this position was dramatically different from the one the OIC had taken in the Rushdie affair.

One sees how in its campaign to get international human rights law to incorporate a duty to combat defamation of Islam, the OIC and its members have moved a great distance away from their former claims that Islamic law was at odds with international human rights law. They are now using stealth tactics, seeking to insert principles that curb rights by the use of Islamic criteria into the UN system, but doing this while making claims that they are wanting to enhance human rights. In 2011, the OIC seemed to shift tactics, recharacterizing its campaign as one aimed at combating intolerance and criminalizing incitement to imminent violence based on religion or belief, which made it sound more congruent with human rights, as evinced by a resolution submitted by Pakistan in March 2011.[101] Whether the OIC would actually back away from its original project to criminalize defamation of Islam remained in doubt.

Summary

The lack of protections for freedom of religion in Islamic human rights schemes is one of the factors that most sharply distinguishes them from international human rights law, which treats freedom of religion as an unqualified right. The refusal to guarantee freedom of religion reveals the enormous gap between their authors' mentalities and the philosophy of human rights. Despite their records of routinely violating the right to freedom of religion, Middle Eastern governments are loathe to make candid avowals of their policies of persecuting people because of their religious beliefs, realizing that their practice is indefensible.

It would be simplistic to blame Islam per se for the lack of religious freedom in the Middle East. In each country, the violations correlate closely with the specific political objectives of the regimes involved. Non-Muslims and persons who convert from Islam are not necessarily the main victims. After all, in the Middle East, believing Muslims live in a climate of intellectual repression where they are regularly exposed to prosecutions for religious crimes merely for expressing ideas at odds with whatever religious doctrines that the local authorities currently endorse. Muslims are exposed to charges of heresy, blasphemy, and apostasy for what is actually political or theological dissent from officially mandated orthodoxy—or for having offended powerful figures. It seems fairer to assess the egregious violations of religious freedom regularly perpetrated in the Middle East as resulting from such factors as states' determination to monopolize religious authority as part of their monopoly of all fonts of power, a disposition to crush all dissent and suppress all critical thought, the wish to placate influential clerics or Islamist factions, and a pattern of pandering to popular prejudices in hopes of shoring up faltering popular support. It is significant that in the wake of the destabilizing changes in Egypt brought about by the Arab Spring, al-Azhar moved away from its previous call for executing apostates, belatedly choosing to present itself as supporting the freedoms of religion, opinion and expression, and scientific research and putting forward a document that endorsed these freedoms—albeit with cautious wording and qualifications that might limit their scope.[102]

There have long been efforts to politicize the international human rights system and to inject bias and selectivity into deciding which countries' human rights violations warrant condemnation. In this respect, the OIC's attempts to get the UN to focus on alleged defamation of Islam occurring in the West while deflecting attention away from OIC members' own egregious human rights violations do not stand out as exceptional. Nonetheless, the OIC campaign to insert in the list of UN human rights principles the duty to combat defamation of Islam does stand out in that it potentially involves a major alteration to the substantive rights set forth in international human rights law. This alteration will introduce a principle that is on its face incongruous, being designed to protect an institution, not the rights of human beings, and that also clashes with long-established human rights principles in areas like freedom of expression and freedom of religion, which will have to be compromised to accommodate it. No country that was genuinely committed to upholding international human rights law would see this alteration as one that would expand protection for human rights.

CHAPTER 10

An Assessment of Islamic Human Rights Schemes

The characteristics of the Islamic human rights schemes examined here should not be ascribed to peculiar features of Islam or Islam's supposed inherent incompatibility with human rights. Instead, these should be seen as part of a broader phenomenon of attempts by elites—the beneficiaries of undemocratic and hierarchical systems—to use religion and culture as devices to legitimize their opposition to international human rights law or to weaken it.

Assessment shows that Islamic human rights schemes, although invoking Islamic tradition, are actually shaped by their authors' negative reactions to ideas of freedom and democracy and to the scope of rights protections afforded by the International Bill of Human Rights. With the heavy investments of states such as Iran and Saudi Arabia in promoting Islamic human rights schemes, they inevitably reflect the attitudes of regimes that are fundamentally hostile to human rights. Significantly, Muslim human rights activists and the burgeoning human rights associations that have altered the political landscape in the Middle East have consistently campaigned to realize the human rights set forth in international law, not watered-down "Islamic" alternatives, such as the ones examined here.

A striking aspect of professedly "Islamic" human rights schemes is their hybridity, which disproves any notion that they represent pure outflowings of the Islamic tradition. Instead, they largely focus on civil and political rights as set forth in the UN system, on which they superimpose Islamic elements that will degrade or nullify them.

This unacknowledged hybridity amounts to an important and problematic feature of Islamic human rights schemes because in theory they derive their authority from their Islamic pedigrees. But, to possess genuine Islamic pedigrees, they would need to rest on methodologies that were designed to ensure that they would set forth authentic, unadulterated Islamic principles on the topic of human rights. Instead of being impelled by efforts to mine the Islamic heritage for guidance, they are replete with concepts and formulations that are patently appropriated from international human rights law and Western constitutions. That the authors borrow so extensively from alien models makes no sense in terms of Islamic jurisprudence, where rules established without respect for Islamic methods and criteria for interpreting the Islamic sources are generally deemed irrelevant. Because the authors are not prepared to confess to making extensive borrowings from outside the Islamic tradition, they naturally fail to propose any adequate theories for integrating such legal transplants in their schemes. Not surprisingly, the resulting admixtures of undigested legal transplants and Islamic elements lack coherence.

Because the authors have no interest in working through the jurisprudential technicalities that are needed to ground human rights in the Islamic tradition, they casually incorporate rules developed by premodern Islamic jurists without examination of the historical context in which these arose and without caring to make any critical assessment of the degree to which these suit the radically altered political, economic, and social circumstances of societies such as those in the contemporary Middle East. Indeed, they consciously avoid acknowledging the grim human rights situation in the contemporary Middle East and the suffocating oppression afflicting people living in that region. Some of the human rights proposed in these schemes are frivolous, while other rights that would be urgently needed to mitigate the abuses prevailing in Middle Eastern countries are completely omitted. Thus, for example, one sees an obligation on the part of believers to treat a corpse with due solemnity, but absolutely no provision for protecting freedom of religion.

Contrary to what their authors would claim, the Islamic restrictions placed on human rights, which are so central to Islamic human rights schemes, are not compelled by unimpeachable Islamic authority; the idea that Islam acts as a constraint on rights is vigorously contested. If the authors' aim had been to advance protection for human rights, they could have located ample raw material in the Islamic heritage, which is replete with values that complement human rights, such as concern for human welfare, compassion for the weak, social justice, tolerance, respect for diversity, and egalitarianism. These and other core principles could provide the basis for constructing a viable synthesis of Islam and international human rights law, as the work of Muslim proponents of democratization and the philosophies of many Muslim human rights activists amply demonstrate.

From an array of options in the Islamic heritage that include principles friendly to rights, the schemes deliberately select those elements that present obstacles to the accommodation of international human rights law—obstacles that are then attributed to Islamic requirements. In reality, it is more accurate to say that the obstacles lie in politics. The authors are interested in rationalizing governmental repression, enforcing social and religious conformity, delegitimizing and even criminalizing dissent, censoring critical perspectives, and perpetuating ingrained hierarchies that include discriminatory treatment of women, non-Muslims, and Muslims belonging to what are locally disfavored sects.

Authors of Islamic human rights schemes seek to convince the world that they constitute valid counterparts of international human rights law. This constitutes a misrepresentation because their objective is inimical to rights—cutting back on the civil and political rights that are afforded by international law. Careful comparisons with international documents inevitably reveal the deficiencies of the Islamic schemes. The latter assert the supremacy of vague Islamic criteria in all areas relevant for the protection of human rights, but these Islamic criteria are left so malleable that they leave those in power with unlimited discretion to interpret them in ways that crush rights.

Even though they are in no sense definitive statements of Islamic positions on human rights, Islamic human rights schemes deserve attention because of their proliferation and their real-world impact. State policy in the Middle East and the ongoing demands for Islamization mean that models embodying the idea that Muslims do have human rights but only subject to significant Islamic qualifications will continue to be promoted and may influence laws and constitutions. Added to this, one observes the proactive roles increasingly assumed in the UN human rights system by the OIC and its members in efforts to inject ideas taken from Islamic human rights schemes into the fabric of international human rights law. The OIC's protracted campaign to alter international human rights law to make it incorporate a rule criminalizing defamation of religions, which ultimately translates into criminalizing defamation of Islam, is one example of the efforts that have been made to smuggle into the corpus of human rights law concerns for protecting Islam at the expense of human rights. This campaign involves prioritizing Islam over civil and political rights in the same way that it is prioritized in Islamic human rights schemes—even though this prioritization is being done under the rubric of combating defamation of religions.

The OIC and its members have dramatically altered their official stances on human rights in the course of the last two decades. Instead of regularly pressing the idea of Islamic cultural particularism being at odds with human rights and boldly asserting that their commitment to Islamic law entails violating international human rights law, they now hypocritically affirm their support for international human rights law and claim that their projects are aligned with its philosophy. Having altered their rhetoric so that it fits better in the human rights mainstream, Middle Eastern countries have been able to make strategic alliances with countries from outside the region, such as Russia, that also want to employ

206 An Assessment of Islamic Human Rights Schemes

stealth tactics to undermine human rights. In Russia's case, it is elevating "traditional values" to a concern of human rights. Working in such alliances has given OIC members expanded influence in the UN human rights system but has also necessitated adjusting their tactics. Thus, when rejecting proposals at the UN that are designed to advance human rights of sexual minorities, they make only occasional objections grounded in Islamic law, for the most part condemning such proposals on grounds that their non-Muslim allies would also endorse.

Ultimately, what should one make of these Islamic human rights schemes? What will be their significance? Is it possible that, despite their obvious deficiencies and flaws, they still serve some constructive function? Viewing the incompleteness of their assimilation of international law, an optimist might nonetheless contend that Islamic human rights do constitute a step forward. After all, they suggest that even Muslim conservatives have become persuaded that human rights are so influential that they have to be addressed. An optimist might speculate that, even if these did not measure up to international standards, their promulgation would nonetheless enhance the legitimacy of human rights in the eyes of some Muslims by associating Islam with human rights.

That is, persons inclined to look for the positive potential of these schemes might view the phenomenon of Islamization of human rights as representing a temporary and transitional phase in the process of assimilating international human rights principles. They might propose that the indigenization of international human rights law requires—at least for many conservative Muslims—that human rights concepts initially pass through a stage in which international human rights are disassembled and readjusted to fit conservative values. The merit of such transitional human rights formulations could be that human rights, introduced gradually and conditionally, might avoid excessive clashes with familiar Islamic strictures.

If viewed in this light, some of the obfuscation that one routinely encounters in these schemes could be seen as facilitating the reception of human rights by avoiding specifics that might highlight inherent conflicts. That is, the evasive tactics and intentionally ambiguous formulations that abound in these schemes could be characterized as helpful in avoiding a premature break with the heritage of premodern *shari'a* rules, a break that could be exploited by adamant opponents of human rights. One might hope that the Islamic features that have been grafted onto imported human rights concepts would be eventually discarded when further developments created space for adopting the international standards.

Alternatively, one could propose a more pessimistic appraisal, which seems to be warranted given that Islamic human rights schemes have been backed by antidemocratic governments, ideologues with philosophies hostile to human rights, and institutions and organizations that adhere to policies at odds with human rights. Where the whole point of an endeavor is to supplant international human rights law with a distinctly inferior version of human rights and to legitimize this by exploiting the prestige of Islam, the outcome should be harmful for the prospects for realizing human rights.

It is hard to see how Islamic human rights schemes, which are all designed to enfeeble the human rights afforded in international law, could have positive impact in the long term. Because Islamization pressures seem likely to continue, models that give governments grounds for claiming that they have broad Islamic warrants for denying the civil and political rights afforded under international law will likely be emulated, which will entail compromising rights. People in the Middle East concerned with advancing human rights realize this. Pro-democracy activists of the Arab Spring have regularly expressed anxieties that Islamist groups may manage to gain the upper hand after old dictatorships are toppled and exploit their political ascendancy to pursue Islamization, which could lead to imprinting the supremacy of Islamic law in any new constitutions that would be adopted. Pro-democracy activists wanting to have constitutions that will buttress freedoms and reinforce protections for human rights see only dangers in the prospect of new constitutions that would stipulate that Islam must be accorded priority. Recalling what happened to the liberal first draft of Iran's postrevolutionary constitution, which clerics managed to rewrite to enshrine the supremacy of Islamic law, and the consequences that Islamization has had for Iranians' human rights, they have every reason to be apprehensive.

Once embodied in law, Islamic criteria limiting rights protections present obstacles to advancing human rights. For example, by incorporating Islamic limitations on human rights in the text of the 1979 Iranian constitution, what were previously *informal* obstacles to realizing international human rights protections were elevated to the stature of *formal* constitutional principles affirming Islamic restrictions on human rights—as shown by the ruling of Iran's Council of Guardians nullifying the attempt to ratify the Women's Convention on the grounds that doing so would violate both Islamic law and the Iranian constitution.

The Islam and human rights nexus has been in a state of acute tension for decades. Every indication is that we are far from having seen the last chapter in Muslims' efforts to settle on the optimal relationship of these two vital factors in contemporary Middle Eastern political life. In the wake of the popular uprisings and mass protests of the Arab Spring, which manifested both a great hunger for democratization and the disposition on the part of many to assume that Islamists offered the best prospects for good governance, one can anticipate debates on Islam and human rights to intensify. In Tunisia in December 2011, one observed the spectacle of Moncef Marzouki, the prominent human rights activist, assuming the office of president, while Hamadi Jebali, a leader of the Islamist Ennahda Party, took the office of prime minister. How they would sort out their respective perspectives on what policies a country that was embarking on a new venture of democratization should adopt would be just one of many experiments with achieving the right balance. And, in Yemen, in the person of Tawakkul Karman, the dynamic pro-democracy activist whose championing of women's rights won her a share in the 2011 Nobel Peace prize, one had a woman with Islamist ties who was also a foe of interpretations of Islam that would limit women's role. Obviously, Karman aspires to combine her Islamic loyalties with a fight to ensure that the end of dictatorship opens the door to women's full participation in society and politics, seeing no necessary opposition between Islam and women's rights. In the wake of the Arab Spring, hers will be only one of many struggles to spread a vision of Islam as supporting aspirations for human rights, difficult struggles that have momentous implications for the future.

Excerpts from the Constitution of the Islamic Republic of Iran of 24 October 1979 As Amended to 28 July 1989*

In the Name of Allah, the Compassionate, the Merciful
We sent aforetime Our apostles with clear signs, and sent down with them
the Book and the Balance that men may uphold justice . . .

Qur'an (57:25)

Preamble

The Constitution of the Islamic Republic of Iran sets forth the cultural, social, political, and economic institutions of Iranian society on the basis of Islamic principles and norms, which represent the earnest aspiration of the Islamic *Ummah* [community] . . .

The Form of Government in Islam

In the view of Islam, government does not derive from the interests of a class, nor does it serve the domination of an individual or a group. It represents rather the crystallization of the political ideal of a people who bear a common faith and common outlook, taking an organized form in order to initiate the process of intellectual

---

*Taken from Albert Blaustein and Gisbert Flanz, eds., *Constitutions of the Countries of the World* (Dobbs Ferry, NY: Oceana, 1992). Various passages corresponding to Arabic quotations in the Persian original have been omitted.

and ideological evolution towards the final goal, i.e., movement towards *Allah*. Our nation, in the course of its revolutionary developments, has cleansed itself of the dust and impurities that accumulated during the *taghuti* [heathenish] past and purged itself of foreign ideological influences, returning to authentic intellectual standpoints and world-view of Islam. It now intends to establish an ideal and model society on the basis of Islamic norms. The mission of the Constitution is to realize the ideological objectives of the movement and to create conditions conducive to the development of man in accordance with the noble and universal values of Islam. . . .

Legislation setting forth regulations for the administration of society will revolve around the Qur'an and the *Sunnah*. Accordingly, the exercise of meticulous and earnest supervision by just, pious, and committed scholars of Islam (*al-fuqaha al-'udul*) is an absolute necessity . . .

Women in the Constitution

Through the creation of Islamic social infrastructures, all the elements of humanity that hitherto served the multifaceted foreign exploitation shall regain their true identity and human rights. As part of this process, it is only natural that women should benefit from a particularly large augmentation of their rights, because of the greater oppression that they suffered under the *taghuti* regime.

The family is the fundamental unit of society and the main centre for the growth and edification of human being[s]. Compatibility with respect to belief and ideal, which provides the primary basis for man's development and growth, is the main consideration in the establishment of a family. It is the duty of the Islamic government to provide the necessary facilities for the attainment of this goal. This view of the family unit delivers woman from being regarded as an object or as an instrument in the service of promoting consumerism and exploitation. Not only does woman recover thereby her momentous and precious function of motherhood, rearing of ideologically committed human beings, she also assumes a pioneering social role and becomes the fellow struggler of man in all vital areas of life. Given the weighty responsibilities that woman thus assumes, she is accorded in Islam great value and nobility.

An Ideological Army

In the formation and equipping of the country's defense forces, due attention must be paid to faith and ideology as the basic criteria. Accordingly, the Army of the Islamic Republic of Iran and the Islamic Revolutionary Guards Corps are to be organized in conformity with this goal, and they will be responsible not only for guarding and preserving the frontiers of the country, but also for fulfilling the ideological mission of *jihad* in God's way; that is, extending the sovereignty of God's law throughout the world. . . .

General Principles

Article 1

The form of government of Iran is that of an Islamic Republic, endorsed by the people of Iran on the basis of their longstanding belief in the sovereignty of truth and Qur'anic justice, in the referendum of [March 29 and 30, 1979], through the affirmative vote of a majority of 98.2% of eligible voters, held after the victorious Islamic Revolution led by the eminent *marji' al-taqlid* [source of emulation], Ayatollah al-'Uzma Imam Khumayni;

Article 2

The Islamic Republic is a system based on belief in:

1. the One God (as stated in the phrase "There is no god except Allah"), His exclusive sovereignty and the right to legislate, and the necessity of submission to His commands;
2. Divine revelation and its fundamental role in setting forth the laws;
3. the return to God in the Hereafter, and the constructive role of this belief in the course of man's ascent towards God;
4. the justice of God in creation and legislation;
5. continuous leadership (*imamah*) and perpetual guidance, and its fundamental role in ensuring the uninterrupted process of the revolution of Islam;
6. the exalted dignity and value of man, and his freedom coupled with responsibility before God; in which equity, justice, political, economic, social, and cultural independence, and national solidarity are secured by recourse to:
   A. continuous *ijtihad* [interpretation] of the *fuqaha* possessing necessary qualifications, exercised on the basis of the Qur'an and the *Sunnah* of the *Ma'sumun* [the Prophet, his daughter Fatima, the Shi'i Imams], upon all of whom be peace;
   B. sciences and arts and the most advanced results of human experience, together with the effort to advance them further;
   C. negation of all forms of oppression, both the infliction of and the submission to it, and of dominance, both its imposition and its acceptance.

Article 3

In order to attain the objectives specified in Article 2, the government of the Islamic Republic of Iran has the duty of directing all its resources to the following goals:

1. the creation of a favorable environment for the growth of moral virtues based on faith and piety and the struggle against all forms of vice and corruption;

2. raising the level of public awareness in all areas, through the proper use of the press, mass media, and other means;
3. free education and physical training for everyone at all levels, and the facilitation and expansion of higher education;
4. strengthening the spirit of inquiry, investigation, and innovation in all areas of science, technology, and culture, as well as Islamic studies, by establishing research centers and encouraging researchers;
5. the complete elimination of imperialism and the prevention of foreign influence;
6. the elimination of all forms of despotism and autocracy and all attempts to monopolize power;
7. ensuring political and social freedoms within the framework of the law;
8. the participation of the entire people in determining their political, economic, social, and cultural destiny;
9. the abolition of all forms of undesirable discrimination and the provision of equitable opportunities for all, in both the material and intellectual spheres;
10. the creation of a correct administrative system and elimination of superfluous government organizations;
11. all round strengthening of the foundations of national defense to the utmost degree by means of universal military training for the sake of safeguarding the independence, territorial integrity, and the Islamic order of the country;
12. the planning of a correct and just economic system, in accordance with Islamic criteria, in order to create welfare, eliminate poverty, and abolish all forms of deprivation with respect to food, housing, work, health care, and the provision of social insurance for all;
13. the attainment of self-sufficiency in scientific, technological, industrial, agricultural, and military domains, and other similar spheres;
14. securing the multifarious rights of all citizens, both women and men, and providing legal protection for all, as well as the equality of all before the law;
15. the expansion and strengthening of Islamic brotherhood and public cooperation among all the people;
16. framing the foreign policy of the country on the basis of Islamic criteria, fraternal commitment to all Muslims, and unsparing support to the *mustad'afun* [oppressed] of the world.

Article 4

All civil, penal, financial, economic, administrative, cultural, military, political, and other laws and regulations must be based on Islamic criteria. This principle applies absolutely and generally to all articles of the Constitution as well as to all other laws and regulations, and the *fuqaha* of the Guardian Council are judges in this matter.

Article 5

During the Occultation of the *Wali al-'Asr* [Shi'i Imam] (may God hasten his reappearance), the *wilayah* [governance] and leadership of the Ummah devolve upon the just (*'adil*) and pious (*muttaqi*) *faqih* [jurist], who is fully aware of the circumstances of his age; courageous, resourceful, and possessed of administrative ability, [he] will assume the responsibilities of this office in accordance with Article 107.

Article 7

In the Islamic Republic of Iran, the affairs of the country must be administered on the basis of public opinion expressed by the means of elections, including the election of the President, the representatives of the Islamic Consultative Assembly, and the members of councils, or by means of referenda in matters specified in other articles of this Constitution. . . .

Article 8

In the Islamic Republic of Iran, *al-'amr bil-ma'ruf wa al-nahy 'an al-munkar* [commanding the good and forbidding the evil] is a universal and reciprocal duty that must be fulfilled by the people with respect to one another, by the government with respect to the people, and by the people with respect to the government. The conditions, limits, and nature of this duty will be specified by law. (This is in accordance with the Qur'anic verse: "The believers, men and women, are guardians of one another; they enjoin the good and forbid the evil" [9:71].) . . .

Article 9

In the Islamic Republic of Iran, the freedom, independence, unity, and territorial integrity of the country are inseparable from one another, and their preservation is the duty of the government and all individual citizens. No individual, group, or authority, has the right to infringe in the slightest way upon the political, cultural, economic, and military independence or the territorial integrity of Iran under the pretext of exercising freedom. Similarly, no authority has the right to abrogate legitimate freedoms, not even by enacting laws and regulations for that purpose, under the pretext of preserving the independence and territorial integrity of the country.

Article 10

Since the family is the fundamental unit of Islamic society, all laws, regulations, and pertinent programs must tend to facilitate the formation of a family, and to safeguard its sanctity and the stability of family relations on the basis of the law and the ethics of Islam.

Article 12

The official religion of Iran is Islam and the Twelver Ja'fari school . . . and this principle will remain eternally immutable. Other Islamic schools, including the Hanafi, Shafi'i, Maliki, Hanbali, and Zaydi, are to be accorded full respect, and their followers are free to act in accordance with their own jurisprudence in performing their religious rites. These schools enjoy official status in matters pertaining to religious education, affairs of personal status (marriage, divorce, inheritance, and wills) and related litigation in courts of law. In regions of the country where Muslims following any one of these schools of *fiqh* [jurisprudence] constitute the majority, local regulations, within the bounds of the jurisdiction of local councils, are to be in accordance with the respective school of *fiqh*, without infringing upon the rights of the followers of other schools.

Article 13

Zoroastrian, Jewish, and Christian Iranians are the only recognized religious minorities, who, within the limits of the law, are free to perform their religious rites and ceremonies, and to act according to their own canon in matters of personal affairs and religious education.

Article 14

In accordance with the sacred verse ("God does not forbid you to deal kindly and justly with those who have not fought against you because of your religion and who have not expelled you from your homes" [60:8]), the government of the Islamic Republic of Iran and all Muslims are duty-bound to treat non-Muslims in conformity with ethical norms and the principles of Islamic justice and equity, and to respect their human rights. This principle applies to all who refrain from engaging in conspiracy or activity against Islam and the Islamic Republic of Iran. . . .

The Rights of the People

Article 19

All people of Iran, whatever the ethnic group or tribe to which they belong, enjoy equal rights; and color, race, language, and the like, do not bestow any privilege.

Article 20

All citizens of the country, both men and women, equally enjoy the protection of the law and enjoy all human, political, economic, social, and cultural rights, in conformity with Islamic criteria.

Article 21

The government must ensure the rights of women in all respects, in conformity with Islamic criteria, and accomplish the following goals:

1. create a favorable environment for the growth of woman's personality and the restoration of her rights, both the material and intellectual;
2. the protection of mothers, particularly during pregnancy and childrearing, and the protection of children without guardians;
3. establishing competent courts to protect and preserve the family;
4. the provision of special insurance for widows, and aged women and women without support;
5. the awarding of guardianship of children to worthy mothers, in order to protect the interests of the children, in the absence of a legal guardian.

Article 22

The dignity, life, property, rights, residence, and occupation of the individual are inviolate, except in cases sanctioned by law.

Article 23

The investigation of individuals' beliefs is forbidden, and no one may be molested or taken to task simply for holding a certain belief.

Article 24

Publications and the press have freedom of expression except when it is detrimental to the fundamental principles of Islam or the rights of the public. The details of this exception will be specified by law.

Article 25

The inspection of letters and the failure to deliver them, the recording and disclosure of telephone conversations, the disclosure of telegraphic and telex communications, censorship, or the willful failure to transmit them, eavesdropping, and all forms of covert investigation are forbidden, except as provided by law.

Article 26

The formation of parties, societies, political or professional associations, as well as religious societies, whether Islamic or pertaining to one of the recognized religious minorities, is permitted provided they do not violate the principles of independence, freedom, national unity, the criteria of Islam, or the basis of the Islamic Republic. No one may be prevented from participating in the aforementioned groups, or be compelled to participate in them.

Article 27

Public gatherings and marches may be freely held, provided arms are not carried and that they are not detrimental to the fundamental principles of Islam.

Article 28

Everyone has the right to choose any occupation he wishes, if it is not contrary to Islam and the public interests, and does not infringe the rights of others. The government has the duty, with due consideration of the need of society for different kinds of work, to provide every citizen with the opportunity to work, and to create equal conditions for obtaining it. . . .

Article 32

No one may be arrested except by the order and in accordance with the procedure laid down by law. In case of arrest, charges with the reasons for accusation must, without delay, be communicated and explained to the accused in writing, and a provisional dossier must be forwarded to the competent judicial authorities within a maximum of twenty-four hours so that the preliminaries to the trial can be completed as swiftly as possible. The violation of this article will be liable to punishment in accordance with the law. . . .

Article 37

Innocence is to be presumed, and no one is to be held guilty of a charge unless his or her guilt has been established by a competent court.

Article 38

All forms of torture for the purpose of extracting confession or acquiring information are forbidden. Compulsion of individuals to testify, confess, or take an oath is not permissible; and any testimony, confession, or oath obtained under duress is devoid of value and credence. Violation of this article is liable to punishment in accordance with the law.

Article 39

All affronts to the dignity and repute of persons arrested, detained, imprisoned, or banished in accordance with the law, whatever form they may take, are forbidden and liable to punishment.

Article 40

No one is entitled to exercise his rights in a way injurious to others or detrimental to public interests. . . .

The Right of National Sovereignty and the Powers Deriving Therefrom

Article 56

Absolute sovereignty over the world and man belongs to God, and it is He Who has made man master of his own social destiny. No one can deprive man of this divine right, nor subordinate it to the vested interests of a particular individual or group. The people are to exercise this divine right in the manner specified in the following articles. . . .

Powers and Authority of the Islamic Consultative Assembly

Article 72

The Islamic Consultative Assembly cannot enact laws contrary to the *usul* and *ahkam* [sources and rules] of the official religion of the country or to the Constitution. It is the duty of the Guardian Council to determine whether a violation has occurred, in accordance with Article 96. . . .

Article 91

With a view to safeguard the Islamic ordinances and the Constitution, in order to examine the compatibility of the legislations passed by the Islamic Consultative Assembly with Islam, a council to be known as the Guardian Council is to be constituted with the following composition:

1. six *'adil fuqaha,* conscious of the present needs and the issues of the day, to be selected by the Leader, and
2. six jurists, specializing in different areas of law, to be elected by the Islamic Consultative Assembly from among the Muslim jurists nominated by the Head of the Judicial Power. . . .

Article 96

The determination of compatibility of the legislation passed by the Islamic Consultative Assembly with the laws of Islam rests with the majority vote of the *fuqaha* on the Guardian Council; and the determination of its compatibility with the Constitution rests with the majority of all the members of the Guardian Council. . . .

The Leader or Leadership Council

Article 107

After the demise of the eminent *marji' al-taqlid* and great leader of the universal Islamic revolution, and founder of the Islamic Republic of Iran, Ayatollah al-Uzma Imam Khumayni . . . who was recognized and accepted as *marji'* and Leader by a decisive majority of the people, the task of appointing the Leader shall be vested with the experts elected by the people. The experts will review and consult among themselves concerning all the *fuqaha* possessing the qualifications specified in Articles 5 and 109. In the event they find one of them better versed in Islamic regulations, the subjects of the *fiqh*, or in political and social issues, or possessing general popularity or special prominence for any of the qualifications mentioned in Article 109, they shall elect him as the Leader. Otherwise, in the absence of such a superiority, they shall elect and declare one of them as the Leader. The Leader thus elected by the Assembly of Experts shall assume all the powers of the *wilayat al-amr* [command] and all the responsibilities arising therefrom.

The Leader is equal with the rest of the people of the country in the eyes of law. . . .

Article 112

Upon the order of the Leader, the Nation's Exigency Council shall meet at any time the Guardian Council judges a proposed bill of the Islamic Consultative Assembly to be against the principles of *Shari'ah* or the Constitution, and the Assembly is unable to meet the expectations of the Guardian Council. Also, the Council shall meet for consideration on any issue forwarded to it by the Leader and shall carry out any other responsibility as mentioned in this Constitution.

The permanent and changeable members of the Council shall be appointed by the Leader. The rules for the Council shall be formulated and approved by the Council members subject to the confirmation by the Leader. . . .

The Presidency

Article 115

The President must be elected from among religious and political personalities possessing the following qualifications:

Iranian origin; Iranian nationality; administrative capacity and resourcefulness; a good past record; trustworthiness and piety; convinced belief in the fundamental principles of the Islamic Republic of Iran and the official *tnadhhab* [school of law] of the country.

The Army and the Islamic Revolution Guard Corps

Article 144

The Army of the Islamic Republic of Iran must be an Islamic Army, i.e., committed to Islamic ideology and the people, and must recruit into its service individuals who have faith in the objectives of the Islamic Revolution and are devoted to the cause of realizing its goals.

The Cairo Declaration on Human Rights in Islam*

The Member States of the Organization of the Islamic Conference,

Reaffirming the civilizing and historical role of the Islamic Ummah which God made the best nation that has given mankind a universal and well-balanced civilization in which harmony is established between this life and the hereafter and knowledge is combined with faith; and the role that this Ummah should play to guide a humanity confused by competing trends and ideologies and to provide solutions to the chronic problems of this materialistic civilization;

Wishing to contribute to the efforts of mankind to assert human rights, to protect man from exploitation and persecution, and to affirm his freedom and right to a dignified life in accordance with the Islamic Shari'ah;

Convinced that mankind which has reached an advanced stage in materialistic science is still, and shall remain, in dire need of faith to support its civilization and of a self motivating force to guard its rights;

Believing that fundamental rights and universal freedoms in Islam are an integral part of the Islamic religion and that no one as a matter of principle has the right to suspend them in whole or in part or violate or ignore them in as much as they are binding divine commandments, which are contained in the Revealed Books of God

---

*United Nations General Assembly. A/CONF.157/PC/62/Add.18. Submitted to the World Conference on Human Rights. Preparatory Committee. Fourth session. Geneva, April 19–May 7, 1993. Item 5 on the provisional agenda. Annex to res. no. 49/19-P.

and were sent through the last of His Prophets to complete the preceding divine messages thereby making their observance an act of worship and their neglect or violation an abominable sin, and accordingly every person is individually responsible—and the Ummah collectively responsible—for their safeguard;

Proceeding from the above-mentioned principles,

Declare the following:

Article 1:

A. All human beings form one family whose members are united by submission to God and descent from Adam. All men are equal in terms of basic human dignity and basic obligations and responsibilities, without any discrimination on the grounds of race, color, language, sex, religious belief, political affiliation, social status or other considerations. True faith is the guarantee for enhancing such dignity along the path to human perfection.

B. All human beings are God's subjects, and the most loved by Him are those who are most useful to the rest of His subjects, and no one has superiority over another except on the basis of piety and good deeds.

Article 2:

A. Life is a God-given gift and the right to life is guaranteed to every human being. It is the duty of individuals, societies and states to protect this right from any violation, and it is prohibited to take away life except for a Shari'ah-prescribed reason.

B. It is forbidden to resort to such means as may result in the genocidal annihilation of mankind.

C. The preservation of human life throughout the term of time willed by God is a duty prescribed by Shari'ah.

D. Safety from bodily harm is a guaranteed right. It is the duty of the state to safeguard it, and it is prohibited to breach it without a Shari'ah-prescribed reason.

Article 3:

A. In the event of the use of force and in case of armed conflict, it is not permissible to kill non-belligerents such as old men, women and children. The wounded and the sick shall have the right to medical treatment; and prisoners of war shall have the right to be fed, sheltered and clothed. It is prohibited to mutilate dead bodies. It is a duty to exchange prisoners of war and to arrange visits or reunions of the families separated by the circumstances of war.

B. It is prohibited to fell trees, to damage crops or livestock, and to destroy the enemy's civilian buildings and installations by shelling, blasting or any other means.

Article 4:

Every human being is entitled to inviolability and the protection of his good name and honor during his life and after his death. The state and society shall protect his remains and burial place.

Article 5:

A. The family is the foundation of society, and marriage is the basis of its formation. Men and women have the right to marriage, and no restrictions stemming from race, color or nationality shall prevent them from enjoying this right.
B. Society and the State shall remove all obstacles to marriage and shall facilitate marital procedure. They shall ensure family protection and welfare.

Article 6:

A. Woman is equal to man in human dignity, and has rights to enjoy as well as duties to perform; she has her own civil entity and financial independence, and the right to retain her name and lineage. The husband is responsible for the support and welfare of the family.

Article 7:

A. As of the moment of birth, every child has rights due from the parents, society and the state to be accorded proper nursing, education and material, hygienic and moral care. Both the fetus and the mother must be protected and accorded special care.
B. Parents and those in such like capacity have the right to choose the type of education they desire for their children, provided they take into consideration the interest and future of the children in accordance with ethical values and the principles of the Shari'ah.
C. Both parents are entitled to certain rights from their children, and relatives are entitled to rights from their kin, in accordance with the tenets of the Shari'ah.

Article 8:

Every human being has the right to enjoy his legal capacity in terms of both obligation and commitment, [and] should this capacity be lost or impaired, he shall be represented by his guardian.

Article 9:

A. The question [*sic*] for knowledge is an obligation and the provision of education is a duty for society and the State. The State shall ensure the availability of ways and means to acquire education and shall guarantee educational diversity in the interest of society so as to enable man to be acquainted with the religion of Islam and the facts of the Universe for the benefit of mankind.

B. Every human being has the right to receive both religious and worldly education from the various institutions of education and guidance, including the family, the school, the university, the media, etc., and in such an integrated and balanced manner as to develop his personality, strengthen his faith in God and promote his respect for and defense of both rights and obligations.

Article 10:

Islam is the religion of unspoiled nature. It is prohibited to exercise any form of compulsion on man or to exploit his poverty or ignorance in order to convert him to another religion or to atheism.

Article 11:

A. Human beings are born free, and no one has the right to enslave, humiliate, oppress or exploit them, and there can be no subjugation but to God the Most-High.

B. Colonialism of all types being one of the most evil forms of enslavement is totally prohibited. Peoples suffering from colonialism have the full right to freedom and self-determination. It is the duty of all States and peoples to support the struggle of colonized peoples for the liquidation of all forms of colonialism and occupation, and all States and peoples have the right to preserve their independent identity and exercise control over their wealth and natural resources.

Article 12:

Every man shall have the right, within the framework of Shari'ah, to free movement and to select his place of residence whether inside or outside his country and if persecuted is entitled to seek asylum in another country. The country of refuge shall ensure his protection until he reaches safety, unless asylum is motivated by an act which Shari'ah regards as a crime.

Article 13:

Work is a right guaranteed by the State and Society for each person able to work. Everyone shall be free to choose the work that suits him best and which serves his interests and those of society. The employee shall have the right to safety and security as well as to all other social guarantees. He may neither be assigned work beyond his capacity nor be subjected to compulsion or exploited or harmed in any way. He shall be entitled—without any discrimination between males and females—to fair wages for his work without delay, as well as to the holidays allowances and promotions which he deserves. For his part, he shall be required to be dedicated and meticulous in his work. Should workers and employers disagree on any matter, the State shall intervene to settle the dispute and have the grievances redressed, the rights confirmed and justice enforced without bias.

Article 14:

Everyone shall have the right to legitimate gains without monopolization, deceit or harm to oneself or to others. Usury (*riba*) is absolutely prohibited.

Article 15:

A. Everyone shall have the right to own property acquired in a legitimate way, and shall be entitled to the rights of ownership, without prejudice to oneself, others or to society in general. Expropriation is not permissible except for the requirements of public interest and upon payment of immediate and fair compensation.
B. Confiscation and seizure of property is prohibited except for a necessity dictated by law.

Article 16:

Everyone shall have the right to enjoy the fruits of his scientific, literary, artistic or technical production and the right to protect the moral and material interests stemming therefrom, provided that such production is not contrary to the principles of Shari'ah.

Article 17:

A. Everyone shall have the right to live in a clean environment, away from vice and moral corruption, an environment that would foster his self-development and it is incumbent upon the State and society in general to afford that right.
B. Everyone shall have the right to medical and social care, and to all public amenities provided by society and the State within the limits of their available resources.
C. The State shall ensure the right of the individual to a decent living which will enable him to meet all his requirements and those of his dependents, including food, clothing, housing, education, medical care and all other basic needs.

Article 18:

A. Everyone shall have the right to live in security for himself, his religion, his dependents, his honor and his property.

B. Everyone shall have the right to privacy in the conduct of his private affairs, in his home, among his family, with regard to his property and his relationships. It is not permitted to spy on him, to place him under surveillance or to besmirch his good name. The State shall protect him from arbitrary interference.

C. A private residence is inviolable in all cases. It will not be entered without permission from its inhabitants or in any unlawful manner, nor shall it be demolished or confiscated and its dwellers evicted.

Article 19:

A. All individuals are equal before the law, without distinction between the ruler and the ruled.

B. The right to resort to justice is guaranteed to everyone.

C. Liability is in essence personal.

D. There shall be no crime or punishment except as provided for in the Shari'ah.

E. A defendant is innocent until his guilt is proven in a fair trial in which he shall be given all the guarantees of defense.

Article 20:

It is not permitted without legitimate reason to arrest an individual, or restrict his freedom, to exile or to punish him. It is not permitted to subject him to physical or psychological torture or to any form of humiliation, cruelty or indignity. Nor is it permitted to subject an individual to medical or scientific experimentation without his consent or at the risk of his health or of his life. Nor is it permitted to promulgate emergency laws that would provide executive authority for such actions.

Article 21:

Taking hostages under any form or for any purpose is expressly forbidden.

Article 22:

A. Everyone shall have the right to express his opinion freely in such manner as would not be contrary to the principles of the Shari'ah.

B. Everyone shall have the right to advocate what is right, and propagate what is good, and warn against what is wrong and evil according to the norms of Islamic Shari'ah.

C. Information is a vital necessity to society. It may not be exploited or misused in such a way as may violate sanctities and the dignity of Prophets, undermine moral and ethical values or disintegrate, corrupt or harm society or weaken its faith.
D. It is not permitted to arouse nationalistic or doctrinal hatred or to do anything that may be an incitement to any form or racial discrimination.

Article 23:

A. Authority is a trust; and abuse or malicious exploitation thereof is absolutely prohibited, so that fundamental human rights may be guaranteed.
B. Everyone shall have the right to participate, directly or indirectly in the administration of his country's public affairs. He shall also have the right to assume public office in accordance with the provisions of Shari'ah.

Article 24:

All the rights and freedoms stipulated in this Declaration are subject to the Islamic Shari'ah.

Article 25:

The Islamic Shari'ah is the only source of reference for the explanation or clarification of any of the articles of this Declaration.

Cairo, 14 Muharram 1411H
5 August 1990

A/HRC/10/L.11
12 May 2009

Human Rights Council
Tenth session
Agenda item 1

10/22 Combating defamation of religions

The Human Rights Council,

Reaffirming the pledge made by all States under the Charter of the United Nations to promote and encourage universal respect for and observance of human rights and fundamental freedoms for all, without distinction as to race, sex, language or religion,

Reaffirming also that all human rights are universal, indivisible, interdependent and interrelated,

Recalling the 2005 World Summit Outcome adopted by the General Assembly in its resolution 60/1 of 16 September 2005, in which the Assembly emphasized the responsibilities of all States, in conformity with the Charter of the United Nations, to respect human rights and fundamental freedoms for all, without distinction of any kind, and acknowledged the importance of respect and understanding for religious and cultural diversity throughout the world,

Recognizing the valuable contribution of all religions to modern civilization and the contribution that dialogue among civilizations can make towards improved awareness and understanding of the common values shared by all humankind,

http://www2.ohchr.org/english/bodies/hrcouncil/docs/10session/A.HRC.10.L.11.pdf

Welcoming the resolve expressed in the United Nations Millennium Declaration, adopted by the General Assembly on 8 September 2000, to take measures to eliminate the increasing acts of racism and xenophobia in many societies and to promote greater harmony and tolerance in all societies, and looking forward to its effective implementation at all levels,

Underlining in this regard the importance of the Durban Declaration and Programme of Action adopted by the World Conference against Racism, Racial Discrimination, Xenophobia and Related Intolerance, held in Durban, South Africa, in 2001, welcoming the progress achieved in implementing them, and emphasizing that they constitute a solid foundation for the elimination of all scourges and manifestations of racism, racial discrimination, xenophobia and related intolerance,

Welcoming all international and regional initiatives to promote cross-cultural and interfaith harmony, including the Alliance of Civilizations and the International Dialogue on Interfaith Cooperation for Peace and Harmony, and their valuable efforts in the promotion of a culture of peace and dialogue at all levels,

Welcoming also the reports of the Special Rapporteur on contemporary forms of racism, racial discrimination, xenophobia and related intolerance submitted to the Council at its fourth, sixth and ninth sessions (A/HRC/4/19, A/HRC/6/6 and A/HRC/9/12), in which the Special Rapporteur highlighted the serious nature of the defamation of all religions and the need to complement legal strategies,

Noting with deep concern the instances of intolerance, discrimination and acts of violence against followers of certain faiths occurring in many parts of the world, in addition to the negative projection of certain religions in the media and the introduction and enforcement of laws and administrative measures that specifically discriminate against and target persons with certain ethnic and religious backgrounds, particularly Muslim minorities following the events of 11 September 2001, and that threaten to impede their full enjoyment of human rights and fundamental freedoms,

Stressing that defamation of religions is a serious affront to human dignity leading to a restriction on the freedom of religion of their adherents and incitement to religious hatred and violence,

Noting with concern that defamation of religions and incitement to religious hatred in general could lead to social disharmony and violations of human rights, and alarmed at the inaction of some States to combat this burgeoning trend and the resulting discriminatory practices against adherents of certain religions and, in this context, stressing the need to effectively combat defamation of all religions and incitement to religious hatred in general and against Islam and Muslims in particular,

Convinced that respect for cultural, ethnic, religious and linguistic diversity, as well as dialogue among and within civilizations, are essential for global peace and understanding, while manifestations of cultural and ethnic prejudice, religious intolerance and xenophobia generate hatred and violence among peoples and nations,

Underlining the important role of education in the promotion of tolerance, which involves acceptance by the public of and its respect for diversity,

Noting the various regional and national initiatives to combat religious and racial intolerance against specific groups and communities and emphasizing, in this context, the need to adopt a comprehensive and non-discriminatory approach to ensure respect for all races and religions,

Recalling its resolution 7/19 of 27 March 2008 and General Assembly resolution 63/171 of 18 December 2008,

1. Takes note of the study of the United Nations High Commissioner for Human Rights on the compilation of existing legislation and jurisprudence concerning defamation of and contempt for religions (A/HRC/9/25) and the report of the Special Rapporteur on contemporary forms of racism, racial discrimination, xenophobia and related intolerance (A/HRC/9/12) presented to the Council at its ninth session;

2. Expresses deep concern at the negative stereotyping and defamation of religions and manifestations of intolerance and discrimination in matters of religion or belief still evident in the world, which have led to intolerance against the followers of these religions;

3. Strongly deplores all acts of psychological and physical violence and assaults, and incitement thereto, against persons on the basis of their religion or belief, and such acts directed against their businesses, properties, cultural centres and places of worship, as well as targeting of holy sites, religious symbols and venerated personalities of all religions;

4. Expresses deep concern at the continued serious instances of deliberate stereotyping of religions, their adherents and sacred persons in the media, as well as programmes and agendas pursued by extremist organizations and groups aimed at creating and perpetuating stereotypes about certain religions, in particular when condoned by Governments;

5. Notes with deep concern the intensification of the overall campaign of defamation of religions and incitement to religious hatred in general, including the ethnic and religious profiling of Muslim minorities in the aftermath of the tragic events of 11 September 2001;

6. Recognizes that, in the context of the fight against terrorism, defamation of religions and incitement to religious hatred in general have become aggravating factors that contribute to the denial of fundamental rights and freedoms of members of target groups, as well as to their economic and social exclusion;

7. Expresses deep concern in this respect that Islam is frequently and wrongly associated with human rights violations and terrorism and, in this regard, regrets the laws or administrative measures specifically designed to control and monitor Muslim minorities, thereby stigmatizing them and legitimizing the discrimination they experience;

8. Reaffirms the commitment of all States to the implementation, in an integrated manner, of the United Nations Global Counter-terrorism Strategy,

adopted without a vote by the General Assembly in its resolution 60/288 of 8 September 2006 and reaffirmed by the Assembly in its resolution 62/272 of 5 September 2008, and in which it clearly reaffirms, inter alia, that terrorism cannot and should not be associated with any religion, nationality, civilization or group, as well as the need to reinforce the commitment of the international community to promote, among other things, a culture of peace and respect for all religions, beliefs, and cultures and to prevent the defamation of religions;

9. Deplores the use of the print, audio-visual and electronic media, including the Internet, and any other means to incite acts of violence, xenophobia or related intolerance and discrimination against any religion, as well as the targeting of religious symbols and venerated persons;

10. Emphasizes that, as stipulated in international human rights law, including articles 19 and 29 of the Universal Declaration of Human Rights and articles 19 and 20 of the International Covenant on Civil and Political Rights, everyone has the right to hold opinions without interference and the right to freedom of expression, the exercise of which carries with it special duties and responsibilities and may therefore be subject to limitations only as provided for by law and are necessary for respect of the rights or reputations of others, protection of national security or of public order, public health or morals and general welfare;

11. Reaffirms that general comment No. 15 of the Committee on the Elimination of Racial Discrimination, in which the Committee stipulated that the prohibition of the dissemination of all ideas based upon racial superiority or *hatred* is compatible with freedom of opinion and expression, is equally applicable to the question of incitement to religious *hatred*;

12. Strongly condemns all manifestations and acts of racism, racial discrimination, xenophobia and related intolerance against national or ethnic, religious and linguistic minorities and migrants and the stereotypes often applied to them, including on the basis of religion or belief, and urges all States to apply and, where required, reinforce existing laws when such xenophobic or intolerant acts, manifestations or expressions occur, in order to deny impunity for those who commit such acts;

13. Urges all States to provide, within their respective legal and constitutional systems, adequate protection against acts of hatred, discrimination, intimidation and coercion resulting from defamation of religions and incitement to religious hatred in general, and to take all possible measures to promote tolerance and respect for all religions and beliefs;

14. Underscores the need to combat defamation of religions and incitement to religious hatred in general by strategizing and harmonizing actions at the local, national, regional and international levels through education and awareness building;

15. Calls upon all States to make the utmost effort, in accordance with their national legislation and in conformity with international human rights and hu-

manitarian law, to ensure that religious places, sites, shrines and symbols are fully respected and protected, and to take additional measures in cases where they are vulnerable to desecration or destruction;

16. Calls for strengthened international efforts to foster a global dialogue for the promotion of a culture of tolerance and peace at all levels, based on respect for human rights and diversity of religions and beliefs, and urges States, non-governmental organizations, religious leaders as well as the print and electronic media to support and foster such a dialogue;

17. Expresses its appreciation to the High Commissioner for Human Rights for holding a seminar on freedom of expression and advocacy of religious hatred that constitutes incitement to discrimination, hostility or violence, in October 2008, and requests her to continue to build on this initiative, with a view to contributing concretely to the prevention and elimination of all such forms of incitement and the consequences of negative stereotyping of religions or beliefs, and their adherents, on the human rights of those individuals and their communities;

18. Requests the Special Rapporteur on contemporary forms of racism, racial discrimination, xenophobia and related intolerance to report on all manifestations of defamation of religions, and in particular on the serious implications of Islamophobia, on the enjoyment of all rights by their followers, to the Council at its twelfth session;

19. Requests the High Commissioner for Human Rights to report to the Council at its twelfth session on the implementation of the present resolution, including on the possible correlation between defamation of religions and the upsurge in incitement, intolerance and hatred in many parts of the world.

43rd meeting
26 March 2009

Glossary

ahl al-kitab People of the book. In Islamic law, the term for Jews and Christians, who are deemed to share the scriptural tradition that culminated in Islam. Some also include Zoroastrians and Sabeans in this category.

Ahmadi Pertaining to the sect founded by Mirza Ghulam Ahmad (d. 1908) in India. Depending on interpretations, he is either to be considered as a new Prophet or as an Islamic reformer. Ahmadis have been accused of heresy for accepting a prophet after the Prophet Muhammad, and Pakistan officially treats them as non-Muslims.

Baha'i Pertaining to a religion established in Iran by Baha Ullah, known as the Bab, and promulgated by his son, Abdul Baha (1844–1921). It honors a line of prophets who include Abraham, Moses, Jesus, Muhammad, the Bab, and Baha Allah, which opens them to charges of apostasy from Islam. Iran's Shi'i clerics long denounced this religion, and since the Islamic Revolution, Baha'is have been the targets of particularly harsh persecution.

burqa A concealing, tent-like covering with a patch of netting in front of the eyes that permits the wearer to peer out. Required of women by social and religious pressures in many conservative areas of Afghanistan and Pakistan.

chador A large semicircle of cloth, today typically black, wrapped in such a way as to conceal all but a woman's face and hands. Commonly worn by lower-class urban women in Iran, it became imposed as the form of Islamic dress favored by officialdom after Iran's Islamic Revolution.

concordisme In the context of the apologetic literature discussed in this book, the retroactive projection of prestigious modern developments in Western civilization into a putative Islamic past in efforts to demonstrate that Islam anticipated these developments.

Copts Depending on the context: the Coptic-speaking, Christian inhabitants of Egypt at the time of the Arab conquest or the remnants of this group. Copts have adopted the Arabic language but retain their Christian affiliation. Their community has been reduced by extensive conversions to Islam and is now a beleaguered minority in Egypt.

cultural relativism The rejection of the idea that universal standards can be validly used to judge individual cultures, based on the assumption that cultures can only be fairly judged in terms of their own internal value systems.

dhimmi A non-Muslim subject living under Muslim rule who enjoys protection in return for paying a special tax to the Muslim ruler and accepting a subjugated status governed by Islamic rules.

Druze Pertaining to a sect that was originally an offshoot of Isma'ili Islam but that is regarded as having broken away from Islam, now concentrated in the Levant, especially in Lebanon.

faqih (**plural**, *fuqaha*) An Islamic scholar possessed of advanced training in Islamic jurisprudence.

hijab (**Arabic**)/*hejab* (**Persian**) A highly ambiguous term used to refer to various versions of Islamic modest dress for women. Potentially signifying everything from very concealing attire such as a *chador* to a head scarf worn with otherwise conventional contemporary clothing.

Islamization The goal of many programs that have been put forward to reverse the Westernization of governments and legal systems in Muslim countries. Treating Islam as an ideology, Islamization programs typically assume that reviving Islamic law and strengthening Islamic morality will cure the ills of Muslim countries, enable them to block Western predations, and usher in an era of justice, prosperity, and social harmony.

jihad A term with a variety of connotations, but essentially connoting a struggle on behalf of Islamic causes. It potentially could include actual warfare against infidels but could also signify the individual believer's struggle to follow the teachings of Islam and to serve the faith.

jizya A tax amounting to a form of tribute required of non-Muslim subjects and paid to their Muslim rulers.

madhhab (plural, *madhahib*) Pertaining to the distinctive strains in jurisprudence that congealed into what are treated as separate schools with their own methodologies and rules.

millet The Ottoman term for the organization of society in which the Sunni rulers allowed separate communities to persist based on religious adherence (Catholics, Greek Orthodox, Jews, and the like). These non-Muslim communities could enjoy a modicum of autonomy and self-government as long as they remained loyal to the Ottoman Sultan and paid the requisite taxes.

muhtasib In traditional Muslim societies, a kind of market and public safety inspector, also tasked with enforcing Islamic morality. In the contemporary context, more likely to be an official charged with the task of identifying and punishing infractions of conservative mores.

Mu'tazila A medieval rationalist current in Islamic thought that has always had some echoes in Shi'i thought and that recently seems to be spreading in influence among Islamic reformers and proponents of progressive positions.

Muslim Brotherhood/*Ikhwan* One of the most influential of all the groups calling for Islamization. Founded in Egypt in 1928, this Sunni group has continued to press its program of remaking government, law, and society along Islamic lines in order to establish the ideal Islamic community. Members of the brotherhood, such as Hassan al-Banna and Sayyid Qutb, have spawned many emulators.

Orientalism Since the 1978 publication of Edward Said's provocative study *Orientalism*, this term has become associated with his critique of Western scholarship that he claimed was designed to portray Middle Eastern Muslims as enmeshed in an exotic and primitive culture. This portrayal was one that could be used by European powers to justify imperialist ventures, depicted as ways to bring progress and enlightenment to a benighted civilization.

purdah A system of keeping women in seclusion and segregated from men to whom they are not related and ensuring that, if they leave their homes, they are veiled and escorted by male family members. This system is often associated with the Indian Subcontinent.

qanun A term derived from the Greek that is used to denote secular law, especially codified laws. (All Islamic legal terminology derives from Arabic.)

shari'a The body of Islamic law, which is derived using approved methodologies from the Islamic sources, the Qur'an and the *sunna*.

Shi'i Pertaining to a branch of Islam whose adherents split from the Sunnis on the basis that the Prophet's divine inspiration had been inherited through his bloodline. Shi'is believe that Ali, the Prophet's son-in-law, was his rightful successor and that only the Prophet's descendants, known as Imams, should rule over the Muslim community.

Sufi Pertaining to the mystical tradition in Islam, in which the believer seeks oneness with God through mystical experiences.

sunna Roughly, the custom of the Prophet Muhammad, which is regarded as normative. Contained in accounts known individually as *hadith*, the sayings and actions of the Prophet Muhammad serve as an important source of guidance for Muslims. The accounts are contained in various collections, the contents of which can differ considerably.

Sunni Pertaining to the majority sect of Islam. The original Sunnis accepted the authority of the Caliphs who succeeded the Prophet Muhammad, rejecting the Shi'i position that his son-in-law Ali was the rightful successor. Over the centuries, Sunnis developed a jurisprudence that differed significantly from the Shi'i tradition, and within their own tradition, four separate schools of jurisprudence congealed.

Twelver Shi'ism The largest branch of Shi'ism. Adherents believe that the last of the divinely inspired Imams was the twelfth. After his disappearance, bereft of leadership, these Shi'is have turned to eminent Islamic clerics for guidance as they await his return. The geographic regions where Twelver Shi'is are concentrated have changed over the centuries. Today they constitute a majority in Azerbaijan, Bahrain, Iran, and Iraq.

ulama Collective term for Islamic scholars and jurists.

umma The Muslim community, often entailing a reference to the early period of Islamic history when Muslims were united in a single religious and political community, which remains an ideal for many.

Wahhabi Pertaining to a puritanical sect of Islam that is dominant in Saudi Arabia and that takes its name from its founder Muhammad ibn 'Abd al-Wahhab (1703–1792).

Bibliography

Given the burgeoning literature and proliferating websites on Islam and human rights in the Middle East, this bibliography can offer only a small and selective sampling. An attempt has been made to list materials covering various topics, without any implication that works not cited lack merit.

The Origins and Premises of the UN Human Rights System

Lindholm, Tore. "Prospects for Research on the Cultural Legitimacy of Human Rights: The Cases of Liberalism and Marxism." In *Human Rights in Cross-Cultural Perspectives: A Quest for Consensus*, ed. Abdullahi An-Na'im. Philadelphia: University of Pennsylvania Press, 1992, 387–426. A significant, original examination of the philosophical basis for the UDHR.

Morsink, Johannes. *The Universal Declaration of Human Rights: Origins, Drafting, and Intent*. Philadelphia: University of Pennsylvania Press, 1999. A valuable, detailed history of the process culminating in the production of the UDHR.

Waltz, Susan E. "Universal Human Rights: The Contribution of Muslim States." *Human Rights Quarterly* 26 (November 2004): 799–844. A review of the significant input from delegates of Muslim countries in the drafting of the human rights instruments.

———. "Universalizing Human Rights: The Role of Small States in the Construction of the Universal Declaration of Human Rights." *Human Rights Quarterly* 23 (2001): 44–72. An important examination of how crucial UN human rights instruments were shaped by delegates from smaller countries.

The Islamic Heritage and Human Rights

Abou El Fadl, Khaled. "The Human Rights Commitment in Modern Islam." In *Human Rights and Responsibilities in the World Religions*, eds. Joseph Runzo,

Nancy M. Martin, and Arvind Sharma. Oxford: Oneworld, 2003, 331–340. Reflections on how Muslims can rethink their religious heritage, identifying Islamic values consonant with human rights.

_____. *Speaking in God's Name: Islamic Law, Authority, and Women.* Oxford: Oneworld, 2003. A vigorous challenge to authoritarian approaches to Islamic law and a lacerating critique of the methods underlying readings of the Islamic sources that call for subjugating Muslim women to male authority.

Cohen, Joshua, and Ian Lague, eds. *The Place of Tolerance in Islam.* Boston: Beacon Press, 2002. Khaled Abou El Fadl examines tolerance; others respond and critique his stance.

Goodman, Lenn. *Islamic Humanism.* Oxford: Oxford University Press, 2003. A study of the humanistic elements that inhere in the Islamic heritage.

Kugle, Scott Siraj al-Haqq. *Homosexuality in Islam: Critical Reflection on Gay, Lesbian, and Transgender Muslims.* Oxford: Oneworld, 2010. A detailed and probing examination of the Islamic heritage as it pertains to contemporary controversies about gay rights.

Kurzman, Charles, ed. *Liberal Islam: A Sourcebook.* Oxford: Oxford University Press, 1998. Writings by a wide range of liberal Muslim intellectuals on subjects including democracy, the rights of women and non-Muslims, and freedom of thought.

Lawyers Committee for Human Rights. *Islam and Equality: Debating the Future of Women's and Minority Rights in the Middle East and North Africa.* New York: Lawyers Committee for Human Rights, 1999. Exchanges among participants at a conference on international law, human rights, and Islam, disputing whether equality can be accommodated within an Islamic framework.

Mernissi, Fatima. *Islam and Democracy: Fear of the Modern World,* trans. Mary Jo Lakeland. Reading, MA: Addison-Wesley, 1992. An argument by a prominent Moroccan advocate of human rights and democracy challenging the barriers that Islam supposedly presents to democracy.

Sadri, Mahmoud, and Ahmad Sadri, eds. *Reason, Freedom, and Democracy in Islam: Essential Writings of Abdolkarim Soroush.* Oxford: Oxford University Press, 2000. See also the website of Soroush, http://www.drsoroush.com/English .htm. Proposals for enlightened, rationalist approaches to understanding Islam by one of Iran's leading philosophers, originally a supporter of the Islamic Revolution and now one of the country's most famous dissidents.

Safi, Omid, ed. *Progressive Muslims: On Justice, Gender, and Pluralism.* Oxford: Oneworld, 2005. A collection of essays by Muslims arguing for progressive interpretations of Islam on a variety of subjects.

Taji-Farouki, Suha, ed. *Modern Muslim Intellectuals and the Qur'an.* Oxford: Oxford University Press, 2004. Essays presenting a variety of current trends in Qur'an interpretation by liberal Muslims, demonstrating the importance of interpretive methodologies for drawing out the implications of the text.

Human Rights and Culture

Engle, Karen. "Culture and Human Rights: The Asian Values Debate in Context." *New York Journal of International Law and Politics* 32 (2000): 291–333. A particularly interesting dissection of the Asian values debate and analysis of how "cultural" objections to international human rights can actually be proxies for other concerns.

Howland, Courtney W., ed. *Religious Fundamentalisms and the Human Rights of Women.* New York: St. Martin's Press, 1999. A collection of essays wrestling with the implications of various fundamentalisms for women's human rights.

Mayer, Ann Elizabeth. "Shifting Grounds for Challenging the Authority of International Human Rights Law: Religion as a Malleable and Politicized Pretext for Governmental Noncompliance with Human Rights." In *Human Rights with Modesty: The Problem of Universalism,* ed. Andras Sajo. Leiden: Martinus-Nijhoff, 2004, 349–374. An analysis of Iran's changing stances on human rights universality over several decades, demonstrating the political contingency of "Islamic" objections to international human rights law.

———. "Universal Versus Islamic Human Rights: A Clash of Cultures or a Clash with a Construct?" *Michigan Journal of International Law* 15 (1994): 307–404. A dissection of how Huntington's clash of civilizations model misrepresents Muslims' reactions to human rights, relating Huntington's thesis to debates at the 1993 Vienna human rights conference.

Feminism and Islamic Feminism

Afkhami, Mahnaz, ed. *Faith and Freedom: Women's Human Rights in the Muslim World.* New York: I. B. Tauris, 1995. A collection of essays on various aspects of women's human rights in Muslim countries.

Afkhami, Mahnaz, and Haleh Vaziri. *Claiming Our Rights: A Manual for Women's Human Rights Education in Muslim Societies.* Bethesda, MD: Sisterhood Is Global, 1996. A pioneering work providing real-life human rights dilemmas for Muslim women to study, discuss in group settings, and resolve.

Mernissi, Fatima. *The Veil and the Male Elite: A Feminist Interpretation of Women's Rights in Islam.* Reading, MA: Addison-Wesley, 1991. Reinterpretations of the Islamic heritage from an Arab feminist's perspective.

Mir-Hosseini, Ziba. *Islam and Gender: The Religious Debate in Contemporary Iran.* Princeton: Princeton University Press, 1999. An important account of competing Iranian feminist and conservative readings of the Islamic sources, with attention to the important feminist work of the cleric Mohsen Saidzadeh.

Moghadam, Val. "Islamic Feminism and Its Discontents: Toward a Resolution of the Debates." *SIGNS: Journal of Women in Culture and Society* 27 (2002): 1136–1171. An insightful comparison of Islamic feminism and its secular counterpart.

Human Rights Issues in the Islamic Republic of Iran

Abrahamian, Ervand. *Tortured Confessions*. Berkeley: University of California Press, 1999. An in-depth assessment of how the practice of torture under the Islamic Republic reflects Iran's Islamic ideology.

Afshari, Reza. *Human Rights in Iran: The Abuse of Cultural Relativism*. Philadelphia: University of Pennsylvania Press, 2001. A vigorous critique of the human rights record of the Islamic Republic with particularly valuable analyses of source material in Farsi.

Khorasani, Noushin Ahmadi. *Iranian Women's One Million Signatures Campaign for Equality: The Inside Story*. Women's Learning Partnership Translation Series. Syracuse, NY: Syracuse University Press, 2009. A firsthand account of how Iranian women sought to mobilize grassroots support for the idea of women's equality.

Mir-Hosseini, Ziba, and Richard Tapper. *Islam and Democracy in Iran: Eshkevari and the Quest for Reform*. London: I. B. Tauris, 2006. An important examination of the political context in which Iran's reformers press for democracy, with assessments of the writings and activities of one of Iran's most eminent dissident clerics.

Schirazi, Asghar. *The Constitution of Iran: Politics and the State in the Islamic Republic*. New York: I. B. Tauris, 1997. A thorough account of Iran's constitution and its political and legal context.

The Politics of Human Rights

Abirafeh, Lina. *Gender and International Aid in Afghanistan: The Politics and Effects of Intervention*. Jefferson, NC: McFarland, 2009. A probing analysis of the pitfalls facing Western aid projects based on a philosophy of gender mainstreaming but lacking familiarity with the realities of Afghan culture and politics.

al-'Azm, Sadiq Jalal. "The Importance of Being Earnest About Salman Rushdie." *Die Welt des Islams* 31 (1991): 1–49. An examination of the context and significance of the Rushdie case by an eminent Arab philosopher.

Bennoune, Karima. "Toward a Human Rights Approach to Armed Conflict: Iraq 2003." *U.C.–Davis Journal of International Law and Policy* 11 (2004): 171–228. An inquiry into how international human rights law as well as international humanitarian law should apply to the US invasion and occupation of Iraq.

Chase, Anthony Tirado, and Amr Hamzawy, eds. *Human Rights in the Arab World: Independent Voices*. Philadelphia: University of Pennsylvania Press, 2006. Essays by both Arab and Western authors on a variety of current controversies about the struggle to advance human rights in Arab societies, including both Islamic and secular dimensions.

Danchin, Peter G. "US Unilateralism and the International Protection of Religious Freedom: The Multilateral Alternative." *Columbia Journal of Transnational Law* 41 (2002): 33–135. A dissection of the US pattern of privileging freedom of religion over other human rights and the unilateralist approach of the US International Religious Freedom Act.

Franks, Mary Ann. "Obscene Undersides: Women and Evil Between the Taliban and the United States." *HYPATIA* 18 (2003): 135–155. An examination of the oppression of Afghan women, finding fault with the policies of both the Taliban and the United States.

Klausen, Jytte. *The Cartoons That Shook the World.* New Haven: Yale University Press, 2009. A solid overview of the Danish cartoons controversy.

Mendez, Juan E., and Javier Mariezcurrena. "Prospects for Human Rights Advocacy in the Wake of September 11, 2001." *Law and Inequality Journal* 22 (2004): 223–263. Appraisals of problematic US policies and actions in the war on terrorism, examining the repercussions of these on the human rights movement.

Risse, Thomas, Stephen Ropp, and Kathryn Sikkink, eds. *The Power of Human Rights: International Norms and Domestic Change.* Cambridge: Cambridge University Press, 1999. Proposal for a schematization of the stages through which international human rights law penetrates into domestic legal systems.

Waltz, Susan E. *Human Rights and Reform: Changing the Face of North African Politics.* Berkeley: University of California, 1995. Based on extensive research, a discussion of how human rights activism developed in North Africa and how it affected the political landscape.

Whitaker, Brian. *Unspeakable Love: Gay and Lesbian Life in the Middle East.* Berkeley: University of California Press, 2006. A probing and sensitive account by an eminent journalist of many dimensions of the difficult lives of gays and lesbians in the Middle East and the surrounding political context.

Wickham, Carrie. "The Problem with Coercive Democratization: The Islamist Response to the US Democracy Reform Initiative." *Muslim World Journal of Human Rights* 1 (2004). Available at http://www.bepress.com/cgi/viewcontent.cgi ?article=1018&context=mwjhr. An insightful analysis of how US initiatives to spread democracy in Arab countries have provoked a backlash among Islamists, who find these initiatives culturally offensive and fraught with double standards.

Internet Sites with Useful Information and Links

AHR. Arab Human Rights Index, offering extensive links to UN human rights committees, country human rights reports submitted to the UN, ratifications of human rights treaties, and some human rights organizations: http://www.arabhumanrights.org/en/

al-bab (Arab Gateway)—Human rights, with links to relevant declarations on human rights, including the UIDHR, human rights reports by NGOs and governments, and reports on specific Arab countries: http://www.al-bab.com/arab/human.htm

Islam and Human Rights, School of Law, Emory University. Website dedicated to the topic of Islam and human rights with extensive links to publications, bibliographies, materials for human rights activism, and other useful resources: http://www.law.emory.edu/IHR/

LGBT Rights. Human Rights Watch has developed a lesbian, gay, bisexual, and transgender program, and its website offers reports on LGBT issues around the world, including many from the Middle East: http://www.hrw.org/en/category/topic/lgbt-rights

Qantara.de. Dialogue with the Islamic World, with many links to human rights institutions and NGOs, human rights documents and reports, including the UIDHR, the Cairo Declaration, and similar documents: http://www.qantara.de/webcom/show_link.php/_c–449/i.html

University of Minnesota Human Rights Library. Islam and human rights links, including the UIDHR: http://www1.umn.edu/humanrts/links/islam.html

University of Minnesota Human Rights Library. Middle East links, some of which relate to Islam and human rights: http://www.umn.edu/humanrts/links/mideast.html

Muslim World Journal of Human Rights. Published by the Berkeley Electronic Press, with scholarly articles on human rights issues in Muslim societies: http://www.bepress.com/mwjhr/

General Indices for Comparative Assessments of Development Records of Middle Eastern Countries

The World Bank Worldwide Governance Indicators: http://data.worldbank.org/data-catalog/worldwide-governance-indicators
  An overview of governance indicators for 212 countries in the period 1996–2008 that illustrates many of the governance shortcomings of Middle Eastern countries, many of which in turn correlate with human rights deficiencies.

United Nations Development Program, Arab Human Development Report 2004. Towards Freedom in the Arab World: http://hdr.undp.org/en/reports/regionalreports/arabstates/name,3278,en.html
  A critical assessment by development experts how lack of freedom in Arab countries relates to the relatively low progress of development.

United Nations Development Program, Arab Human Development Report 2005. Towards the Rise of Women in the Arab World: http://hdr.undp.org/en/reports/regionalreports/arabstates/name,3403,en.html
    A study of the situation of Arab women that analyzes the factors holding Arab women back, assigning a relatively low weight to the impact of religion.

World Economic Forum, The Global Gender Gap Report 2010: http://www3.weforum.org/docs/WEF_GenderGap_Report_2010.pdf
    A review of women's status around the world with data showing how wide the inequality is between men and women in the Middle East.

Internet Sites for Women's Rights

UN Division for the Advancement of Women. Many links and resources, including reports on the meetings of the Committee on the Elimination of Discrimination Against Women, where Muslim countries' defenses of their stances on women's rights through 2007 can be found: http://www.un.org/womenwatch/daw/

From 2008 onward, the material is available at: http://www2.ohchr.org/english/bodies/cedaw/index.htm

Women Living Under Muslim Laws. A feminist NGO studying the rights of women in Muslim countries, with many links: http://www.wluml.org/

Women's Human Rights Resources, Bora Laskin Law Library, University of Toronto. Extensive materials and links for all dimensions of women's human rights, relevant international law, and literature on the topic of women's rights: http://www.law-lib.utoronto.ca/diana/

Women's Learning Partnership. Material to empower women and girls in the Global South through leadership training, capacity building, and help women use new technologies to generate and receive information and knowledge: http://www.learningpartnership.org/

Notes

Preface

1. Aspects of these adjustments and reformulations are discussed in Bassam Tibi, *The Crisis of Modern Islam: A Preindustrial Culture in the Scientific Technological Age*, trans. Judith von Silvers (Salt Lake City: University of Utah Press, 1988); Bassam Tibi, *Islam and the Cultural Accommodation of Social Change*, trans. Clare Krojzl (Boulder: Westview Press, 1990); Olivier Roy, *Globalised Islam: The Search for a New Ummah* (London: Hurst, 2004); and Gilles Kepel, *The Revenge of God: The Resurgence of Islam, Christianity, and Judaism in the Modern World* (Malden, MA: Polity Press, 2004).

Chapter One

1. See Virginia Sherry, "The Human Rights Movement in the Arab World: An Active and Diverse Community of Human Rights Advocates Exists in Several Countries of the Region," Special Middle East Watch Issue, *Human Rights Watch* 4 (Fall 1990): 6–7; Kevin Dwyer, *Arab Voices: The Human Rights Debate in the Middle East* (Berkeley: University of California Press, 1991); Susan Waltz, *Human Rights and Reform: Changing the Face of North African Politics* (Berkeley: University of California Press, 1995); *Cairo Papers in Social Science. Human Rights: Egypt and the Arab World* 17 (Fall 1994); Anthony Tirado Chase and Amr Hamzawy, eds., *Human Rights in the Arab World: Independent Voices* (Philadelphia: University of Pennsylvania Press, 2006); Shirin Ebadi, *Iran Awakening. A Memoir of Revolution and Hope* (New York, Random House, 2006); Valentine Moghadam, *From Patriarchy to Empowerment: Women's Participation, Movements, and Rights in the Middle East, North Africa, and South Asia* (Syracuse: Syracuse University Press, 2007). One can also get information from individual human rights NGOs, such as The Arab Organization for Human Rights, http://aohr.org/; The Egyptian Organization for Human Rights, http://www.eohr.org/; The Ibn Khaldun Center for Development Studies, http://www.eicds.org/; The Human

Rights Commission of Pakistan, http://www.hrcp-web.org/; and Women Living Under Muslim Laws, http://www.wluml.org/.

2. Neil MacFarquhar, "Saudi Arabia's King Employs Royal Treasury to Keep Peace," *The New York Times*, June 8, 2011, A1.

3. See Alan Watson, *Legal Transplants: An Approach to Comparative Law* (Edinburgh: Scottish-Academic Press, 1974), 6–9.

4. Perverse mischaracterizations that are deployed by persons who are determined to discredit critical examinations of this topic are exemplified by the unfounded accusations that hostile reviewers have hurled at earlier editions of this book. These include charges that the book presents Islam as a monolithic model, that it suggests that Islam is static and inherently opposed to rights, that it argues for the superiority of Western law, and that it asserts that "contemporary Muslims do not possess the culture that entitles them to be concerned with human rights." See, for example, the extremely misleading reviews by Ahmad Dallal, *Middle East Studies Association Bulletin* 26 (1992): 245–246; Ridwan al-Sayyid, "Contemporary Muslim Thought and Human Rights," *IslamoChristiana* 21 (1995): 27–41; and Shamsheer Ali, "Review Article: Misguided Theorizing and Application," *Journal of Muslim Minority Affairs* 19 (1999): 299–320, to which I responded in Ann Elizabeth Mayer, "Misguided Interpretation: Ann Elizabeth Mayer's Response to Shamsheer Ali's Review Article," *Journal of Muslim Minority Affairs* 20 (2000): 181–184. See especially the wildly inaccurate charges in John Strawson, "A Western Question to the Middle East: 'Is There a Human Rights Discourse in Islam?'" *Arab Studies Quarterly* 19 (Winter 1997): 31–58, to which I responded in Ann Elizabeth Mayer, "A Rebuttal," *Arab Studies Quarterly* 20 (Winter 1998): 95–97, available at http://www.findarticles.com/p/articles/mi_m2501/is_n1_v20/ai_20791170.

See also an article on my website dissecting the canons of pseudo-scholarship in this area, "*Not* Taking Rights Seriously: Hallmarks of the Frivolous Human Rights 'Critique,'" available in the writings section at http://lgst.wharton.upenn.edu/mayera/. A partisan of this movement to discredit critical appraisals of Islamic human rights schemes, Mashood Baderin, makes the outlandish claim that this book asserts that "Western culture should serve as the universal normative model for the content of international human rights law." See Mashood A. Baderin, *International Human Rights and Islamic Law* (Oxford: Oxford University Press, 2003), 10. Elsewhere, Baderin concocts an accusation that I have written that supporting "universalism"—*his* term, one not used in the passage referred to—entails agreeing that "Islamic law has no normative value and enjoys little prestige." See ibid., 12. Discussions of what I have actually written have been deliberately—and most conveniently—disregarded by these authors, whose political agendas dictate their recourse to misrepresentations of work supporting Muslims' entitlement to human rights, pretending that all such work aims to denigrate Islam.

5. There are important exceptions to the uncritical approach that dominated until recently. See, for example, Abdullahi An-Na'im, *Toward an Islamic Reformation: Civil Liberties, Human Rights, and International Law* (Syracuse, NY: Syracuse University Press, 1990); Sami Aldeeb Abu Sahlieh, *Les Musulmans face aux droits de l'homme: Religion et droit et politique. Etude et documents* (Bochum, Germany: Verlag Dr. Dieter

Winkler, 1994); Jack Donnelly, "Human Rights and Human Dignity: An Analytic Critique of Non-Western Conception of Human Rights," *American Political Science Review* 76 (1982): 306–316; Tore Lindholm and Kari Vogt, eds., *Islamic Law Reform and Human Rights: Challenges and Rejoinders* (Copenhagen: Nordic Human Rights Publications, 1993).

6. See, for example, Ahmed Rashid, *Militant Islam, Oil and Fundamentalism in Central Asia* (New Haven: Yale University Press, 2001).

7. Edward Said, *Orientalism* (London: Routledge and Kegan Paul, 1978).

8. Some implications of Said's work for legal scholarship are considered in William Lafi Youmans, "Edward Said and Legal Scholarship," *UCLA Journal of Islamic and Near Eastern Law* 3 (2003–2004): 107–116.

9. Said's analyses of Orientalist stereotypes have counterparts in assessments made in Sadiq Jalal al-'Azm, "Orientalism and Orientalism in Reverse," in *Forbidden Agendas: Intolerance and Defiance in the Middle East*, ed. Jon Rothschild (London: Al-Saqi Books, 1984), 349–381. See also "The Importance of Being Earnest About Salman Rushdie," *Die Welt des Islams* 31 (1991): 1–49, by the same author.

10. An important essay by Said's colleague Tony Judt has reminded us of Said's actual views on issues of human rights. See Tony Judt, "The Rootless Cosmopolitan," *The Nation*, July 19, 2004, available at http://www.thenation.com/doc/20040719/judt.

11. One of the influential voices expressing the critical mindset that is becoming more common is that of Khaled Abou El Fadl. See *Speaking in God's Name: Islamic Law, Authority and Women* (Oxford: Oneworld, 2003), and "The Human Rights Commitment in Modern Islam," in *Human Rights and Responsibilities in the World Religions*, eds. Joseph Runzo, Nancy M. Martin, and Arvind Sharma (Oxford: Oneworld, 2003), 331–340.

12. See Baderin, *International Human Rights*, 27.

13. A good illustration of this position can be found in Adamantia Pollis and Peter Schwab, "Human Rights: A Western Construct with Limited Applicability," in *Human Rights: Cultural and Ideological Perspectives*, eds. Adamantia Pollis and Peter Schwab (New York: Praeger, 1979), 1–18.

14. Ibid., 14.

15. Fernando Teson, "International Human Rights and Cultural Relativism," *Virginia Journal of International Law* 25 (1985): 875.

16. United Nations General Assembly. Thirty-Ninth Session. Third Committee. Sixty-fifth meeting, held on Friday, December 7, 1984, New York. A/C.3/39/SR.65. In a book that presents Iran's stances on human rights in the most favorable light, the statement that Iran would not hesitate to violate human rights has been excised from the quoted passage. See Baderin, *International Human Rights*, 30.

17. See Ann Elizabeth Mayer, "Universal Versus Islamic Human Rights: A Clash of Cultures or a Clash with a Construct?" *Michigan Journal of International Law* 15 (1994): 317–320, 371–377, 392.

18. "Women in Iran: An Online Discussion," *Middle East Policy* 8 (December 2001): 128–143.

19. For a critical evaluation of cultural relativists' tendency to totalize and reify Islamic culture, see Mayer, "Universal Versus Islamic Human Rights," 379–402; and Reza Afshari, "An Essay on Islamic Cultural Relativism in the Discourse on Human Rights," *Human Rights Quarterly* 16 (1994): 235–276.

20. Louis Muñoz, "The Rationality of Tradition," *Archiv für Rechts und Sozialphilosphie* 68 (1981): 212.

21. "Islam Guarantees Rights, Says Saud," *Riyadh Daily*, June 17, 1993, available in LEXIS/Nexis Library, ALLWLD File.

22. Press release of Iran's permanent mission to the United Nations, "Statement by H. E. Dr. Mohammad-Javad Zarif, Deputy Foreign Minister and Head of Delegation of the Islamic Republic of Iran Before the World Conference on Human Rights," Vienna, 18 June 1993.

23. The resolution is called "Promoting human rights and fundamental freedoms through a better understanding of traditional values of humankind" A/HRC/12/L.13/Rev.1.

24. United Nations, "Traditional Values," Resolution adopted at Twelfth Session of HRC Source: WLUML Networkers, available at http://www.wluml.org/node/5581.

25. Nick Cumming-Bruce, "Iran Defends Human Rights Record Before U.N. Council," *The New York Times*, February 16, 2010, available at http://www.nytimes.com/2010/02/16/world/middleeast/16geneva.html.

26. For examples of how Muslims are meshing human rights ideas with the Islamic tradition, see Abdullahi An-Na'im, *Toward an Islamic Reformation: Civil Liberties, Human Rights, and International Law* (Syracuse, NY: Syracuse University Press, 1990); Lindholm and Vogt, *Islamic Law Reform and Human Rights*; Lawyers Committee for Human Rights, *Islam and Justice: Debating the Future of Human Rights in the Middle East and North Africa* (New York: Lawyers Committee for Human Rights, 1997); Khaled Abou El Fadl, "The Human Rights Commitment in Modern Islam," in *Human Rights and Responsibilities in the World Religions,* eds. Joseph Runzo, Nancy M. Martin, and Arvind Shama (Oxford: Oneworld, 2003), 301–364; and Abdolkarim Soroush, *Reason, Freedom, and Democracy in Islam: Essential Writings of Abdolkarim Soroush,* trans. and ed. Mahmoud Sadri and Ahmad Sadri (Oxford: Oxford University Press, 2000). Works of Soroush are available at http://www.drsoroush.com/English.htm. The ideas of Islamic feminists, discussed in Chapter 6, also show how Islam can be harmonized with human rights.

27. See the Casablanca Declaration, available at http://www.al-bab.com/arab/docs/international/hr1999.htm.

28. Beirut Declaration on the Regional Protection of Human Rights in the Arab World, available at http://www.cihrs.org/focus/almethaq/beirut-declaration.htm.

29. Amitabh Pal, "Shirin Ebadi," *The Progressive*, September 2004, available at http://www.progressive.org/sept04/intv0904.html.

30. Ibid.

31. Regarding the Western tendency to consider it incongruous for "Orientals" to have modern ideas, see Rhoda E. Howard, "Cultural Absolutism and the Nostalgia for Community," *Human Rights Quarterly* 15 (1993): 315–338.

32. Teson, "International Human Rights," 895.

33. Jack Donnelly, "Cultural Relativism and Universal Human Rights," *Human Rights Quarterly* 6 (1984): 411.

34. See, for example, the discussions among Islamists and human rights activists in Lawyers Committee, *Islam and Justice*, showing how Islamists seek to associate their goals with human rights. See also Khaled Elgindy, "The Rhetoric of Rashid Ghannouchi," *Arab Studies Quarterly* (Spring 1995): 101–119.

35. Ann Elizabeth Mayer, "The Fundamentalist Impact on Law, Politics, and Constitutions in Iran, Pakistan and the Sudan," in *Fundamentalisms and the State: Remaking Polities, Economics, and Militance*, eds. Martin Marty and Scott Appleby (Chicago: University of Chicago, 1993), 110.

36. Ibid.

37. Sherif Tarek, "Emad El-Din Abdel Ghafour, Chairman of the Salafist Nour Party," *ahramonline*, Dec. 12, 2011, available at http://english.ahram.org.eg/NewsContent/1/64/29157/Egypt/Politics-/Emad-ElDin-Abdel-Ghafour,-chairman-of-the-Salafist.aspx.

38. According to the margin of appreciation doctrine, instead of requiring uniform application of the European Convention on Human Rights throughout the Council of Europe, national authorities are accorded a certain flexibility in deciding on the definition, interpretation, and application of the basic human rights guarantees contained in the treaty. See, for example, Howard Charles Yourow, *The Margin of Appreciation Doctrine in the Dynamics of European Human Rights Jurisprudence* (The Hague: Martinus Nijhoff, 1996).

39. Lawyers Committee, *Islam and Justice*.

40. The declaration from the meeting is presented in German translation in Bassam Tibi, "Bericht über das Kolloquium Arabischer Wissenschaftler und Schriftsteller: *Multaqa Tunis al-thaqafi 'an al-hurriyat al-dimuqratiya fi al-'alam al-'arabi*/Das kulturelle Tunis-Kolloquium über die Demokratischen Freiheiten in der Arabischen Welt im Centre Culturel de Hammamet, April 1–3, 1983," *Orient* 24 (1983): 398–399.

41. The serious consequences of the freedom deficit in Arab countries have been analyzed in the studies by the United Nations Development Program and the Arab Fund for Economic and Social Development; see, e.g., *Arab Human Development Report 2002* (New York: United Nations Publications, 2002), also available at http://www.undp.org/rbas/ahdr/english2002.html.

42. See, for example, the statement of Saad Eddin Ibrahim, the prominent Egyptian campaigner for democracy, made in July 2002 before he was yet again dragged off to prison for daring to challenge Egypt's repressive system. "What After the Law? Statement from Saad Ibrahim, July 29, 2002," available at http://www.nearinternational.org/alerts/egypt120020731en.html.

43. "Doha Declaration for Democracy and Reform," *Daily Star*, June 29, 2004, available at http://www.journalofdemocracy.org/Articles/Documents-Doha-Declaration-15-4.pdf.

44. The Pakistani ideologue Mawdudi made a similar assertion, claiming, "When we speak of human rights in Islam we mean those rights granted by God. Rights

granted by kings or legislative assemblies can be withdrawn as easily as they are conferred; but no individual and no institution has the authority to withdraw the rights
conferred by God." Abu'l A'la Mawdudi, *Human Rights in Islam* (Leicester, UK: Islamic
Foundation, 1980), 15.

45. "Islam Guarantees Rights, Says Saud."

46. See, generally, Baderin, *International Human Rights and Islamic Law.*

47. See this interpretation in Tore Lindholm, "Prospects for Research on the Cul-
tural Legitimacy of Human Rights: The Cases of Liberalism and Marx," in *Human
Rights in Cross-Cultural Perspectives: A Quest for Consensus,* ed. Abdullahi An-Na'im
(Philadelphia: University of Pennsylvania Press, 1992), 397.

48. Ibid., 396–397.

49. See, for example, Susan Waltz, "Universalizing Human Rights: The Role of
Small States in the Construction of the Universal Declaration of Human Rights,"
Human Rights Quarterly 23 (2001): 59–60; Mary Ann Glendon, "Foundations of
Human Rights: The Unfinished Business," *American Journal of Jurisprudence* 44
(1999): 4.

50. Mary Ann Glendon, *A World Made New: Eleanor Roosevelt and the Universal
Declaration of Human Rights* (New York: Random House, 2001), 185.

51. Glendon, "Foundations of Human Rights," 6.

52. Fereydoun Hoveyda, "The Universal Declaration and 50 Years of Human Rights,"
Transnational Law and Contemporary Problems 8 (1998): 432.

53. Susan E. Waltz, "Universal Human Rights: The Contribution of Muslim
States," *Human Rights Quarterly* 26 (November 2004): 799–844.

54. See, for example, Michael Ignatieff, "Human Rights as Idolatry," in *Human
Rights as Politics and Idolatry,* ed. Amy Gutman (Princeton: Princeton University Press,
2001), 58–60, 183.

55. Johannes Morsink, *The Universal Declaration of Human Rights: Origins,
Drafting, and Intent* (Philadelphia: University of Pennsylvania Press, 1999), 25–26.

56. Ibid., 25.

57. Waltz, "Universal Human Rights," 815.

58. Ibid., 822.

59. Ibid., 820.

60. Ibid.

61. Ibid., 821.

62. Morsink, *The Universal Declaration,* 25.

63. Waltz, "Universal Human Rights," 823.

64. Ibid., 841.

65. Morsink, *The Universal Declaration,* 26.

66. Waltz, "Universal Human Rights," 839.

67. Ibid., 822–823.

68. Ibid., 824.

69. Ibid., 828–833.

70. Ibid., 840.

71. The human rights treaty ratifications can be researched on the UN website on the Status of Treaties Deposited with the Secretary General, available at http://untreaty .un.org/ENGLISH/bible/englishinternetbible/partI/chapterIV/chapterIV.as.

72. Ann Elizabeth Mayer, "The Internationalization of Religiously Based Resistance to International Human Rights Law," in *Global Justice and the Bulwarks of Localism: Human Rights in Context,* eds. Christopher L. Eisgruber and Andras Sajo (Boston: Martinus Nijhoff, 2005), 223–255.

73. Karen Engle, "Culture and Human Rights: The Asian Values Debate in Context," *New York University Journal of International Law and Politics* 32 (2000): 291–332.

Chapter Two

1. Leo Strauss, *Natural Right and History* (Chicago: University of Chicago Press, 1953), 181–182.

2. J. Roland Pennock, "Rights, Natural Rights, and Human Rights: A General View," in *Human Rights: NOMOS XXIII,* eds. J. Roland Pennock and John W. Chapman (New York: New York University Press, 1981), 1.

3. The status of ratifications and reservations regarding the ICCPR can be found at http://untreaty.un.org/ENGLISH/bible/englishinternetbible/partI/chapterIV/treaty5.asp.

4. Louis Henkin, "International Human Rights as Rights," in *Human Rights: NOMOS XXIII,* eds. J. Roland Pennock and John W. Chapman (New York: New York University Press, 1981), 258–259.

5. The translation is taken from "Constitution of the Islamic Republic of Iran of 24 October 1979 as amended to 28 July 1989," *Constitutions of the Countries of the World,* ed. Albert Blaustein and Gisbert Flanz (Dobbs Ferry, NY: Oceana, 1992).

6. The Cairo Declaration was submitted to the United Nations by the OIC prior to the World Conference on Human Rights in Vienna. See UN GAOR, World Conference on Human Rights, 4th Session, Agenda Item 5, UN Doc. A/CONF.157/PC/ 62/ Add.18 (1993).

7. See Ann Elizabeth Mayer, "Universal Versus Islamic Human Rights: A Clash of Cultures or a Clash with a Construct?" *Michigan Journal of International Law* 15 (1994): 375.

8. Ibid., 371–379.

9. See Isabelle Vichniac, "La Commission internationale de juristes dénonce un projet de 'déclaration des droits de l'homme en Islam,'" *Le Monde,* February 13, 1992.

10. "Closing Session of Teheran's Islamic Summit Delayed," *Deutsche PresseAgentur,* December 11, 1997, available in LEXIS/Nexis Library, ALLWLD File.

11. See "Saudi Arabia: The New Constitution," *Arab Law Quarterly* 8 (1993): 258–270; Rashed Aba-Namay, "The Recent Constitutional Reforms in Saudi Arabia," *International and Comparative Law Quarterly* 42 (1993): 295–331.

12. Article 7 of the law said that the government derived its power from the Islamic sources, the Qur'an and the custom of the Prophet, and Article 1 asserted that Saudi Arabia was an Islamic state.

13. See Lawyers Committee for Human Rights, *The Justice System of the Islamic Republic of Iran* (May 1993), 47–50.

14. Constitutional developments in Iran are discussed in Said Arjomand, ed., *Authority and Political Culture in Shi'ism* (Albany: State University of New York Press, 1988); and Janet Afary, *The Iranian Constitutional Revolution, 1906–1911: Grassroots Democracy, Social Democracy, and the Origins of Feminism* (New York: Columbia University Press, 1996).

15. The amendments are discussed in Asghar Schirazi, *The Constitution of Iran: Politics and the State in the Islamic Republic*, trans. John O'Kane (London: I. B. Tauris, 1997), 95, 110–111, 234–237.

16. Due to space limitations, the voluminous reports reviewing the human rights situations in these countries cannot be listed. One can consult the relevant sections in *Amnesty International Report, Human Rights Watch World Report*, and *US State Department Country Reports on Human Rights Practices*, all issued annually. See also topical reports prepared by the Africa, Asia, and Middle East regional sections of Human Rights Watch and also by Amnesty International, and the Lawyers Committee for Human Rights (renamed Human Rights First). Reports by local human rights groups can be useful if made by independent entities.

17. Human Rights Watch/Middle East, *Iran: Power Versus Choice. Human Rights and Parliamentary Elections in the Islamic Republic of Iran* (March 1996).

18. "Ayatollah Yazdi Denounces 'Conspiracy' Aimed at Undermining Country," *BBC Summary of World Broadcasts*, November 24, 1997, available in LEXIS/Nexis Library, ALLWLD File.

19. Ann Elizabeth Mayer, "Islamic Law as a Cure for Political Law: The Withering of an Islamist Illusion," *Mediterranean Politics* 7 (Autumn 2002): 117–142.

20. Reza Afshari, *Human Rights in Iran: The Abuse of Cultural Relativism* (Philadelphia: University of Pennsylvania Press, 2001); Ervand Abrahamian, *Tortured Confessions* (Berkeley: University of California Press, 1999).

21. Quoted by Edward Mortimer, "Islam and Human Rights," *Index on Censorship* 12 (October 1983): 5.

22. See, for example, Charles Kurzman, "Critics Within: Islamic Scholars' Protests Against the Islamic State in Iran," *International Journal of Politics, Culture and Society* 15 (2001): 341–359; Ziba Mir-Hosseini and Richard Tapper, *Islam and Democracy in Iran: Eshkevari and the Quest for Reform* (London: I. B. Tauris, 2006).

23. Mayer, "Islamic Law as a Cure for Political Law," 117–142.

24. See Ladan Boroumand and Roya Boroumand, "Illusion and Reality of Civil Society in Iran: An Ideological Debate," in "Iran Since the Revolution," special issue, *Social Research* 67 (Summer 2000): 303–344.

25. Useful background is provided in J. Millard Burr and Robert O. Collins, *Requiem for the Sudan: War, Drought, and Disaster on the Nile* (Boulder: Westview Press, 1995); Human Rights Watch/Africa, *Civilian Devastation: Abuses by All Parties in the War in Southern Sudan* (New York: Human Rights Watch, 1994); Ann Lesch, *The Sudan: Contested National Identities* (Bloomington: Indiana University Press, 1998);

and Human Rights Watch, *Sudan, Oil, and Human Rights* (New York: Human Rights Watch, 2003).

26. *BBC Summary of World Broadcasts*, May 1, 1984, ME/7631/A/8.

27. "The Transitional Constitution of the Republic of the Sudan, 1985," in *Constitutions of the Countries of the World*, eds. Albert Blaustein and Gisbert Flanz (Dobbs Ferry, NY: Oceana, 1989). Article 3 made constitutional principles supreme so that they would prevail over other laws; Article 5 said that the state shall strive to "eradicate racial and religious fanaticism"; and Article 17, that all persons would be equal before the law.

28. See the reports from Africa Watch, *Denying "the Honor of Living." Sudan: A Human Rights Disaster* (March 1990); *Threat to Women's Status from Fundamentalist Regime* (March 1990); *New Islamic Penal Code Violates Basic Human Rights* (April 1991); *Inside al-Bashir's Prisons* (February 1991); *The Ghosts Remain: One Year After an Amnesty Is Declared, Detention and Torture Continue Unabated* (February 1991); and *Eradicating the Nuba* (September 1992).

29. On the various pseudo-constitutionalist initiatives taken by Bashir's government, see Peter Nyot Kok, "Codifying Islamic Absolutism in the Sudan: A Study in Constitution-Making Under al-Bashir," *Orient* 36 (1995): 673–706.

30. "Sudan Says UN Human Rights Text Offends Islam," *Agence France Presse*, February 23, 1994, available in LEXIS/Nexis Library, ALLWLD File.

31. "Sudan Calls UN Official a Blasphemer," *International Herald Tribune*, March 9, 1994, available in LEXIS/Nexis Library, ALLWLD File.

32. See Amnesty International, *Sudan: North-South Peace Deal Leaves Future of Human Rights Uncertain*, AI Index: AFR 54/002/2005 (Public) News Service No. 003, January 7, 2005.

33. As noted, President Zia was allied with such groups as Mawdudi's Jama'at-i-Islami. "Emir" is the term Mawdudi advocated for the leader of an Islamic government.

34. "Political Plan Announced, Seventh Session of Federal Council. Address by President General Muhammad Zia ul-Haq, Islamabad, August 12, 1983. Supplement to the Constitution of the Islamic Republic of Pakistan," in Blaustein and Flanz, eds., *Constitutions*, 182.

35. See Rubya Mehdi, *The Islamization of the Law in Pakistan* (Chippenham, England: Nordic Institute of Asian Studies, 1994).

36. Relevant analyses include Olivier Roy, *Afghanistan: From Holy War to Civil War* (Princeton: Darwin Press, 1995); Ahmed Rashid, *Taliban: Militant Islam, Oil, and Fundamentalism in Central Asia* (New Haven: Yale Nota Bene, 2001).

37. A particularly useful collection of Human Rights Watch reports on aspects of the deplorable human rights situation in Afghanistan is available at http://www.hrw.org/asia/afghanistan.

38. This topic is discussed in Aba-Namay, "Recent Constitutional Reforms," 295–331, and is critically evaluated in Middle East Watch, *Empty Reforms: Saudi Arabia's New Basic Laws* (May 1992).

39. For discussions of the petitions that had preceded the Basic Law, see Middle East Watch, *Empty Reforms*, 59–62.

40. Ann Elizabeth Mayer, "Conundrums in Constitutionalism: Islamic Monarchies in an Era of Transition," *UCLA Journal of Islamic and Near Eastern Law* 1 (2002): 190–204.

41. Middle East Watch, *Empty Reforms*, 2.

Chapter 3

1. See A. J. Arberry, *Sufism: An Account of the Mystics of Islam* (New York: Macmillan, 1950).

2. Khaled Abou El Fadl, "The Human Rights Commitment in Modern Islam," in *Human Rights and Responsibilities in the World Religions*, eds. Joseph Runzo, Nancy M. Martin, and Arvind Sharma (Oxford: Oneworld, 2003), 331–340.

3. Ibid., 336.

4. Ibid., 301–364; Lenn Goodman, *Islamic Humanism* (Oxford: Oxford University Press, 2003).

5. Majid Khadduri, *The Islamic Conception of Justice* (Baltimore: Johns Hopkins University Press, 1984), 78–105.

6. The struggles between proponents of reason and Revelation in Islamic intellectual history are described in A. J. Arberry, *Revelation and Reason in Islam* (London: Allen and Unwin, 1957) and Mohamed El-Shakankiri, "Loi divine et loi humaine et droit dans l'histoire juridique de Islam," *Studia Islamica* 59 (1981): 161–182.

7. The ideas of the Mu'tazila are discussed in George Hourani, *Islamic Rationalism: The Ethics of 'Abd al-Jabbar* (Oxford: Clarendon Press, 1971); and Chikh Bouamrane, *Le problème de la liberté humaine dans la pensée musulmane: Solution mu'tazilite* (Paris: J. Vrin, 1978).

8. Bouamrane, *Le problème de la liberté humaine*, 344–345.

9. For an introduction to his ideas, see *Reason, Freedom, and Democracy in Islam: Essential Writings of Abdolkarim Soroush*, eds. and trans. Mahmoud Sadri and Ahmad Sadri (Oxford: Oxford University Press, 2000); and his website, http://www.drsoroush.com/.

10. Khomeini's views are presented in Farhang Rajaee, *Islamic Values and World View: Khomeyni on Man, the State, and International Politics* (Lanham, MD: University Press of America, 1983): 42–45.

11. See Noel Coulson, "The State and the Individual in Islamic Law," *International and Comparative Law Quarterly* 6 (1957): 49–60.

12. See Erwin J. Rosenthal, *Political Thought in Medieval Islam: An Introductory Outline* (Cambridge: Cambridge University Press, 1962).

13. One finds elements in Islamic legal thought that are akin to the natural law approach to rights in the West. See Myres McDougal, Harold Lasswell, and Lung-chu Chen, *Human Rights and World Order: The Basic Policies of an International Law of Dignity* (New Haven: Yale University Press, 1980), 68–71.

14. Coulson, "The State and the Individual," 50.

15. Examples of works that document the humanism that was and continues to be part of the Islamic tradition are Mohammed Arkoun, *L'humanisme Arabe au ive/ve siècle:*

Miskawayh, philosophe et historien (Paris: J. Vrin, 1970), and *Rethinking Islam: Common Questions, Uncommon Answers* (Boulder: Westview Press, 1994); Marcel Boisard, *L'humanisme de l'Islam* (Paris: Albin Michel, 1979); Hisham Djait, *La Personnalité et le devenir arabo-islamiques* (Paris: Albin Michel, 1974); Joel Kraemer, *Humanism in the Renaissance of Islam: The Cultural Revival During the Buyid Age* (Leiden: Brill, 1986); Fazlur Rahman, *Islam and Modernity: Transformation of an Intellectual Tradition* (Chicago: University of Chicago Press, 1982); and Goodman, *Islamic Humanism*.

16. Some examples are given in Franz Rosenthal, *The Muslim Concept of Freedom Prior to the Nineteenth Century* (Leiden: Brill, 1960), 100–101, 105, 144.

17. Elie Adib Salem, *Political Theory and Institutions of the Khawarij* (Baltimore: Johns Hopkins University Press, 1965); Khadduri, *The Islamic Conception of Justice*, 20–23.

18. Hani Shukrallah, "Human Rights in Egypt: The Cause, the Movement and the Dilemma," *Cairo Papers in Social Science. Human Rights: Egypt and the Arab World. Fourth Annual Symposium* 17 (Fall 1994): 55. For a discussion of the tensions between these value systems as they are embodied in the current political struggles in Morocco, see Fatima Mernissi, *Islam and Democracy: Fear of the Modern World*, trans. Mary Jo Lakeland (Reading, Mass.: Addison-Wesley, 1992); and Ann Elizabeth Mayer, "Moroccans: Citizens or Subjects? A People at the Crossroads," *New York University Journal of International Law and Politics* 26 (1993): 63–105.

19. See, for example, Omid Safi, ed., *Progressive Muslims: On Justice, Gender, and Pluralism* (Oxford: Oneworld Publications, 2005); Joshua Cohen and Ian Lague, eds., *The Place of Tolerance in Islam* (Boston: Beacon Press, 2002).

20. See Said Amir Arjomand, "Constitutions and the Struggle for Political Order: A Study in the Modernization of Political Traditions," *European Journal of Sociology* 33 (1992): 39–82.

21. See Farhat Ziadeh, *Lawyers, the Rule of Law, and Liberalism in Modern Egypt* (Stanford: Hoover Institution, 1968); Nathan Brown, *The Rule of Law in the Arab World: Courts in Egypt and the Arab States of the Gulf* (Cambridge: Cambridge University Press, 1997).

22. See Albert Hourani, *Arabic Thought in the Liberal Age, 1798–1939* (Oxford: Oxford University Press, 1967).

23. See Abdol Karim Lahidji, "Constitutionalism and Clerical Authority," in *Authority and Political Culture in Shi'ism*, ed. Said Arjomand (Albany: State University of New York Press, 1988), 133–158; and Abdul-Hadi Hairi, *Shi'ism and Constitutionalism in Iran* (Leiden: Brill, 1977).

24. The Basic Law disavows any intention to be a constitution, calling itself *al-nizam al-asasi li'l-hukm,* or "basic regulation for government." Article 1 maintains that the country's "constitution," or *dustur,* is the Qur'an and the *sunna.* The Basic Law is compared with the Moroccan constitution in Ann Elizabeth Mayer, "Conundrums in Constitutionalism: Islamic Monarchies in an Era of Transition," *UCLA Journal of Islamic and Near Eastern Law* 1 (Spring/Summer 2002): 183–228.

25. A. K. Brohi, "The Nature of Islamic Law and the Concept of Human Rights," in International Commission of Jurists, Kuwait University, and Union of Arab Lawyers,

Human Rights in Islam: Report of a Seminar Held in Kuwait, December 1980 (International Commission of Jurists, 1982), 43–60.

26. A. K. Brohi, "Islam and Human Rights," *PLD Lahore* 28 (1976): 148–160.

27. A. K. Brohi, "The Nature of Islamic Law and the Concept of Human Rights," *PLD Journal* (1983): 143–176.

28. Brohi, "The Nature of Islamic Law" (Kuwait seminar), 48.

29. Brohi, "Islam and Human Rights," 150.

30. Ibid., 151.

31. Ibid., 152.

32. Ibid., 159.

33. For other perspectives resembling Brohi's, see Abdul Aziz Said, "Precept and Practice of Human Rights in Islam," *Universal Human Rights* 1 (1979): 73–74, 77; M. F. al-Nabhan, "The Learned Academy of Islamic Jurisprudence," *Arab Law Quarterly* 1 (1986): 391–392; Taymour Kamel, "The Principle of Legality and Its Application in Islamic Criminal Justice," in *The Islamic Criminal Justice System,* ed. Cherif Bassiouni (New York: Praeger, 1982), 169; and Cherif Bassiouni, "Sources of Islamic Law and the Protection of Human Rights," in *The Islamic Criminal Justice System,* ed. Cherif Bassiouni (New York: Praeger, 1982), 13–14, 23.

34. Abu'l A'la Mawdudi, *The Islamic Law and Constitution* (Lahore: Islamic Publications, 1980), 252. The original, in a more accurate translation, reads: "Hearing and obeying are the duty of a Muslim man both regarding what he likes and what he dislikes." Ibn al-Farra' al-Baghawi, *Mishkat Al-Masabih*, vol. 2, trans. James Tobson (Lahore: Muhammad Ashraf, 1963), 780.

35. Jack Donnelly, "Human Rights as *Natural* Rights," *Human Rights Quarterly* 4 (1982): 391.

36. Mawdudi, *Human Rights*, 37.

37. Claims that the dead have human rights are rare. If one had a coherent philosophy that the dead do have human rights, one would likely propose other rights for the dead as well. See Raymond Belliotti, "Do Dead Human Beings Have Rights?" *Personalist* 60 (1979): 201–210.

38. Ibid., 24–25.

39. Ibid., 24.

40. Ibid., 36.

41. Ibid.

42. Ibid., 17.

43. Universal Islamic Declaration of Human Rights (UIDHR), Article 1.b.

44. Mawdudi, *Human Rights*, 18.

45. Cairo Declaration on Human Rights in Islam, Article 14.

46. Mawdudi, *Human Rights,* 18.

47. UIDHR, Article 20.e.

48. Mawdudi, *Human Rights,* 38.

49. Ibid., 22.

50. UIDHR, Arabic version, Article 14.

51. Searches for cultural identity go on in many formerly colonized societies. See Borhan Ghalioun, "Identité, culture et politique culturelle dans les pays dépendants," *Peuples Méditerranéens* 16 (1981): 31–50.

52. Abu'l A'la Mawdudi, *Purdah and the Status of Women in Islam* (Lahore: Islamic Publications, 1979), 45. Cited are figures such as "Judge Ben Lindsey, President of the Juvenile Court of Denver" (59), "Dr. Kraft Ebing [*sic*]" (116), and "Wester Marck [*sic*]" (127) to show that there was a scientific justification for *shari'a* rules. Even statements in the popular US monthly *Reader's Digest* were deemed worthy of citation.

53. Sultanhussein Tabandeh, *A Muslim Commentary on the Universal Declaration of Human Rights*, trans. F. J. Goulding (Guildford, England: F. J. Goulding, 1970), 15.

54. See, for example, Asghar Schirazi, *The Constitution of Iran: Politics and the State in the Islamic Republic* (New York: I. B. Tauris, 1997), 162–172.

55. See the UIDHR and the work of Tabandeh and Mawdudi, where sources are cited without showing how the rights supposedly inhering in them have been derived.

56. International Commission of Jurists, *Human Rights in Islam*, 9. See also remarks on pages 11 and 34.

57. Ibid., 54.

58. "Islam a Champion of Human Rights, Official Says," *Compass Newswire*, October 28, 1997, available in LEXIS/Nexis Library, ALLWLD File.

59. Tabandeh, *A Muslim Commentary*, 85.

60. Mawdudi, *Human Rights*, 15.

61. Ibid., 39.

62. For example, see Mawdudi, *Human Rights*, 15, 17–22.

63. International Commission of Jurists, *Human Rights in Islam*, 7.

64. Ibid., 49–55.

65. See Abdullahi An-Na'im, *The Second Message of Islam* (Syracuse, N.Y.: Syracuse University Press, 1987); and his *Toward an Islamic Reformation: Civil Liberties, Human Rights, and International Law* (Syracuse, N.Y.: Syracuse University Press, 1990).

66. See, for example, Khaled Abou El Fadl, "A Distinctly Islamic View of Human Rights—Does It Exist and Is It Compatible with the Universal Declaration of Human Rights?" in *Islam and Human Rights: Advancing a US-Muslim Dialogue,* ed. Shireen Hunter (Washington, DC: CSIS Press, 2005), 27–42.

67. See Arkoun, *Rethinking Islam*, and the critique of religious thought by Sadiq Jalal al-'Azm, *Naqd al-fikr al-dini* (Beirut: Dar al-tali'a, 1972); and Muhammad Sa'id al-Ashmawy, *Against Islamic Extremism*, ed. Carolyn Fluehr-Lobban (Gainesville: University Press of Florida, 2001).

68. See, for example, Suha Taji-Farouki, ed., *Modern Muslim Intellectuals and the Qur'an* (Oxford: Oxford University Press, 2004).

Chapter Four

1. Rosalyn Higgins, "Derogations Under Human Rights Treaties," *British Yearbook of International Law* 48 (1976–1977): 281.

2. Myres McDougal, Harold Lasswell, and Lung-chu Chen, "The Aggregate Interest in Shared Respect and Human Rights: The Harmonization of Public Order and Civic Order," *New York Law School Law Review* 23 (1977–1978): 183.

3. Ibid., 201–202.

4. Ibid., 202.

5. Universal Declaration of Human Rights (UDHR), Articles 1, 7, 10, and 16, respectively.

6. UDHR, Article 18, and International Covenant on Civil and Political Rights (ICCPR), Article 18.

7. UDHR, Article 23, and International Covenant on Economic, Social, and Cultural Rights (ICESCR), Article 6.

8. Johannes Morsink, "The Philosophy of the Universal Declaration," *Human Rights Quarterly* 6 (1984): 318.

9. UDHR, Articles 19, 20, and 21, respectively.

10. ICCPR, Articles 6 and 9, respectively.

11. Ebow Bondzie-Simpson, "A Critique of the African Charter on Human and Peoples' Rights," *Howard Law Journal* 31 (1988): 660–661.

12. See Courtney W. Howland, "The Challenge of Religious Fundamentalism to the Liberty and Equality Rights of Women: An Analysis Under the United Nations Charter," *Columbia Journal of Transnational Law* 35 (1997): 327–331.

13. Yves Linant de Bellefonds, *Traité de droit musulman comparé*, vol. 1, *Théorie de l'acte juridique* (Paris: Mouton, 1965), 18–50; and Noel Coulson, *A History of Islamic Law* (Edinburgh: Edinburgh University Press, 1964), 21–119.

14. Islamic reformist thought is assessed in Malcolm Kerr, *Islamic Reform* (Berkeley: University of California Press, 1966); Charles Adams, *Islam and Modernism in Egypt: A Study of the Modern Reform Movement Inaugurated by Muhammad Abduh* (New York: Russell and Russell, 1968); and Aziz Ahmad, *Islamic Modernism in India and Pakistan, 1857–1964* (London: Oxford University Press, 1967).

15. See, for example, Abdolkarim Soroush, *Reason, Freedom, and Democracy in Islam: Essential Writings of Abdolkarim Soroush*, trans. and eds. Mahmoud Sadri and Ahmad Sadri (Oxford: Oxford University Press, 2000); Mohammed Arkoun, *The Unthought in Contemporary Islamic Thought* (London: Saqi Books, 2002); Khaled Abou El Fadl, *Speaking in God's Name: Islamic Law, Authority and Women* (Oxford: Oneworld 2003); and Omid Safi, ed., *Progressive Muslims: On Justice, Gender, and Pluralism* (Oxford: Oneworld Publications, 2005).

16. See Ervand Abrahamian, *Khomeinism* (Berkeley: University of California Press, 1993).

17. See Abdul-Hadi Hairi, *Shi'ism and Constitutionalism in Iran* (Leiden: Brill, 1977), which gives many examples of the objections raised by the *ulama* to the proposed constitution.

18. One eyewitness to a religious demonstration against the proposed constitution reported that a mullah proclaimed that constitutionalists were to be killed in

as great numbers as possible, egging on his followers to beat two constitutionalists to death. The naked mangled bodies of the constitutionalists were then displayed. Ibid., 218.

19. The phenomenon of the *ulama* misconstruing the purport of Western freedoms is examined in many parts of Hairi's book. See ibid.

20. Abid Al-Marayati, *Middle Eastern Constitutions and Electoral Laws* (New York: Praeger, 1968), 17–20.

21. Shaul Bakhash, *The Reign of the Ayatollahs* (New York: Basic Books, 1984), 77.

22. Ibid., 78.

23. Ibid.

24. *Qavanin* (pl. of *qanun*) would normally refer to secular laws. However, with the modifications by the adjective "Islamic," as here, *qavanin* seems to mean "Islamic principles." This application of the term contrasts with the use of *qavanin* in Article 4, where the reference can only be to secular law because there it is stated that laws, *qavanin*, should be based on (and qualified by) "Islamic principles," *mavazin-e eslami*.

25. See Lawyers Committee for Human Rights, *The Justice System of the Islamic Republic of Iran* (New York: Lawyers Committee for Human Rights, 1993).

26. See, for example, Ziba Mir-Hosseini and Richard Tapper, *Islam and Democracy in Iran: Eshkevari and the Quest for Reform* (London: I. B. Tauris, 2006).

27. An example of how calculations of political interests could override any concern for fidelity to *shari'a* law can be seen in Khomeini's assertion on January 7, 1988, that his government was free to undertake any actions that it deemed in the interests of Islam. He claimed that Iran's Islamic government was among the most important divine institutions and had priority over such secondary institutions as prayers, fasting, and the pilgrimage. See Asghar Schirazi, *The Constitution of Iran: Politics and the State in the Islamic Republic*, trans. John O'Kane (London: I. B. Tauris, 1997), 229–231.

28. Space does not allow discussion of the council here, but it is examined in Schirazi, *The Constitution of Iran*.

29. Examples of the problems of translating the UIDHR are illustrated by attempts to provide literal translations of the Arabic version into English and French that resulted in inconsistencies. See *Islamo Christiana* 9 (1983): 103–120 (English) and 121–140 (French).

30. In the English-language pamphlet version of the UIDHR published by the Islamic Council, these notes are placed on page 16 after the rights provisions.

31. In the Arabic counterpart of this article, one discovers that it actually offers a "right" to propagate Islam.

32. *Al-intiqal* in the Arabic, but translated into English as "transfer."

33. See, for example, Abu'l A'la Mawdudi, *Purdah and the Status of Women in Islam* (Lahore: Islamic Publications, 1979), 145–147, 200–209.

34. Sultanhussein Tabandeh, *A Muslim Commentary on the Universal Declaration of Human Rights*, trans. F. J. Goulding (Guildford, England: F. J. Goulding, 1970), 20.

35. Tabandeh, *A Muslim Commentary*, 73.

262   Notes to Chapter Five

36. Abu'l A'la Mawdudi, *Human Rights in Islam* (Leicester, England: Islamic Foundation, 1980), 28–29.

37. See "Transitional National Assembly Approves Document on Human Rights," *BBC Summary of World Broadcasts*, July 20, 1993, available in LEXIS/Nexis Library, ALLWLD File.

38. Constitution of the Islamic Republic of Afghanistan, available at http://www .oefre.unibe.ch/law/icl/af00000_.html.

39. For background, see Nathan J. Brown, "Iraq's Constitutional Process Plunges Ahead," in *Carnegie Endowment for International Peace Policy Outlook*, July 2005.

40. Law of Administration for the State of Iraq for the Transitional Period, available at http://www.cpa-iraq.org/government/TAL.html.

41. U.S. Commission on International Religious Freedom Tells U.S. Ambassador Draft Constitution Fails to Protect Fundamental Rights," July 26, 2005, available at http://www.uscirf.gov/mediaroom/press/2005/july/07262005_iraq.html.

42. James Glanz, "U.S. Builds Pressure for Iraq Constitution as Deadline Nears," *New York Times*, August 14, 2005, 6.

43. See the translation of the Iraqi constitution, available at http://www.washington post.com/wp-dyn/content/article/2005/10/12/AR2005101201450.html.

44. Khalilzad Speeches, "Iraqi Draft Constitution Balances Islam, Democracy, Envoy Says," August 23, 2005, available at http://iraq.usembassy.gov/iraq/20050823 _khalilzad_press_conference.html.

Chapter Five

1. An introduction to these two aspects of the Islamic heritage is Louise Marlow, *Hierarchy and Egalitarianism in Islamic Thought* (Cambridge: Cambridge University Press, 1997).

2. A summary of the rules on personal status can be found in Joseph Schacht, *Introduction to Islamic Law* (Oxford: Clarendon Press, 1964), 24–33.

3. An example is the condemnation of the principle of equality in the supplement to the first Iranian constitution, signed by a number of prominent Shi'i clerics. See Abdul-Hadi Hairi, *Shi'ism and Constitutionalism in Iran* (Leiden: Brill, 1977), 221–222, 232–233.

4. Abu'l A'la Mawdudi, *Human Rights in Islam* (Leicester, England: Islamic Foundation, 1980), 28–29.

5. Ibid., 21.

6. Ibid., 32.

7. The translation is taken from "Constitution of the Islamic Republic of Iran of 24 October 1979 As Amended to 28 July 1989," in *Constitutions of the Countries of the World*, eds. Albert Blaustein and Gisbert Flanz (Dobbs Ferry, NY: Oceana, 1992).

8. The texts cited are 3:64, "None of us shall take others for lords besides Allah," and 49:13, "We have created you male and female." These were not historically interpreted to mandate equality.

9. Sultanhussein Tabandeh, *A Muslim Commentary on the Universal Declaration of Human Rights*, trans. F. J. Goulding (Guildford, England: F. J. Goulding, 1970), 15.

10. Ibid., 19.

11. Ibid., 20.

12. Jacobus Ten Broek, *The Antislavery Origins of the Fourteenth Amendment* (Berkeley: University of California Press, 1951).

13. Early Muslim interpretations of the principle of equality are discussed in Hairi, *Shi'ism and Constitutionalism*, 224–234.

14. This was the interpretation of Mirza Muhammad Hussain Na'ini, a leading Shi'i cleric who endeavored to show that constitutional rights accorded with Islam. Ibid., 224.

15. Relevant analysis is provided in Courtney W. Howland, "The Challenge of Religious Fundamentalism to the Liberty and Equality Rights of Women: An Analysis Under the United Nations Charter," *Columbia Journal of Transnational Law* 35 (1997): 329–330.

16. For example, the Prophet is quoted as saying that there can be no superiority of the Arab over the non-Arab, of the red (meaning "white" in contemporary American usage) over the black, or of the black over the red save in piety; the Prophet is further quoted as saying that if his own daughter stole, her hand would be cut off like that of any other thief.

17. Because the Arabic and English categories do not correspond and because the English translation is obviously only a very rough approximation of the Arabic, the English cannot be used to clarify the meaning of the ambiguous terms *jins* and *'irq*. Because other provisions of the UIDHR mandate sex-based discrimination, reading *jins* in Article 3.b to mean "sex," which might seem natural, entails internal inconsistencies in the document. But, given the lack of consistency in the English and Arabic versions, one might anticipate some provisions barring sex-based discrimination and others mandating such discrimination.

18. *Ansar Burney v. Federation of Pakistan*, PLD FSC, 1983, 73.

19. Ibid., 93.

20. This provision affords yet another example of the discrepancies between the Arabic and English versions, with the English version designed to convey the impression that it resembles international human rights law.

21. Nuri was active in the revolutionary committees and the Revolutionary Guards, in the debates over the postrevolutionary constitution, and in the Majles after the revolution. This information was kindly provided by Professor Hamid Algar.

22. Yahya Noori [Nuri], "The Islamic Concept of State," *Hamdard Islamicus* 3 (1980): 78.

23. Ibid., 83.

24. Ibid., 70–80.

25. Orwell's work enjoyed enormous popularity in Iran since the revolution. By 1984, a Persian translation of *Animal Farm* had become one of Iran's best-sellers and George Orwell Iran's best-selling author. See "Book Boom in Tehran," *Index on Censorship* (October 1984), 9.

Chapter Six

1. The reforms made by the Qur'an are presented schematically in a volume produced under the auspices of the Giant Forum and Global Issues Awareness for National Trust in collaboration with the Women's Development Fund, Canadian International Development Agency (CIDA), Islamabad, Pakistan. See *International Conference on Islamic Laws and Women in the Modern World: Islamabad, December 22–23, 1996* (Islamabad: Giant Forum, 1996), 20–21. Hereafter, cited as *International Conference on Islamic Laws.*

2. Fazlur Rahman, "The Status of Women in the Qur'an," in *Women and Revolution in Iran*, ed. Guity Nashat (Boulder: Westview Press, 1983), 38.

3. Jane Smith, "Women, Religion, and Social Change in Early Islam," in *Women, Religion, and Social Change*, eds. Yvonne Haddad and Ellison Findley (Albany: State University of New York Press, 1985), 19–35.

4. See the examination of disparities between the original sources and later interpretations in Barbara Stowasser, "The Status of Women in Early Islam," in *Muslim Women*, ed. Freda Hussain (New York: St. Martin's Press, 1984), 11–43; Asma Barlas, *"Believing Women" in Islam: Unreading Patriarchal Interpretations of the Qur'an* (Austin: University of Texas Press, 2002); and Fatima Mernissi, *The Veil and the Male Elite: A Feminist Interpretation of Women's Rights in Islam* (Reading, MA: Addison-Wesley, 1991).

5. Rahman, "The Status of Women," 37.

6. Introductions to aspects of women's status in the *shari'a* can be found in Joseph Schacht, *Introduction to Islamic Law* (Oxford: Clarendon Press, 1964), 126–127; Yves Linant de Bellefonds, *Traité de droit musulman comparé*, vol. 2, *Le Mariage: La Dissolution du mariage* (Paris: Mouton, 1965); Noel Coulson, *Succession in the Muslim Family* (Cambridge: Cambridge University Press, 1971); Ghassan Ascha, *Du statut inférieur de la femme en Islam* (Paris: L'Harmattan, 1987); and *International Conference on Islamic Laws.*

7. A summary of these changes can be found in J. N. D. Anderson, *Law Reform in the Muslim World* (London: Athlone, 1976). See also Tahir Mahmood, *Personal Law in Islamic Countries* (New Delhi: Academy of Law and Religions, 1987); and *International Conference on Islamic Laws*, 185–453.

8. A perfect embodiment of this response can be found in Abu'l A'la Mawdudi, *Purdah and the Status of Women in Islam* (Lahore: Islamic Publications, 1979). Many aspects of this literature are reviewed by Ascha, *Du statut inférieur.*

9. For a learned discussion of contraception and abortion in Islamic jurisprudence, see Basim Musallam, *Sex and Society in Islam: Birth Control Before the Nineteenth Century* (Cambridge: Cambridge University Press, 1983).

10. See Abdullahi El-Naiem [An-Na'im], "A Modern Approach to Human Rights in Islam: Foundations and Implications for Africa," in *Human Rights and Development in Africa*, eds. Claude Welch Jr. and Ronald Meltzer (Albany: State University of New York Press, 1984), 82; and Mernissi, *The Veil and the Male Elite.*

11. Works that show the growth and influence of feminism include Mernissi, *The Veil and the Male Elite*; Riffat Hassan, "Feminist Theology: The Challenges for Muslim Women," *Critique: Journal for Critical Studies of the Middle East* (Fall 1996): 53–66; Mahnaz Afkhami, ed., *Faith and Freedom: Women's Human Rights in the Muslim World*; Mahnaz Afkhami and Erika Friedl, eds., *Muslim Women and the Politics of Participation: Implementing the Beijing Platform* (Syracuse, NY: Syracuse University Press, 1997); Ziba Mir-Hosseini, *Islam and Gender: The Religious Debate in Contemporary Iran* (Princeton: Princeton University Press, 1999), and *Feminism and the Islamic Republic: Dialogues with the Ulema* (Princeton: Princeton University Press, 1999); Shaheen Sardar Ali, *Gender and Human Rights in Islam and International Law* (The Hague: Kluwer Law International, 2000); Val Moghadam, "Islamic Feminism and Its Discontents: Toward a Resolution of the Debates," *SIGNS: Journal of Women in Culture and Society* 27 (2002): 1136–1171; Khaled Abou El Fadl, *Speaking in God's Name: Islamic Law, Authority and Women* (Oxford: Oneworld Publications, 2003).

12. This is a consistent theme of Mawdudi's writings. For an example of his arguments, see Mawdudi, *Purdah and the Status of Women*, 21–24.

13. Ibid., 73–74.

14. Ibid., 24.

15. Thus, in most Muslim countries, the choice has been to compromise, keeping some *shari'a* rules but including many reforms improving the rights of women. See *International Conference on Islamic Laws*, 185–453; and Lynn Welchman, *Women and Muslim Family Laws in Arab States: A Comparative Overview of Textual Development and Advocacy* (Amsterdam: Amsterdam University Press, 2007).

16. See Jane Connors, "The Women's Convention in the Muslim World," in *Human Rights as General Norms and a State's Right to Opt Out: Reservations and Objections to Human Rights Conventions*, ed. J. P. Gardner (London: British Institute of International and Comparative Law, 1997), 85–103.

17. See, for example, Rana Husseini, "Women Activists Welcome Endorsement of Government Decision to Lift Reservation on CEDAW Article," *Jordan Times*, May 20, 2009, available at http://www.jordantimes.com/?news=16860; "Morocco Withdraws Reservations to CEDAW," *Magharebia/ADFM*, December 18, 2008, available at http://www.wluml.org/node/4941.

18. Hossam Bahgat and Wesal Alfi, "Sexuality Politics in Egypt," in *SexPolitics. Reports from the Front Lines*, eds. Richard Parker, Rosalind Petchesky, and Robert Sember, 58–62, available at http://www.sxpolitics.org/frontlines/book/pdf/sexpolitics.pdf.

19. Ann Elizabeth Mayer, "Rhetorical Strategies and Official Policies on Women's Rights: The Merits and Drawbacks of the New World Hypocrisy," in *Faith and Freedom*, ed. Afkhami, 105–119, and "Religious Reservations to CEDAW: What Do They Really Mean?" in *Religious Fundamentalism and the Human Rights of Women*, ed. Courtney Howland (New York: St. Martin's Press, 1999), 105–116.

20. Sultanhussein Tabandeh, *A Muslim Commentary on the Universal Declaration of Human Rights*, trans. F. J. Goulding (Guildford, England: F. J. Goulding, 1970), 1.

21. See, for example, his comments on Article 16 of the UDHR. Ibid., 41–45.

22. Ibid., 40.

23. Ibid., 58.

24. Ibid., 51.

25. Abu'l A'la Mawdudi, *The Islamic Law and Constitution* (Lahore: Islamic Publications, 1980), 262–263; and *Purdah and the Status of Women*, passim, and on divorce, 151.

26. Mawdudi, *Purdah and the Status of Women*, 12.

27. Ibid., 12–15, 26–71.

28. Ibid., 15.

29. Ibid., 73.

30. Abu'l A'la Mawdudi, *Human Rights in Islam* (Leicester, England: Islamic Foundation, 1980), 18.

31. Mawdudi, *Human Rights*, 18.

32. Indeed, restrictions on women's testimony in the *shari'a* rules of evidence can make it especially difficult for a woman to prove such an offense.

33. Naturally, the sordid details of these incidents were publicized in India, Pakistan's enemy. See, for example, Amita Malik, *The Year of the Vulture* (New Delhi: Orient Longman, 1972). Mawdudi and his followers had backed the efforts of the Pakistani government to crush the movement to establish an independent Bangladesh, and he preferred to pretend that no rapes had resulted.

34. According to the preface, Mawdudi's human rights pamphlet is translated from a speech delivered on November 16, 1975, at the Civil Rights and Liberties Forum in the Flatties Hotel in Lahore. Mawdudi, *Human Rights*, 7. Mawdudi and his audience in Lahore, capital of the Punjab, which has traditionally supplied most of Pakistan's military manpower, must have been aware of how the Bengali mass rapes had tarnished Pakistan's image.

35. See Shahla Haeri, "The Politics of Dishonor: Rape and Power in Pakistan," in *Faith and Freedom*, ed. Afkhami, 161–174; and Rubya Mehdi, "The Offence of Rape in the Islamic Law of Pakistan," *Women Living Under Muslim Laws: Dossier* 18 (July 1997): 98–108. The sexism of the Pakistani laws on rape in the wake of Islamization is dissected in Asifa Quraishi, "Her Honor: An Islamic Critique of the Rape Laws of Pakistan from a Woman-Sensitive Perspective," *Michigan Journal of International Law* 18 (1997): 287–320.

36. According to the choice-of-law rules in Islam and in the law of Muslim countries, Islamic criteria are used to judge the validity of a mixed marriage. See Klaus Wahler, *Interreligiöses Kollisionsrecht im Bereich privatrechtlicher Rechtsbeziehungen* (Cologne: Carl Heymanns Verlag, 1978), 157–158.

37. Examples of such rules are discussed in Mahmood, *Personal Law*, 275–276.

38. These references appear on p. 19 of the English version.

39. For example, see Mawdudi's invocation of this verse; Mawdudi, *Purdah and the Status of Women*, 149.

40. Yves Linant de Bellefonds, *Traité de droit musulman comparé*, vol. 3, *Filiation: Incapacités, Liberalités entre vifs* (Paris: Mouton, 1965), 81–142.

41. In theory, the guardian could also marry off a male ward without his consent, but because a Muslim man can easily terminate an unwanted marriage, this has little practical significance.

42. Anderson, *Law Reform in the Muslim World*, 102–105.

43. Robert F. Worth, "Tiny Voices Defy Child Marriage in Yemen," *The New York Times*, June 29, 2008, available at http://www.nytimes.com/2008/06/29/world/middle east/29marriage.html?pagewanted=all.

44. See, for example, Mawdudi, *Purdah and the Status of Women*, 144–155.

45. Noel Coulson, *Succession in the Muslim Family* (Cambridge: Cambridge University Press, 1971), 214.

46. Linant de Bellefonds, *Traité de droit musulman comparé*, vol. 2, 451–470.

47. The translation is from "Constitution of the Islamic Republic of Iran of 24 October 1979 as Amended to 28 July 1989," in *Constitutions of the Countries of the World*, eds. Albert Blaustein and Gisbert Flanz (Dobbs Ferry, NY: Oceana, 1992).

48. Eliz Sanasarian, *The Women's Rights Movement in Iran: Mutiny, Appeasement, and Repression from 1900 to Khomeini* (New York: Praeger, 1982), 94–97. The situation of women in the aftermath of the suspension of the Family Protection Act is examined in Ziba Mir-Hosseini, *Marriage on Trial: A Study of Islamic Family Law. Iran and Morocco Compared* (New York: I. B. Tauris, 1993).

49. Shahla Haeri, *Law of Desire: Temporary Marriage in Iran* (London: I. B. Tauris, 1989).

50. *International Conference on Islamic Laws*, 316.

51. Parvin Paidar, *Women and the Political Process in Twentieth-Century Iran* (Cambridge: Cambridge University Press, 1995), 303–335.

52. Ibid., 286–289.

53. See Ziba Mir-Hosseini, "The Politics and Hermeneutics of Hijab in Iran: From Confinement to Choice," *Muslim World Journal of Human Rights* 4 (2007), 1–19, available at http://www.bepress.com/mwjhr/vol4/iss1/art2/.

54. See UN High Commissioner for Human Rights, "Situation of Human Rights in the Islamic Republic of Iran: Iran (Islamic Republic of) 15/10/97," A/52/472, available at http://www.iran.org/humanrights/UN971015.htm.

55. "Iranian Team Set for Atlanta Despite Visa Bother," *Deutsche Presse-Agentur*, July 9, 1996, available in LEXIS/Nexis Library, ALLWLD File.

56. Nikki Keddie, "Women in Iran Since 1979," Special Issue, Iran Since the Revolution, *Social Research* 67 (Summer 2000): 417–419.

57. See Ann Elizabeth Mayer, "Islamic Rights or Human Rights: An Iranian Dilemma," *Iranian Studies* 29 (Summer-Fall 1996): 284–288.

58. "Iranian Cleric Blasts Taleban for Defaming Islam," *Reuters North American Wire*, October 4, 1996, available in LEXIS/Nexis Library, ALLWLD File.

59. "Iranian Leader Warns Women Against Copying Western Feminist Trends," *Agence France Presse*, October 22, 1997, available in LEXIS/Nexis Library, ALLWLD File.

60. Mahsa Sherkarloo, "Iranian Women Take on the Constitution," *MERIP Online*, July 21, 2005, available at http://merip.org/mero/mero072105.html.

61. See Mehrangiz Kar, Ludovic Trarieux Prize Winner 2002, available at http://www.ludovictrarieux.org/uk-pages3.1.plt.htm.

62. See Mehrangiz Kar, "Iranian Law and Women's Rights," *Muslim World Journal of Human Rights* (2007): 1–13, available at http://www.bepress.com/mwjhr/vol4/iss1/art9/.

63. See Noushin Ahmadi Khorasani, *Iranian Women's One Million Signatures Campaign for Equality: The Inside Story* (Women's Learning Partnership Translation Series, 2009), available at http://www.learningpartnership.org/iran-oms; Iran's One Million Signatures Campaign, available at http://learningpartnership.org/iran-oms.

64. See "Women Ejected by Force from Iran Stadium," *Iran Focus*, March 6, 2006, available at http://www.iranfocus.com/modules/news/article.php?storyid=6091.

65. Saeed Kamali Deghan, "Iran Jails Director Jafar Panahi and Stops Him Making Films for 20 Years," *The Guardian*, December 20, 2010, available at http://www.guardian.co.uk/world/2010/dec/20/iran-jails-jafar-panahi-films.

66. "Mahmoud Ahmadinejad Blasts Fifa 'Dictators' as Iranian Ban Anger Rises," *The Guardian*, June 7, 2011, available at http://www.guardian.co.uk/football/2011/jun/07/iran-anger-ahmadinejad-fifa-ban/.

67. See Sarah Menkedick, "Iran Wins Membership to the U.N Commission on the Status of Women, Women's Rights," May 08, 2010, change.org, available at http://news.change.org/stories/iran-wins-membership-to-the-un-commission-on-the-status-of-women; Elizabeth Weingarten, "At Last Minute, East Timor Beats Out Iran for Chair of New UN Body," *The Atlantic*, November 10, 2010, available at http://www.theatlantic.com/international/archive/2010/11/at-last-minute-east-timor-beats-out-iran-for-chair-of-new-un-body/66397/.

68. *The Meaning of the Glorious Koran,* trans. Marmaduke Pickthall (Albany: State University of New York Press, 1976).

69. See, for example, Tabandeh, *A Muslim Commentary*, 51–52; and Mawdudi, *Purdah and the Status of Women*, 185–201.

70. A critique of how the concept of '*ird* has been used to deny Arab women their humanity and basic rights can be found in Nawal El-Saadawi, *The Hidden Face of Eve: Women in the Arab World* (Boston: Beacon Press, 1981), 7–90.

71. The other two countries that recognized the Taliban government were Pakistan and the United Arab Emirates.

72. Declarations and Reservations to the Convention on the Elimination of All Forms of Discrimination Against Women, available at http://www.unhchr.ch/html/menu3/b/treaty9_asp.htm.

73. See Human Rights Watch, "Perpetual Minors: Human Rights Abuses Stemming from Male Guardianship and Sex Segregation in Saudi Arabia," April 19, 2008, available at http://www.hrw.org/en/reports/2008/04/19/perpetual-minors-0.

74. United Nations CEDAW/C/SAU/2 Convention on the Elimination of All Forms of Discrimination Against Women Distr.: General 29 March 2007; English Original:

Arabic 07–29667 (E) 120507 230507*0729667* Committee on the Elimination of Discrimination against Women. Consideration of reports submitted by States Parties under article 18 of the Convention on the Elimination of All Forms of Discrimination against Women. Combined initial and second periodic reports of States Parties. Saudi Arabia, available at http://daccess-dds-ny.un.org/doc/UNDOC/GEN/N07/296/67 /PDF/N0729667.pdf?OpenElement.

75. The Global Gender Gap Report 2010, available at http://www3.weforum .org/docs/WEF_GenderGap_Report_2010.pdf.

76. Committee on the Elimination of Discrimination Against Women. Pre-session working group. Fortieth session 14 January–1 February 2008. Responses to the list of issues and questions contained in document number CEDAW/C/SAU/Q/2, A.H. 1428 (A.D. 2007), available at http://www2.ohchr.org/english/bodies/cedaw/docs /CEDAW.C.SAU.Q.2.Add.1.pdf.

77. Ibid.

78. Zinnia Shah, "Saudi Arabia: Battle to Overturn Ban on Women Driving Is First Step to Women's Full Integration into Society," *Women Living Under Muslim Laws*, July 25, 2011, available at http://www.wluml.org/node/7459.

79. Neil MacFarquhar, "Saudis Arrest Woman Leading Right-to-Drive Campaign," *The New York Times*, May 23, 2011, available at http://www.nytimes.com/2011/05 /24/world/middleeast/24saudi.html.

80. Suo Moto No. 1/K of 2006, Pakistan Citizenship Act. 1951, In Re: Gender Equality, available at http://federalshariatcourt.gov.pk/Leading%20Judgements/Suo %20Moto%20No.1-K%20of%202006.pdf.

81. Ibid., par. 3.

82. Ibid., par. 28.

83. Ibid., par. 27.

84. See "Pakistan: Whether the Spouse of a Citizen of Pakistan Can Acquire Citizenship; If So, Information Requirements, Procedures and Documents Needed," *Refworld*, October 28, 2010, available at http://www.unhcr.org/refworld/country ,,IRBC,,PAK,,4dd1028e2,0.html.

85. Amnesty International, *Women in Afghanistan: A Human Rights Catastrophe*, AI Index: ASA 11/03/95.

86. See, generally, Nancy Hatch Dupree, "Afghan Women Under the Taliban," in *Fundamentalism Reborn: Afghanistan and the Taliban*, ed. William Maley (New York: New York University Press, 1998), 145–166; and Marjon E. Ghasemi, "Islam, International Human Rights, and Women's Equality: Afghan Women Under Taliban Rule," *Southern California Review of Law and Women's Studies* 8 (Spring 1999): 445–467.

87. See, for example, John Burns, "Sex and the Afghani Woman: Islam's Straightjacket," *The New York Times*, August 29, 1997, A4; "Islamic Rule Weighs Heavily for Afghans," *The New York Times*, September 24, 1997, A6.

88. See Anne E. Brodsky, *With All Our Strength: The Revolutionary Association of the Women of Afghanistan* (New York: Routledge, 2003).

89. Benazeer Roshan, "The More Things Change, the More They Stay the Same: The Plight of Afghan Women Two Years After the Overthrow of the Taliban," *Berkeley Women's Law Journal* 19 (2004): 270–286.

90. "Afghanistan 'Most Dangerous Place for Women,'" *Al Jazeera,* June 15, 2011, available at http://english.aljazeera.net/news/asia/2011/06/201161582525243992.html.

91. Lila Abu-Lughod, "Do Muslim Women Really Need Saving? Anthropological Reflections on Cultural Relativism and Its Others," *American Anthropologist* 104 (2002): 787; Mary Ann Franks, "Obscene Undersides: Women and Evil Between the Taliban and the United States," *HYPATIA* 18 (2003): 135–155.

92. See, for example, Condoleezza Rice's televised comments on the US involvement in the constitution drafting and her claim that "the United States stands for equality for women worldwide," adding: "We've communicated that very clearly to the Iraqi government," available at http://www.pbs.org/newshour/bb/white_house/july-dec05/rice_7–28.html.

93. See the discussions in Mayer, "Rhetorical Strategies," 104–114, and "Internationalization of the Conversation on Women's Rights: Arab Governments Face the CEDAW Committee," in *Islamic Law and the Challenge of Modernity,* eds. Yvonne Haddad and Barbara Freyer Stowasser (Walnut Creek, Calif.: Altamira Press, 2004), 147–154.

94. Tabandeh, *A Muslim Commentary,* 39.

95. Ibid., 41.

96. Ibid., 51.

97. Ibid., 52.

98. Mawdudi, *Purdah and the Status of Women in Islam,* 113–122.

99. Ibid., 120.

100. Ibid., 121–122.

101. Javad Bahonar, "Islam and Women's Rights," *al-Tawhid* 1 (1984): 160.

102. Ibid., 161.

103. Ibid., 165.

104. Ibid., 161.

105. Ibid., 164. Of course, since he was trying to show the Islamic treatment of women in a positive light, Bahonar had reason to avoid mentioning the discriminatory features of the inheritance scheme.

106. Hammed Shahidian, "Contesting Discourses of Sexuality in Post-Revolutionary Iran," in *Deconstructing Sexuality in the Middle East: Challenges and Discourses,* ed. Pinar Ilkkaracan (Burlington,VT: Ashgate, 2008), 117.

107. See Ann Elizabeth Mayer, "Islam and Human Rights: Different Issues, Different Contexts. Lessons from Comparisons," in *Islamic Law Reform and Human Rights: Challenges and Rejoinders,* eds. Tore Lindholm and Kari Vogt (Oslo: Nordic Human Rights Publications, 1993), 121–125.

108. Mary Daly, *The Church and the Second Sex* (Boston: Beacon Press, 1985), 85.

109. Ibid., 88.

110. Ibid., 154.

111. Ibid., 115.

112. Ibid.

113. Ibid., 87.

Chapter Seven

1. Bernard Lewis, *The Emergence of Modern Turkey* (London: Oxford University Press, 1961), 104–106, 113–115, 131.

2. The theme that European rule was needed to protect minorities from oppression permeates the thinking in Lord Cromer [Evelyn Baring], *Modern Egypt*, 2 vols. (New York: Macmillan, 1908), especially vol. 2, 123–259.

3. For background, see Peter Holt, *Egypt and the Fertile Crescent* (Ithaca: Cornell University Press, 1966); Bernard Lewis, *The Middle East and the West* (New York: Harper, 1964), and the sources cited therein; and Elizabeth Monroe, *Britain's Moment in the Middle East, 1914–56* (Baltimore: Johns Hopkins University Press, 1981).

4. The Casablanca Declaration, available at http://www.al-bab.com/arab/docs /international/hr1999.htm.

5. These attitudes are exemplified in Ayatollah Khomeini's thinking. See Imam [Ruhollah] Khomeini, *Islam and Revolution: Writings and Declarations of Imam Khomeini*, trans. Hamid Algar (Berkeley: Mizan Press, 1981).

6. Information about the Commission on International Religious Freedom is available at http://www.uscirf.gov/countries/countriesconcerns/index.html.

7. Lee Romney, "Battle Urged Against Religious Persecution," *Los Angeles Times*, October 20, 1997.

8. The circumstances of the early Islamic community are described in W. Montgomery Watt, *Muhammad, Prophet and Statesman* (Oxford: Oxford University Press, 1971).

9. The law of *jihad* is discussed in Rudolph Peters, *Jihad in Classical and Modern Islam* (Princeton: Markus Wiener, 1996), 1–54.

10. For the evolution of *jihad* doctrine, see ibid., 55–159; and Ann Elizabeth Mayer, "War and Peace in the Islamic Tradition and in International Law," in *Just War and Jihad: War, Peace, and Statecraft in the Western and Islamic Traditions*, ed. James Johnson and John Kelsay (Westport, CT: Greenwood Press, 1991), 195–226.

11. For background, see A. S. Tritton, *The Caliphs and Their Non-Muslim Subjects: A Critical Study of the Covenant of Umar* (London: Cass, 1970); and Antoine Fattal, *Le Statut légal des non-musulmans en pays d'Islam* (Beirut: Imprimerie Catholique, 1958).

12. Zoroastrians and Sabeans are sometimes also included in this category.

13. See, for example, the studies in Benjamin Braude and Bernard Lewis, eds., *Christians and Jews in the Ottoman Empire*, 2 vols. (New York: Holmes and Meier, 1982).

14. See Bernard Lewis, *The Jews of Islam* (Princeton: Princeton University Press, 1984).

15. Introductions to the impact of nationalism can be found in Albert Hourani, *Arabic Thought in the Liberal Age, 1798–1939* (London: Oxford University Press, 1962); and Lewis, *The Emergence of Modern Turkey*.

16. Jeffrey Fleishman, "Islamist Parties' Electoral Success in Egypt has Copts Worried," *Los Angeles Times*, Dec. 11, 2011, available at http://articles.latimes.com/2011/dec/11/world/la-fg-egypt-christians-muslims-20111212.

17. Samer al-Atrush, "Salafis, Dark Horse of Egypt's Vote, Seek to Assure Copts," *Agence France Presse*, Dec. 1, 2011, available at http://www.google.com/hostednews/afp/article/ALeqM5jCBsKRkdn4xIuLdXTcJ_a8_MFG3w?docId=CNG.0dce4efdb83eeb8aa808cbba95edd57a.481.

18. Yasmine Fathi, "Egypt Copts React to Islamist Electoral Win," ahramonline, December 4, 2011, available at http://english.ahram.org.eg/~/NewsContent/1/64/28346/Egypt/Politics-/Egypt-Copts-react-to-Islamist-electoral-win.aspx.

19. Subhi Mahmassani, *Arkan huquq al-insan* (Beirut: Dar al-'ilm li'l-malayin, 1979), 260–264, 281.

20. Ibid., 260–264.

21. S. M. Haider, "Equality Before Law and Equal Protection of Laws as Legal Doctrines for the Prevention of Discrimination and Protection of Minorities," in *Islamic Concept of Human Rights*, ed. S. M. Haider (Lahore: Book House, 1978), 213–237; Recep Senturk, "Minority Rights in Islam: From *Dhimmi* to Citizen," in *Islam and Human Rights: Advancing a U.S. Muslim Dialogue*, ed. Shireen T. Hunter (Washington, DC: CSIS Press, 2005), 67–99.

22. Al-Bishri's ideas are discussed in Leonard Binder, *Islamic Liberalism* (Chicago: University of Chicago Press, 1988), 246–292.

23. Ibid., 287–288.

24. See the critique of the treatment of non-Muslims in Egypt in Abdullahi An-Na'im, "Religious Freedom in Egypt: Under the Shadow of the Islamic *Dhimma* System," in *Religious Liberty and Human Rights in Nations and Religions*, ed. Leonard Swidler (Philadelphia: Ecumenical Press, 1986), 43–59.

25. Courtney W. Howland, "The Challenge of Religious Fundamentalism to the Liberty and Equality Rights of Women: An Analysis Under the United Nations Charter," *Columbia Journal of Transnational Law* 35 (1997): 329–330.

26. Sultanhussein Tabandeh, *A Muslim Commentary on the Universal Declaration of Human Rights*, trans. F. J. Goulding (Guildford, England: F. J. Goulding, 1970), 18.

27. Ibid., 17.

28. Ibid., 36.

29. Ibid.

30. Ibid.

31. Ibid., 70.

32. Ibid., 71.

33. Abu'l A'la Mawdudi, *Human Rights in Islam* (Leicester, England: Islamic Foundation, 1980), 30. His calls for respecting non-Muslims did not stop him from attacking "heretical" Ahmadis.

34. The translation is taken from "Constitution of the Islamic Republic of Iran of 24 October 1979 As Amended to 28 July 1989," in *Constitutions of the Countries of the World*, ed. Albert Blaustein and Gisbert Flanz (Dobbs Ferry, NY: Oceana, 1992).

35. See "Senior Iran Cleric Calls Non-Muslims 'Animals,'" *Iran Focus*, November 20, 2005, available at http://www.iranfocus.com/modules/news/article.php?storyid=4505.

36. See, for example, Shaul Bakhash, *The Reign of the Ayatollahs* (New York: Basic Books, 1984), 226.

37. Supporting this is the section of the preamble that provides that the goal of the army is "accomplishing an ideological mission, that is, the 'Jihad' for the sake of God, as well as for struggling to open the way for the sovereignty of the Word of God throughout the world."

38. Abu'l A'la Mawdudi, *The Islamic Law and Constitution* (Lahore: Islamic Publications, 1980), 188–189, 274–276.

39. Human Rights Watch/Middle East, *Iran: Religious and Ethnic Minorities. Discrimination in Law and Practice* 9, no. 7 (September 1997), available at http://www.hrw.org/reports/1997/iran/Iran-06.html; Amnesty International, Document-Iran: Human Rights Abuses Against the Baluchi Minority, September 17, 2007, Index Number: MDE 13/104/2007, available at http://www.amnesty.org/en/library/asset/MDE13/104/2007/en/160fb9c4-d370-11dd-a329-2f46302a8cc6/mde131042007en.html.

40. Human Rights Commission of Pakistan, *State of Human Rights in Pakistan 1993* (Lahore: Human Rights Commission of Pakistan, n.d.), 45–48.

41. Roger Cooper, *The Baha'is of Iran*, Minority Rights Group Report 51 (London: Minority Rights Group, 1982), 7–8, 10.

42. Ibid., 11.

43. Cooper, *The Baha'is of Iran*; Douglas Martin, "The Persecution of the Baha'is of Iran, 1844–1984," *Baha'i Studies* 12–13 (1984). See also the reports of the US Commission on International Religious Freedom, available at http://www.uscirf.gov/.

44. "Iran Rejects US Allegation on Violation of Religious Freedom," *BBC Monitoring Middle East*, October 8, 1999, available in Lexis, News library.

45. Mawdudi, *Human Rights*, 21–22.

46. Mawdudi, *The Islamic Law and Constitution*, 288–291.

47. Ibid., 191–193.

48. Ibid., 297–298.

49. Ibid., 276.

50. Ibid., 287.

51. The 1953 disturbances and the views of both the Ahmadis and their opponents are discussed in *Report of the Court of Inquiry Constituted Under Punjab Act II of 1954 to Enquire into the Punjab Disturbances of 1953* (Lahore: Superintendent, Government Printing, Punjab, 1954).

52. The ordinance is discussed in Nadeem Ahmad Siddiq, "Enforced Apostasy: *Zaheeruddin v. State* and the Official Persecution of the Ahmadiyya Community in Pakistan," *Law and Inequality* 14 (1995): 275–338.

53. This case is critically evaluated in Siddiq, "Enforced Apostasy," and Tayyab Mahmud, "Freedom of Religion and Religious Minorities in Pakistan: A Study of Judicial Practice," *Fordham International Law Journal* 19 (1995): 40–100.

54. For the text of the 1991 bill, see Rubya Mehdi, *The Islamization of the Law in Pakistan* (Richmond, England: Curzon Press, 1994), 324–329.

55. *Zaheeruddin v. State*, 26 S.C.M.R. (S.Ct.) 1718 (1993) (Pak.), 1773–1774.

56. See Human Rights Watch, "Denied Dignity. Systematic Discrimination and Hostility Toward Saudi Shia Citizens," September 3, 2009, available at http://www .hrw.org/node/85348 and Human Rights Watch, "The Ismailis of Najran: Second-Class Saudi Citizens," September 22, 2008, available at http://www.unhcr.org/refworld /docid/48d8a4712.html.

57. See, for example, Human Rights Watch, "Bad Dreams. Exploitation and Abuse of Migrant Workers in Saudi Arabia," July 14, 2004, available at http://www.unhcr .org/refworld/publisher,HRW,,SAU,412ef32a4,0.html.

58. Details are set forth in the *Annual Report of the United States Commission on International Religious Freedom*, May 2005, 27–37, 113–120, available at http://www .uscirf.gov/countries/publications/currentreport/2005annualRpt.pdf#page=37.

59. For coverage of the ongoing problems affecting non-Muslims, see the Saudi Arabian chapter in the *USCIRF 2011 Annual Report*, available at http://www.uscirf .gov/images/book%20with%20cover%20for%20web.pdf.

60. *The USCIRF 2011 Annual Report*, 215, available at http://www.uscirf.gov /images/book%20with%20cover%20for%20web.pdf.

61. *The USCIRF 2011 Annual Report*, 88, available at http://www.uscirf.gov/images /book%20with%20cover%20for%20web.pdf.

62. See the discussion in Ann Elizabeth Mayer, "The Fatal Flaws in the U.S. Constitutional Project for Iraq," *Journal of International Affairs. Religion & Statecraft* 61 (Fall/Winter 2007), 153–169.

Chapter Eight

1. See the Yogyakarta Principles, available at http://www.yogyakartaprinciples.org/.

2. Statement of Louse Arbour, UN High Commissioner for Human Rights, Launch of the Yogyakarta Principles, November 7, 2007, United Nations, New York, available at http://ypinaction.org/files/02/74/10_Statement_of_Louise_Arbour_on _YPs_Nov_07__2_.pdf.

3. See Michael O'Flaherty and John Fisher, "Sexual Orientation, Gender Identity and International Human Rights Law: Contextualising the Yogyakarta Principles," *Human Rights Law Review* 8, no. 2 (2008): 207–248, available at http://www.yogyakarta principles.org/yogyakarta-article-human-rights-law-review.pdf.

4. See Sonia Katyal, "Exporting Identity," *Yale Journal of Law & Feminism* 14 (2002): 97–176; Jeffrey A. Redding, "Human Rights and Homo-sectuals: The International Politics of Sexuality, Religion, and Law," *Northwestern University Journal of International Human Rights* 4 (2006): 436–492; O'Flaherty and Fisher, "Sexual Orientation," 232.

5. See Negar Azimi, "Prisoners of Sex," *The New York Times Magazine*, December 3, 2006, available at http://www.nytimes.com/2006/12/03/magazine/03arabs.html.

6. See, generally, Brian Whitaker, *Unspeakable Love: Gay and Lesbian Life in the Middle East* (Berkeley: University of California Press, 2006).

7. See Daniel Ottosson, *State-Sponsored Homophobia: A World Survey of Laws Prohibiting Same Sex Activity Between Consenting Adults* (Brussels: International Lesbian and Gay Association, 2009), available at http://ilga.org/historic/Statehomophobia /State_sponsored_homophobia_ILGA_07.pdf; Human Rights Watch, "'We Are a Buried Generation.' Discrimination and Violence Against Sexual Minorities in Iran," December 15, 2010, available at http://www.hrw.org/en/reports/2010/12/15/we-are -buried-generation; Amnesty International, "Egypt Torture and Imprisonment for Actual or Perceived Sexual Orientation," December 19, 2001, available at http://www .amnesty.org/en/library/asset/MDE12/033/2001/en/4925e77c-d8af-11dd-ad8c-f3d 4445c118e/mde120332001en.html.

8. See "Persecution of Homosexuals (Saudi Arabia)," WikiIslam, available at http://www.wikiislam.net/wiki/Persecution_of_Homosexuals_(Saudi_Arabia).

9. See, generally, Barrak Alzaid, "Fatwas and Fags: Violence and the Discursive Production of Abject Bodies," *Columbia Journal of Gender & Law* 19 (2010): 617–648. See also Human Rights Watch, *'They Want Us Exterminated': Murder, Torture, Sexual Orientation and Gender in Iraq* (New York: Human Rights Watch, 2009), available at http://www.hrw.org/node/85050.

10. This and many other examples of the heinous tortures perpetrated under Mubarak are discussed in Human Rights Watch, "Work on Him Until He Confesses," available at http://www.hrw.org/reports/2011/01/30/work-him-until-he-confesses.

11. Whitaker, *Unspeakable Love*, 48–50; Hossam Bahgat, "Explaining Egypt's Targeting of Gays," *MERIP*, July 23, 2001, available at http://www.merip.org/mero /mero072301; Scott Long, "The Trials of Culture: Sex and Security in Egypt," *MERIP*, MER230, Spring 2004, available at http://www.merip.org/mer/mer230/trials-culture.

12. Redding, *Human Rights*, 445.

13. Long, "Trials of Culture."

14. Whitaker, *Unspeakable Love*, 50.

15. See Raha Bahreini, "From Perversion to Pathology: Discourses and Practices of Gender Policing in the Islamic Republic of Iran, *Muslim World Journal of Human Rights* 5 (2008): 2, 19, available at http://www.bepress.com/mwjhr/vol5/iss1/art2/.

16. Ibid., 3.

17. Scott Siraj al-Haqq Kugle, *Homosexuality in Islam: Critical Reflection on Gay, Lesbian, and Transgender Muslims* (Oxford: Oneworld, 2010), 258–266.

18. "No Homosexuals in Iran": Ahmadinejad, Agence France Presse, September 24, 2007, available at http://afp.google.com/article/ALeqM5hATGOzv6YSmgeMY 1zdYbdpyrG2cw.

19. See Bahreini, "From Perversion to Pathology," 2–51.

20. See "Be Like Others," available at http://www.belikeothers.com.

21. See Rasha Moumneh, "The Gulf's Gender Anxiety," *The Guardian*, July 7, 2011, available at http://www.guardian.co.uk/commentisfree/2011/jul/06/gulf-gender -anxiety-transgender.

22. Human Rights Watch, "Halt Dress Code Crackdown," March 30, 2008, available at http://www.hrw.org/en/news/2008/03/30/kuwait-halt-dress-code-crackdown.

23. Ibid.

24. Ibid.

25. Ibid.

26. Basim Usmani, "Pakistan to Register 'Third Sex' Hijras: A Court Ruling Follows a Bid to Improve Life for Pakistan's Impoverished Transgender, Transvestite and Eunuch Community," *The Guardian,* July 18, 2009, available at http://www.guardian.co.uk /commentisfree/2009/jul/18/pakistan-transgender-hijra-third-sex/; "Pakistan Transgenders Pin Hopes on New Rights," *BBC News South Asia*, April 25, 2011, available at http://www.bbc.co.uk/news/world-south-asia-13186958.

27. See Sonia Katyal, "Exporting Identity."

28. Homosexuals Demand Rights at Istanbul's Gay Pride March, *Turkish Weekly*, June 29, 2011, available at http://www.turkishweekly.net/news/117727/homosexuals -demand-rights-at-istanbul%E2%80%99s-gay-pride-march.html.

29. See, generally, Vanja Hamzic, "The Case of 'Queer Muslims': Sexual Orientation and Gender Identity in International Human Rights Law and Muslim Legal and Social Ethos," *Human Rights Law Review* 11 (2011): 237–274, available at http:// hrlr.oxfordjournals.org/content/11/2/237; and Kugle, *Homosexuality in Islam*.

30. Kugle, *Homosexuality in Islam*, 2.

31. Ibid., 51–63, 166; Whitaker, *Unspeakable Love*, 183–194.

32. Kugle, *Homosexuality in Islam*, 157–166.

33. See ibid., 4, 129.

34. *Dudgeon v. United Kingdom*, Appl. No. 7525/76, Council of Europe: European Court of Human Rights, 22 October 1981.

35. A list of activist groups can be found at Gay and Lesbian Arabs, al-bab.com, available at http://www.al-bab.com/arab/background/gay.htm.

36. Whitaker, *Unspeakable Love*, 50, 66–71, 111, 148; Long, "Trials of Culture"; Redding, "Human Rights," 483–491.

37. See "Interview with Egyptian Human Rights Activist. Hossam Bahgat Talked with Alasdair Soussi," *The New Internationalist*, Issue 424, July 1, 2009, available at http://www.newint.org/columns/makingwaves/2009/07/01/hossam-bahgat/.

38. Whitaker, *Unspeakable Love*, 114–115.

39. Ibid., 66–70

40. Hamzic, "The Case of 'Queer Muslims.'"

41. *Toonen v. Australia*, Communication No. 488/1992, U.N. Doc CCPR/C/50/ D/488/1992 (1994), available at http://www1.umn.edu/humanrts/undocs/html/vws 488.htm.

42. For more details, see O'Flaherty and Fisher, "Sexual Orientation," 214–218.

43. Human Rights Watch, "UN: General Assembly Statement Affirms Rights for All. 66 States Condemn Violations Based on Sexual Orientation and Gender Identity," December 18, 2008, available at http://www.hrw.org/en/news/2008/12/18/un-general -assembly-statement-affirms-rights-all.

44. Action on Resolution on Human Rights, Sexual Orientation and Gender Identity, available at http://www.ohchr.org/en/NewsEvents/Pages/DisplayNews.aspx?News ID=11167&LangID=E.

45. "UN Issues First Report on Human Rights of Gay and Lesbian People," *UN News Centre*, Dec. 15, 2011, available at http://www.un.org/apps/news/story.asp?News ID=40743&Cr=discrimination&Cr1=#.

46. See O'Flaherty and Fisher, "Sexual Orientation," 228.

47. Mashood Baderin, *International Human Rights and Islamic Law* (Oxford: Oxford University Press, 2005), 117.

48. Response to SOGI Human Rights Statement, read by Syria, 18 Dec 2008, ILGA ASIA, available at http://ilga.org/ilga/en/article/mkjJMT21ax; Response read by Syria to Statement on Human Rights and the so-called notions of "Sexual Orientation" and "Gender Identity," UN General Assembly, December 18, 2008, available in audio-visual form at http://www.un.org/webcast/ga2008.html.

49. See *Lawrence v. Texas*, Scalia, J., dissenting, available at http://www.law.cornell .edu/supct/html/02–102.ZD.html.

50. General Assembly, GA/SHC/3997 Sixty-Fifth General Assembly, Third Committee, 46th Meeting (AM) "General Assembly Will Hold 'World Conference on Indigenous Peoples' in 2014, Under Terms of Resolution Recommended by Third Committee," available at http://www.un.org/News/Press/docs/2010/gashc3997.doc.htm.

51. "United Nations Human Rights Council Establishes Mandate on Côte d'Ivoire, Adopts Protocol to Child Rights Treaty, Requests Study on Discrimination and Sexual Orientation," Human Rights Council, June 17, 2011, available at http://www.ohchr .org/en/NewsEvents/Pages/DisplayNews.aspx?NewsID=11167&LangID=E.

Chapter Nine

1. See the excellent critical analysis in Abdullah Saeed and Hassan Saeed, *Freedom of Religion, Apostasy, and Islam* (Burlington, VT: Ashgate, 2002).

2. See, for example, Mohamed Talbi, "Religious Liberty: A Muslim Perspective," in *Religious Liberty and Human Rights in Nations and Religions*, ed. Leonard Swidler (Philadelphia: Ecumenical Press, 1986), 175–188.

3. Saeed and Saeed, *Freedom of Religion*, 69–73.

4. Talbi, "Religious Liberty," 205.

5. See Saeed and Saeed, *Freedom of Religion*, 61–68.

6. Subhi Mahmassani, *Arkan huquq al-insan* (Beirut: Dar al-'ilm li'l-malayin, 1979), 123–124.

7. Sami Aldeeb Abu Sahlieh, "Les Droits de l'homme et l'Islam," *Revue general de droit international public* 89 (1985): 637.

8. Sources on this subject include Navid Kermani, "Die Affäre Abu Zayd: Eine Kritik am religiösen Diskurs und ihre Folgen," *Orient* 35 (1994): 25–49; "Shari'a or Civil Code? Egypt's Parallel Legal Systems: An Interview with Ahmad Sayf al-Islam," *Middle East Report* (November-December 1995): 25–27; Nasr Abu Zaid, "The Case of Abu Zaid: Academic Freedom in Egypt," *Index on Censorship* 4 (1996): 30–39; and Kilian Bälz, "Submitting Faith to Judicial Scrutiny Through the Family Trial: The Abu Zayd Case," *Die Welt des Islams* 37 (1997): 135–155.

9. Bjazet [pseud.], "La tradition? . . . Quelle tradition?" *Monde arabe: Maghreb Machrek* (January-March 1996): 23–31; and Kermani, "Die Affäre Abu Zayd," 29.

10. Kermani, "Die Affäre Abu Zayd," 29.

11. Ibid., 35.

12. Ibid., 33–34.

13. Ibid.

14. Bälz, "Submitting Faith to Judicial Scrutiny," 149.

15. Kermani, "Die Affäre Abu Zayd," 48.

16. See statement issued by the International Islamic Conference on "True Islam and Its Role in Modern Society," Amman, Jordan, July 6, 2005, available at http://www .kingabdullah.jo/news/details.php?kn_serial=3409&menu_id=26&lang_hmka1=1.

17. The author's translation of a French translation from the Arabic offered in Sami Aldeeb Abu Sahlieh, "Liberté religieuse et apostasie dans l'Islam," *Praxis juridique et religion* 23 (1986): 53.

18. Aldeeb Abu Sahlieh, "Liberté religieuse," 61–66.

19. Sultanhussein Tabandeh, *A Muslim Commentary on the Universal Declaration of Human Rights,* trans. F. J. Goulding (Guildford, England: F. J. Goulding, 1970), 70.

20. Ibid., 71.

21. Ibid.

22. Ibid.

23. Ibid., 71–72. One can find similar defenses being offered by an Egyptian author for the application of the death penalty for apostasy. These are discussed in Aldeeb Abu Sahlieh, "Les Droits de l'homme et l'Islam," 643–644.

24. Tabandeh, *A Muslim Commentary,* 72.

25. Ibid., 59.

26. Ibid.

27. It should be recalled that Tabandeh's intended audience consisted of persons attending an international human rights conference in Iran.

28. J. Roland Pennock, "Rights, Natural Rights, and Human Rights: A General View," in *Human Rights: NOMOS XXIII,* eds. J. Roland Pennock and John W. Chapman (New York: New York University Press, 1981), 14.

29. The meaning of the phrase *takhdhil li'l-umma* is obscure. A related verb with the same root occurs in the Qur'an (3:160) in the sense of "forsake." One can predict that the prohibited speech targeted here involves ideas that are deemed harmful to the Islamic community, but exactly what constitutes *takhdhil* is open to speculation.

30. The International Commission of Jurists (ICJ) invoked the UIDHR provision granting freedom of religion when protesting the execution of Mahmud Muhammad Taha, discussed later in this chapter. The ICJ, *Human Rights Internet Reporter* 10 (January-April 1985). Apparently, the ICJ mistakenly concluded that the UIDHR prohibited executions for apostasy.

31. *The Meaning of the Glorious Koran,* trans. Marmaduke Pickthall (Albany: State University of New York Press, 1976).

32. Firuz Kazemzadeh, "The Baha'is in Iran: Twenty Years of Repression," Special Issue, Iran Since the Revolution, *Social Research* 67 (Summer 2000): 535–558.

33. Douglas Martin, "The Persecution of the Baha'is of Iran, 1844–1984," *Baha'i Studies* 12–13 (1984): 49, 54–56, 58, 65; and Human Rights Watch/Middle East, *Iran: Religious and Ethnic Minorities. Discrimination in Law and Practice* 9, no. 7 (September 1997): 10–15.

34. Martin, "The Persecution of the Baha'is," 54.

35. Roger Cooper, *The Baha'is of Iran,* Minority Rights Group Report 51 (London: Minority Rights Group, 1982), 13–14; Economic and Social Council, *Report on the Human Rights Situation in the Islamic Republic of Iran,* E/CN.4/1987/20 (January 28, 1987): 20.

36. Human Rights Watch/Middle East, *Iran,* 10.

37. This translation is taken from "Constitution of the Islamic Republic of Iran of 24 October 1979 as Amended to 28 July 1989," in *Constitutions of the Countries of the World,* ed. Albert Blaustein and Gisbert Flanz (Dobbs Ferry, NY: Oceana, 1992).

38. A collection of his writings with valuable background material is afforded in Ziba Mir-Hosseini and Richard Tapper, *Islam and Democracy in Iran: Eshkevari and the Quest for Reform* (London: I. B. Tauris, 2006).

39. See ibid., 173–174; Human Rights Watch, "Iran: Prosecution of Independent Cleric Condemned," October 11, 2000, available at http://hrw.org/english/docs/2000/10/11/iran683_txt.htm.

40. Saeed Kamali Dehghan, "Ahmadinejad Allies Charged with Sorcery," *The Guardian,* May 5, 2011, available at http://ww w.guardian.co.uk/world/2011/may/05/ahmadinejad-allies-charged-with-sorcery.

41. His views are set forth in a book translated by Abdullahi Ahmed An-Na'im, *The Second Message of Islam by Ustadh Mahmoud Mohamed Taha* (Syracuse, NY: Syracuse University Press, 1987).

42. Aldeeb Abu Sahlieh, "Liberté religieuse," 51.

43. Abdullahi An-Na'im, "The Islamic Law of Apostasy and Its Modern Applicability: A Case from the Sudan," *Religion* 16 (1986): 207.

44. Ibid., 209. The Muslim World League is the parent organization of the Islamic Council, which sponsored and published the UIDHR. According to one account, the

Muslim World League later congratulated Nimeiri for executing Taha. Aldeeb Abu Sahlieh, "Les Droits de l'homme et l'Islam," 707.

45. Ibid.

46. *Report of the Court of Inquiry Constituted Under Punjab Act II of 1954 to Enquire into the Punjab Disturbances of 1953* (Lahore: Superintendent, Government Printing, Punjab, 1954), 218.

47. Saeed and Saeed, *Freedom of Religion*, 35–50.

48. "Factbox: Pakistan's Blasphemy Law Strikes Fear in Minorities," Reuters, January 5, 2011, available at http://www.reuters.com/article/2011/01/05/us-pakistan -blasphemy-idUSTRE7041DQ20110105.

49. Salman Taseer, "Thousands Mourn Pakistan Governor," *BBC News South Asia*, January 5, 2011, available at http://www.bbc.co.uk/news/world-south-asia-12116764.

50. Jane Perlez, "Extremists Are Suspected in Killing of Pakistani Minister," *The New York Times*, March 2, 2011, available at http://www.nytimes.com/2011/03/03 /world/asia/03pakistan.html?pagewanted=all.

51. See, for example, Human Rights Watch, "Denied Dignity. Systematic Discrimination and Hostility Toward Saudi Shia Citizens," September 3, 2009, available at http://www.hrw.org/en/node/85347/section/2; and Human Rights Watch, "The Ismailis of Najran," September 22, 2008, available at http://www.hrw.org/en/node /75197/section/2.

52. Human Rights Watch, "Saudi Arabia: Witchcraft and Sorcery Cases on the Rise," November 24, 2009, available at http://www.hrw.org/en/news/2009/11/24 /saudi-arabia-witchcraft-and-sorcery-cases-rise; "Saudi Arabia Beheads Woman for 'Sorcery,'" *Al-Jazeera*, December 13, 2011, available at http://www.aljazeera.com/news /middleeast/2011/12/2011121302059182183.html.

53. See Abdul Waheed Wafa and Carlotta Gall, "Afghan Court Gives Editor 2-Year Term for Blasphemy," *The New York Times*, October 24, 2005, A3; Griff Witte, "Post-Taliban Free Speech Blocked by Courts," *Washington Post,* December 11, 2005, A24.

54. Carlotta Gall, "Afghans Pick Rival of Karzai as a Chairman in Parliament," *The New York Times*, December 22, 2005, A19.

55. See US Commission on International Religious Freedom, "The Religion-State Relationship and the Right to Freedom of Religion or Belief: A Comparative Textual Analysis of the Constitutions of Predominantly Muslim Countries," available at http://www.uscirf .gov/countries/global/comparative_constitutions/03082005/03082005_study.html.

56. See *The Annual Report of the United States Commission on International Religious Freedom*, May 2011, 10–13, available at http://www.uscirf.gov/images/book%20with %20cover%20for%20web.pdf.

57. For a critique of this initiative, see Peter G. Danchin, "US Unilateralism and the International Protection of Religious Freedom: The Multilateral Alternative," *Columbia Journal of Transnational Law* 41 (2002): 33–135.

58. Ann Elizabeth Mayer, "Clashing Human Rights Priorities: How the United States and Muslim Countries Selectively Use Provisions of International Human Rights

Law," *Satya Nilayam: Chennai Journal of Intercultural Philosophy* 9 (2006), available at http://them.polylog.org/6/ama-en.htm.

59. See "Muslim Cartoon Fury Claims Lives," *BBC NEWS*, February 6, 2006, available at http://news.bbc.co.uk/2/hi/4684652.stm.

60. See Guy E. Carmi, "Dignity Versus Liberty: The Two Western Cultures of Free Speech," *Boston University International Law Journal* 26 (2008), 277–374.

61. For background on the Rushdie affair, see Lisa Appignanesi and Sara Maitland, eds. *The Rushdie File* (London: Fourth Estate, 1989); Aamir Mufti, "Reading the Rushdie Affair: An Essay on Islam and Politics," *Social Text* 29 (1991): 95–116; Malise Ruthven, *A Satanic Affair: Salman Rushdie and the Rage of Islam* (London: Chatto & Windus, 1990); Brian Finney, "Demonizing Discourse in Salman Rushdie's *The Satanic Verses*," available at http://www.csulb.edu/~bhfinney/SalmanRushdie.html.

62. Sheila Rule, "Khomeini Urges Muslims to Kill Author of Novel," *The New York Times*, February 15, 1989, available at http://www.nytimes.com/books/99/04/18/specials/rushdie-khomeini.html.

63. Various representative reactions and comments, largely from Muslims, can be found in *Index on Censorship* (May 1989): 7–18. For other responses, see Appignanesi and Maitland, *The Rushdie File*.

64. See, for example, the book *For Rushdie: Essays by Arab and Muslim Writers in Defense of Free Speech* (New York: Braziller, 1994). The volume includes contributions from many of the cultural luminaries of the Muslim world.

65. "Islamic Conference Calls Only for Ban on 'Satanic Verses,'" *Los Angeles Times*, March 17, 1989, available at http://articles.latimes.com/1989-03-17/news/mn-1643_1_islamic-conference.

66. See Ann Elizabeth Mayer, "Islamic Rights or Human Rights: An Iranian Dilemma," *Iranian Studies* 29 (Summer-Fall 1996): 290–292.

67. "Iranian Political Factions in Row over Rushdie Affair," *Agence France Presse*, April 21, 1997, available in LEXIS/Nexis Library, ALLWLD File.

68. "Palestinian Affairs: Iranian Envoy Calls UN Draft Resolution on Human Rights Baseless, Irrelevant," *BBC Summary of World Broadcasts*, December 15, 1995, available in LEXIS/Nexis Library, ALLWLD File.

69. "UN Condemns Iran on Human Rights," *Agence France Presse*, March 8, 1995, available in LEXIS/Nexis Library, ALLWLD File.

70. On these resolutions, see, generally, Allison G. Belnap, "Defamation of Religions: A Vague and Overbroad Theory That Threatens Basic Human Rights," *Brigham Young University Law Review* (2010): 635–685. The resolutions can be accessed on the websites of the UN Human Rights Council and the UN General Assembly.

71. Ten-year Programme of Action to Meet the Challenges Facing the Muslim Ummah in the 21st Century. Third Extraordinary Session of the Islamic Summit Conference, December 8, 2005, available at http://www.oic-oci.org/ex-summit/english/10-years-plan.htm.

72. Resolution No. 34/34-POL on Combating Islamophobia and Eliminating Hatred and Prejudice Against Islam, The 34th Session of the Islamic Conference of Foreign Ministers, May 15–17, 2007, available at http://www.oic-oci.org/34icfm /english/resolution/34ICFM-POL-07-RES-FINAL-ENG.pdf.

73. Ibid.

74. NGOs: ARTICLE 19 and The Cairo Institute for Human Rights Studies (CIHRS), "Joint Written Statement Submitted by ARTICLE 19, a Non-Governmental Organisation on the Roster, and the Cairo Institute for Human Rights Studies (CIHRS), a Non-Governmental Organisation in Special Consultative Status," September 11, 2008, available at http://www.article19.org/pdfs/press/un-resolutions-on-combating-defamation -of-religions.pdf.

75. Ibid.

76. Ibid., par. 18.

77. "Women Living Under Muslim Laws Demands the UN Resolution on Combating Defamation of Religions Be Revoked," April 7, 2009, available at http://www .wluml.org/ar/node/5181.

78. See, for example, Human Rights First, "Violence Against Muslims," March 2011, available at http://www.humanrightsfirst.org/wp-content/uploads/pdf/3-2010 -muslim-factsheet-update.pdf.

79. Ibid.

80. ARTICLE 19 and CIHRS, par.10.

81. Ibid., par. 11.

82. Reporters Without Borders, "UN Human Rights Council Turns Special Rapporteur on Free Expression into Prosecutor," March 31, 2008, available at http://www .rsf.org/UN-Human-Rights-Council-turns.html.

83. Speech of H. E. Ambassador Saad Eddine Taib, adviser to the Secretary-General, on the OIC Inter-Institutional Forum on Universal Shared Values: Challenges & New Paradigms to Commemorate the 60th Anniversary of the Universal Declaration of Human Rights, Geneva, December 19, 2008, available at http://docs.google.com /gview?a=v&q=cache:PesVd_Q3SUQJ:www.oic-un.org/forum/Saadeddin_TAIB.pdf +cultural+diversity+saad+eddin+taib&hl=en&gl=us.

84. Ibid.

85. Jytte Klausen, *The Cartoons That Shook the World* (New Haven: Yale University Press, 2009), 15.

86. Ibid., 86–89.

87. Ibid., 89

88. Ibid.

89. Ibid., 91.

90. Ibid., 34.

91. Jason Keyser, "Egypt's Media Stoked Soccer Fan Anger with Algeria," Associated Press, November 22, 2009, available at http://www.breitbart.com/article.php?id =D9C4OOJ01&show_article=1.

92. Klausen, 39.

93. Ibid., 36.

94. Statement of Secretary-General at The First International Conference Organized by OIC, "Challenging Stereotypes in Europe and the Islamic World," February 5, 2006, available at http://www.oic-oci.org/topic_detail.asp?t_id=2318&x_key =van gogh.

95. P. K. Abdul Ghafour and Abdul Hannan Faisal Tago, OIC, "Arab League Seek UN Resolution on Cartoons," *Arab News*, January 30, 2006, available at http://www .arabnews.com/?page=1&section=0&article=77052&d=30&m=1&y=2006.

96. "OIC Denounces Cartoons Violence," *BBC News*, February 21, 2006, available at http://news.bbc.co.uk/2/hi/south_asia/4736854.stm.

97. Ibid.

98. "The Interview of the Secretary-General with the Danish Daily *Jyllands Posten*," October 28, 2008, available at http://www.oic-oci.org/english/article/Jyllands%20Posten %20Interview.pdf.

99. Marie Louise Sjølie, "The Danish Cartoonist Who Survived an Axe Attack," *The Guardian*, January 4, 2010, available at http://www.guardian.co.uk/world/2010 /jan/04/danish-cartoonist-axe-attack.

100. "The OIC General Secretariat Condemns the Reported Attempt on the Life of Danish Cartoonist," January 3, 2010, available at http://www.oic-oci.org/topic _detail.asp?t_id=3171.

101. U.N. Human Rights Council, "Combating Intolerance, Negative Stereotyping and Stigmatization of, and Discrimination, Incitement to Violence, and Violence Against Persons Based on Religion or Belief: Resolution Adopted by the Human Rights Council," April 12, 2011, available at A/HRC/RES/16/18, http://www.unhcr.org /refworld/docid/4db960f92.html.

102. See Shari'ah Staff, "Al-Azhar Document for Basic Freedoms," *onislam*, 455396, January 15, 2012, available at http://www.onislam.net/english/shariah/contemporary -issues/islamic-themes/455396-al-azhar-basic-freedoms-document.html.

Index

Iran human rights/constitution
  1997 elections, 36
  2001 elections, 36
  Ahmadinejad and, 37
  Baha'is and, 135, 144, 144–145, 171,
    176, 180–181
  bar association and, 33, 34
  Cairo Declaration and, 31
  CEDAW and, 117, 207
  clerical dissent and, 36
  constitution (1906–1907), 33–34, 71
  constitution (1979) and, 30–31,
    33–34, 35, 49
  Council of Guardians, 37, 76, 117, 207
  cultural relativism/cultural
    particularism and, 9–10, 12–13
  disagreements on human rights, 36
  dissident clerics vs. ruling clerics, x
  draft/rewriting constitution, 72
  dress code/enforcement, 10, 116
  equal protection and, 73, 95–97
  equality and, 87–88
  Expediency Council and, 76
  freedom of association and, 72, 74
  freedom of religion and, 169, 180–182
  Green Movement, 37
  hejab rules, 116
  ideologization of Shi'ism, 143
  Islam as state religion/state ideology, 75
  Islamic clerics (*fuqaha*) and, 35–36
  Islamic criteria priority, 72–73, 75–76
  Khamene'i on human rights, 36
  Mehrangiz Kar and, 118
  morality police, 116
  Muslim sects conflicts/discrimination,
    143
  occupation "choice," 72, 74
  Olympics and, 116–117
  One Million Signatures Campaign
    and, 118
  overthrow of shah, 33, 34
  overview, 71–76
  political freedom and, 74
  political law and, 36

  publications/press, 72, 73
  religious minorities, 95, 142–145
  respect and, 117, 119
  sexual minorities, 153, 155–156
  shah's Westernization, 33
  Shi'i clerics and, 34
  Taliban and, 117
  "temporary marriages," 115
  theocracy, 34, 35–36
  Twelver Shi'ism, 29, 31, 45, 49, 115, 142
  UDHR and, 72, 76
  ulama and constitution (1906–1907),
    71
  UN Human Rights Council and,
    12–13
  UN human rights positions/system
    and, 12–13, 119, 142
  UN Women and, 119
  women and sports/sporting events,
    116–117, 118–119
  women's inequality/oppression, 10, 73,
    95, 114–119, 153
  World Conference on Human Rights
    (1993/Vienna), 11
  See also specific individuals
Iranian Committee for the Defense of
  Freedom and Human Rights, 72
Iranian Family Protection Act (1967), 115
Iran's High Council for Human Rights,
  12–13
Iraq
  Cairo Declaration and, 31
  constitution, 32, 81–82, 83–84, 96,
    97, 127, 148–150
  Muslim sects conflict/discrimination,
    31, 136
  opposition to Islamization, 34
  religious minorities and, 31, 136,
    149–150
  sexual minorities, 154
  Shi'is and, 31, 136
  Sunnis and, 31, 136
  TAL (Transitional Administrative Law),
    82–84